The Plundering Time

The Plundering Time

Maryland and the English Civil War
1645–1646

TIMOTHY B. RIORDAN

BALTIMORE
MARYLAND HISTORICAL SOCIETY

Library of Congress Cataloging-in-Publication data
Riordan, Timothy B.
The plundering time : Maryland and the English Civil War, 1645–1646 / Timothy B. Riordan.
p. cm.
Includes bibliographical references and index.
ISBN 0-938420-89-5 (alk. paper)
1. Maryland—History—Colonial period, ca. 1600–1775. 2. Maryland—Politics and government—To 1775. 3. Privateering—Maryland—History—17th century. 4. Pillage—Maryland—History—17th century. 5. Ingle, Richard, 1609–1653. 6. Pirates—Maryland—Biography. 7. Catholics—Maryland—History—17th century. 8. Protestants—Maryland—History—17th century. 9. Great Britain—History—Civil War, 1642–1649—Influence. I. Title.
F184.R54 2003
975.2'02—dc22

2003059996

The paper used in this publication meets the minimum requirements of the American National Standard for Information Sciences Permanence of Paper or Printed Library Materials ANSI Z39.48-1984.

Dedicated to

Diane Marie Velasquez-Riordan

1952–2000

Contents

Preface & Acknowledgments

In the summer of 1986, as part of my position as Field Archaeologist at Historic St. Mary's City, I had the opportunity to help excavate a site known as "Mr. Pope's Fort," a ditch-and-bank, palisaded enclosure that played an important part in the events of the Plundering Time. Little was known about either the period or the fort. Although the fort's existence was known, questions about who built it and why, and what part it played in the little-known events of the time were still hotly debated. For two summers, our archaeological field school probed the layout of the fort, tested its construction, and dated the associated artifacts. During the course of excavation and analysis, we learned a great deal about the fort's archaeology but could not answer the basic historical questions of why it was built and who built it.

Garry Wheeler Stone, then Director of Research at Historic St. Mary's City, pointed me to some partial transcripts that had been made of court cases related to these events. Earlier, he had hired a researcher at the Public Records Office in London to make a calendar of all the associated testimony in the various cases resulting from these actions. Using this information I was able to obtain microfilmed copies of the originals and spent a number of years transcribing the testimony. In this mass of material lay a wealth of names, descriptions, and surprising details. I also went through the published volumes of the *Archives of Maryland,* cross-referencing the names from the court cases and making connections between events. Things I had read many times before, and to which I had never paid much attention, suddenly seemed more significant in light of the new information. Patterns began to emerge, and the complex motives of the participants became clearer.

What emerged from this research was a radically different view of the Plundering Time and a new perspective on colonial history in general. Earlier studies viewed the events of the Plundering Time as a simple act of revenge by Richard Ingle. The period was seen as an aberration, something outside the general flow of Maryland's early history. It is now clear that the causes of this rebellion can be traced to fundamental flaws in the social order initially brought to Maryland, and that it was the first of a series of such eruptions that shook the colony in the seventeenth century.

Equally important is placing this episode in a global context. There is a tendency to see the Plundering Time, and Maryland history in general, as isolated from other world events. Maryland was a tiny frontier settlement on the edge of the English world. It was, at best, only in sporadic contact with ideas and news from England. Nevertheless, a significant aspect of this research was how closely events in Maryland paralleled those in England. Perhaps the connection is more obvious because at the time they occurred the events in Maryland were related to a major upheaval in the English political system. I believe the same connection underlies all colonial history. Every ship that crossed the Atlantic to the English colonies brought eagerly awaited news from home. The news was told, retold, and argued over for months. More importantly, in the seventeenth century every ship disgorged a large number of people directly from England, imbued with new ideas and new ways of thinking about things. Their impact on colonial society was considerable.

Many people helped in the research leading to this book and in refining the writing of it. Great thanks go to Lois Green Carr and to Russell Menard, who ably blazed the trail by challenging the accepted view of Ingle's Rebellion. Garry Wheeler Stone provided the foundation for my project by sharing his own research. Without their pioneering studies and encouragement, even the first steps would not have been possible. It is with deep gratitude that I acknowledge Brenda Rodgers, Interlibrary Loan Librarian at St. Mary's College of Maryland. She not only found impossible things but had them delivered to the library so that I could review them. I, and the readers of this book, owe a great debt to Robert I. Cottom, editor of the Press at the Maryland Historical Society, who took my arcane and sometimes awkward prose and made it both understandable and enjoyable to read. To my colleagues at Historic St. Mary's City, Henry Miller, Silas Hurry, and Ruth Mitchell, thank you for being there. Whether they knew it or not, they were my sounding board for trying out new ideas. We may not have always agreed on some things but, their careful and considered responses have made this a better study than it would have been.

A number of individuals shared their specialized expertise and insights with me during the course of my research. Conversations with John Krugler, whose knowledge of the Calverts and their place in English history is unsurpassed, greatly aided my understanding of the English political situation. Charles Fithian provided invaluable insights on weapons, fortifications, and especially the militia structure in England and Maryland. Virginia Busby shared her knowledge of Native Americans and the Contact Period in the Chesapeake. I thank all three for their interest in the project and for their encouragement.

Finally, I am deeply grateful for the support of my family and many friends who always knew that the book could be written. Their support through the years was invaluable in getting the research completed.

Timothy B. Riordan
Historic St. Mary's City, Maryland
August 20, 2003

The Plundering Time

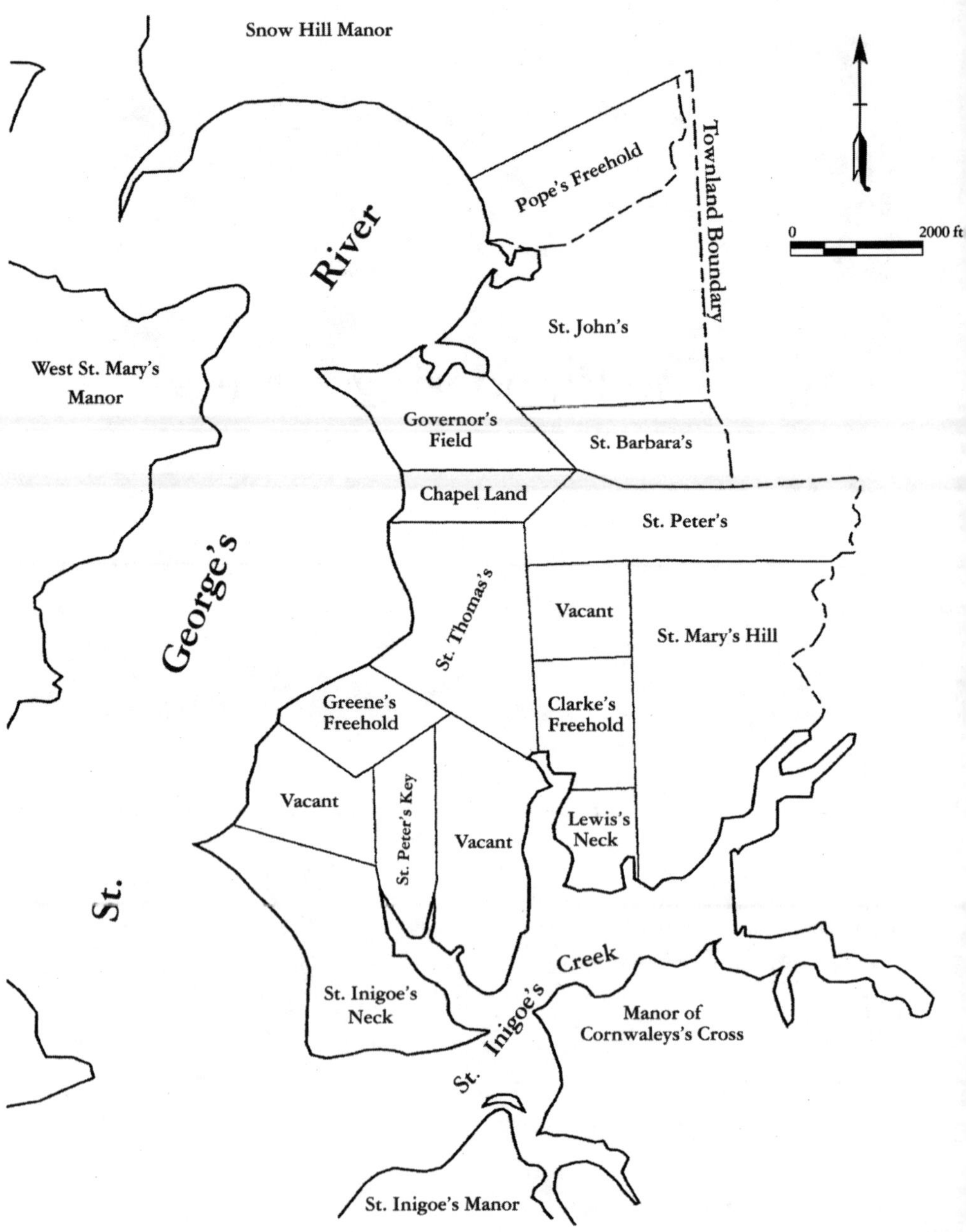

Map showing early Maryland settlement near the St. Mary's (St. George's) River and St. Inigoe's Creek.

INTRODUCTION

"They came in arms . . . and ransacked every place"

Maryland's "Plundering Time" was one of the most violent and unsettled periods of its history.[1] In 1645 the colony was invaded by a band of privateers under the leadership of Richard Ingle who, with the aid of many Protestant settlers, overthrew the Proprietary government of Lord Baltimore. For almost two years the rebels ruled the colony by force of arms, plundering their opponents and bringing Maryland close to the brink of ruin. The rebellion was finally suppressed late in 1646 when Governor Leonard Calvert returned from Virginia with a force comprising exiled Marylanders and mercenary Virginians and restored Proprietary rule. Not surprisingly, these events caused a major disruption in the colony's growth. It has been estimated that St. Mary's County, the main place of settlement in Maryland, fell from approximately five hundred to a mere one hundred settlers by the end of the troubles.[2] Kent Island, the other center of population in the young colony, was said to have suffered a similar decline. Significantly for later history, the rebellion dealt a fatal blow to Lord Baltimore's vision of an aristocratic, manorial society. The Maryland that emerged from these "troubled times" was very different from what had existed before the rebellion.[3]

Early studies of the Plundering Time concentrated on Richard Ingle himself without attempting to understand the context in which he operated. They attributed the conflict to Ingle's revenge for an attempted arrest the year before. Richard Ingle is vitally important to the understanding of this period, but the story is much larger than the anger of one man. Ingle was only in Maryland for a few months in 1645. Protestant settlers kept the rebellion alive for two years after his departure. Earlier histories also leave the impression that on Ingle's arrival, Catholics and loyal Protestants either ran away or surrendered, yet there is evidence of active resistance to Ingle by the Proprietary government in the spring of 1645. Ingle indeed provided the spark for the conflict, but issues among the Marylanders themselves supplied the fuel.[4]

Recently historians have begun to take a broader view of these events. Russell R. Menard has suggested that the Proprietary government was ready to collapse in 1645, before Ingle arrived, and that the anarchy precipitated by Ingle's raid was the inevitable result of flaws in the structure of a government that had been stretched to the breaking point by depressed tobacco prices and elevated expectations. Garry Wheeler Stone has argued that Maryland was a stable, if flawed, society and would have adjusted to its problems had it not been for the disruptive influence of the English Civil War.[5] Lois Green Carr has addressed this stability in the first decade of settlement:

> The first ten years of Maryland settlement had seen considerable success. In 1644, immigrants, servant and free, were continuing to arrive, former servants were becoming planters, planters were growing and marketing tobacco, community networks were forming, courts and assemblies were functioning. Quarreling leaders did work out compromises. From this point of view, there is no reason to suppose that the colony at Ingle's arrival was close to collapse. . . . By this interpretation, Ingle's Rebellion was an offshoot of the English Civil War that happened to wreak havoc in a small settlement where religious tensions were inevitably severe.[6]

Neither viewpoint is sufficient to explain the Plundering Time. Carr and Stone convincingly demonstrate that early Maryland society was stable and not on the brink of collapse in 1644. Maryland's gentry, despite their squabbles, could and did act together when the need arose. Nevertheless, the Plundering Time must be interpreted within the context of the English Civil War. The ideas and rhetoric of the main players in this drama were shaped by contemporary events in England. Whatever legal pretext Ingle had for making war on Maryland stemmed from his letter of marque. Without it his actions would have been simple piracy and freebooting. Ingle's invasion was not an isolated event but part of a larger attempt to overthrow Royalist governors and replace them with those well affected to Parliament. If Ingle was not carrying out the specific orders of the Parliamentary government, he was at least following the plan that they had proposed for Virginia the year before. In any case, it was civil unrest in England that allowed Ingle to make his attack on Maryland.[7]

Menard is correct in tracing the causes of rebellion to basic flaws in Maryland society. It is no coincidence that the conflict was cast in terms of Catholic and Protestant rather than Royalist and Roundhead. Had Ingle not invaded, the rebellion eventually might have occurred anyway, because the roots of the conflict were set down in the earliest days of settlement.

New historical and archaeological evidence has accumulated in the past few years and can be used to reinterpret much of the older material. What emerges is a very different picture from the traditional view of the period and better explains the motives of those involved and the implications they created for Maryland's subsequent history. The central theme of this book is that Maryland's Plundering Time should not be viewed as one man's act of revenge nor, solely, as an extension of the English Civil War to America. Both are involved to be sure, but, more importantly, the seeds of conflict were already present in Maryland before Ingle arrived. The Plundering Time represents the first of the many rebellions that rocked Maryland's colonial history. It is not an isolated incident but fits well into the recurring cycle of revolution and counterrevolution that is characteristic of early Maryland's political climate.

The object of this book is to tell the story of the Plundering Time as fully as the evidence will permit. The period is more dramatic than anything a novelist could invent. It involves friendship and betrayal, loyalty and rebellion, honor and deceit. Any compelling story, be it historical or fictional, must have a central conflict arising from tensions between the main characters, and Maryland's early colonial history is rife with such friction. Menard has identified three causes behind the events of the Plundering Time: religious tension between Catholics and Protestants, conflict between Marylanders and Virginians, and disagreement over the direction in which Maryland society should evolve.[8] These themes provide the framework for understanding why events occurred and why major characters chose the courses they did. Each must be reviewed briefly before any interpretation can be attempted.

Throughout Maryland's colonial history, the issue of religion was never far from the surface. Lord Baltimore tried to maintain a careful balance between Catholics' quest for freedom of worship, English laws against recusants (i.e., those who refused to attend Church of England services), and the sensibilities of Maryland Protestants. In his instructions to the colonists, written before the voyage began, Baltimore required Catholics to worship in private and to be silent on matters of religion, points that were restated in a proclamation issued by Governor Leonard Calvert after the colonists arrived in Maryland. Lord Baltimore and his appointed officials did everything in their power to grant Catholics freedom of worship without threatening the legal status of the charter of Maryland. The balance was delicate and constantly under threat from fanatics on both sides.[9]

The extent to which Maryland authorities tried to maintain this balance and the attitudes that ultimately doomed it are well illustrated in the case of William Lewis, a Catholic and the overseer on the Jesuit Plantation at St. Inigoes.[10] On Sunday, 1 July 1638, Lewis urgently called on Captain Thomas Cornwaleys, one of the Commissioners of Maryland, with some disturbing news. Robert Sedgrave, Lewis's servant, had drawn up a petition to the governor and council of Virginia accusing Lewis of forbidding his servants the use of Protestant books and demeaning all Protestant ministers as "instruments of the divell." Lewis told Cornwaleys that Sedgrave and Francis Gray, a Protestant freeman, were on their way to the chapel to get the Protestant freemen to sign the petition. This was a serious charge in the fledgling colony not only because of the religious issue but because of the implication that Virginia had the right to intervene in Maryland's internal affairs.

Cornwaleys spied Sedgrave and Gray heading to the chapel at St. Mary's City and called them into his house to question them. They knew they were in serious trouble, and their answers to Cornwaleys's questions, when compared to their later testimony, showed they tried to downplay the whole affair. Gray had the petition on his person and yielded it to the captain. The petition implored Virginia authorities, "that you who have power that you will doe in what lieth in you to have these absurd abuses and hereticulous crimes to be reclaymed."[11]

When asked about the petition, Gray claimed that he did not know of its existence until Sedgrave gave it to him and, further, that he had not taken time to read it. He said that Sedgrave had written it and asked him to get some of the freemen to sign it. Gray believed that it was intended for presentation to the governor and council of Maryland. Cornwaleys ordered all of the parties to be on good behavior and to return that afternoon to see if the matter warranted a court hearing. Apparently it did, for a trial was held two days later.

Word of the trial traveled fast in this small community, and when the court met on 3 July 1638 a large crowd gathered. The court consisted of Governor Leonard Calvert, the provincial secretary, John Lewgar, and Captain Cornwaleys. All three were Catholics and large investors in the Maryland venture. For Robert Sedgrave and Francis Gray, the future did not look bright.

When Calvert questioned Sedgrave about writing the petition, he confessed to writing it but swore that Francis Gray had asked him to do it. He further testified that he was to keep the petition until Gray had a chance to talk to Thomas Copley, a Jesuit and head of the Maryland mission, about Lewis's activities. On the Sunday they had been caught, according to Sedgrave, Gray informed him that he had talked to the Jesuit and that Copley had blamed Lewis for his misplaced zeal. Sedgrave claimed that they had decided not to present the petition and were only going to the chapel for services.

Francis Gray was then called to testify and admitted that he had lied to Cornwaleys during the initial questioning. It was he, not Sedgrave, who had thought of the petition. He carefully sidestepped the fact that the document was addressed to the governor of Virginia, not Maryland. Calvert's answer to this evasion has not been recorded, but the trial now took a decided turn.

The court agreed to hear testimony against Lewis on the charges listed in the petition. Ellias Beech, another of Lewis's servants, testified that he was present in Lewis's house when Sedgrave and Gray were reading aloud from a book of sermons by a Mr. Smith passages that labeled the pope as the Antichrist and claimed the Jesuits were Antichristian ministers. According to Beech, Lewis came into the room and said the book was an instrument of the devil. Sedgrave defiantly asked Lewis if all Protestant books were the same, but Beech could not remember what answer Lewis had given. William Lewis, in his own defense, testified that his servants read the book aloud just so that he would hear it. He told them that the book was a lie and that it came from the devil, as all lies did. He further stated that the author of the book, by publishing such lies, was an instrument of the devil.

Additional witnesses were called against William Lewis, two of whom testified that Lewis said all Protestant ministers were ministers of the devil. Sedgrave further swore that Lewis forbade his servants to have any Protestant books, an allegation Lewis, who must have been disturbed by the turn of events, strongly denied. In exasperation, he said that he expressly permitted his servants to have and use Protestant books as long as they did not read them so as to disturb him in his own house. He had forbidden only that particular book because it was so obnoxious to his own beliefs.

Uncomfortable at the testimony against him, Lewis attempted to bring the trial back to its original purpose. He alleged that the intention of the petition was to combine the Protestants against him so that the governor and council of Virginia would charge him with treason. He claimed that he had a witness to testify to that effect, and the court called the witness, John Thornton, only to learn that he was on a trading voyage. Governor

Calvert deferred the trial of Sedgrave and Gray until Thornton could be produced, and no further action against Sedgrave and Gray appears in the Maryland records.

The governor then asked Secretary Lewgar for his opinion on the charges against Lewis. Lewgar found him guilty of offensive and "indiscrete" speeches and of forbidding a book that could be legally read in England. He did not find him guilty of forbidding all Protestant books. The governor and Cornwaleys agreed with Lewgar's verdict and fined Lewis five hundred pounds of tobacco, the currency of the young colony. He was also required to put in a bond of three thousand pounds of tobacco that he would not "offend the peace of the colony or of the inhabitants thereof by iniurious & unnecessary arguments or disputations in matter of religion; or shall use any ignominious words or speeches touching the books or ministers authorised by the State of England."[12]

This case clearly demonstrates how far the Maryland authorities were willing to go in pacifying the Protestant faction. The court, comprising only Catholics, imposed a heavy fine on Lewis, a fellow Catholic, but did not punish Sedgrave or Gray at all. Lewis was certainly guilty of disobeying Lord Baltimore's instructions and Governor Calvert's proclamation by proselytizing and by "unnecessary" religious disputation as even Thomas Copley, the Jesuit, admitted. But, the judgment would seem to be unfair to William Lewis. Sedgrave and Gray proved themselves untrustworthy in their testimony by repeatedly lying. Gray's testimony leaves the impression that he knew he was in trouble and was making up any excuse to avoid punishment. In light of their duplicity, it seems likely, as Lewis stated, that Sedgrave and Gray had been intentionally taunting Lewis in his own house. When he reacted as they knew he would, they attempted to raise the religious issue against the Catholic government by writing to the governor of Virginia, implying that no justice was to be had under Catholic rule.

Francis Gray bears most of the responsibility in this case. He seems to have been the instigator of events. Gray was present in the house when the book was being read, it was his idea that Sedgrave write the petition, and he was going to get the Protestant freemen to sign it. Lewis claimed that the petition was aimed against him personally, but the request for assistance is not specific and could have been used as an excuse for overthrowing the Proprietary government. In this case, and in his later actions, Gray proved himself the first of many Marylanders who were not content under a policy of toleration but strove for the restriction of religious freedom. Occurring only four years after the initial settlement, this case demonstrates that one of the central flaws in Maryland society was already evident. It may be that Cornwaleys's prompt action was the only thing that kept the first Protestant rebellion from occurring in 1638.

While Marylanders on both sides tried to maintain the delicate balance between religious freedom and majority opinion, others were not so willing to grant religious freedom to their opponents. It is likely that the religious issue separating Catholics and Protestants was present in most events in early Maryland, perhaps not openly expressed but always in the background. Religion deeply divided colonial Maryland with a chasm that could not easily be crossed. Sometimes conflicts erupted in rebellions, as during the Plundering Time. More often they were expressed in subtle ways.

A second cause contributing to the events of the Plundering Time was the stormy relationship between Maryland and Virginia. The enmity between Virginia and the Calvert family pre-dated the founding of Maryland, the second colony established by the Calverts. The first, Avalon, was located in Newfoundland and by all accounts was a financial disaster. Begun in 1621 as a fishing station, the colony struggled along for almost a decade. In 1627, George Calvert, first Lord Baltimore, visited Avalon and in 1628 spent a terrible winter there. That was enough to convince him that the climate of Newfoundland was too harsh. He began to look southward for a new place to colonize and in 1629 sailed to Virginia.[13]

Arriving at Jamestown on 1 October 1629, Lord Baltimore was met with open hostility. Virginians suspected Calvert's religion and would not permit him to settle in Virginia until he swore an oath of allegiance to the king and to the Church of England. Calvert submitted an alternative oath that allowed him to be faithful to his king and his own conscience. The Virginians did not accept his compromise, and life in Jamestown was not pleasant. Calvert was openly reviled on the street and, at one point, threatened with violence. Despite the hostility, he began looking for a place to found a new colony. Later in 1629 he sailed up the Chesapeake to look over the land. He may have inquired about the area south of Virginia as well. In any case, he was convinced that somewhere in this region a colony could succeed and prosper. Taking ship for England, he set out to persuade the king to grant him a charter for a new settlement near Virginia.

Many Virginians also opposed the idea of any new colonies in the Chesapeake, which they considered to be theirs alone. This group, led by William Claiborne, Secretary of State for Virginia, had their own plans for the region and sought to do everything in their power to block a grant to Calvert. Claiborne was soon on a ship trailing Calvert to England, but he failed in his mission. Calvert's application for a grant of land north of Virginia received the crown's approval over the Virginians' protests, because the Crown was worried about Dutch encroachment in Delaware Bay. Calvert was thought better able to fund a colony that could hold the Dutch in check. George Calvert died before he fulfilled his ambition, but on 20 June 1632 his son Cecil, second Lord Baltimore, received approval for the Charter of Maryland. In spite of this official blessing, events did not progress smoothly for the new colony.[14]

In 1631, at least in part to keep Calvert from claiming the upper Chesapeake, William Claiborne began a trading post on Kent Island. The settlement was successful, and by 1634 when St. Mary's City was founded, about a hundred colonists lived on the island. The Kent Islanders conducted a profitable fur trade that became a sore point between themelves and the new Maryland government. Early in 1635, Claiborne's men seized a ship from St. Mary's that had been trading in the vicinity of Palmer's Island in the upper reaches of the bay and sent its crew home on foot. Maryland retaliated by capturing a boat called the "Long Tayle" in the Patuxent River. Clashes between rival fur traders continued for several years and culminated in a bloody confrontation on the Pocomoke River in 1637 that left four dead. Kent Island was finally subdued in 1638 when Governor Calvert led a force of thirty musketeers onto the island. Although Kent Island officially became part of Maryland, it retained an undercurrent of hostility against the Proprietary government, and many of its settlers remained loyal to Claiborne and Virginia.[15]

Having lost Kent Island, William Claiborne developed other interests in Virginia, but he never gave up hope of recovering the island. As late as 1676, almost forty years after the seizure, he was petitioning Charles II to grant it back to him, and during the 1640s he took every opportunity to cause trouble for the Maryland government. Occasionally this meant raising a rebellion on Kent Island, either by his presence or by his orders. Most of the time, Claiborne expressed his hostility by using his position in Virginia and his contacts in England to obstruct and hinder the development and security of Calvert's colony. The hatred Claiborne and his faction bore for Maryland played an important part in the events leading up to Ingle's invasion and in subsequent developments. In fact, as some historians have suspected, Claiborne seems to have been more active in the conflict than previously thought.[16]

The third cause leading to Ingle's "raising a rebellion" in Maryland was a conflict over the direction in which Maryland would evolve. Unlike the first two, this one may not have been as obvious to the settlers themselves, but in hindsight it is clear that early Maryland society was plagued by an incipient class struggle that contributed to the events of the Plundering Time. The Lords Baltimore had planned Maryland as a stratified, aristocratic, manorial society. Theirs was a conservative plan that called for transplanting English rural society to the New World. This social system, already in decline in England by the time Maryland was founded, was familiar to most of Maryland's early settlers. Consisting of large land grants tilled by tenant farmers who paid rents to landlords who in turn provided the government necessary to perpetuate the system, it was the traditional lifestyle of rural England and, not surprisingly, was associated with areas of high recusancy and Catholic activity. It also required stability and a general acceptance of the existing social order. While Protestant areas of England were moving toward open agriculture, the beginnings of the enclosure movement, and incipient industrialization, Catholic areas maintained a rural lifestyle based on cattle-raising and traditional lord-tenant relations.[17]

The struggle between the gentry and the poorer classes was not peculiar to Maryland nor to England, but it was part of the overall breakdown of the medieval political order as the Renaissance swept across northern

Europe. This movement put a greater emphasis on the individual and the nuclear family at the expense of lineage and the established social order, as Lawrence Stone expressed clearly when discussing changes that took place in England:

> The fundamental shift in human values and in the social arrangements that went with them in the period from 1560 to 1640 has been well described by one historian as a shift from a "lineage society" characterized by bounded horizons and particularized modes of thought, to the more universalistic standard of values of a "civil society." The causes of this vast change are clear enough: the Reformation with its powerful drive for the christianization of society . . . the growth of more commercialized relations between man and man; the rise of "possessive market individualism" that was slowly beginning to erode old communal affiliations. Finally there was the institutional expansion of the nation state. . . . The consequent decline of kinship and clientage was a major cause of the rise of the nuclear family.[18]

All of these pressures were accentuated in the fragile settlement of the Maryland frontier. The population of early Maryland consisted primarily of young males with few family ties. Lineage-based decisions concerning marriage or inheritance such as Stone discusses for contemporary English society were not a matter of concern. Lord Baltimore's plan for Maryland called for transferring the traditional clientage relationships to the New World, but it was obvious within the first years of settlement that the lure of cheap land was too great for the plan to succeed. Men chose to acquire their own land rather than remain a tenant on someone else's property. The dispersed settlement pattern of early Maryland doomed the development of any "communal affiliations" such as were common in the smallest of English villages.[19]

The result of these pressures was a more open society where upward mobility was a real possibility. Unlike England, where land was expensive and wages were low, Maryland was described as a "good poore man's Country." The progression from servant to tenant to freeholder became a demonstrated reality by 1642. Although it was clearly stratified, early Maryland society was closer to the individualistic, "civil" society that Stone saw emerging in England. Maryland freemen could and did take an active part in the government of the colony. They twice rejected the code of laws sent by Lord Baltimore and jealously guarded their rights as English subjects in opposition to his claims for feudal control of the colony. They sought many of the same rights for their Assembly that would eventually lead to a civil war in England between the king and Parliament. On important local issues such as fee schedules, Indian policy, and taxes, the freemen often voted along class lines.[20]

These flaws, religious, political and social, were present from the beginning of Maryland's settlement and were accentuated by the isolated, demographically skewed nature of the immigrating society. Like tinder, they awaited a spark. The English Civil War provided that spark, and Richard Ingle bore the torch. It is probable that Protestant rebellions were inevitable given these flaws, yet they did not occur in isolation from political events in England. Without some hope of support or legitimization from England, no group would dare to upset the established order. The Plundering Time, although its root causes were grown at home, cannot be understood without reference to events in England.

In the early 1640s, England was undergoing a constitutional crisis much more serious than, but similar to, Maryland's own. Questions of religious practice, taxation, the place of a monarch in a constitutional system, and the general structure of society were hotly debated. The causes that led to the English Civil War are complex and have occupied historians for three centuries. Our purpose here is not to describe in detail the origins of the conflict but to present the events that led up to the war and to provide a basis for understanding their effects on Maryland.[21]

Charles I ascended the throne in 1625 amidst great rejoicing, but by the late 1620s the joy had faded. Serious disagreements had developed between the king and Parliament. Although the issues were diverse, the main areas of friction appear to have been Charles's attempts to raise taxes without Parliament's consent and his arbitrary imprisonment of royal enemies. Parliament, for its part, was greatly frustrated at not having the authority to hold its own meetings—the power to call or dissolve parliamentary sessions resided with the throne. Charles had successively dissolved two Parliaments when they began to debate questions that irritated him and was about to dissolve a third by royal order in 1629, but when the Speaker rose from his chair, a signal that debate was over, two members of the House of Commons grabbed him and violently sat him down again. After the reading of a protestation against the king's abuses, Parliament dissolved itself.[22]

The king, having had enough problems with balky Parliaments, refused to call another one for eleven years. During the 1630s, Charles I *was* the government of England. To support personal rule without an elected Assembly he had to devise ways of raising money and sought to raise taxes wherever and whenever he could, though it never seemed to be enough. Still this was a peaceful and prosperous period and might have continued longer if the Charles had not stumbled into a war with Scotland.

That war, brought on by the king's insistence that the Scottish church adopt an Anglican prayer book, went badly for the English and was concluded by the Treaty of Berwick in June 1639. The treaty was unsatisfactory from the English point of view, and Charles desperately needed money to renew the war. His advisors suggested that he call a new Parliament and rely on the patriotic support of the people. This proved to be a mistake. The session started where the last had ended. Grievances that had not been satisfied eleven years before were now debated. Charles dissolved what would become known as the "Short Parliament" after only three weeks. War with Scotland broke out again late in 1640, and the king was forced to call another Parliament to pay for it. This body, known since as the "Long Parliament," first met on 3 November 1640 and, with some interruptions, stayed in power until 16 March 1660. But that was well in the future. For now, it busied itself in a struggle with the king for control of the government.

As the tobacco fleet made ready to sail from London on its outward voyage to the Chesapeake in the autumn of 1641, Parliament was considering a "Grand Remonstrance" to be presented to King Charles. This long document, which detailed Parliament's conflict with the king and demanded control of royal appointments, was quickly followed by bills for Parliamentary control of the church and of the militia. When Charles refused to surrender control of the militia, Parliament passed an ordinance giving themselves the necessary powers. Meanwhile, the king, having sent the queen abroad for safety, was traversing the country attempting to raise support for the contest he knew was in the offing.[23]

When the tobacco fleet returned to London the following spring, an uneasy peace existed between the two sides. King and Parliament continued to trade charges, but both hesitated to open hostilities. In April, Charles tried to seize the arsenal at Hull but was refused admittance. Numerous ports and towns were declaring support for Parliament, and the entire navy followed suit as well. By June, Parliament had raised between four and five thousand volunteers and had begun training them. The king hastily granted commissions for the raising of cavalry troops and assembled his own fighting force.

The onset of the Civil War was now only a matter of time. When the tobacco fleet slipped down the Thames and began its outward voyage in the fall of 1642, it would carry the news that England was at war. That news, transformed by colonial conditions, would strike the flawed foundation of Lord Baltimore's planned manorial society and forever change the direction of Maryland's development. In order to appreciate the interaction of these forces on the frontier settlement of colonial Maryland, we must look at how the first decade of Maryland settlement had progressed.

CHAPTER ONE

"Our present estate every day bettering itt selfe"

In the eight years since its founding in 1634, the province of Maryland had prospered and grown, navigating through the tempests of religious bigotry, hostile neighbors, and a swelling wave of cultural change. Religious toleration was the accepted, if not the preferred, practice for both Catholics and Protestants. Kent Island had been firmly established as part of Maryland, and the hostile faction in Virginia had been temporarily silenced.

While adjusting to these disruptive influences and adapting to a new environment, the colony had seen continued growth and settlement. The colonists were not crowded into the restricted area of the St. Mary's fort but had spread out and occupied widely dispersed plantations. By the end of 1642 they had surveyed and patented about 37,000 acres. The largest settlement was still along the St. Mary's River in St. Mary's, St. Michael's, and St. George's Hundreds, but important settlements had been established at St. Clement's, about twenty miles up the Potomac, and at Mattapany, some nine miles upriver on the Patuxent. The Kent Island settlement continued to grow. The population of St. Mary's County in 1642 is estimated to have been between 340 and four hundred. Although this is still a small number, it represents more than a 250 percent increase in population since the original settlement. If Kent Island is added, the total population of Maryland was almost six hundred.[1]

Construction of Lord Baltimore's envisioned conservative, agricultural society was well under way. Dotted with manors, the province was assuming a stratified social order.[2] The Catholic gentry was trying hard to impose Lord Baltimore's vision on the rough Maryland frontier, and if they had not yet completely succeeded, they had come close in many ways. The geographic constraints of this manor system set the conditions for settlement. Those freemen who held their own land did so on the edges of the manors or in areas between them. Manor lands were worked by tenants. If these were not life tenants, as was common in England, neither were they transients. Many stayed on for six or seven years, working the land and paying rent.[3]

In spite of the economic gains that had been made since the initial settlement, Maryland's political foundation remained fragile. The institutions of English government and society, buttressed and defended by ancient tradition in their native land, had to be adapted or redefined in building a new society. The political system Lord Baltimore wanted to establish in Maryland had already broken down in England and was soon to be swept away in the Civil War. In Maryland, it was in an even more perilous condition because of Maryland's demographic profile. The population was overwhelmingly male, young, and unmarried. Freed from the social restraints of family-based kinship networks and with their own vision of economic advancement, these young men constituted a powerful disruptive force.[4] "A young man not yet burdened by family responsibilities could afford the consequences of political assertion more easily than an older man with wife and children to support," Russell R. Menard has noted. "The dispersed pattern of settlement, the fragility of the new institutions, and the limited police power at the disposal of the proprietary officials made it difficult for the gentry to effectively deal with unrest."[5]

Most of those young men were Protestants already accustomed to the more individualistic ways of life developing in England. They chafed under the conservative rule of Catholic gentry. Conditions in Maryland aided rather than hindered the trend toward "possessive market individualism" and a modern capitalistic society. Provincial society was characterized not by a change from a lineage-based family to a nuclear family but to one of no family. The majority of Maryland settlers lived for long periods either by themselves or with partners and servants. Such loose associations fostered few restraints on the actions of the individual.[6]

Arrayed against these strong, almost irresistible, trends were a handful of Catholic manor lords committed to imposing a traditional society and settlement on the Maryland landscape, but even among the gentry the commitment to Lord Baltimore's vision was not unanimous. Some of the manor lords, in particular Thomas Cornwaleys, held a progressive view of the world that frequently brought them into conflict with his Lordship's government. Despite their quarrels, Maryland's leaders cooperated in the establishment of a turbulent but seemingly permanent community. The glue that held the province's disparate elements together was the authority invested in the stratified social order central to Lord Baltimore's plan.

That social order was given form in the structure of the Maryland government. As governor of Maryland, Leonard Calvert held the highest position. He was the second son of George Calvert, first Lord Baltimore. In 1642 he was thirty-two years of age and had already lived an adventurous life. In a time when most people did not travel far from their homes, he had already crossed the Atlantic Ocean at least five times before reaching the age of twenty-five years.[7]

When only eighteen, he accompanied his father to Avalon in Newfoundland. The colony was being harassed by the French, and the Calverts captured six French vessels. In the fall of 1628, George Calvert sent Leonard back to England with the prize ships to represent him in the Admiralty Court. Leonard then petitioned the king for a ship to carry provisions back to Newfoundland and to defend the colony. He was given command of the *St. Claude,* a large ship the English had captured from the French in 1625. Late in March 1629, the king granted him a letter of marque for the *St. Claude,* and on 20 April he sailed from England as its captain. Leonard Calvert was back in Newfoundland by August 1629 and probably accompanied his father to Jamestown.[8]

When the Maryland venture was taking shape, Cecil Calvert, second Lord Baltimore, entrusted his younger brother with the responsibility of establishing the colony and governing in his name. Leonard was in the colony from its founding, with only brief trips to Virginia during the next eight difficult years. No sooner had the settlement been established, a strenuous task in itself, than the Marylanders found themselves in a war with the Kent Islanders, a conflict that dragged on for four years until Governor Calvert forcefully solved the problem by invading Kent Island in 1638.[9]

Modern historians have questioned Leonard Calvert's role as a leader. Several studies have characterized him as weak and vacillating or as aloof and incapable of inspiring loyalty. They often make a comparison between Calvert and William Claiborne, who, it is said, inspired intense loyalty among the Kent Islanders. These studies fail to note that Claiborne was of the same religion as the people he was governing, that those people came from a colony that had been established for a quarter of a century, and that many were his employees. Personal loyalty may have contributed to Claiborne's success in raising rebellion on Kent Island, but other factors were at work. In the end, what decided the issue was the personal interest of the Kent Islanders. When Claiborne attempted to persuade them to march on St. Mary's in the 1640s, they were willing to follow him until they learned that he had no authority from any legitimate government to do so. Despite their supposed personal loyalty, the islanders were not willing to risk their lives and estates for him.[10]

In some respects, history has been unfair to Leonard Calvert. He was, after all, in the unenviable position of being caught between Lord Baltimore and the colonists. All of his authority derived from the commission granted by his brother. This legal authorization and simple family loyalty guaranteed that Leonard Calvert would carry out his brother's wishes. Yet there were times where the situation in Maryland or simple fairness required that Calvert not carry out those instructions. To his credit, he was able to make those decisions.

The record during the first decade of settlement shows him to have been a fair and practical leader who was not afraid to take decisive action. Despite being a Catholic himself, he enforced Lord Baltimore's instruction that Catholics were to worship privately and that religious disputation be kept to a minimum. In the case of William Lewis, Calvert went out of his way to accommodate the Protestant faction. He effectively ended the Kent Island dispute by force of arms but did not exact a heavy toll on the islanders themselves. He did not dispossess them but had them take out patents under Lord Baltimore, and he wisely chose to make a friend out of John Butler, one of the island's leaders, rather than send him into exile or execute him. Such a leader was needed to control the men who came to Maryland.[11]

As the personal representative of Lord Baltimore in the province, Leonard Calvert's position was one of great responsibility and encompassed most of the executive functions of the government. Not only was he governor, he was also lieutenant general of the militia, admiral, chief justice, and chancellor. Lord Baltimore required the governor to participate in every important decision that might affect the province. The governor had the power to call and dismiss assemblies, establish ports or market fairs, grant land, and hear and decide all cases civil and criminal.[12]

To help him govern the colony, Leonard Calvert called on the provincial secretary, John Lewgar, and the Council of Maryland. Early in 1642 the council consisted of two men besides Lewgar: Thomas Cornwaleys and Giles Brent. Each played an important part in the drama of the Plundering Time. We must therefore assess the kind of men the councilors were in order to understand how they reacted in the crisis.[13]

Next to the governor himself, John Lewgar held the most important office in Maryland. As secretary of the province, Lewgar had many responsibilities. In addition to being a councilor, he was a judge in cases involving probate or matrimony, keeper of all of the provincial records, and recorder of all grants of land and all acts of the Assembly. Most of what is known about early Maryland we owe to Lewgar's diligent recordkeeping. He was also designated as Lord Baltimore's collector and receiver for all rents, customs, fines, and other money due the proprietor.[14]

Secretary Lewgar was the perfect choice for this position and competently handled all of the mundane administrative details of the colony. He was clearly Lord Baltimore's man and faithfully followed his instructions as far as he could. Cecil Calvert, Lord Baltimore, had a high regard for Lewgar, for he not only made him secretary but entrusted Lewgar with his personal estate. Lewgar was loyal to Leonard Calvert as well. On several occasions he upheld this personal loyalty at great personal risk and expense. A highly educated man, his interests ran more to the spiritual and academic than the functional matters of a frontier settlement. Perhaps because of this scholarly demeanor, he was easily swayed by some of the other Maryland leaders and subsequently appears at times to have vacillated.

We know a good deal about Lewgar's early life in England. He was born in 1602 and attended Trinity College at Oxford in 1616. While there he made the acquaintance of Cecil Calvert, a friendship that would serve him well for the rest of his life. He graduated in 1619 with a bachelor of arts degree, received a master of arts degree in 1622, and in 1627 became an Anglican minister. He accepted the position of rector of the parish of Laverton in Somerset and in 1632 was ordained a priest in the Church of England after receiving a bachelor of divinity degree.

His might have lived out his life as an academic and country pastor had it not been for the whim of his close friend William Chillingsworth. Lewgar had met Chillingsworth at Oxford and regarded him as one of the brightest students in his class. When Lewgar left Oxford, Chillingsworth stayed on and helped prepare arguments against the Counter-Reformation. Later, Chillingsworth had a change of heart and converted to Catholicism. Lewgar, in an early example of how easily he could be persuaded, decided to argue his friend out of his error, only to end up trapped in it himself. He became convinced that the Catholic Church was the true church and was undoubtedly surprised when his friend ssubsequently renounced Catholicism and returned to the Church of England.[15]

The decision to become a Catholic cost Lewgar dearly. Before his change of faith, he had a secure position as rector and was amply prepared for a successful religious, academic, or civil career. Afterward, like all Catholics in England, he was barred from almost all civil and academic activities. Making his position worse was the fact that he had a wife and a small son to support. It is typical of Lewgar that, having convinced himself of the rightness of a proposition, he carried through with it despite the cost to himself and others.[16]

Following his conversion, Lewgar moved to London in search of work. There he met his other friend from Oxford, Cecil Calvert, who hired him for various tasks. Eventually, Calvert appointed Lewgar to be Secretary of the Province of Maryland, and in 1637, accompanied by his family, Lewgar crossed the Atlantic on the ship *Unity*.[17] During his tenure as secretary, he faithfully carried out Lord Baltimore's policies even when he disagreed with their wisdom. As a judge, he had a strong sense of the law and almost ruined himself to uphold the principle. Garry Wheeler Stone describes him as "ambitious, decisive, and unexperienced. . . . politically naive and inept but a competent administrator and an outstanding judge."[18]

While the governor and secretary managed the daily tasks of the provincial government, the council was less active. They were to meet with the governor when he called them to discuss matters of importance to the colony. The councilors also served as local justices of the peace and decided whether to bind prisoners over for the provincial court, where they often sat as justices. There was no set number of councilors, and during this period the number varied between three and six. Early in 1642, Thomas Cornwaleys and Giles Brent were the only other members of the council. Each made significant contributions to the founding of Maryland and were important figures in the events of the Plundering Time.

While we know a fair amount about his family, little is known about the early life of Thomas Cornwaleys before his involvement in the Maryland venture. He was born in 1605, the son of Sir William Cornwaleys of London. His family had good connections to the throne and a strong Catholic tradition. Sir Thomas Cornwaleys, his great-grandfather, had been comptroller of the household of Queen Mary. Charles Cornwaleys, his grandfather, was ambassador to Spain and treasurer for Henry, Prince of Wales. His father had served in Ireland and had been knighted by the Earl of Essex. Thomas Cornwaleys was the second son of Sir William and would have inherited little from his father—the reason usually given for his interest in Maryland. His life in the province shows him to have been well educated, but there seems to be no record of his attending a university in England. Perhaps he was educated on the Continent because of his Catholicism. An old reference suggests that he was a merchant before coming to Maryland. Certainly he was one of the most prominent merchants in Maryland, was familiar with trade, and was well connected to business interests in London. Leonard Calvert and the other Maryland leaders seem to have relied on him for military advice and leadership, and it is possible that he had some military training or had seen service on the Continent. During a visit to England in 1640 he joined the king's army in preparation for the second war against the Scots. He seems to have been the most active, pragmatic, and level-headed of the provincial Catholic gentry.[19] Cornwaleys accompanied Leonard Calvert to Maryland as one of Lord Baltimore's original commissioners and in eight short years made his mark on the colony. In 1642, he was thirty-seven years old, in the prime of life, and actively engaged in all aspects of the Maryland venture—political, military, and economic.

As captain and chief military officer of Maryland throughout this troubled period, Cornwaleys saw considerable action. In 1635 he was involved in several naval battles with ships from Kent Island that were trading without a license from Lord Baltimore. Cornwaleys was in charge of the Maryland vessels in the Battle of the Pocomoke when Lt. Ratcliffe Warren and three others were killed. When Leonard Calvert determined to force the submission of Kent Island in 1638, he placed Cornwaleys in command of the thirty musketeers raised for the expedition. Cornwaleys also led the second expedition to Kent Island to put down Thomas Smith's rebellion.[20]

Cornwaleys, more than any of the other investors in early Maryland, was an entrepreneur. He set up the first mill in the colony and built a large, framed house as an example to others. His original economic interest was in the fur trade. He was a shareholder in the joint stock company established by Lord Baltimore for trading with the Indians and held a one-eighth share of the *Dove,* the company trading vessel. By 1639, Cornwaleys, in partnership with Governor Leonard Calvert, controlled all of the fur trade in the upper Chesapeake. Cornwaleys was also a major participant in the tobacco trade, despite his personal misgivings about the value of the plant. He reportedly sent 33,000 pounds of tobacco to England in 1639, which placed him in the top 10 percent of British tobacco merchants. Most of this tobacco was not grown on Cornwaleys's plantations but was payment for credit extended to other planters. In 1642, the court records reveal that Cornwaleys lent credit amounting to 40,056 pounds of tobacco, an amount almost twice as large as the next highest lender and which represented almost a third of the total debt recorded in the court records. All of this activity indicates that Cornwaleys was the richest man in Maryland and that the "Poore younger brother's fortune" that he brought with him was not as small as he would make it seem.[21]

Thomas Cornwaleys presents a most interesting contrast to the other leaders of early Maryland. While most of the Catholic gentry were intent on reproducing the conservative, communal social structure of rural England, Cornwaleys seems to have identified more with the modern, capitalistic society that placed an emphasis on the value of the individual. This often placed him in opposition to the rest of the gentry and gave him the support of most of the freemen. Very early on he expressed many of the concerns for freedom that would come to characterize the American experience. At one point, Cornwaleys, closely allied with the Jesuits, reminded Lord Baltimore that "Securety of Contiens" was his first requirement from the government. Although this is often cited as an early expression of the concept of separation of church and state, we should not lose sight of the fact that it was set in the context of an argument supporting special privileges for the Jesuits. Nevertheless, the idea that individuals should be free to follow their own religion without government interference is a basic concept in the American creed. Later in the same letter he wrote, "I love to bee the manager of my own affairs, which favors, if your Lordship be pleased to grant me, I shall not care for other approbation." In both of these statements, Cornwaleys associated himself with the modern ideal that places more emphasis on the individual. These concerns extended beyond his personal affairs to the community in general. In the first Assembly for which we have a record, Cornwaleys was one of the leaders who opposed the code of laws sent over by Lord Baltimore, asserting the right of freemen to initiate the legislation that affected their lives. He was also one of the judges that convicted William Lewis, a fellow Catholic, of interfering in the free practice of his servants' religion.[22] Historians have greatly underrated the role that Thomas Cornwaleys played in early Maryland.[23]

The other member of the council early in 1642 was Giles Brent, youngest son of Sir Richard Brent, Lord of Lark Stoke and Admington in Gloucestershire, where the Brent family had been important since the fifteenth century. Sir Richard was a locally prominent landowner and had served as sheriff of Gloucestershire in 1614. He had thirteen children, of whom Giles was the seventh, being born about 1607. Little is known about Giles Brent before he came to Maryland. In 1637 he sent five servants to Maryland and in 1638 arrived himself in the company of his older brother, Fulke, his sisters Margaret and Mary, and at least nine servants.[24]

The Brents were precisely the sort of people Lord Baltimore wanted to attract to his new colony. They had a strong Catholic background, and during the English Civil War the Brent estates in Gloucestershire were sequestered by the Parliamentary government because of their faith. The Brents immigrated as a family and in Maryland continued to be closely allied to the church. They were an important part of Baltimore's plan for transplanting a rural English society in the province, a classic example of the family with strong lineage that had provided much of the stability for English country life in earlier centuries. Such a family places great emphasis on the bonds between siblings and respect for the eldest son as heir. In many ways this is the kind of relationship that existed between Lord Baltimore and Leonard Calvert, and it was clearly the case for the Brents. From very early after their arrival in the colony, the Brent estates seem to have been managed as a family venture, with Margaret Brent supervising those at St. Mary's and Giles Brent taking care of those on Kent Island.[25]

Giles Brent combined within himself both good and bad aspects of this system. On the positive side he was intensely loyal to his family. It was unfortunate for Lord Baltimore that most of the Catholic gentry did not have these kinds of family ties in the province. Brent's family background gave him the confidence to play an active part in governing the province, and he held many offices in the 1640s, including those of deputy governor, councilor, treasurer, commander of Kent, judge, and burgess. Finally, his role as manor lord and commander of Kent put him in a position of authority over many of the planters. Within the framework of a paternalistic, lineage-based society, he recognized his responsibility to care for and foster their interests. In the Assembly he championed their freedom to leave the province without a pass and argued against the right of Lord Baltimore or his governor to adjourn the Assembly without their consent.[26]

On the other hand, Giles Brent was a difficult man to govern. His cantankerousness kept him at odds with Maryland authorities for most of the 1640s and eventually led him to abandon Maryland for the northern neck of Virginia in 1649. Perhaps because he was a younger son and realized that the position he held in Maryland was one that he could not have hoped to hold in England, Brent was sensitive about his rank and prerogatives. This trait is evident in a number of places in the records and made it difficult for the other Maryland leaders to work with him. Brent was also accused, several times, of bending justice to his own ends and profit. He had a tendency to become jealous, petty, and argumentative. It is likely that all of these characteristics played a part in shaping his actions during the opening stages of the Plundering Time.

These four men—Calvert, Lewgar, Cornwaleys, and Brent—were the Maryland government in early 1642. Serving them were the sheriffs, constables, coroners, justices of the peace, clerks, and other minor officials who carried out their orders. In many cases, those minor officials were their personal servants, overseers, tenants, and clients. The governmental structure reflected and supported the manorial system and was buttressed by the mutual rights and duties expected between lord and tenant. It was also a system that was medieval in origin and out of step with conditions in Maryland.[27]

During the 1630s an undercurrent of resistance to this antiquated system began to stir. Because of the nature of the provincial social structure, this resistance was most often cast in religious terms. It became evident in the case against William Lewis in 1638 and, early in 1642, in the petition of the "Protestant Catholicks of Maryland" against Thomas Gerard for locking their chapel and keeping the key. During the 1640s, under pressure from events in England, the undercurrent would coalesce into a determined party that was both Protestant and Parliamentarian. By early 1642, the outlines of this development were just becoming evident.[28]

There is no way of knowing whether, if left to itself, the fledgling opposition would have grown sufficiently strong to challenge Lord Baltimore's government, but hastening its development a few years later was the arrival of a dedicated leader with a strong military force and a plan of action. That leader was Richard Ingle, ship's captain, merchant, and Parliamentarian. Without Ingle, the events of the Plundering Time might never have occurred as savagely they did, or perhaps tensions within Maryland society might have resolved themselves in a different way altogether. Yet Ingle, with his ship, crew, and mercenaries clearly served to galvanize Protestant opposition to feudal, Catholic Maryland. Had the province not already been split by this conflict, Ingle would have been just another pirate. To understand Ingle's contribution to this drama, we must first explore his background and his connections with Maryland.

In 1642, Richard Ingle, an experienced mariner and merchant, had close economic ties with several of the Catholic leaders and was described as the chief trader to Maryland. He was thirty-three years old and by his own testimony had been in the Virginia trade for ten years. Ingle was often referred to as "of London," because it was the port from which his ships sailed. The Maryland indictment against Ingle in 1644 described him as "late of Redriff in commit Surrey." The county of Surrey extends along the south side of the Thames River adjacent to London. There seems to be no place in that county named Redriff. A town named Redhill exists, but it is far south of London and the river. In his 1645 deposition, Ingle described himself as being from Stepney in county Middlesex. The city of London is in Middlesex County and the parish of Stepney is east of London on the Thames. Early in the seventeenth century, the waterfront in Stepney underwent rapid expansion and became the main area for shipping and ship fitting—and the home of a great many of England's daring sea captains. At the time in question, Stepney was divided into four hamlets, the most populous of which was Ratcliff. This village of 3,500 inhabitants had been an area of shipbuilding in the Middle Ages but led the change to trading and ship fitting in the seventeenth century. Ratcliff was often called Redcliff in this period, making it likely that this was Ingle's home and that the writer of the Maryland indictment mistook the county in which it was located.[29]

No information survives on Ingle's family or early years. He probably came from a middle-class background. The typical master of a merchant ship in the seventeenth century has been described as being from "a moderately prosperous stratum of society, sons of small merchants, ships' officers or shipbuilding craftsmen." Ingle likely received some schooling and was clearly literate. He probably went to sea at an early age and received much of his education as an apprentice to a ship's captain. Although he claimed in 1642 to have been in the tobacco trade for ten years, the first record of him as a master of a vessel appears in 1639. Accordingly, there were at least seven years where he must have been working his way up the chain of command.[30]

The earliest record of Ingle dates to 10 September 1639, when he is described as the master of the ship *Blessing* of London. At the time, the ship was preparing for a trip to Virginia, and Thomas Cornwaleys paid ten shillings export duty for three pieces of cloth, valued at £10, that he put aboard. That was the beginning of a close and profitable relationship between the two men. In 1645, Cornwaleys testified that he had met Ingle six years earlier and thought "the said Richard Ingle to be a very able, honest and careful man." Through Cornwaleys, Ingle was introduced to the other Maryland leaders. On the return voyage, Thomas Gerard of St. Clement's Manor and possibly Thomas Cornwaleys booked passage back to England. It is also likely that Ingle carried back much of the Maryland tobacco crop at the same time.[31]

By October 1640, Ingle had a new ship, called the *Richard and Anne,* which was preparing for a voyage to Virginia. On this voyage, Cornwaleys exported cloth valued at £56 and paid a duty of £2,16s. On the same ship, Leonard Calvert is said to have exported shoes, stockings, hose, cloth, groceries, and sugar valued at £14 14s 8d. The ship arrived in Maryland late in 1640 or early in 1641. At that time, Calvert hired Ingle to transport forty thousand pipestaves from Kent Island to London. These were formerly the property of Claiborne, Cloberry & Company but had been seized when Calvert took the island in 1638. Despite reservations, conveniently remembered and recorded at a later date, Ingle gladly took the contract.[32]

Ingle by his own and others' testimony was now the chief merchant trading to Maryland, trading with and accepted by all of the Maryland gentry. But Ingle's trading interests extended beyond Lord Baltimore's province. He had very good ties with the settlement at Accomac on the lower eastern shore of Virginia. In 1640, Nathaniel Littleton of Accomac exported £12 16s 8d worth of cloth from London in the *Richard and Anne.* Ingle traded more than goods and tobacco, he traded servants as well. While in Accomac in early 1641, he sold an indentured servant named Sarah Hickman who had been consigned to him by Anthony Pennistone, a London merchant. Ingle shows up frequently in the Accomac court records and traded with many of the leading settlers of that place, including William Stone, who served as Ingle's factor, Argall Yeardley, Nathaniel Littleton, and William Roper. All of these men served as justices of the county court.[33]

By 1642, Ingle was master of yet another ship, the *Ellinor* of London. He accepted a bill of exchange from Margaret Brent in Maryland and gave testimony on 25 April 1642 at the Accomac County Court. At this time he was about to begin his homeward voyage and was laden with Maryland and Virginia tobacco. Caught in a severe storm after leaving Accomac, the *Ellinor* was laid over on her side for two and a half hours and only righted when the crew cut her masts away. She limped into Boston harbor for repairs and stayed until 4 June. During the time she was being repaired, Ingle was impressed with the Bostonians and claimed he had never had such a reception in the ten years he had traded in the Chesapeake.[34]

In three years, Ingle served as master of three different ships. He was obviously hired for his experience in the tobacco trade and was not financing these voyages himself. It is interesting that he appears in the Maryland and Virginia records as master of a vessel at just about the same time. It may be that the *Blessing* was his first command. Later, he would be referred to as part owner of the ships that he sailed, but at this point in his career, it is not known what stake he had in the ships. His business connections were growing. In addition to his own trading, Ingle was well connected to some of the most prominent tobacco merchants in London. On several occasions, he was listed as factor or merchant for Anthony Pennistone and for Thomas Allan & Company. Pennistone had been in the Virginia tobacco trade for ten years, and his relationship with Ingle lasted several years at least. Beginning with his outward voyage in the fall of 1642, Ingle would sail as captain of the *Reformation* for the next three years.

To judge from what has been written about him, Ingle was either the worst villain and pirate to sail the Chesapeake or a man of principle set upon by men of lesser virtue for their own gain. In evaluating Ingle's character, it is difficult to separate the rhetoric from the facts, but it is possible to briefly sketch some important aspects of his personality. Richard Ingle was a man of strong convictions. Some have called him a Puritan, though this highly charged term overstates the case. There is no doubt that he was on the Parliamentary side in the English Civil War. He may have been one of the earliest ship's captains to sign the National Covenant for Parliament. It is also certain that he was a Protestant, but no evidence associates him with the religious ideals implied by the term Puritan. One could be a Parliamentarian without being a Puritan. Parliament's efforts to force the king's submission was obviously a cause in which he vehemently believed.[35]

Although the Parliamentary cause was important to him and he had a strong dislike of the Catholic church, Ingle was a businessman first. His scruples did not stop him from transporting Jesuits and other Catholic priests to Maryland. When he got in trouble at Accomac for his Parliamentary opinions, he later sought and obtained forgiveness so that he could continue trading there. After his ship was seized and later rescued, Ingle worked out an arrangement with the Maryland authorities so that he could complete his trading in the province. The next year he sailed for

Maryland with the intention of trading again. Convictions were important, but he could not let them interfere with a successful trading voyage.[36]

In his business dealings, Ingle was not above bending the law or increasing his profit at the expense of others. Sarah Hickman, the servant Ingle sold in 1641, probably served twice as long as she should have because of him. Samuel Chandler, a merchant and planter of Accomac, testified that Ingle had told him and another merchant that Mr. Pennistone had bound Hickman to serve for two years but that he, Ingle, had sold her for four. At the same court, Ingle was accused of taking three hogsheads of tobacco that had been shipped on the *Ellinor* by Richard Smith as payment of a debt owed to Ingle by Argall Yeardley. This action caused confusion in the court and could not be resolved, because Ingle had already left the country. Though the outcome of these cases is not recorded, they do indicate that Ingle sought his own profit even if it took less than legal means to find it.[37]

Ingle's most serious flaw was his inability to contain a violent temper. Not only did he hold strong opinions on the events of his day, but he was more than ready to defend them with force. In the course of a political argument, he threatened the sheriff of Accomac with a cutlass and kidnapped a number of Virginians to satisfy his anger. He seems to have been a man given to violent outbursts, many of which he regretted later. An official of the Admiralty later called him a "mad Captain" and recommended that the navy would be better without him. After each outburst, Ingle sought conciliation for business purposes, but it is obvious that he continued to harbor a grudge against those whom he thought had wronged him. This made him all the more likely to blow up at the next perceived threat. Ingle's tendency to right cumulative wrongs in a violent fashion is important to understanding his behavior in the Plundering Time.[38]

CHAPTER TWO

"They slew the men . . . we had there and carried away our goods"

In June 1642, as his newly repaired ship made its way from Boston to London, Richard Ingle was still a friend of Maryland, and if the people of the province thought of him at all it was with anticipation of the goods he would bring back in trade. The planters had more immediate concerns. Late in May or early in June, they began transplanting the young tobacco seedlings from the beds to newly cleared fields. The growing cycle that had begun eight years before continued in the spring of 1642, but this season would differ from the others. Some of the planters would not live to harvest their crop, and Maryland's government would experience a crisis parallel to that occurring in England. These changes were set in motion by the Susquehannock Indians, who suddenly attacked Maryland.

The early history of Maryland's relations with the native inhabitants of the Chesapeake was unlike that of Virginia. The Virginians fought the groups nearest them for food and land while making alliances with those living farther from their settlements. The opposite was true in Maryland. From the beginning relations between the local Piscataway and the Maryland colonists were peaceful and cooperative. This friendship might have been extended to other groups, like the Susquehannocks, were it not for the enmity of first the Kent Islanders and then the Dutch and Swedes on Delaware Bay.[1]

For all these European factions, the main area of interest was the northern Chesapeake and the flow of beaver pelts from the interior to the coast. The beaver trade was a major element in the economic rationale for the founding of Lord Baltimore's colony and the only reason for the establishment of the Kent Island settlement. It was also important in drawing the Swedes and the Dutch to the Delaware country. Most of Maryland's troubles with the Indians derived from the contest to control the beaver trade of the northern Chesapeake. Key to winning that contest was an alliance with the Susquehannocks, who controlled the Indian side of the trade.[2]

The Marylanders were under a disadvantage in seeking such an alliance for two reasons. First, they had settled in the middle of a war zone. The Susquehannocks and the Piscataways were engaged in their own violent battle for control of the bay, and the Piscataways were losing. In the eyes of the Susquehannocks, Lord Baltimore's colonists had established themselves in enemy territory and had made an alliance with their rivals. Consequently the Susquehannocks viewed them with suspicion. Additionally, the Kent Islanders already had a strong partnership with the Susquehannocks and actively encouraged their hostility to the new interlopers. William Claiborne was arrested in Virginia for threatening to use the Indians against Maryland, and one of his agents did urge the Susquehannocks to attack a vessel that came to trade in 1634.[3]

Nevertheless, it is important to note that the Susquehannocks did not attack the ship, nor did they refuse to trade with the Marylanders. In fact, they sent for more furs to trade with them. In the end, the traders got 250 beaver pelts which would have been worth approximately £60, a not inconsiderable sum at the time. During the 1630s, both before and after Leonard Calvert's invasion of Kent Island, the Susquehannocks carried on at least some trade with Maryland. Nor is there any indication that the hostility between the two groups was ever serious. The Indians were willing to trade with anyone who could supply what they wanted. Not until the early 1640s did the Susquehannocks become an enemy of Maryland.[4]

What caused this change? The reason, it has been argued, was Indian "loyalty" to their old trading partner, Claiborne, when the beaver trade that had been going to Kent Island shifted to New Sweden on the Delaware after 1638. Some have suggested that Calvert's taking of Palmer's Island in 1638, so close to their homeland, had angered the Susquehannocks. Certainly Claiborne and his agents tried to turn the Indians against Maryland, and their efforts may have contributed to shaping later events. But if Claiborne had such influence with the Indians, why did they wait four years before attacking Maryland? If loyalty and offended patriotism were an issue, why did they not begin raiding Maryland in 1639?[5]

It is more likely that the Susquehannocks were, as they should have been, loyal to themselves, and we must seek an answer in their self-interest. By 1638 the Susquehannocks were beginning to feel pressure from the Iroquois, whom the Dutch were supplying with guns. The Susquehannocks thought themselves at a disadvantage and sought weapons where they could find them. They were already getting them, directly or indirectly, from the Dutch. As early as 1634, during the high point of Claiborne's trading, the Susquehannocks were trading with the Dutch in Manhattan and went to war against the Delawares to protect that trade. It is not known if the Kent Islanders were trading guns for beaver, but the St. Mary's people did not. The establishment of New Sweden in 1638 and the apparent willingness of the Swedes to trade guns and ammunition for beaver was very attractive to the Susquehannocks. One reference suggests that the Swedes began training the Indians not only in the mechanics of the weapons but in their tactical use as well. Because of this (to the Susquehannocks) helpful policy and their ability to undersell the Dutch, the Swedes captured most of the beaver trade in the early 1640s. They had what the Indians wanted. Moreover, they were closer to them than the Dutch. There is ample evidence to support the idea that these issues, rather than any personal attachment to a non-resident Virginian, were responsible for a shift in trade after 1638.[6]

Although a reasonable case can be made to explain the Susquehannocks' shift in trading partners, the case for why they began actively raiding Maryland in 1642 is much less clear. William Claiborne was not even in the

Chesapeake in 1642 when the raids began and can hardly be blamed for them. It has been suggested that the Susquehannocks sought to capture trade goods circulating in the Chesapeake area, though if they were as well supplied by the Swedes and the Dutch as they appear to have been, this is a poor reason for the beginning of hostilities. One looks in vain for some incident or occasion that could be responsible for the increasingly violent raids of 1641–42.[7]

In fact, the causes may have been cumulative and related to the changing nature of the fur trade in the northern Chesapeake. Beginning in 1638, control of Maryland's fur trade underwent major revisions that left many of the original investors, including the Jesuits, believing that Lord Baltimore had betrayed them. At least partly for this reason, the Jesuits were allowed to establish missions among the local Indians and to convert them to Christianity. Despite their limited numbers, the Jesuits were remarkably successful over the next three years. In July 1640, the Tayac of the Piscataways was baptized, and several other Indian chiefs sought instruction in the Christian faith. Along with their preaching, the Jesuits also carried on a trade with the Indians, which undoubtedly had a major impact on the local economy.[8]

The increasingly close alliance between the Piscataways and the Jesuits must have alarmed the Susquehannocks. Their old enemies, whom they had all but vanquished, were now growing stronger and wealthier. Furthermore, they were gaining strength from the Englishmen's religion and its power. Not surprisingly, the Susquehannocks moved to challenge this alliance before it became too great. If this indeed was the cause of hostilities, then it was hardly by chance that the Maryland settlement that first suffered the Susquehannocks' fury was the Jesuit storehouse and mission at Mattapany, the center of Jesuit trading activity.

By March 1641, only eight months after the baptism of the Tayac, the Susquehannocks were spoiling for a fight. Into this situation sailed the Jesuit pinnace on a trading voyage under the command of Mathias de Sousa, a free black and an experienced Indian trader. His instructions were to proceed to Kent Island and hire additional crew. De Sousa was probably looking for an interpreter or someone who had experience dealing with the Susquehannocks, both of which would be available on Kent

Island. During that voyage the boat was threatened and possibly attacked by the Indians. De Sousa later testified that if it were not for the presence of John Prettiman, the pinnace and men would have been destroyed. Relations between the Indians and the colonists continued to deteriorate through the year. In July, the governor issued a proclamation authorizing the Kent Islanders to kill any Indian they found on the island. There was very little trade in beaver at the head of the bay that summer.[9]

The troubles on Kent Island and at the head of the bay were but the first act in this drama. In the summer of 1642 the Susquehannocks threatened to sweep down the Chesapeake, destroying Indian villages and English settlements alike. Anticipating the imminent advance of raiding parties, Governor Calvert, on 23 June, issued a proclamation for the safety of the colony. No Indians were to be given shot or powder, and none were to be allowed inside a house. Each head of a household was to provide firearms for all the men in his house, and no man was to go any distance without a loaded gun. The signal of approaching danger would be three shots fired within the space of fifteen minutes. Those hearing the alarm were to duplicate it.[10]

While these preparations were necessary against the threat of Susquehannock raids, neither the governor nor the freemen seemed to be overly worried. Leonard Calvert had determined as early as April to hold a session of the Assembly that summer. Originally the session was scheduled for 1 June but was postponed to 18 July. When it met, the burgesses conducted substantial business, but very little of it had anything to do with Indians. When the session began, Robert Vaughan of Kent Island offered a motion in the name of all the burgesses that the Assembly be divided into upper and lower houses and that the lower house have the right to veto all legislation they did not like. Governor Calvert, aware that this would limit his ability to control the Assembly, and having no authority from Lord Baltimore to allow it, denied the request. Although Calvert was able to dismiss this attempt by the burgesses to exert control over the legislative process, the problem would not go away. The Assembly was aware of the struggle over Parliamentary rights being waged in England, and echoes of those conflicts were already beginning to appear in Maryland.

The next important piece of business was a motion for a march against an unspecified group of Indians. Perhaps still stinging from their recent defeat, the burgesses raised a great opposition. The governor curtly told them that he did not need their permission to wage war as that power was his alone. He brought the subject to their attention merely to see what they would contribute to the expedition. John Lewgar, probably by prearrangement, moved for a levy of twenty pounds of tobacco per head. The burgesses would have none of it and asked to review Lord Baltimore's patent. The records contain no further mention of a march against the Indians in this session. The only other matters dealing with them were a complaint from Henry Bishop about the Patuxents killing his swine and a bill against giving the Indians guns. While they may have recognized a growing threat, the Assembly was unable or unwilling to take the steps necessary to effectively combat it.[11]

The records do not tell us when the Susquehannocks attacked, but scattered clues exist. Late in August there was a sudden increase in activity. On the eighteenth, Thomas Cornwaleys was authorized to raise men to "castigate enemies and vanquish them." Calvert wrote to the governor of Virginia on 23 August, reporting that John Angud, a Virginia merchant, and four others of that colony had been killed and asking for help. Maryland lost eight settlers in Indian attacks that summer. Calvert suggested that the two colonies mount a joint attack on the Susquehannocks with each contributing one hundred men, a plan that reveals the magnitude of the threat. The largest expedition Maryland had sent against the Indians to that time consisted of only thirty men. Unfortunately, no help was forthcoming from Virginia.[12]

Another clue to the timing of the attacks comes from an investigation of the deaths of several of the eight slain settlers. Since each was tied into the commercial network of the colony, owing debts or being owed by others, there should be inventories or estate accounts for them, but the records contain not even a brief description of who was killed or when. Only one suggestion hints at the identity of some of the victims. An administration of the estates of Richard Lusthead, Thomas Charinton, and John Machin was granted on 22 August 1642. All lived in Mattapanient

Hundred. Lusthead and Charinton were freemen, and Machin was a servant of the Jesuits. We do not know exactly when they died, but Lusthead and Charinton were both listed in a tax list compiled on 2 August 1642. These men and a Jesuit servant by the name of James were killed between 2 August and 18 August.[13] The Jesuit letter of 1642 records these events and reveals confusion on the part of the colonists:

> An attack having been recently been made on a settlement of ours, they slew the men whom we had there, and carried away our goods, to our great loss. And unless they are brought to subjection by force of arms, which we little expect from the consels of the English who disagree among themselves, we shall not be safe there.[14]

Later documents, written in 1644, suggest that the Jesuit house at Mattapany was attacked twice with the loss of life in both cases. The last attack probably came before 18 August, when Cornwaleys was given his commission to march against the Indians. Cornwaleys led his men over to Mattapany, but they do not seem to have encountered the enemy. An inventory of the goods of Richard Lusthead taken on 31 August 1642 includes a reference to bacon and a hog eaten by the soldiers. These facts suggest that the brunt of the attack came at Mattanany in early August.[15]

Although not unexpected, the attacks were a shock to the colonists. Giles Brent strongly urged the governor to authorize a march against the Susquehannocks. His property on Kent Island, if it had not already been attacked, was, because of its location, in extreme danger. It was generally conceded that a march against the Indians was a necessity. Governor Calvert issued a proclamation on 22 August requiring all freemen, in person or by proxy, to attend an Assembly at St. Mary's on 5 September to consult on matters important to the safety of the colony. On the first day twenty-one men attended, holding proxies for 135 others. Giles Brent held the largest group of proxies, for seventy-three inhabitants of Kent Island. Thomas Cornwaleys with eighteen and Thomas Greene with nine had smaller but significant collections of proxies. Together, these three men controlled two-thirds of the votes in the Assembly and consistently voted against the government. They might be referred to as the freemen's party. Governor Calvert, Secretary Lewgar, and their adherents formed a much smaller group that might be called the government party. The first matter, after settling the orders of the house, was to appoint a committee to draw up the bill for an expedition against the Indians. That committee consisted of Calvert, Lewgar, Cornwaleys, Brent, and several others. They were scheduled to meet in the afternoon to draft the necessary legislation and were also authorized to consider what other bills might be necessary to protect the colony.[16]

While the Indian threat was the main concern, the political climate ensured that other issues would surface as well. That same morning, Giles Brent, for his proxies on Kent Island, asked the house to declare that the freemen had the right to leave the province without seeking permission whenever they chose if they were not in debt or obnoxious to justice. This issue was important to the Kent Islanders, because many of them still had strong ties to Virginia and were used to moving freely between the colonies. During the July Assembly, this right of free movement had been restricted by an act requiring a pass before any debtor could be transported out of the province. Now the combined threat of more Indian raids and the expenses sure to occur in warding off these attacks probably made many of the planters think about temporarily removing to Virginia. It did not help that Kent Island lay in the Susquehannocks' path. As with other issues of parliamentary or individual rights, Calvert quickly put an end to the discussion by stating that he did not consent to the question being decided by or in the Assembly. He then adjourned the house until that afternoon.

By the afternoon session, the committee had drafted a bill for a war on the Susquehannocks. The bill as read in the house authorized the pressing of every third man in the province for the expedition. It is not certain if this referred only to freemen or if servants were to be counted as well. If only freemen, the total number would have been around fifty men. Each soldier was to be provided with a gun, two pounds of powder, eight pounds of shot, a sword, and two months' provisions. In order to pay for and support the expedition, the committee devised another act making it lawful for the governor to press men, vessels, and supplies needed for the expedition. The costs were not to exceed six thousand pounds of tobacco in one year, with four thousand pounds coming from St. Mary's County and two thousand from Kent Island.

After the bill was read, Calvert demanded that a clause be inserted exempting himself and his servants from the levy. Although this demand seems high-handed, he was following the precedent set in Virginia two years earlier. In an Assembly held at Jamestown in January 1640, the burgesses voted to exempt each of the council members and ten of their servants from all public charges. It is also possible that Calvert wanted to keep his servants around his house to guard the records of the province. But this was Maryland, not Virginia, and when the issue was put to a vote, Calvert lost by a wide margin. The governor ended the first day of the session by adjourning the house.[17]

The next morning, Giles Brent once again raised the question of the freemen's right to leave the province without permission from the government. Again the governor denied the Assembly's right to debate the question. Secretary Lewgar rose to say that in his opinion Lord Baltimore's most recent instructions did give the Assembly the right to decide such issues. Lewgar's intrusion was totally unexpected, and Calvert was now trapped. If he let the vote proceed, he was sure to lose, and the Assembly would have set an important precedent. Trying to stave off defeat, Calvert declared that every freeman had the right to depart from the province if he was not in debt or obnoxious to justice, and no great dangers threatened the safety of the province. He added that there were times when provincial well-being could override the right to depart. For the moment, this compromise satisfied both sides. Left unsaid was whether the current situation was one of those emergencies to which Calvert referred.

The calling of this Assembly so soon after the last one had an unexpected effect. At the end of July, the Assembly had passed more than thirty laws, each containing the statement that they would endure until the next Assembly. When the September Assembly ended, these laws would be null and void, so it became necessary to enact them all again. A committee was formed to decide which laws should be presented to the house. They agreed on twenty-five bills, including the one for an expedition against the Indians. The full house met again on the morning of 12 September, and the twenty-five bills were read to the members. Governor Calvert objected immediately to a provision in each that they would endure for three years and insisted on the standard language stipulating that they would expire at the next Assembly. The question was voted upon and, led by Cornwaleys and Brent, the Assembly decided overwhelmingly that they should endure for three years. Later that afternoon the debate turned harsh as each side tried to force its own way. Giles Brent continued his attack on the power of the government to restrict movement out of the province, presenting an unsigned protest, in the name of the house, regarding certain liberties. Calvert refused to receive it. Someone brought up the endurance clause again, and once more it was voted overwhelmingly to be three years. The governor had the bill for an expedition against the Indians read and held a vote on whether it should be engrossed, that is written in legal and final form so that it could be officially voted upon. This proposition went down to a crushing defeat, probably 119 voices against and only thirty supporting.

Then one of the great, unrecorded moments in Maryland political history occurred. Somehow—perhaps it was late and everyone wanted to go home—a deal was made. All of the bills, including the Indian war bill, were read again, and all were voted to be engrossed. Satisfied with the proceedings, the governor adjourned the Assembly for the night.

Whatever led to the compromise was missing the next morning. Apparently the clause stating that the bills were to endure for three years was in each of them except the first, which gave Lord Baltimore a custom duty on tobacco exported to non-English ports. When this bill was read, the governor refused to support it if it did not last three years like the rest. The Assembly passed the bill, but Calvert refused to enact it. All twenty-five bills then foundered because of this problem. The Assembly had come to a complete standstill.

Someone, probably Brent, then read a protest against Lord Baltimore's power to adjourn the Assembly. Although this protest is only mentioned in two lines of the record and is never seen again, it provides an important insight into the whole controversy over the endurance of laws. According to the charter, only Lord Baltimore or his governor had the right to call an Assembly. Perhaps because the settlement was so young, Assemblies had been called almost every year, and the laws they passed often contained a clause stating they would continue until the next Assembly. So long as there was an Assembly every year, this was not a problem. But what if Lord Baltimore or his governor decided not to convene one?

That such a concern was not without foundation is shown by the history of the English Parliament. Only the king had the right to convene Parliament, and Charles I chose not to do so from 1629 to 1640. He might not have called another had he been able to raise the money he needed to fight a war. However, in 1640 he could avoid it no longer, and Parliament, called back after such a lengthy absence, began to redress old grievances. In 1641, Parliament forced the king to accept the Triennial Act, which required him to call a Parliament at least once every three years, and another act that forbade him from dissolving Parliament without its consent. In England, Parliament began limiting the power of the king and seeking its independence.[18]

In the same vein, Virginians had but recently gained a measure of control over the legislative process. When Governor Berkeley arrived in the colony early in 1642, he carried a set of instructions from the king regarding the government. One of these instructions required the governor to call an Assembly at least once a year. That which King Charles was not willing to grant his English subjects he required of his colonists in Virginia. In all likelihood the Marylanders were aware of this newly won right, and it served as one more reminder of Lord Baltimore's arbitrary power over them.[19]

It is within this context that the debate over the endurance of laws in Maryland must be viewed. Cornwaleys and Brent cannot be construed as Parliamentarians in the sense that the word would acquire over the next few years. Yet, like many of their class in England, they were beginning to believe that the people had the right to a voice in their government, and they sought to put limits on the arbitrary use of power by those in authority. By setting a limit on the laws they passed, they hoped to ensure that an Assembly must be held every three years.

Whatever his personal opinions, Leonard Calvert was charged with upholding his brother's authority and prerogatives. By this point, though, it had become clear that he could not continue to obstruct the Assembly and still protect the province against the Susquehannocks. In the end, the three-year clause was added to all of the laws. Calvert was also forced to recast his statement regarding provincial emergencies and declared, "it is the Common right of all the inhabitants to depart out of the Province at their Pleasure unless indebted or obnoxious to Justice."[20]

On the afternoon of 13 September 1642, all of the bills were passed unanimously and enacted by the governor. Included was the bill for an expedition against the Indians. Although it passed, it did so over the objection of Captain Cornwaleys and his proxies. The captain still objected to the exemption granted to the governor and his servants. That the governor was excluded from the costs of this expedition incensed Cornwaleys and would soon have disastrous consequences for the colony.

Having succeeded in getting the war bill through the Assembly, Calvert wasted no time in acting upon it. On the same day the bill finally passed, he issued a proclamation declaring the Susquehannocks, Wicomesis, and Nanticokes to be enemies of the province and called for an attack to be made against them. The expedition would tax the resources of the province and required careful planning. Most of all, it needed a capable leader. The natural choice would have been Captain Cornwaleys because of his proven skill in military matters, but Cornwaleys was still upset over the Assembly debates and had effectively withdrawn from the government. When on 16 September he was asked to renew his oath as a member of the council, he flatly refused. With Cornwaleys unwilling to participate, the governor had to find someone else to lead the march against the Indians. He turned to Giles Brent, who had been one of the most vocal in advocating the expedition.[21]

Calvert, Lewgar, and Brent carefully worked out a plan for war against the Susquehannocks. The sheriff of St. Mary's was called upon to press twenty soldiers for duty, and Brent was authorized to press twenty more from Kent Island. If this was not every third man in the province, it was still a large force. Lewgar organized the logistics of the expedition. He hired two boats to transport the men and personally provided most of the supplies, including 426 pounds of beef, nine pecks of salt, a barrel of corn, two bushels of peas, and eight pounds of powder. While the soldiers were on Kent Island, Lewgar had an ox killed, which provided an additional five hundred pounds of meat. Despite his unwillingness to be an active participant, Cornwaleys was asked to provide ten pounds of powder and 106 pounds of bullets and lead for the war. With these preparations completed, Governor Calvert issued a commission to Giles Brent on 21 September, making him captain of the expedition. The boats sailed from St. Mary's and headed up the bay to the rendezvous on Kent Island, carrying with them Maryland's hope that a decisive victory would force the Indians to sue for peace or at least avoid raiding the settlements next season.[22]

Sometime after leaving St. Mary's, Giles Brent began to have second thoughts about the venture. These doubts hardened when he arrived at Kent and discovered that, since Brent would be away on the march against the Indians for at least two months, Calvert had taken the precaution of commissioning William Brainthwaite to be commander of Kent in Brent's absence. Overseeing the island was a position Brent had held since 1640, and the announcement that he was to be replaced came as an unpleasant surprise. He seems to have taken it as an affront to his dignity and perhaps more importantly a threat to his control over the economy of the island. At this point, Brent lost all enthusiasm for the expedition.

Nevertheless, he went through the motions of carrying out his duty. He assembled the freemen at Kent Fort and told them of his commission, letting them know that twenty men were needed but assuring them that no one would be pressed against his will. Brent then asked for volunteers. Not surprisingly, not a man stepped forward for so dangerous a mission. Claiming that there were some illegalities in the commission, he dismissed the freemen while he considered his next move.

Undoubtedly he pondered the difficult nature of his position and how to save himself. Calvert was counting on him to conduct the expedition which he, Brent, had first suggested. Could he simply ignore the commission without incurring the governor's wrath? A further complication arose from the presence of the soldiers from St. Mary's on the island. They were waiting for the expedition to get started and were using supplies intended for the trip. Brent concluded that he had no choice but to proceed. Despite his earlier promises to the freemen, he issued warrants for the impressment of twenty men and the collection of powder and shot. In due time, the drafted men assembled at Kent Fort with their arms and ammunition, complaining loudly about the expense and the danger of Indian reprisals but evidently agreeing to go on the expedition. Brent, who was no longer committed to the expedition anyway, seized on their complaints as an excuse permitting him to safely extricate himself. By blaming the failure of the venture on their unwillingness, Brent thought he could shift the responsibility from his own shoulders. Eventually, Brent let the islanders go home without accomplishing anything. The expedition headed for home on or about 9 October and arrived the next day.

Brent presented his excuses, but Calvert refused to hear them, and, incensed, the governor immediately began proceedings against him. Calvert had heard rumors that Brent was stirring up the islanders against the government and feared that he was trying to raise a rebellion. He required Brent to give a bond of ten thousand pounds of tobacco on the condition that he would not return to Kent before answering the charges brought against him, nor would he try to sow dissension against the government. Brent refused to sign the bond, and Calvert commanded him not to leave St. Mary's Hundred (the area directly around St. Mary's) before the next court.

Brent realized that he was in serious trouble and reacted in a way that would best protect his interests. Calvert was threatening large fines and possibly other penalties that would greatly reduce Brent's estate. To forestall the event, Brent on the same day the charges were made against him transferred all of his land, goods, debts due, cattle, and servants to his sister, Margaret. The only stipulation in the deed was that she pay his debts. The Brents used this technique on several occasions, transferring property or developing false lawsuits to confuse the issue and protect their assets. In essence, he created a legal trust with a commingling of both estates and presented an impediment to the seizure of any of the assets. It is a clear example of the workings of a lineage-based family. Henceforth, all of the Brent estate in Maryland was treated as joint property. While the deed seems to indicate that Giles Brent was giving up control of his assets, it is obvious that he retained a significant stake in them. The deed of transfer was signed on 10 October but was not registered until after the formal presentment of charges against Brent. Perhaps he was waiting to see if the governor was serious about the indictment.

He found out how serious Calvert was at a court held on 17 October, where John Lewgar, his Lordship's attorney, presented the case against him. In his argument, Lewgar pointed out that the march against the Indians had been Brent's idea, that he had taken an active part in planning the enterprise, and that he had accepted a commission to carry it out. He went on to stress the great charge incurred and how the honor and safety of the province had been riding on the success of the expedition. Lewgar charged that Brent's actions, or lack of them, had led directly to the failure of the venture. Finally, he reported that the debacle had prompted contempt for the government and disgrace among Maryland's Indian allies, and had set a bad example to others who now might feel they could ignore a commission with impunity. Lewgar asked that Brent be called to answer for his misdemeanors and "that such proceedings & sentence may be had & used against him as justice shall require."

Following Lewgar's reading of the charges, Calvert issued commissions for the collection of testimony in the case. Brent submitted a list of seven questions to be asked of the witnesses on his behalf. From those questions we can surmise that Brent's main defense was the unwillingness of the Kent Islanders to join in the expedition. Their complaints, according to Brent, centered on three issues: the threat of reprisals, the shortage of powder, and the need to house their crops before they rotted. Brent's final question to the witnesses was whether they had brought up these complaints on their own or at his instigation.

While Brent's questions are elaborately framed and full of legalistic hedging, the government's questions were simple. They contained only three points. First, was the witness present when Brent announced his commission? Second, what words did he use then, or since, concerning the commission? The third question asked if the individual was pressed into service, whether he reported for duty, and how was he discharged? Lewgar contended that the freemen's complaints were immaterial to the case. The commission authorized Brent to press men for the expedition, and the whole point of that authorization was that their willingness did not matter. It was Brent's own reluctance that allowed him to utilize their excuses. All of these examinations were to be kept secret and returned to the court by 3 November. Unfortunately, none of the depositions were recorded; they undoubtedly contained much information pertinent to the events on Kent Island.

The anger against Brent led to the investigation of a number of other charges, and Calvert asked William Brainthwaite to collect testimony concerning them. Brent was accused of being more concerned with his own profit than with justice when he was judge on Kent Island. Reports alleged that when a defendant was brought before him, Brent first looked to his account book and, if the defendant owed him money, had him sign over his crop before making judgment, leaving the plaintiff little or nothing to collect. The rivalry between Brent and William Brainthwaite seems to have run deep. Brent complained that soldiers under Brainthwaite's command had killed one of his sheep on Popelies Island during the late expedition.

In the course of the next month, John Lewgar and Giles Brent traded increasingly acrimonious charges and answers. The case reached a turning point in November, when Brent answered one of Lewgar's charges with a statement that contained "scandalous and contemptuous implications to his Lordship and his authority." The court, with Leonard Calvert and John Langford sitting as judges, found Brent guilty of the charges. John Lewgar asked that Brent's answer be taken out of the record and the judgment against him entered. Brent, feeling the pressure of the charges, delivered an impassioned speech to the court on 8 November:

> I desire and intend to have it enquired of by Counsell learned in the Law in England, whether I have had wrong in the judgment passed against me in this Court yesterday being the 7th of November, or whether not, if in the opinion of such Counsell I have had wrong in it, I intend to seek my right at the

> hands of our Soveraigne the king and for this reason I desire that my answere and the complaint against me, and the judgment & all other the proceedings in this cause may still remaine upon record.[23]

Lewgar countered that Brent's complaint was immaterial and that the judgment should be entered. The court agreed and struck Brent's scandalous answer from the record. However, just in case it was needed, the court ordered that the answer be kept on file. Brent clearly had lost the case, but Lewgar unknowingly opened a loophole through which he would escape. The draft of the indictment which Lewgar presented to the judges to sign stated that Brent had been offered his choice of trial by the court or by a jury. Brent complained that he did not remember such an offer. Leonard Calvert then stated that if Brent would now accept the trial, Calvert would refrain from entering the judgment and let the case be tried by a jury. Brent twice asked for additional time to think about the offer but eventually agreed to the terms. The previous judgment and Brent's answer were annulled, and Brent was again required to answer the charges.

Giles Brent had either a good legal mind or a strong survival instinct. Through November and early December he managed to confound the justice system and completely extricate himself from any penalty. On 14 November, he answered the charges with a plea of not guilty. He claimed that he delayed carrying out his commission because he was waiting for further orders from the governor. Later he complained that the charges were not clear, and he could not tell if he was being sued civilly for damages or being charged criminally. Lewgar responded by presenting a civil suit for six thousand pounds of tobacco as the cost of the expedition and a trial date was set for 1 December.[24]

The importance of the trial was underscored by the presence of four justices on the bench, Calvert, Lewgar, Langford, and Captain William Blount. Previously, the greatest number of sitting judges was three; most often it was only two. The sheriff brought in twelve jurors who were duly sworn. Brent objected to one of them, Mr. George Binx, claiming that he had already expressed his opinion in the case, and it was not favorable to Brent. The court did not allow the exception. In looking at the men on the jury, it is interesting to note that they were evenly divided between those who supported Brent and Cornwaleys in the recent Assembly and those who supported the governor.[25]

The trial began with Calvert instructing the jury on the facts of the case. The jury objected that this was testimony and not under oath. The governor then was sworn, and the jury heard his evidence. No other witnesses or depositions were recorded in this case. Next the jury was given a written copy of the indictment and went out to deliberate. On their return, they declared Brent not guilty of the charges.

The jury's decision meant that Brent was not liable for the six thousand pounds of tobacco, but he still had to face a charge of criminal contempt for neglecting to carry out his commission. On 3 December, John Lewgar filed the criminal bill against Brent and required Brent to answer it. Fresh from his previous acquittal, Brent denied any wrongdoing and confidently asked to be tried by a jury. In this request he was to be disappointed and rudely surprised. As his Lordship's attorney pointed out, probably with a smile, the charge of contempt was a criminal case and could not be decided by a jury. The case had to be tried by the judges of the Provincial Court. Brent had not anticipated this turn of events. He was unlikely to receive the same gentle treatment from the court as he had from a jury and asked for more time to consider and amend his answer.

By this time, both sides had played out their hands as best they could, much of the anger had subsided, and a compromise was in the air. Brent knew he would be found guilty by the court and would lose his official position in the community. Cornwaleys could walk away from the government without a second look, but for Brent this would be a serious loss of prestige. As far as the government was concerned, there was no further profit in pursuing this case. The greatest fine they could levy was one thousand pounds of tobacco and, given Brent's transfer of property to his sister, they might not even get that. The fine, if it were collectible, would not compensate Lord Baltimore or the province for the loss of a competent, if difficult, official nor for his and his family's probable departure with a considerable estate.

Brent filed his answer on 5 December, and the tone was much different from his earlier ones. He made no further attempt to blame others and offered no legal obfuscation but simply replied that he had done what he thought best for the honor and benefit of both his Lordship and the colony. He said that his actions were not prompted by contempt for the government and pleaded not guilty of the charge. This answer was sufficient for Calvert, who accepted his excuses and acquitted him of all charges.

So ended Maryland's first attempt to make war on the Susquehannocks. The expedition cost the colony six thousand pounds of tobacco but did nothing to avenge the raids of 1642 or make the province safer in the future. What it did do was discredit Maryland in the eyes of her Indian allies. When the next raiding season began, Maryland would be even more exposed. But the Indian threat was just one of the crises facing Leonard Calvert in the winter of 1642.

CHAPTER THREE

"Security of contiens was . . . expected from this government"

No sooner had the Indian war subsided for the season than a crisis of a different kind broke on the Maryland shore. When the shipping arrived that winter, it brought several dispatches for Leonard Calvert from his brother in London. Included in the usual instructions and requests was a letter in which Lord Baltimore upbraided his brother for granting land to the Jesuits against his orders and launched into a fantastic description of Jesuit intentions:

> I am (upon very good reason) satisfied in my judgment that they do designe my destruction and I have too good cause to suspect, that if they can not make or mainteine a partie by degrees among the English, to bring their ends about they will endeavour to do it by the Indians within a verie short time by arming them etc. against all those that shall oppose them and all under pretence of God's honor and the propagation of the Christian faith, which shall be the maske and vizard to hide their other designs withall.[1]

This document reveals how strained relations were between Lord Baltimore and the Jesuits by late 1642. His accusation that they were in league with the Indians against the colonists is, from our perspective, patently absurd. Ironically, this was the same charge used by the Protestants against the Catholic government any time they chose to raise a rebellion. On the frontier, it evoked an emotional response without requiring proof. For Lord Baltimore, removed from Maryland and already disposed to see Jesuit actions in a bad light, such a charge would seem plausible and even probable. Baltimore relied on various correspondents to keep him informed of conditions in Maryland. Few were objective observers, and it is likely that the suggestion of conspiracy came from one with a grudge against the Jesuits. While this may have been the source, it would never have gained credence if serious problems had not already existed between the spiritual and temporal realms in Maryland. To understand how these problems developed, we must explore the ambiguous position of the Jesuits in the early Maryland colony.

As plans for the Maryland venture were being formulated in 1633, both Cecil Calvert and the Jesuits were eager to establish a Jesuit presence in the new colony, but they arrived at this juncture from different viewpoints and harbored different expectations. Lord Baltimore desired their presence for reasons both spiritual and secular. The spiritual welfare of his colonists was certainly part of his concern, as was the need, stated in the Charter of Maryland, to bring the Christian faith to the Indians. But the Jesuits were attractive for secular reasons as well. They were an important part of Catholic survival in England, a position they acquired by associating with powerful and influential landowners—the very class from which Lord Baltimore hoped to draw settlers and capital for his venture. In fact, the Jesuit missionary network running through those households was important in publicizing the venture. More practically, the Jesuits brought twelve people into the province with the first expedition and within four years could claim rights for more than fifty individuals, a significant addition to the population. From Lord Baltimore's perspective, the Jesuit mission was a spiritual and economic success.[2]

For their part, the English Jesuits saw Maryland as a chance to extend their work to a new pagan population. Theirs was a missionary order, and the opportunity was too attractive to ignore. In the sixteenth and early seventeenth centuries, English Jesuits, barred from missionary activity in English colonies, found useful work in India, Brazil, and the Far East. The opening of the English mission held promise for a while, but by the early seventeenth century many English Jesuits felt that being a chaplain to a wealthy landowner was too limiting. It was particularly so in light of the glowing reports sent back by French Jesuits in Canada. Maryland promised to be an exciting project, where benighted souls could be brought to the light of truth. Also, given the nature of the enterprise, neither Lord Baltimore nor the Jesuits expected that the colony would be predominantly Catholic. This gave the Jesuits the possibility to work among the Protestants in an atmosphere relatively free of the penal laws then current in England.[3]

The objectives of Lord Baltimore and the Jesuits were not mutually exclusive and, in many ways, supported each other. They should have had a close, working relationship. The problems that arose came from the expectations each side brought to the project and centered on the position the Jesuits would hold in the new society.[4]

Jesuit practice was to attach themselves to a locally prominent, Catholic landowner as his chaplain and often as a tutor for his children. From this position, Jesuits served not only the family but the population on the patron's estate as well. Their employers supported them and provided a salary, and the landowners' prominence and influence provided protection for the missionaries as they went about their work. Such relationships were becoming all the more common in the 1620s and 1630s, but such dependence brought its own problems. The arrangement gave the gentry great power over the clergy and reversed the traditional relationship that had existed during the Middle Ages. Priests were now dependent upon their patron not only for a livelihood but, because they were considered outlaws by the state, for their safety. It is through the lens of this client-patron relationship that one must view the Jesuit mission to Maryland.[5]

Jesuits began by regarding all of Maryland as Lord Baltimore's estate.

They expected to be supported and protected by their patron, and they were surprised to discover that Cecil Calvert had no intention of supporting them either from his own pocket or from a common source within the colony. Calvert made it clear that if the Jesuits wished to participate in the Maryland venture, they would have to act like, and could expect to be treated as, gentlemen adventurers. That meant they had to provide for their own support by importing their own servants, growing crops, and bartering for supplies. Lord Baltimore promised only that their position would be equal to that of the other gentlemen. They could expect the same benefits and would be under the same obligations, including the acquisition and holding of land.[6]

Lord Baltimore had little choice in this arrangement. Whatever his personal opinions, granting any special privileges to the Jesuits would have been politically dangerous. The whole concept of allowing a Catholic to found a colony was suspect in English Protestant eyes. The Charter of Maryland had come under attack even before the ships left England. Further, even if Lord Baltimore wanted to support the clergy, there was the real possibility that he could not afford it while footing the bill for a new colony. Given the circumstances, the client-patron relationship common in England could not be extended to Maryland. The conditions proposed by Lord Baltimore and reluctantly accepted by the Jesuits were the best that could be made at the time. Had they been fully accepted by both sides, the early history of Maryland might have been much smoother, but both the Jesuits and Lord Baltimore clung persistently to the parts of the client-patron relationship that most benefited their side, and that was a recipe for trouble.

Settled in a new land under a Catholic proprietor, the Jesuits expected to be freed from the restrictions imposed on them in England. Even more than simple freedom, they sought the position that the clergy held in other Catholic countries. In many ways, their expectations were fulfilled. In Maryland, Jesuits were accorded an exemption from normal political activity. They did not participate in elections, were excused from attending the Assembly, and did not serve on juries. There was no probate of Jesuit estates, although a number of priests and brothers died during this period. Finally, despite Father Copley's complaint about being asked to pay fifteen hundred pounds of tobacco toward building a fort, the Jesuits do not appear on any surviving tax list.[7]

Although Lord Baltimore's official policy was to treat the Jesuits as gentlemen, his officials were willing to grant them a special respect. It hardly could have been otherwise, given the personal histories of the men who made up the government. All were Catholics who had suffered discrimination for remaining in or converting to the Catholic faith. Having in part come to Maryland so that they could practice their religion, it would have been too much to expect them not to accord their priests the respect and exemptions given in Catholic countries.

The granting of such privileges by Lord Baltimore or his officials was politically dangerous. The colony was founded under suspicion and in an atmosphere that fostered paranoia. Lord Baltimore put a strong emphasis on discovering who among the colonists was conspiring with his enemies against the new government. Wary of any action that might give his opponents an excuse for limiting or revoking the Charter, Cecil Calvert tried to make Maryland conform as much as possible to English law and practice. As part of that effort he sent a body of laws to Maryland with John Lewgar in 1637, but in an Assembly held early the next year, freemen flatly rejected the code. The details of this set of laws is not known. From later comments it is obvious that they tended to favor Lord Baltimore to the disadvantage of the colonists. More importantly for the Jesuits, the laws not only failed to extend any special consideration to the clergy, but an act entitled "for settling the glebe" seemed to suggest that they had to give land on their manors for the support of a Protestant minister. Further, John Lewgar, his Lordship's secretary, was apparently of the opinion that the Jesuits were to be held to their bargain.[8]

Jesuit reaction was predictable but can only be understood in light of the client-patron relationship. Thomas Copley, head of the mission, wrote to Lord Baltimore after the Assembly had completed its business and commented on the laws that were being sent to England for his approval. Copley made a strong effort to show that he had nothing to do with them and had only glimpsed them briefly. He went on to discuss the implications of this new code for the colony, and in the process offered his opinion on how the laws would affect the church:

> First there is not any care at all taken to promote the conversion of the Indians, to provide or to show any favor to Ecclesiastical persons, or to preserve for the church the Immunitye and priviledges which she enjoyeth everywhere else . . . that they may proceed with Ecclesiasticall persons as with others, and accordingly they seem to resolve to bind them to all there laws, and to exacte of them as of others.[9]

Later in the letter, Father Copley outlined his expectations for the position of the church in Maryland in a series of requests to Lord Baltimore. These can be grouped into two different categories. The first set of requests had to do with the position of the church in relation to the civil authority. Copley asked that the Jesuit church and their houses be considered as Sanctuary. This privilege, which had existed since Saxon times in England but had been swept aside by the Reformation, provided protection from the law for anyone who asked for and was granted Sanctuary. In practice, it extended beyond the actual church or house to the limits of the property. Although this might appear to have been an unusual request, it clearly fit with Copley's view of the church's position. The privilege, if granted, would place all "Ecclesiasticall" persons beyond the reach of the sheriff or the Assembly and was a step toward the official establishment of the Catholic church in Maryland. His second request extended that program. He asked that the Jesuits, their domestic servants, and half of their planting servants be exempt from taxes and from public service, presumably in such organizations as the militia. Then he requested that while the Jesuits had to have their cases tried in the civil courts, the magistrates be instructed that they did so as representatives of the church and only because there was no ecclesiastic jurisdiction established in Maryland. Finally, Copley asked that the church might be allowed whatever privileges she enjoyed in Catholic countries so long as they did not raise problems with the English authorities. These requests would have given the Catholic church the kind of position in Maryland that it had not had in England for almost one hundred years.

Father Copley also made a number of requests that directly related to the conditions of the Maryland mission. He wanted priests given the freedom to visit and live with the Indians without asking permission from the civil authorities. One of the Jesuits' reasons for undertaking the mission to Maryland was to carry the gospel to the Indians and, up to this point, they had not been permitted to do more than visit the neighboring villages. Anxious to get started, they chafed under the limitations imposed by a cautious administration. In order to support the mission, Father Copley asked for Lord Baltimore's permission to trade freely with the Indians for beaver and corn. The potentially lucrative fur trade had been assigned to Lord Baltimore by the recent Assembly, and Governor Calvert, writing at the same time, reported that only Thomas Cornwaleys should be permitted a portion of this trade. Finally, the Jesuits asked to be allowed to take up such land as they needed now but reserve their other claims until they needed more.

What Father Copley requested went far beyond equal treatment for Jesuits; he would establish a special position for the church in Maryland. While the church could not have the privileges it enjoyed in Catholic countries, Copley's plan, if granted, would come very close. This was a far cry from Lord Baltimore's instruction on the privacy of Catholic worship, and he wrote on the letter "herein are demands of very extravagant privileges."[10]

The disagreement between the Jesuits and Lord Baltimore exposed the different views held by each side, but more importantly, it also created an ethical problem for the Catholic gentry. Thomas Cornwaleys voiced his objections to the body of laws in a letter written at the same time as Father Copley's. His opinion must have been influenced by discussion with his Jesuit confessor, for during the Assembly, Cornwaleys is recorded as only objecting to two laws: capital offenses and support of the proprietor. Most of the laws the Jesuits opposed were passed with no dissenting votes, yet Cornwaleys was vehement in his later objections:

> I will rather sacrifice myself and all I have in defense of Gods Honor and his churches right, then willingly Consent to anything that may not stand with the Good Contiens of A Real

> Catholick. Which resolution if your Lordship doe not allsoe make good by A Religious Care of what you send Authorized by your Consent, I shall with as much Convenient speede as I can with draw myself.[11]

This sudden change in Cornwaleys's opinions may be explained by Father Copley's statement regarding his participation in the Assembly. He had studiously avoided being part of the process and only read the laws after they were passed and were being sent to England for approval. It must have come as a rude awakening to see that the special position granted to the Jesuits by the local authorities was now to be eliminated.[12]

Father Copley's objections must have surprised John Lewgar. When Lewgar presented the original code of laws to the Assembly and helped revise the set passed in that session, he shared Lord Baltimore's assumption that the Jesuits had agreed to be treated as other gentlemen. After the session, when confronted by a different view, Lewgar tried to reconcile allegiance to his adopted faith with his employer's practical need to control events in Maryland. The result was a series of questions that Lewgar submitted to the Jesuit Provincial in London. These questions, called the "twenty cases," outline the tension of a private conscience in conflict with public policy. Lewgar had to know if he risked excommunication by enforcing laws similar to those of Protestant England. Ultimately, the answers to the questions would determine if Catholics could function in a secular society. The echoes of the twenty questions reverberate even today. Lewgar's cases cover all of Father Copley's objections and the body of laws passed by the Assembly. They include concerns about clerical exemptions, the secular probate of wills, the secular institution of marriage, etc. The most important question, on which all of the others are based is the first, general case:

> Whether a lay Catholick can with a safe conscience take charge of government or of an office in such a country as this, where he may not nor dare discharge all the dutyes and obligations of a Catholick magistrate nor yield and maintayne to the Church all her rights and libertyes which she hath in other Catholick countryes?[13]

Father Copley opened another front in the battle by writing his own letter to his English Provincial and one directly to the General of the Society of Jesus in Rome. These letters were not only to report on events but were probably intended to put pressure on Lord Baltimore from another source. General Vitelleschi's answer in September 1639 supported Copley's position. He also commended the "uprightness of that magistrate who, desiring to be reckoned a Catholic, will I trust, determine on no measure against ecclesiastics without referring to the chief Pastor." This magistrate was undoubtedly John Lewgar. At the same time, the general wrote to Edward Knott, soon to be English Provincial, stating that conscience was not to be sacrificed in the Maryland matter.[14]

In the interim, a compromise was somehow reached. There is no evidence that the concept of Sanctuary was ever granted to the Jesuits, but they were treated, as they had been, in a special manner. For the first time they were allowed to live with the Indians, they could trade for beaver and corn, and they seem to have been exempted from public taxes and military service. They were treated as a corporate body rather than as individuals. For its part, the civil government went ahead with its plans to establish English law in Maryland dealing with such matters as marriage, probate, and the administration of legacies.

As far as the documents reveal, Lewgar never received an answer to his questions. Almost a year later, in January 1639, he wrote to Cecil Calvert still seeking a reply on the proper conduct of a Catholic magistrate in a Protestant country. Nevertheless, he reported that there were no differences between the government and the Jesuits at that time. It is clear from this letter that Father Copley's politicking and letter writing had some effect. Lewgar went to some trouble to assure Lord Baltimore that neither he nor the governor had shown any disrespect to the priests nor had they been denied any of their rights and liberties so far as that was possible. When the next Assembly met in March 1639, one of the bills considered was an Act for Church Liberties that guaranteed the "Holy Church within this Province shall have all her rights, liberties and immunities safe whole and inviolable in all things." This phrasing became part of the Ordinance that passed at the end of the session. While some have argued over which "Holy Church" the act referred to, it is clear that the Jesuits were the ones to benefit by it. Compare this bill to John Lewgar's statement to Lord Baltimore in January: "I professe before Almighty God, that I am not conscious of any thing yet done out of disrespect to their persons, functions, or rightful liberties; & that hereafter they shall find me as ready [to] serve and honor them as your Lordship can wish." This may have settled, for the time being, the issue of church rights in Maryland, but it was only the beginning of the conflict between church and state.[15]

Another, equally serious issue that created a rift between Lord Baltimore and the Jesuits was the question of landholding. The Jesuit mission had to be self-supporting. Needing land and servants to grow tobacco and thus build a strong foundation for the mission, they imported servants and acquired land rights for others, until by 1638 they held land rights for sixty-two individuals, more than the number held by Leonard Calvert and Thomas Cornwaleys, the largest landowners, together. Under the various conditions proposed by Lord Baltimore, the Jesuits were entitled to 15,700 acres of manorial land and 455 acres of town land in St. Mary's. That would have been a princely estate and, if developed, could have adequately supported all of their missionary activities. As it happened, this legitimate claim got caught up in a larger dispute over land titles.[16]

Lord Baltimore's Charter granted him title to all of the lands that were later erected into Maryland. Much ink and some blood has been spilled over the phrase "not yet cultivated or planted" in the preamble of the Charter, but several times in the 1630s and early 1640s, the royal government supported Calvert's interpretation of this statement and repeatedly dismissed his critics. The result, though, was anything but certain at the time. William Claiborne and his partners claimed that they had purchased the title to Kent Island from the Indians and therefore were not covered by Calvert's grant. Had that precedent been allowed to stand, it would have endangered Lord Baltimore's title to the province. One of the pieces of legislation proposed in the Assembly of 1638, perhaps part of the code of laws sent over by Lord Baltimore, was an act for maintaining the Lord Proprietor's title. The wording has not survived but a similarly titled act was introduced the next year. It outlawed the acceptance of any title to land in Maryland from anyone other than Lord Baltimore, and the second paragraph specifically forbade the purchase or acceptance of land from the Indians. The act effectively negated Claiborne's title to Kent Island and any grants derived from him, and it formed the legal basis for Leonard Calvert's demand that the Kent Islanders have their grants reissued under Lord Baltimore's title.[17]

It was this act to which Father Copley referred when, in his letter to Lord Baltimore, he wrote, "I am resolved to take no land but under your Lordship's title." But he then went on to caution that circumstances might require the Jesuits to accept land from the Indians for a church or a house and suggested that to restrict that liberty might be grounds for excommunication. In light of later events, this paragraph is of great interest. Traditionally, the dispute over land began with the Jesuit acceptance of the farm at Mattapany from the king of the Patuxents. Because of the importance of this issue, we must carefully look at the chronology of the Indian grant.

Father Copley's letter to Lord Baltimore was written on 3 April 1638 and contains two pieces of conflicting information. We have just discussed the paragraph that suggests the possibility that the Jesuits might accept Indian land. This is seventh in Copley's list of points for Baltimore to consider. Listed third is Father Copley's complaint that because of the law for assigning manors, they risked having to choose between Mr. Gerard's manor (St. Inigoes) or "Metapanian." This choice was not, as has been suggested, an attack on mission property. Father Copley was commenting on the Jesuit situation, but the law applied to all of the settlers. More importantly, his complaint implies that Mattapany was already owned by the Jesuits. The question of when the Indian grant was made becomes vitally important at this point.[18]

The gift of Mattapany was probably given to the Jesuits some time in mid- to late 1638, based on evidence derived from the annual letters of the Jesuits for 1638 and 1639, written by the English Provincial who collected the information and sent it on to Rome. To understand the dating of these letters, we must compare the events reported with known events in Maryland and attempt to determine the period of time covered by each letter.[19]

The deaths of two Jesuits are recorded in the beginning of the 1638 letter. Brother Thomas Gervase died in August 1637 and Father John Knowles died in September of the same year. These are the only two events that can be dated with certainty, though the death of another person may offer a clue to the period covered by the letter. Near the end of the document the Jesuits report the death of one of the "chief men" who had been living in Virginia for some time. Possibly this individual was Jerome Hawley, one of the commissioners of Maryland, who died in July 1638. If this identification is correct, then the events recorded in the letter could have occurred as late as August 1638. Almost as important as the events recalled in the letter are those not reported. The Jesuits waited until the Annual Letter of 1639 to announce the arrival of Father Poulton in Maryland, even though he was in the province by 22 November 1638. Thus, the events covered by the 1638 letter must date between October 1637 and October 1638.

The date is important. When the letter was written the Jesuits had not begun their mission work among the Indians, because, it reported, the authorities had not yet permitted the priests to live among the natives. As late as April 1638, Father Copley sought permission from Lord Baltimore to let the Jesuits live freely with the Indians. Support for the dating of the annual letter may reside in a letter written by Father Andrew White to Lord Baltimore in February 1638 in which White barely mentioned the Indians and then only to comment on how hard the language was to learn. Since it was through the missionary efforts of Father White that the Indian grant was obtained, it seems likely that by early 1638, very little missionary activity had been carried out among the Patuxents.[20]

The annual letter of 1639 suffers from some ambiguity in its dating. Only two datable events are recorded in this document The first was the arrival of Father Ferdinand Poulton in November 1638, and the second was the move of Father Andrew White from Patuxent to Piscataway in June 1639. By then the situation had entirely changed. Of the five Jesuits in Maryland, only Thomas Copley was left at St. Mary's. All of the others were out with the Indians or living in a settlement near them. Unlike the previous letter, descriptions of the Indian missions filled page after page, while the events of the settlement at St. Mary's formed but one paragraph at the end of the selection.

One event mentioned in the letter can be dated by reference to other events and documents. The Jesuits reported the case of an Indian who was brought to St. Mary's to be tried for killing an Englishman. After his trial, the Jesuits were able to convert him, and he died a Christian. His baptism and death had an impact on the Tayac of Piscataway and hastened the Tayac's own conversion and baptism. When did this execution take place? The court records regarding it do not survive. The existing court records for the period between August 1638 and August 1642 deal only with estates and inventories. The council minutes do offer one possible piece of information. On 3 February 1640 a warrant was issued to an unnamed person to press three men from Mattapany Hundred and to arrest an Indian from Aquascack town on the Patuxent River for killing an Englishman. If this is the same Indian mentioned in the annual letter, his trial and execution would have taken place early in 1640. The Tayac of Piscataway was eager to be baptized after the trial and execution but was persuaded to postpone the occasion until it could be done with proper degree of ceremony. Accordingly, the baptism was delayed until Pentecost Sunday, 5 July 1640. While his intention is reported in the annual letter of 1639, the actual event is not reported until the letter of 1640. This suggests that the information was transmitted to the English Provincial at least as late as February or March of 1640.[21]

Between the letters of 1638 and 1639 a significant change had taken place in the Jesuit mission. The Fathers had entered the Indian missions with gusto and could already report significant converts. That they could do so supports the contention that some kind of settlement had been reached between Lord Baltimore and the Jesuit Provincial in England. John Lewgar referred to this agreement, in a letter of 5 January 1639 responding to Lord Baltimore's letters of 30 July and 2 August 1638 and a letter Lord Baltimore sent to Father Poulton on 30 July. We can surmise that the letters written in the spring of 1638 by the Jesuits and other

Marylanders had produced such negotiations in England. Lewgar, while still looking for an answer to his twenty cases, repeated Lord Baltimore's statement that the Jesuit hierarchy had agreed there was to be lay jurisdiction in Maryland. It was probably soon after the receipt of these letters, in the autumn of 1638, that the Jesuits were allowed to begin mission work among the Indians.[22]

At this time, Father Andrew White began the mission with Maquacomen, Tayac of Patuxents. One result of this missionary work was a grant of land made at Mattapany from the Indians to the Jesuits. The grant had to have been made when Father White was at Patuxent, sometime between October 1638 and June 1639. Since Maquacomen would gradually become disillusioned with the Jesuits, the grant of land probably was made early in this period, perhaps in the fall of 1638. If that is the case, it is difficult to explain how Father Copley could refer to Mattapany as if it were already Jesuit property in April 1638 when the missionary work that would produce the grant did not begin until the following fall.

Perhaps some of the confusion stems from the loose meaning of the term Mattapany itself. Although the Jesuits may not have received an Indian grant until late 1638, considerable development was already underway in the lower Patuxent region before 1638. All of this area seems to have been known as "Mattapany." The earliest record of the Assembly, in January 1638, recognized Mattapany as an administrative unit equal to St. Mary's and St. George's Hundreds. Eight freemen were identified as living in Mattapany Hundred, representing one-sixth of all the freemen who are identified by place of residence. Of these, six had been servants to the Jesuits before gaining their freedom. Another, Richard Garnett, had immigrated with his family late in 1637 and would soon patent his own manor on the Patuxent. He had arrived on the same ship with Father Copley and had maintained a close relationship with the Jesuits throughout this period. The Society of Jesus obviously played an important part in developing the lower Patuxent region in the 1630s, and even before they began to work with the Indians, it seems that the Jesuits had laid claim to part of the area. It is very likely that most of the freemen from Mattapany were tenants on Jesuit land.[23]

The question we must ask is how the society could have acquired rights to this land if not from an Indian grant? Part of the answer lies in the history of Indian warfare in the 1630s. At the time of European settlement, the local Indians were moving farther inland to avoid exposure to Susquehannock war parties that frequently swept down the bay and up the rivers. Their movements are recorded in several different sources from the 1630s. As early as 1608, John Smith found no Indian settlements on the peninsula between the St. Mary's and Patuxent Rivers south of the future site of St. Mary's, and few settlements on either shore of the Patuxent south of the Tayac's village. This is in strong contrast to the area north of Patuxent, where villages, including the Tayac's, occurred with regularity on each bend in the river. Susquehannock pressure created an uninhabited zone near the mouths of the rivers in southern Maryland and facilitated the settlement of the area by Europeans.[24]

Into this almost abandoned area came the Maryland settlers. Within months of the first landing, Lord Baltimore's commissioners began parceling out provisional land grants to the gentlemen adventurers. Although records of these grants are rare, one or two have survived. More importantly, these provisional grants were often confirmed at a later date in patents from Lord Baltimore. For example, the commissioners granted West St. Mary's Manor to Henry Fleet in May 1634, but it was not patented until 1640, before which time the records reveal considerable development in the area had taken place. The same may be true of Governor Calvert's three manors south of St. Mary's City. The Jesuits are remarkably absent from any of this early development and do not seem to have had any manor land in the St. Mary's area until they purchased St. Inigoes Manor from Richard Gerard. If the Jesuits were occupying land like other gentlemen, where was their provisional grant of manor land? It is possible that Conception Manor, as they originally called their settlement at Mattapany, was their provisional grant. This would explain how they could have a number of tenants on the property as early as 1637. At least one other adventurer, Jerome Hawley, had a provisional grant along the Chesapeake shore at St. Jerome's. Not all of the provisional grants had to be in the St. Mary's River drainage.[25]

The assumption that the Jesuits were given Conception Manor as their provisional grant answers many questions. It explains why Thomas Copley would mention having to choose between two properties already owned by the society and reveals how Mattapany Hundred could be so developed by the beginning of the Assembly of 1638. However, it leaves unresolved the question of the Indian grant, and the controversy it caused.

One must look at all of the Jesuit land along the Patuxent River. In November 1639, Father Poulton had three parcels of land surveyed. The largest, Conception Manor, was 4,500 acres and was centered on Cedar Point on the south side of the Patuxent. Also on the south side of the river was a thousand-acre tract centered on Myrtle Point, identified as St. Gregories Manor. Finally, there was a 3,200-acre tract located on the north side of the river, stretching from Solomon's Island to St. Leonard's Creek, which most likely contained the site of the Indian town of Patuxent. None of these tracts bore the name of Mattapany.[26]

The location of Patuxent village was depicted on John Smith's 1612 map of the Chesapeake and was designated by the symbol for a king's house. Smith placed this symbol on the south bank of St. Leonard's Creek within the area later claimed by Father Poulton. Several of the early Maryland accounts report that Patuxent was the seat of the Tayac or Indian king of the Patuxent Indians, and it was to this town that Father White came in late 1638 to begin his Indian mission. When the Tayac made a gift of land to the Jesuits, it was probably part of this property. The survey refers to Patuxent town in the past tense and probably indicates that the Indians had moved farther upriver. They may have given this property to the Jesuits not out of piety but to put the English between themselves and the Susquehannocks.

One piece of evidence suggesting this piece of property was, or included, the Indian grant can be found in the wording of the 1639 survey. Between Point Patience and Back Creek was a landmark known as Morley's Marsh. In most contemporary land surveys, a natural feature like a marsh or swamp was named after the individual who lived near it. Walter Morley was a Jesuit brother who came to Maryland in November 1638 with Father Poulton. The marsh had to be named after him in the year between

December 1638 and November 1639. This seems to indicate that Brother Morley was living north of the Patuxent in 1639. The significance of this fact is evident when it is compared to the Jesuit annual letter for that year, which reports that Father Poulton, with a Jesuit brother, remained in the plantation given by the Tayac of Patuxent. Walter Morley was the only Jesuit Brother in Maryland at the time. These data suggest that the Indian grant was not the land of Conception Manor but the area north of the Patuxent River.[27]

It was this grant from the Indians that is most often seen as the cause of alienation between Lord Baltimore and the Society of Jesus in the 1640s, but it was only a symptom of a much larger dispute. The Indian land grant merely served to focus both sides on the larger issues involved. Although the Jesuits freely admitted accepting Indian lands, that was not the basis of their claims to the Patuxent properties. When Father Poulton had the tracts surveyed in 1639, they were part of a demand for 11,700 acres that was solidly based on the land rights the Jesuits had acquired in the usual manner. There was no attempt to patent land based on Indian claims. No patents were granted for this land even though they were due to the Jesuits by the Conditions of Plantation and were requested in the normal fashion. The reason for denying the patents had nothing to do with the Indian grant but hearkened back to the controversy surrounding the place of religion, specifically the Catholic religion, in Maryland.[28]

Lord Baltimore expected the Jesuits to behave like secular gentlemen in all things, as they were forced to do in England. For their part, the Jesuits expected to be treated as they were in Catholic countries. Nowhere was this difference of opinion more obvious than in the question of land rights. The Jesuits did not think of themselves as individuals but as part of a larger, corporate body. They held land not as individuals but as a group. Further, even though the land might be granted to the Jesuits, it automatically became the property of the Catholic church and could not be alienated without special permission from the Pope. Property so attached was described as being in mortmain.

In England, where they were considered to be outlaws, the Jesuits often had a lay trustee hold land for them. By the use of such trusts, they avoided the Statutes of Mortmain that had been passed since the reign of Henry VIII, laws that made it illegal to sell or donate land to a religious order without special permission of the king. A lay trustee, who did not hold the land in mortmain, would not be subject to these laws. The religious order would have to depend on the good will and loyalty of the lay trustee. Using a lay trustee would solve the problem over land titles, an idea Lord Baltimore suggested to Father Henry More, the English Provincial as early as August 1638.[29] "It were indeed a very good course for the avoiding of present difficulties," John Lewgar commented, "but Mr. Poulton (whome I acquainted with it) doth not know of any such order taken as yet."[30]

The order Lewgar mentioned did not and would not come from England. The subject of mortmain in Maryland and the problem of clerical exemptions were being debated among the English Jesuit hierarchy and by letter with the Jesuit General in Rome. In September 1639, Father More was replaced as English Provincial by Father Edward Knott. The new Provincial was instructed by the general to maintain opposition to the new laws and to support clerical exemptions. With this hardened attitude, the Jesuits were ready to pressure Lord Baltimore into granting the virtual establishment of the Catholic religion in Maryland.[31]

Father Poulton, in Maryland, opened this phase of the conflict in November 1639 by trying to patent the Jesuit lands in his own name. While John Lewgar made the necessary surveys, Leonard Calvert, on his brother's orders, refused to issue patents for the properties. Cecil Calvert was now precariously balanced between the demands of the state and those of the church. To have granted the lands directly to the Jesuits might have cost him the Maryland Charter, while refusing to do so risked excommunication and damnation. Not being able to move either way safely, the matter of land titles apparently lay idle for a year.[32]

Intense negotiations may have been going on behind the scenes but very little activity appears in the records. The Annual Letter of 1640 recorded a general peace between the government and the Jesuits. The governor and secretary along with two of the Jesuits were reported to have taken a prominent part in the baptism of the Tayac of Piscataway, and the letter mentions no disputes concerning land or other matters. On the other side of the Atlantic, between July and September the Jesuit General wrote three letters concerning the Maryland mission, none of which mention difficulties with the authorities or land disputes. Instead, they offer support for the mission and a desire for more Jesuits to be sent there.[33]

The documents available for this period show the Jesuits in full possession of their Patuxent properties. Father Poulton, described as "of Conception Hundred," was authorized in September to hold an election for a delegate to the upcoming Assembly. References to Conception and St. Gregories Manors appeared in a survey for St. Richard's Manor registered on 4 December 1640. Conception Manor was also referred to in the patent for Snow Hill Manor on 12 February 1641. These references treat the Jesuit properties as any other developing plantation. They indicate that the society was in quiet and peaceful possession of the land.[34]

Shortly afterward, according to Father Thomas Hughes, S.J., the great chronicler of the Jesuits in Maryland, the government seized the Patuxent properties by force and gave them to other settlers. He based his theory on two documents written by the English Provincial, one dated 17 November 1641 and the other composed some time in 1642. Both documents recount how the Tayac of Patuxent gave certain lands to the society to support the priests while they instructed the Indians. In the next sentence, Hughes translated the phrase "ipso facto" to mean "by main force," indicating a violent seizure. This seems to stretch the Provincial's meaning beyond his intention. The phrase normally means "by that very fact" and, in this context, suggests that the fact of an Indian title was being used as an excuse to deprive the society of their land. Such an interpretation certainly fits the available data better than Hughes's vision of the Catholic gentry forcibly dispossessing their priests.

To understand the meaning of these documents, we must consider the date of this supposed seizure and compare it to the subsequent history of the Patuxent properties. Hughes suggests that the expropriation of the Patuxent mission took place some time between September 1640, when Father Poulton was addressed as "of Conception Hundred" in an election warrant, and May 1641, when he addressed a letter to the English Provincial. As there was no mention of the seizure in this letter, Hughes assumed that the information had already been communicated to England by that time. This window can be narrowed further by reference to contemporary documents. The Jesuit annual letter of 1640 recorded events as late as 15 February 1641 and made no reference to land issues. If an appropriation of mission property took place, it had to have occurred between March and May of 1641. There is no evidence in any Maryland records that such an action took place, and some evidence that it did not. The Provincial reports that the land was seized and given to others. No surveys or patents were granted to anyone for these properties during this period.[35]

Maryland documents show the Jesuits in full possession of their Patuxent properties. The election warrant to Father Poulton, dated in September 1640, authorized him to supervise an election for a delegate to the upcoming Assembly and described him as living in Conception Hundred. References to the properties as Jesuit manors occurred as late as 12 February 1641. These references treat the Jesuit properties as any other developing plantation and indicate the society was in quiet and peaceful possession of the land. Later, during the Indian raids of 1642, the Jesuits reported that one of their settlements was attacked. Other references indicate that the stricken settlement was Mattapany House, located on Conception Manor, facts that tend to indicate that the society continued to hold these properties throughout the period.[36]

If the Maryland Jesuits were still in control of these tracts, to what could the English Provincial have been referring when he wrote about the seizure? He may have been responding to a number of Lord Baltimore's actions, both public and secret, that threatened the Jesuit position in Maryland. Among the earliest of these was a document containing four points that Lord Baltimore sought to have approved by the Jesuit Provincial.

Although the document was not dated, it must have been prepared before September 1641. The four points directly deny the privileges Father Copley requested in 1638: the Jesuits could not trade with the Indians without a license, only Lord Baltimore could accept land from the Indians, clergy were to be treated as laymen according to the laws of England, and wills, marriages, and other matters normally handled by church courts would be subject to secular jurisdiction. Naturally the Jesuit Provincial, who was maintaining a hard line against encroachments on clerical privileges, strongly objected.[37]

Apparently at the same time, Calvert was talking with some secular priests in England. This was the same group that his father had battled in the controversy over Bishop Smith's jurisdiction. They were of the opinion that because he was an Englishman and subject to the laws of that realm, his property—Maryland—must conform to those laws as well. Calvert must have liked what he heard, because he began to recruit secular priests for Maryland. Before he could put this plan into action, he had to get approval from the church. A petition, supposedly from the Catholics of Maryland, was presented to the Sacred Congregation for the Propagation of the Faith in Rome, which had to approve new missions. The petition reported that there were many Catholics in Maryland who needed the assistance of priests but failed to mention that the Jesuits had been there for seven years.[38]

On 2 July 1641 the Sacred Congregation passed a decree approving the plan for a mission, asking for more information about Maryland, and seeking a list of qualified priests to be sent. The decree was addressed to Mgr. Rosetti, the Papal Nuncio in Belgium, who began making inquiries about Maryland and the possibility of a new mission. By 7 September information was on its way to Rome, including a description of Maryland and the position of the church there. But the document sent to Rome omitted a vital paragraph that detailed Lord Baltimore's actions against the Jesuits. The missing section reported his attempt at establishing a secular jurisdiction, mentioned the four points proposed, and stated the Jesuit opposition to them as contrary to the dignity of the church. It described Baltimore's discussions with the secular priests, their opinion in his favor, and the fact that the proprietor was trying to put these points into law with the result that the Jesuits might be forced to abandon their mission to the Indians.

Hughes sought to identify the editor who removed this paragraph from the original and implied strongly that Lord Baltimore or his agents were responsible. Certainly it was in Baltimore's interest to have this section deleted, but there is an inherent problem with Hughes's argument. He claimed that the document was edited after it came from England to Belgium and described two distinct changes. The first involved stripping the report of what Hughes referred to as its "true Italo-Anglo style" by removing all of the superlatives. To Hughes, this betrayed an English editor, since English expression was plainer than Italian. Yet the document, in all of its presumably florid style, was written in England and only edited when it reached Mgr. Rosetti. As an example, Hughes cited the passage where the words "Illustrissimo Barone" are replaced by simply "Barone." Compare this to a certificate written by Lord Baltimore himself for the Jesuit Provincial to sign in 1642, in which he referred to himself as "Illustrissimo Barone." If Lord Baltimore was responsible for editing the report on Maryland, why do his own documents not reflect the same plain style?[39]

The second change in the report was the removal of the paragraph previously discussed. If the missing section was part of the original, as it was received by Mgr. Rosetti, he must have known of its contents and approved the removal. Further, he must have been the one who authorized its removal. Whether this was out of respect for the wishes of Lord Baltimore or out of a realization that the mission would not be approved if this paragraph were included, cannot be demonstrated at this point. Whatever the cause, the editing had to have taken place with the full knowledge and approval of Mgr. Rosetti. To insinuate that Lord Baltimore had an active hand in it stretches the truth. With the removal of this material the report became innocuous and the Sacred Congregation was happy to signify its approval for founding the new mission on 12 November 1641.

Another of Lord Baltimore's initiatives in the summer/fall of 1641 addressed the question of the validity of Indian land titles. In August

1641, Baltimore or one of his agents submitted the case of Indian land titles to Doctor Francis Silvius, a noted scholastic theologian at the college at Douai. The case was presented in a series of four questions regarding the rights of a certain Baron Nicholas (Lord Baltimore) over land held by the barbarians within his proprietary colony. Answers supporting Lord Baltimore's position were submitted for Doctor Silvius to consider. The fourth question cuts to the heart of the matter:

> In case a donation . . . has been made by the barbarians to a subject of King N., whether he was qualified or not to that effect by Nicholas, is not Nicholas bound . . . at least in conscience to ratify the said donation . . . or can he dispose of the gift . . . to another or to any other uses . . . whether that . . . subject of King N. were a layman or a cleric; and whether the purposes for which the barbarians made the grant, gift, or sale were pious or profane?[40]

If Dr. Silvius, as a representative of the church, could be persuaded to acknowledge Lord Baltimore's exclusive right to acquire land from the Indians, it would force the Jesuits to only accept land from him and make moot any discussion of mortmain in Maryland. Since Lord Baltimore would be the only source from which land could be acquired, he could force them to accept a lay trustee and avoid the whole question. Under this guise, the Maryland government could conform to the English Statutes of Mortmain while the gentry could privately support various Catholic institutions.

Confident of his ultimate victory, Cecil Calvert proposed a new set of conditions for acquiring land in Maryland. These conditions originally had six articles, although only four were enacted in the province. The fifth and sixth articles, which were eventually abandoned, extended the Statutes of Mortmain to Maryland and disqualified individuals who were members of a corporate body from acquiring land. They also prohibited others from donating land to such bodies or from acting as a trustee for such property.[41]

While some have seen these two articles as a direct attack on the Jesuits by a frustrated Lord Baltimore, they can more properly be seen as an attempt to make Maryland conform to English law and to maintain the Proprietor's title. On the surface, the prohibition against being a lay trustee would seem to indicate a change in attitude since Baltimore's letters of 1639. However, it is necessary to distinguish between public law and private conscience. In England, an individual acting as a lay trustee for Catholic properties was subject to potentially heavy fines. Yet it is clear that such arrangements were both common and well known in England.

> On the financial side, it was well established in practice that bodies of clergy were entitled to own such property as they might be endowed with by their flocks, though arrangements for holding it would naturally include a complicated set of trusts, designed not so much to conceal their purpose as to maintain the fiction that nothing of the kind was occurring.[42]

This distinction between public law and private conscience was quite in keeping with the society Cecil Calvert was trying to shape. He sought to extend his experience as a member of the English Catholic community to the new settlement. Realistically, there was little else he could hope to do. Calvert never intended to allow a Catholic establishment in Maryland, and these new conditions were designed to clarify the situation. He recognized, if others did not, that English law had to apply to Maryland if the Charter was to be protected.

While Lord Baltimore might believe these conditions were necessary, he realized that the Jesuits would have another opinion. To get a sense of their reaction, he instructed John Lewgar to discuss the new conditions with the Maryland Jesuits. Their opinion was that it would be a mortal sin for anyone to cooperate with putting such conditions into effect and that it might be grounds for excommunication. Lewgar advised Lord Baltimore that if the Jesuits were proved correct in their opinion, none of the Catholics would accept the conditions.[43]

The English Provincial was not unaware of these actions during their preparation. He heard rumors concerning Baltimore's questions to Dr. Silvius, the four points, and the new conditions. On 22 September, he wrote a letter to Lord Baltimore defending the rights of the Indians to dispose of their own lands and suggesting that the extension of the Statutes of Mortmain to Maryland would bankrupt the mission, leaving the priests no choice but to become beggars. From this letter it is clear that the Jesuits were still not prepared to accept a minority status in Maryland but would continue to press for a Catholic establishment or, at a minimum, an expanded status over what they had in England. This was a politically dangerous and unrealistic hope.[44]

The futility of it was made clear to the Provincial when Lord Baltimore delivered the new conditions of plantation in early November. Accompanying the other documents was a draft of a certificate for the Provincial to sign. It stated that there was nothing in the conditions that was criminal, nor would they bring Lord Baltimore, his officials, or anyone accepting the conditions under the censure of excommunication. This draft certificate was never signed or authorized by the Jesuits. At the same time, the Provincial received a copy of the four points demanded by Lord Baltimore.

That was the final straw for Father Knott. On 17 November he wrote a letter to Mgr. Rosetti submitting the whole issue to his consideration. He sent Lord Baltimore's four points and his own observations on the issues involved and concluded that the dispute had reached a point at which it could only be solved by arbitration from Rome. Knott also reported that Lord Baltimore would not let any priest sail for Maryland who did not agree with him—of the three priests slated to go to Maryland, only one was allowed to sail. Further, he told Rosetti that he was aware of the efforts of the secular priests to found a mission and suggested that Rosetti should stop them until the issues were decided.

Knott's observations on the Maryland crisis covered a broad range of issues. He began with the conditions under which the Jesuits agreed to found the Maryland mission and the difficulties involved, then defended the rights of the Indians to dispose of their land, specifically mentioning the Patuxent properties. This was the first of the two references used by the historian Father Thomas Hughes as evidence of a violent seizure of those properties. Father Knott discussed the troubles with the Assembly, stating that it was under Lewgar's control and consisted mostly of Protestants. He reported in a stricken tone that Lord Baltimore sought to extend the English laws against Catholics to Maryland—then had the nerve to ask to be exempted from sin for doing so. In the end, Knott requested that the dispute be submitted to the Pope for arbitration and, if the Jesuit position should be upheld, asked that all clergy be required to accept it. For his part, and that of the Jesuits, he would abide by whatever decision came from Rome.[45]

The life of the Jesuit mission to Maryland was now hanging by a very thin thread. On all fronts, the Society of Jesus seemed to be losing ground, both figuratively and literally. Father Knott wrote to the General in Rome suggesting that the mission might have to be abandoned. The General replied that he would be sorry if that came to pass but left the decision to the judgment of the Provincial.

It must have appeared to Lord Baltimore that he had almost achieved his ambition of making Maryland conform to English law, but he had not counted on the ability of the Jesuits to manipulate the powers of the Catholic Church. Father Knott, seemingly despondent in November, had by January completed a vehement memorial to the Holy Office in Rome. The Holy Office was the most important of the Vatican bureaucracies, chaired by the Pope himself. The memorial essentially repeated Knott's observations in stronger language. This time the document was sent to the General in Rome, not to Mgr. Rosetti, and it produced swift results.[46]

On 1 February 1642 the Holy Office wrote to Mgr. Rosetti reporting that they had received disturbing news of Maryland and ordering him to stop all action on the new mission. It went even further and required that if he had given authorization to someone else to act, he was now to order them to wait until further notice. Clearly the charges in the memorial had struck a nerve in the Holy Office, which curtly summarized its wishes so that there would be no question over what to do. "In short, through your prompt action, we desire to have the mission put off, until such time as the Sacred Congregation shall have examined some points, and determined that which is best to do for the greater service of God ever blessed and for the propagation of the holy faith."[47]

Whether or not the points to be examined were those proposed by Lord Baltimore, this was clearly a major blow to his plans. It delayed indefinitely the secular mission and ensured that for the time being the Jesuits would be the only priests in Maryland. The result would probably have been more disturbing to the proprietor had he not been already involved in a more serious dispute with his church.

At about the same time that Father Knott was beginning his memorial to the Holy Office, Dr. Silvius had produced his opinion on the Indian land title cases and completely supported the Jesuit position. He concluded that the Indians were the masters of their own property and could dispose of it as they saw fit. In his summary, he specifically declared that Baltimore could not in good conscience expropriate lands that had been granted by the Indians to the Jesuits or any one else. Lord Baltimore was now in a precarious position with the church. Not only did Silvius's opinion support the Jesuit position on the validity of Indian land titles but it implied that church land was to be held in mortmain. Even worse, by extension it gave validity to Claiborne's title to Kent Island, which Calvert had expropriated, and suggested that anyone who could convince the Indians to sell them land owed no loyalty or rent to Lord Baltimore's government. Such conditions would have made Lord Baltimore's title to Maryland untenable.[48]

Throughout 1642, both sides tried various maneuvers, most of which will never be known, but occasionally evidence has been preserved that sheds light on these developments. The secular priests, apparently unaware of events in Rome, were impatient to develop their mission. As late as 21 July 1642 they had no word on the status of their request. A letter was sent to Bishop Smith on the continent, as the symbolic head of the English church, seeking his approval to begin the mission without authorization from Rome. The letter mentioned repeated attempts to obtain a response from Mgr. Rosetti, who seems to have been ignoring the problem. As the secular priests wanted to sail with this year's shipping, they felt the need to take action. Their argument, which in many ways is close to Cecil Calvert's own, was that Maryland was still part of the English realm and that their faculties authorized them to perform their duties in any of the king's dominions. While we do not know what Bishop Smith's answer was, Mgr. Rosetti was swift to reply to this suggestion. By August 10, he wrote to the Holy Office that he had spoken to the secular priests and convinced them that they needed authorization from Rome and that they should not take any further action until it came.[49]

At the same time, the Jesuits were applying to Lord Baltimore to allow more of their order to go to Maryland. In the previous year, 1641, the Provincial had accepted three priests for service in Maryland, Fathers Rigby, Hartwell, and Cooper. But because of the difficulties that arose that year, Lord Baltimore refused to let any priest go to Maryland who did not agree with his position. Only after great but unspecified difficulties was Father Rigby allowed to sail for Maryland. The other two priests had to remain in England. Relations between Lord Baltimore and the Jesuits had not improved by the time the question came up again. The Jesuits sought permission to send the two priests and enlisted the aid of Lord Baltimore's brother-in-law, William Peasley. Baltimore agreed to let the Jesuits sail if he received "satisfaction in his just and reasonable demands."[50]

These demands, which were set forth in the draft assignment that Baltimore sent to Father Knott, called for the complete surrender of Jesuit property in Maryland. Specifically, the deed mentioned the Patuxent properties but was much more inclusive. It called for the surrender of all properties, no matter how they were obtained, and recognized Lord Baltimore's government as the only legitimate source from which the church could acquire land. This struck not only at the Indian lands, but also at such properties as St. Inigoes, which the Jesuits had legitimately purchased from another settler. The effect of this assignment was to enforce the discredited paragraphs of the 1641 Conditions and bring the Statutes of Mortmain to the province.[51]

Father Knott must have realized that this was a point Lord Baltimore would not concede. He wrote to the General in Rome requesting that permission be obtained from the Holy Office to relinquish the lands. The General replied that he would seek the necessary faculties. But the Holy Office had other ideas, and in December, the General wrote to Father Knott that Lord Baltimore's demands were not to be allowed and that no men were to be sent to Maryland.[52]

While the Jesuit recruits were held up in England, the secular priests somehow managed to get their authorization from Rome. Lord Baltimore's letter of November 1642 reveals that Father Gilmett, who was to be superior of the mission, had sailed in Richard Ingle's ship in early November. He was followed by Father William Territt shortly thereafter. There is no record of how or through whom the secular mission received permission to sail for Maryland. It seems unlikely that they would proceed on their own after Mgr. Rosetti warned them not to do so. Nor do the Jesuits complain about them coming to Maryland without proper authority. We can only assume that they managed to satisfy the Holy Office about conditions in Maryland.[53]

A good portion of Lord Baltimore's letter to his brother was concerned with these new priests and their situation in Maryland. Baltimore was faced with the same problem that he had when Maryland was founded. He wanted priests there, but how were they to be supported? Clearly, the experiment of treating them as independent gentlemen had not worked as Baltimore had hoped. Fathers Gilmett and Territt were not to be treated as ordinary gentlemen but were to be supported as priests. Lord Baltimore hoped they would be maintained by the colonists, especially Leonard Calvert, but if necessary, he agreed to pay them himself, at least for awhile.

It seems ironic that Lord Baltimore's experience with the Jesuits and their demands for a quasi-establishment of the Catholic church led him to sanction the same kind of arrangement with the secular priests. Since he could not trust them to act independently as other gentlemen did, he was forced to find some way of limiting their actions. He chose to treat them in the client-patron relationship common to the English gentry. Since he was not only part of that class but head of the government as well, this amounted to a de facto church establishment in Maryland. Having tried, and failed, to get the Jesuits to support themselves while remaining under the restrictions imposed by the larger Protestant society, Lord Baltimore had no choice but to step in and order things in the best interest of Maryland.

By the time the secular priests sailed for Maryland, Lord Baltimore had been arguing with the Jesuits for four years over the place of religion in Maryland. The questions of clerical exemption, sanctuary, mortmain, and land titles had created serious tension between religious and civil authorities. This tension went well beyond religion and touched on Lord Baltimore's title and his right to govern. Strangely, all of these problems came from people and institutions which should have sympathized with Lord Baltimore's predicament. Instead they tried to force him into a position that would threaten his charter and promise financial ruin. It is a testament to Cecil Calvert's faith in the Catholic Church that he did not let its flawed representatives drive him from its communion.

It is within this context that Baltimore's paranoiac letter must be understood. He held the Jesuits responsible for the defeat of his legislative plan, for threatening his officers with excommunication, for causing arguments within his own family, and for causing problems that threatened the very existence of Maryland. Undoubtedly, other pressures were put on him through Jesuit influence in the English Catholic community. It is little wonder that he took the dispute personally, and this makes his outburst about the Jesuits arming the natives at least more understandable.

Despite all of the problems between Lord Baltimore and the Jesuits, the effects of this dispute in Maryland were minimal. Whatever the status of their land claims, the Jesuits had more land than they could handle. In Maryland they had a status different from that of an ordinary gentleman, even if it was not the fully clerical role they desired. The Catholic gentry, although they might be split politically, were united in their support for the church. Even John Lewgar, who was singled out for special complaint in several letters, was on sufficiently good terms with the Maryland Jesuits to be asked to serve as a lay trustee for their land at Piscataway. This amity and community was soon to undergo severe stress as the religious dispute came crashing onto the Maryland shore.

The touchstone of this phase of the dispute was an action taken by Leonard Calvert against his brother's wishes in July 1641. At the same time that Lord Baltimore was preparing the new Conditions of Plantation which disqualified any member of a corporate body from holding land and any lay person from acting as a trustee for them, the governor was setting up just that kind of arrangement with the Jesuits. On 27 July 1641, Father Thomas Copley submitted a demand for four hundred acres of town land and three thousand acres to be erected into a manor. Right after the demand was recorded, he deeded his interest in these properties to Cuthbert Fenwick, the overseer and factor for Thomas Cornwalyes. Fenwick had the properties surveyed in his name, and legally he was the owner. But this was no simple land transaction, and everyone in the government knew it. The first property surveyed was the twenty-five-acre parcel known as the Chapel Land, and the survey mentions the chapel itself. There could have been no question at the time, and subsequent history demonstrates, that Fenwick was acting as a lay trustee for the Jesuits and that Leonard Calvert and John Lewgar were aware of it.[54]

Lord Baltimore did not become aware of this grant until late in 1642, sixteen months after the fact. Given the speed at which other news traveled, one has to assume that this was not something of which the governor or secretary wanted to make an issue. Their reluctance probably stemmed from the arrival, soon after the grant was made, of the new Conditions of Plantation which specifically denied the validity of land held in trust.[55]

When Lord Baltimore learned of the grant his reaction was understandable. After condemning the Jesuits for plotting his destruction and defending his actions against them, Baltimore mentioned that he had heard about grants of land at St. Mary's and St. Inigoes that the governor had made to the Jesuits. He chided his brother for putting conscience before duty and reminded him that the power to grant land was Baltimore's prerogative—Leonard Calvert had no right, whatever the cause, to assign land against his brother's wishes. Some of the pressure Cecil Calvert felt may be seen in his comment that it was the governor's job to do what he was told and not to force Baltimore to do what others thought was right. He closed this part of the letter with very specific instructions:

> I do once more strictly require you not to suffer anie grants of anie Lands for the future to pass my Seale here to anie Member of the Hill there nor to anie other person in trust for them upon anie pretence whatsoever without especiall Warrant under my hand and Seale to bee hereafter obteyned for me for that purpose.[56]

Given his brother's orders against it, why would Leonard Calvert take the initiative in this matter? This incident was more of a misunderstanding between the two than the governor's attempt to set policy. Governor Calvert did not, despite Lord Baltimore's claim, grant land to the Jesuits. All of the land included in this patent legally belonged to Cuthbert Fenwick and none of it was held in mortmain. This was the arrangement Lord Baltimore himself had suggested in 1639 and which the Jesuits had so strongly resisted. Apparently, Governor Calvert assumed that it was still a viable compromise in 1641 and, with certain restrictions, would satisfy his brother's concerns.

If we look at the land patented by Fenwick, we can see how careful Leonard Calvert was to follow his brother's wishes. All of the land Fenwick claimed had been part of the more than ten thousand acres Father Poulton had asked for in 1639. In order to gain Governor Calvert's approval, the land tainted by an Indian title was eliminated from the demand. The only land asked for by Copley and deeded to Fenwick were tracts either purchased from other settlers, who had a good title, or St. Mary's town lands that could be claimed by headright. The clear land title was an important issue, but equally important was the use of a lay trustee. Fenwick could acquire the land without ensnaring it in mortmain. From Lord Baltimore's perspective, this was as important as anything else.

That both elements, a lay trustee and a clear title, were important to the compromise became evident a week later when Father Copley applied for four hundred acres of land at Piscataway. Apparently the Jesuits and the Catholic community assumed that the use of a trustee would be sufficient to allow them to acquire land. Father Copley deeded the rights to the land at Piscataway to John Lewgar, who probably agreed to act as a trustee. Lewgar, as surveyor general, laid out the parcel and prepared the patent. However, the land at Piscataway was Indian land and, even though it was claimed by headright, it was unacceptable to the governor. As a result, the patent was neither signed nor sealed. Again it is evident that Governor Calvert took his oath to Lord Baltimore seriously and was careful to compromise only within the boundaries set forth in his orders.[57]

Lord Baltimore's discussion of the land controversy and his brother's failings therein was based on two misconceptions. The first was that Leonard Calvert had granted land to the Jesuits, which is what Lord Baltimore had been told. That was not true. The Jesuits would not own land in Maryland, in their own name, until the 1660s. The second misconception or problem was one that Lord Baltimore himself mentioned in the letter. The governor had no way of knowing what recent events or changes had occurred in England. He could not have known that Lord Baltimore was preparing a new set of conditions for the granting of land that would eliminate the option of using a lay trustee to hold church land. By the time this information reached Maryland, the grant had already been made.

Hughes has portrayed the Fenwick grant as an attempt by Father Copley to "save" what was left of the mission, assuming that the government had seized the Patuxent properties, but this misses the real implication of this compromise. The importance of the grant was not that the Jesuits acquired land but that it represented a major change in Jesuit policy. It was a repudiation of the position they had held from the founding of Maryland. They had been arguing for what amounted to a de facto establishment of the Catholic Church with mortmain and clerical exemption. The acceptance of a lay trustee by the Jesuits was a major break with this policy.[58]

It is not hard to postulate a cause for this change with careful review of the chronology of certain events. The first shot fired in the land dispute was Father Poulton's demand for land in his own right in 1639. Over the next four years, it was Father Poulton with whom the governor and secretary had to negotiate. Probably on orders from the Provincial, Father Poulton was a strong defender of the Jesuit position. In June 1641 he met an untimely death, and Father Copley became the head of the mission. Under his leadership, within a month of Father Poulton's death, the concept of a lay trustee was accepted by the Jesuits. Father Copley had already shown himself to be more of a pragmatist than a doctrinarian and, from the time he became Superior, the Jesuits in Maryland seemed more willing to compromise with the civil authorities.[59]

With at least some compromise over land and the prospect of further accommodation on both sides in Maryland, it seemed as though the crisis had passed. True, there were still differences between Lord Baltimore and the English Provincial, and the status of the Patuxent properties was still in question, but a basic understanding had evolved. The Catholic community in Maryland had avoided a serious split over the issue. Only time would tell if their luck would continue.

CHAPTER FOUR

"The tymes now doe seeme perillous"

The same ships that sailed with Lord Baltimore's priests and letters also brought news of a disturbing nature to Maryland. As the tobacco fleet was preparing for its voyage in the late summer of 1642, civil war broke out in England, pitting Charles I against Parliament. Both sides had been making preparations for the conflict since May, when the king had rejected the "Nineteen Propositions" presented to him by Parliament, a plan that would have left Charles a figurehead. In the absence of compromise, war was inevitable.[1]

During the summer both parties raised, equipped, and trained armies. The first major battle occurred at Edgehill in October, where Royalist chances for success were lost when their undisciplined cavalry left the field too soon. In the end, both sides claimed the victory but neither was ready to fight another battle. Except for minor skirmishes, the armies went into winter quarters to await better weather in the spring.

Those events would soon have a major impact on Maryland, but in late 1642 the ripples they cast were mild. London shipping made ready for its outward voyage to the New World with little or no delay. Although the war had been on for three months and a major battle had been fought, Lord Baltimore did not see fit to mention these things in his letter to Leonard Calvert. He was still in London and seems to have had little trouble sending his secular priests off to Maryland despite Parliament's strong anti-Catholic stance. At this early stage of the war, there seems to have been little disruption of the economic lifelines tying the province to the Mother Country.[2]

Still, issues that would soon drag Maryland into the fray and nearly destroy the colony were apparent. As always, religion was foremost. The conflict between king and Parliament was primarily over constitutional issues, but it had more than a hint of religious dispute as well. Even though this conflict was between two Protestant factions, English Catholics could not avoid becoming a part of it. Father Thomas Hughes noted that while England divided itself between Royalists and Parliamentarians, both parties were openly anti-Catholic. Certainly it was a bad time to be Catholic in England.[3]

Nevertheless, the picture was not as bad as some have painted it. Royalists, though unwilling to grant full emancipation to Catholics, were receptive to their aid. The Catholic Marquis of Winchester was a mainstay of support to the king throughout the war, spending £600,000 of his own money in the cause. Nor were Catholics backward in taking up arms in the Royalist cause. Though the Oath of Supremacy barred Catholics from bearing arms, the king relaxed this rule and on 27 September called on the Catholics for armed support. Many Catholic landowners joined the Royalist side, including Lord Baltimore's brother-in-law, Sir Thomas Arundel, who raised a regiment of horse for the king and eventually died of wounds received in battle.[4]

The acceptance of Catholics by Royalist forces was bound to cause a reaction in Parliamentary circles. Both at Parliament and in the field, Catholic and Royalist were assumed to be synonymous. Their reaction was predictable. "The soldiery of the parliament ran riot everywhere with barbarous violence against the Catholics; and many of the laity as well as our own Fathers had infinite occasions for the practice of patience," wrote Father Henry More in his contemporary history.[5]

With the supporters of Parliament exhibiting such virulent anti-Catholic sentiments and Royalists welcoming them, one would expect Lord Baltimore to have been active in supporting his king, but there is little direct evidence to ascertain Lord Baltimore's feelings about the war. That lack of evidence has led many to assume that Baltimore sought to remain neutral despite his assumed Royalist leanings out of an understandable desire to preserve his estate in case one side should win an overwhelming victory. To support this view, they point to Lord Baltimore's negotiations with both Charles and Parliament. Certainly self-preservation was an important part of Cecil Calvert's character, but to ascribe his behavior to that quality alone is to oversimplify his reaction to the war. It also assumes that he maintained the same position during the entire course of the conflict when evidence exists suggesting he changed his attitude over time. Lacking specific information on Baltimore's opinions, historians must rely on circumstantial evidence concerning where he was at specific times, to whom he was talking, and what events were taking shape around him.

Late in 1642, while he was still in London, Lord Baltimore was probably as confused and worried as most Englishmen over the events of the previous months, and like most he undoubtedly thought hard about what course to follow in the crisis. Several scholars have suggested that Baltimore sensibly chose neutrality out of fear of backing the losing side and as a consequence being ruined by the victors. That overlooks part of his problem, for if he failed to support the winning side, even if it was through neutrality, the results might be the same. In pragmatically assessing his prospects, Lord Baltimore had to consider a number of things.

Clearly he could not expect a friendly reception from the Parliamentary side, which equated Catholics with Royalists from the beginning. Early in the conflict, Parliament gave their local committees the right to seize Royalist estates. This same ordinance allowed them to seize two-thirds of Catholic estates even if their owners were not in arms against Parliament. As far as Parliament was concerned, there were no Catholic neutrals. Lord Baltimore's religion had never been a secret, and even in the 1630s his government in Maryland had raised questions at home. Because of their religion he and his officers were already suspect. More than once the charge had been leveled against him that Maryland was a refuge for priests and Jesuits. In the face of anti-Catholic propaganda put forth by Parliament early in the war, there is little chance Lord Baltimore could have thought of supporting this side. Even the question of neutrality must have seemed risky.[6]

On the other hand, Cecil Calvert had very good reasons to be a Royalist. The Calvert family fortune was intimately tied to the monarchy. The colonies of Avalon and Maryland, as well as his family's Irish estates, had been direct gifts from the Stuart kings. Whatever influence the Calverts had stemmed from their connections with the royal court. In the dispute over Kent Island, Charles and his government had been repeatedly supportive of Lord Baltimore. Out of simple loyalty and self-interest, Cecil Calvert therefore had a strong incentive to actively support his king.

If such reasons were not enough, many of Lord Baltimore's relatives and friends were active Royalists. In addition to his brother-in-law, Sir Thomas Arundel, who raised a regiment of horse to serve the king and actively campaigned with them, there was the example of Arundel's wife. So strongly Royalist was Lady Blanche Arundel that she made a legend of herself in defending Wardour Castle, the family home, from a large Parliamentary force for five days. She was, and is, celebrated as a heroine of the Royalist cause. It is well to remember that Wardour Castle itself was barely a mile and a half from Hook Farm, where Cecil Calvert was living. After the castle finally fell to the Parliamentary forces, Henry Arundel, son of Sir Thomas and nephew of Lord Baltimore, besieged it with a force of Royalists. Eventually he set off mines that destroyed the house and forced the defenders to surrender. Another of Baltimore's brothers-in-law, William Arundel, also garrisoned his mansion, Woodhouse, for the king only to see it fall to Parliamentary forces.[7]

The Arundels were not the only Catholics in Lord Baltimore's immediate sphere who were active Royalists. Lady Arundel's father was Edward Somerset, Fourth Earl of Worcester. Before the war Worcester House, in London, was a major center of Catholic activity and the family was closely tied to the Jesuits. The Earl of Worcester was a major financial supporter of the Royalist cause. During the war, Henry Somerset, his son and First Marquis of Worcester, was an important Royalist commander who held the rank of lieutenant general under the Prince of Wales. He would later become the king's representative in an abortive attempt to raise an army of Irish Catholics to fight for the Crown. The ironworks owned by the Somerset family was vital to the Royalist war effort.[8]

Finally, if loyalty and family connections were not enough, one other trend should have been. At this point early in the war, the Royalists were winning. The battle at Edgehill looks in hindsight like a stalemate, but appearances were quite different at the time. When the two sides met, the Parliamentary cavalry and half the infantry fled the field, actions that could not have inspired much confidence in Parliament's ability to defend itself. Prince Rupert's raid on London later that season only served to underscore how fragile the Parliamentary cause was at this time.

Although it seems clear that Lord Baltimore did not participate in the military contest, it is difficult to believe that he did not support the Royalist cause. Over the next year, his actions indicate that he did. Later, when the king's defeat became certain, Calvert, like many other Englishmen, began to look after his own estate by submitting to Parliament and claiming to have been neutral all along, but in this earliest phase of the war he probably maneuvered on a different tack. With Royalist hopes running high, it is likely that he sought some way to prove his loyalty. That effort would soon doom Maryland to two years of conflict and would put an end to Baltimore's vision of a society based on a rural English model.

While Lord Baltimore was agonizing over his loyalties in the emerging conflict, others had no such problems. Captain Richard Ingle was an ardent supporter of the Parliamentary cause from the beginning. Given his upbringing and his strong connections to the London merchant community, there could be little doubt where his sympathies lay. Ingle was moving up in that community and gaining a sense of his place in it. To this point, Ingle had been master of three ships in three years. With this voyage, he had a new ship, the *Reformation,* of which he was part owner. This ship marked a change in his life and gave him the luxury of a stable command. For the next three years, he would sail it to the Chesapeake.

Little specific information is available on the *Reformation.* If we assume that she was a typical London tobacco ship of the 1640s, some of her characteristics can be imagined. Virtually all English ships of this period except the very smallest had three masts. The first two, called the fore and main masts, carried the large square sails that drove the ship. The third mast, closest to the stern, was known as the mizzen mast and carried a lateen sail, large, triangular, and supported by a long yard arm that was often set at forty-five degrees to the mast. If in fact the *Reformation* was rigged in that manner, she shared the profile of virtually every merchant ship depicted in seventeenth-century prints and paintings. The number of masts and the rigging are the only things we can assume with confidence.[9]

Her size can be estimated but never ascertained. In the seventeenth century, a ship's size was related to the type of trade it pursued. A vessel too large or too small for its trade was uneconomical and therefore unprofitable. Ships engaged in the same trade tended to be about the same size. London tobacco ships ranged in size from fifty to four hundred tons with most between 150 and 250 tons. There is some reason to believe that the *Reformation* was near the middle of this range, based on the number of guns she carried and the size and complexity of her crew.[10] English ships were usually heavily armed for protection and to capitalize on any privateering opportunity that might present itself. One writer has described the English ship-building tradition as producing "miniature warships." For more than half a century before the Civil War, he found, "English shipwrights . . . were committed to the substantially built, heavily masted and well-gunned ship for mercantile purposes as for privateering or the navy. English ships sailed triumphantly in waters from which Spanish and Italian shipping had been driven by corsairs and foreign owners sought to buy English-built merchantmen."[11]

One of the few facts known about the *Reformation* is that she carried twelve guns. Weapons varied widely according to the type of trade and the perceived dangers of the voyage. One of the most dangerous trades, from England to the Levant, had a standardized ratio of 12.5 tons per gun, and this may be seen as the maximum. Given that the route to the Chesapeake was not nearly so dangerous, a ratio of 15–20 tons per gun might be appropriate. That would mean that the *Reformation* weighed 180–240 tons, which would be well within the range for London ships.[12]

The ship had a crew of thirty, including, in addition to her captain, a master's mate, a boatswain, two coopers, two gunners, a surgeon, and a servant to the captain. The first three positions were standard on any trading ship. Most ships trading for tobacco carried a cooper, but two was unusual. Perhaps the second cooper was a cooper's mate, or apprentice. The same may be true of one of the gunners. It was unusual to have more than one gunner except on the largest of ships. In any case, the presence of multiple specialists in these positions indicates that the *Reformation* was relatively large. The presence of a surgeon is reportedly indicative of a ship in the range of two hundred tons.[13]

Although exact data on crew size and number of specialists is difficult to obtain, the voyages of a ship called *Abraham* are instructive. She was a ship of two hundred tons that made trading voyages between England and Barbados in the 1630s. Her crew consisted of the master, master's mate, boatswain, boatswain's mate, gunner, gunner's mate, carpenter, carpenter's mate, cook, surgeon, and nineteen sailors, a list approximating that of the *Reformation*. The specialist—a carpenter—missing from the *Reformation* list may simply not have testified.[14]

A look at the size of the ship relative to the crew is also revealing. The *Abraham* carried one man for every 6.7 tons of weight, well within the range for other ships of the period, whose ratios varied from five to eight tons per man. The relationship was codified in 1662 when the government decreed that ships sailing to the Mediterranean must carry thirty-two men for two hundred tons, or a ratio of 6.25. Somewhat later, the Levant Company mandated that its ships carry a ratio of fifteen men for every hundred tons or 6.7 tons per man. With a crew of thirty, it can be posited that the *Reformation* had a total weight of around two hundred tons. This estimate of crew number and ship's size provides a fairly accurate description of Captain Ingle's ship.[15]

As far as anyone can tell, the crew was all English and, not surprisingly, from the London area. They lived in places like Shadwell, Barking, Wapping, Whitechapel, Gravesend, and Stepney. These were all located in London or on the Thames River near the capital and all were associated with maritime enterprises. The crew, especially the junior officers, were all devoted to their captain, and some made multiple voyages under Richard

Ingle. We can assume that most of them shared his sympathy for the Parliamentary cause.[16]

The *Reformation* began its outward voyage to Maryland by slipping down the Thames and within a day or two was at Gravesend, about twenty miles from London and the last port before leaving the river. The town of Gravesend was an important milestone on any voyage from London, for it was the last place for the passengers to bid farewell to relatives and friends or to conveniently send messages. From the time they signed on in London until they cleared Gravesend, the crew was on half pay or "river pay," so the leaving of Gravesend was significant to them as well.[17] In the uncertain times of 1642, Gravesend was where Parliament granted letters of marque to merchant ships sailing to the New World and other places. It was there on 20 November 1642 that Richard Ingle, "not having the feare of God before his eies, but instigated by the instigation of the divell, & example of other traitors & enemies of his majesty traitorously & as an enemy of our Lord the King, did levie war & beare arms against his majesty and accept & exercise the command & captainship of the said town of Gravesend, against the king, for & under the king's enemies contrary to his allegience & contrary to the peace, etc."[18]

This last bit of business concluded, the *Reformation* left Gravesend and headed for the Downs, a protected area of the coast where ships waited for a favorable wind to begin their journey. The wait varied according to the season of the year and could be anywhere from a few days to a few weeks. The *Reformation* was not delayed long and soon sailed out of the Downs, along the southern coast of England and out into the open ocean. With her she carried the infection of war, which she would soon spread to Maryland.

Richard Ingle sailed on what was known as the northern route. This track went from the coast of England in a southwesterly direction until the Newfoundland shore was sighted. From there it was a simple matter to navigate down the eastern seaboard to the Chesapeake. The route was much shorter and safer than sailing through the Caribbean, and it was the one Ingle had followed the previous spring on his return voyage to England. The average length of passage was seven to eight weeks from the

Downs to the Virginia Capes. The *Reformation* seems to have made the voyage in about twelve weeks, although it is possible that Ingle stopped in Boston where he had enjoyed a warm reception the previous May.[19]

By mid-February, the *Reformation* had rounded Cape Charles and anchored at Accomac, Virginia, where Ingle had well-established trading interests. She was shortly followed into Accomac by the *Gabriel and Elinor*, whose master, Edward More, was mentioned in Lord Baltimore's letter to Leonard Calvert. The arrival of the two ships must have aroused considerable interest among Virginia planters eager for news of events in England. In addition to the news provided by crews and passengers, the authorities sought written information in some of the letters the ships carried. Lord Baltimore's dispatches, borne by Mr. Gilmett and Mr. Territt, the secular priests, were apparently safe from prying eyes, but other letters were not. On 20 February 1642 a Northampton County Court reported:

> Whereas by information unto this Court there were certayne Lettres directed to the Province of Maryland which Lettres likewise by Information did concerne the state of England as alsoe of this Collony And whereas the tymes now doe seeme perillous. It was therefore thought Fitt and soe ordered by this Court that the said Lettres should bee brooke open And findinge noe matter of consequence and weight therein they were Sealed upp agayne and sent to the place to which they were directed.[20]

The letters violated by the court, were addressed to Andrew White and Thomas Copley, of Maryland, both of whom were Jesuits. They were written by William Webb of London to introduce a Mr. Cobbs and assure him a warm welcome. Cobbs was to be secretary to Sir Edmund Plowden, who had come to Virginia in December. Plowden, also a Catholic, was trying to organize the colony of New Albion along the Delaware River in New Jersey. This plan had many similarities to Maryland, including a strong Catholic element. Given that the letters were both addressed to Jesuits and are quite vague in their expression, one wonders if Cobbs was a Jesuit himself, perhaps the elusive stowaway about whom Lord Baltimore was so concerned. The letter addressed to Father Copley expressed the hope "that my true friend . . . may be accepted of and assisted in the ways you trace there in your plantation," which sounds very much like some one trying to hide the real meaning. For lack of evidence, this must remain speculation.

A more serious problem concerns how the Court could open these letters. Both refer to Cobbs as the "bearer of these lines." It is unlikely that they were stolen, nor is it likely that Cobbs would surrender them to the court. It is also possible that Cobbs did not survive the trip across the Atlantic. On 24 February, only four days after the letters were opened, Edward More, master of the *Gabriel and Elinor,* petitioned the court for advice. He had transported two servants and two others for a Mrs. Troughton of Maryland. Apparently three of these people were now dead, and he was worried about his passage money. The person who had arranged passage for the four was a Mrs. Poultney, which may be a corruption of Poulton. Mrs. Troughton's maiden name was Poulton, and she may well have been the sister of Father Ferdinand Poulton. Cobbs may have been part of this party or he might have died of the same causes as these others.[21]

The fact that the court not only opened the letters but recorded the contents, suggests a strong desire to know as much as possible concerning the conflict in England. The civil war was a major topic of conversation, and undoubtedly tempers flared here as in England. Most such arguments passed without any notice by the authorities or by historians, but one would take on major significance in the next few years.

On 22 February, the *Reformation* was riding in the harbor at Accomac and trading with the planters. As was the custom, a number of visitors were on board, between eighteen and twenty according to accounts, trading or just talking with the crew. Captain Ingle entertained in the great cabin some of the more important guests, including Argall Yeardley, the commander of Northampton County, and his younger brother Captain Francis Yeardley. When the subject of the troubles in England came up, as it inevitably must, Francis Yeardley, who like most Virginians supported the king, said something disparaging about Parliament and the "Rundheads." Ingle took offense. "All those that are of the King's side are Rattleheads," he retorted. Argall Yeardley cautioned his brother to hold his tongue until they were ashore, fearing that they were vulnerable on Ingle's ship. The young man did not listen, and the argument grew loud enough to be heard all over the ship. Ingle, "in a discontented passion," left the cabin and went on deck. Not finished with the argument, Francis Yeardley followed him above and the argument began to get out of control.[22]

Ingle returned to the cabin, grabbed a pole-axe and a cutlass, and came back on deck. Argall Yeardley, who had also come up on deck, saw Ingle and came out of the Roundhouse saying, "What is the reason that you are Arm'd here in harbour. It is not an usual thing." Ingle replied that he would walk his own ship as it pleased him. Yeardley asked, "Whoe doe you weight for, doe you weight for my brother?" Ingle replied that he was not and probably added something else because Yeardley, as commander of Accomac, arrested him in the name of the king. Ingle answered, "If you had arrested mee in the King and Parliaments name I would have obeyed it for soe it is now." With that, he drew his cutlass and thrust it at Yeardley's chest, threatening but not striking him. Ingle ordered all of the Virginians ashore and told his crew to weigh anchor for Maryland. The Yeardleys and several others did go ashore, but eighteen or more of the Virginians were caught unaware and got a free, if unasked for, trip to Maryland.

Those who were caught on board the ship when it left Accomac testified that Ingle "gave the Virginians good Language untill they came to Maryland." Several men who must have been below deck when the altercation took place asked Ingle why he was carrying them up to Maryland. Ingle replied, "You may all thank Franck Yardley your Commanders brother for had not they both Affronted me I had stayed Att Accomack with my ship." When the ship arrived at an unspecified place in Maryland, a large number of local settlers came aboard and Ingle bragged to them of his escape. He held up his weapons and said, "With this Powle Axe and Cuttlas I seazed the Commaunder of Accomack and his brother."

The testimony of the Virginians concerning Ingle's bravado on his arrival in Maryland matches well with charges later brought against him in a Maryland court. Ingle had strong opinions concerning affairs in England

and was not reticent about sharing them. In addition to boasting about his dispute with the Yeardleys, Ingle proclaimed his loyalty to Parliament up and down the province. On 30 March, in the St. Mary's River, Ingle said that King Charles was no king if he did not join with Parliament, and on 5 April, while the *Reformation* was at St. Clements Island, Ingle reportedly slandered the honor of Prince Rupert. At Kent Island around the same time, he announced that he was a captain of Gravesend for the Parliament against the king. No one in Maryland could have doubted where Ingle's sympathies lay. Yet the Maryland government seems to have taken no notice of these obviously traitorous speeches.[23]

As Ingle's temper began to cool, he resumed the business of a tobacco trader. On 6 March, he was in court at St. Mary's demanding six hundred pounds of tobacco owed by Jane Cockshott to Anthony Penniston, a London merchant. Early in April, he was at Kent Island where he loaded over 2,500 pounds of tobacco owed to Thomas Cornwaleys by various planters and gathered for him by Giles Brent. On 11 April, he gave a deposition before Leonard Calvert regarding a disputed bill of exchange that he had received from Margaret Brent the previous year. His Parliamentary sympathies do not seem to have gotten in the way of his business interests.[24] He even sent a message back to Accomac to try to smooth the waters. Richard Lemmon, one of those carried up to Maryland in Ingle's haste, testified that the captain had asked him to, "remember his love to Mr. Argoll Yardley and did desire if hee had done Mr. Yardley any wrong which hee did not acknowledge any hee would make him satisfaction in any submissive way which hee should desire."[25]

It is important to note in light of later events that Ingle's conflict with the Yeardley brothers was well known in Maryland in the spring of 1643. It would have been hard for anyone not to have heard of it. Yet, no one in the government made an effort to prosecute him for it—and that fact is significant.

CHAPTER FIVE

"Whereas I am determined to goe for England"

The controversy raised by Captain Ingle's opinions was less troubling to the Maryland government than the immediate problem of the Indian war. Maryland had made no effective response to the Susquehannock raids of the previous summer. Giles Brent's aborted expedition left the province looking weak in the eyes of the Indians, and many of the colonists were nervous over the possibility of renewed warfare in the spring. Also, many feared the cost of defending the frontier or sending an expedition against the Indians after the last failed, but expensive, attempt.

By mid-January, colonists' fears had grown acute. Governor Calvert issued a proclamation assuring them that Lord Baltimore would shoulder the burden and began taking steps to prepare the colony for the expected attack. One of his first actions was to restrict the movement of Indians along the Patuxent frontier by authorizing the settlers in that area to shoot any who did not have a white flag or did not surrender when ordered. This was not a call for a general massacre of the Indians nor an order given in desperation; two weeks later the governor forced a reluctant jury to convict a colonist for killing an Indian near St. Mary's. The shoot-to-kill order was issued only for the Patuxent frontier where Indian raids had been most destructive and contained specific conditions for the use of force.

Calvert took another step by making a peace treaty with the Nanticoke Indians of the Eastern Shore. They were one of three tribes earlier declared to be enemies of the province, and this eliminated a third of the Indian threat.[1]

Calvert concluded that these preparations would not stop the Susquehannocks from raiding the settlements. The only way to bring peace was to carry the war to them and demonstrate the dangers of continued hostility. A march or expedition against the Susquehannocks was necessary, but because the colonists were reluctant to fund or even participate in such a venture Calvert was forced to make some extraordinary arrangements. To begin with, Lord Baltimore would honor his pledge to pay for the necessary supplies, ammunition, and transport. Any captured plunder that should have gone to the government to defray the cost of the expedition, would be given to the soldiers who volunteered to go. The expedition would be planned to avoid conflict with the planting schedule, making it easier for men to volunteer. Finally, Calvert negotiated with the major creditors in the colony and got them to agree to postpone collecting debts from the soldiers until the next year. These conditions, so Calvert felt, would be enough to recruit a sizable force.

To lead the expedition, the governor selected Thomas Cornwaleys, the one man in the colony who possessed strong military skills. Cornwaleys had been only marginally involved in the last expedition because of a dispute with the government. He refused to take the oath of a councilor and from September through December 1642 had little to do with the Maryland government. There is no indication of what changed his mind, but now he was willing, even eager, to lead this force of volunteers. But inducements and an able commander notwithstanding, nothing was done. By April, Calvert reported that the means were not available to support the expedition. As a result, he revoked all orders and commissions related to it. The frontier remained at the mercy of the Susquehannocks.[2]

At St. Mary's meanwhile, the Catholic community was undergoing significant changes. The secular priests had arrived in early March and almost doubled the number of clerics in the colony. The governor and Secretary Lewgar probably welcomed Fathers Gilmett and Territt as allies in the struggle with the Jesuits, but in a short time, they discovered their error. According to the Jesuits, when the case was fully explained to them the secular priests defended the Jesuit position. This unexpected turn of events would have made it impossible for the government to implement Lord Baltimore's policy of making Maryland conform to English law. Baltimore, no closer to settling the land issue, now had two priests and their servants to support out of his personal estate.[3]

The question of how to support this new mission or where it was to be located was never fully thought through in the rush to get the clerics to Maryland. In many ways, Lord Baltimore thought of the secular priests as his chaplains rather than as missionaries. As such, he was willing to pay their expenses and instructed his brother to provide them with what they needed and to draw up bills of exchange addressed to him in England to pay for it. This was an important point in keeping up the appearance that they were his private chaplains. Baltimore could have told the governor to pay for these expenses out of his estate in Maryland, but it was often difficult to separate his personal estate from the government and to have done so might have given the appearance of establishing the Catholic religion in Maryland. His support for the priests was not unqualified, and he cautioned his brother to limit his expense in this matter. He hoped the Maryland Catholics could help to support them as well.[4]

An equally vexing question was where the priests would live and where they might perform their function. Lord Baltimore had sent them to Maryland without a specific plan in mind. He requested that Leonard Calvert keep Father Gilmett with him and that a suitable place be found for Father Territt. In the surviving documents there is no indication of their purpose in coming to Maryland or where they were to perform their priestly duties. Baltimore would soon take steps to rectify that problem.

At the time the ships sailed in November, Cecil Calvert steadfastly opposed the Jesuits sending more men to Maryland. Two priests had been waiting more than a year to sail, but his opposition had kept then in London. By April, Fathers Bernard Hartwell and John Cooper, the delayed Jesuits, had arrived in Maryland. Notice of their arrival was added to the end of the Annual Letter for 1642, where it is recorded that their voyage took fourteen weeks, an exceptionally long crossing. If they arrived early in April, the latest they could have left London was late December, hence some kind of compromise had to have been worked out between Lord Baltimore and the Jesuits in December 1642. Part of that agreement involved the lands granted to the Society of Jesus at St. Mary's in 1641, which Lord Baltimore only learned about in November 1642. Since these lands were held in trust for the society and were not technically church lands, no special license was required to sell them. Lord Baltimore was allowed to purchase them and the improvements on them, including a public Catholic chapel.[5]

It is likely that the same ship that brought the new Jesuits also carried Lord Baltimore's instructions for the purchase of the Chapel Land. On 8 April, Father Copley wrote a letter to the general in Rome asking whether the chapel, while not consecrated, enjoyed all of the indulgences of a Jesuit church. If he intended or even knew of the plans to sell the chapel, why would he ask this question? That is another indication of the ship's late arrival. With Lord Baltimore's instruction in hand, on 12 April 1643 the Maryland commissioners of the treasury, Governor Calvert, Secretary Lewgar, and John Langford, prepared a bill of exchange drawn on Lord Baltimore for £200 sterling. The bill was given to Thomas Cornwaleys, who was acting as trustee for the Jesuits.[6]

The price of £200 was a very large sum for Maryland at this time. It is almost certain that the purchase included more than the twenty-five acres of the Chapel Land. Lord Baltimore's agents probably purchased all four hundred acres of town land granted to Fenwick in 1641. Historical evidence from a later period links the Chapel Land (twenty-five acres), St. Mary's Hill (255 acres), and St. Inigoes Neck (120 acres) together as the Chapel Freehold. Such a purchase would have provided Lord Baltimore's priests with a chapel in which to say Mass and a substantial house on St. Mary' Hill, which had been the Jesuit mission headquarters. Yet, even with this extra land and improvements, Lois Green Carr has argued convincingly that the value of the property would be only £130 sterling. She suggests that the purchase may have included some of the vessels and accouterments for saying Mass at the chapel. Given what the Jesuits later claimed to have lost during Ingle's raid, this seems like a plausible explanation of the difference.[7]

The sale of the Chapel Freehold seemed to have been an amicable solution to a difficult problem. It was not the final answer to the land dispute, but it defused an important issue concerning the Catholic chapel at St. Mary's. Now that Lord Baltimore owned it, he could claim that it was a private chapel and not an open violation of English law. He could establish his own chaplains there and confirm its private nature. As it happened, this solution would break down into a dispute over the price, and the animosity arising from the breakdown would strain the unity of the Maryland gentry at just the wrong time. Still, early in 1643 the compromise seemed to be working.

Seven priests were now in Maryland, which would not see this many priests again until the 1680s. The two secular priests were established at the chapel in St. Mary's while the Jesuits were scattered at Mattapany, Portobacco, St. Inigoes, and distant Indian villages. Since the annual letter has not been preserved, there is no direct information on their activities in 1643. Indirect comments by the general of the society indicate that the priests were reaping a bountiful harvest. In a letter of 1 August, the general told Father Knott, the English Provincial, that he looked forward to hearing of the advance in faith being made in Maryland in contrast to Europe. On the same day he wrote an even more optimistic letter to Father Copley in Maryland. He expressed his happiness that the door to Maryland was wide open for publicly preaching the gospel. Both of these letters reflect the general's belief that the compromise reached in December 1642 was working and had settled the dispute with Lord Baltimore.[8]

But the land dispute was not over. It boiled up again in September. Father Knott wrote to the general and informed him of continuing difficulties with Lord Baltimore. The provincial reported that Baltimore was still demanding the surrender of lands accepted without his prior consent and that he wanted the Jesuits to swear not to accept any other land except from him. In response to these demands, Father Knott suggested three courses of action and asked the general's advice on which to follow. The first course of action was probably to give in on all points. On 31 October the general wrote that this course was not possible. He suggested that the Jesuits could promise not to take any other land without Baltimore's consent. As for land already accepted, that had passed into church jurisdiction and could only be alienated by special permission from the Pope.[9] He went on to conclude:

> However, I do not think that it can be of such great consequence; and I suppose his lordship is willing to approve of a fitting subsistence being provided for ours according to our institute; wherefore he will probably consent that the said property serve that purpose. If not, please inform me anew and I will try whether perchance we may not be able to obtain from the Apostolic See the powers necessary to release our claim.[10]

What was of little consequence to the general was a real problem for Lord Baltimore. The Jesuit promise not to accept new land and their willingness to acknowledge Baltimore's property rights might have helped to pacify Cecil Calvert, but the simple fact of Jesuit land ownership in Maryland was still a threat to his control of the province. With the increasingly anti-Catholic sentiment in England, it was even more important that Maryland conform to English laws concerning mortmain. Lord Baltimore would continue to press for the surrender of the Indian lands both for his own property rights and to avoid difficulties with the English government. But, so far as the Maryland council and the local Jesuits were concerned, this dispute was out of their hands and they could only wait until it was settled by those with more authority.

There was another, unexpected result of this late shipping to Maryland. Governor Calvert decided to return to England with this year's fleet. On 11 April 1643 he noted, "Whereas I am determined to goe for England, I doe hereby publish and declare to all inhabitants of this Province, that I have . . . appointed & elected Mr. Giles Brent Esq. to be Lieutenant General of this Province of Maryland . . . until further order from his Lordship therein."[11] This declaration appears in the records with no forewarning and no explanation. We are left to wonder if he made the decision suddenly, perhaps as the result of news brought by the late shipping to Maryland, or if this was a trip that Calvert had been planning for some time. Nor is there any information on why he chose this particular time to leave. A period of civil war would appear to be a poor time to return home. In the absence of specific information, all that remains is informed speculation.

Governor Calvert's actions leading up to the declaration do not indicate that he was preparing to leave Maryland. Through February and March he performed his normal governmental duties with no sign of an impending change. Early in February he called an Assembly but had to cancel it at the last moment. He tried again on 3 April, but there is no evidence that this Assembly ever met. Calvert also sat on the provincial court through the month of March and as late as 9 April was still acting as a judge. The governor signed land warrants throughout the first part of the year with the last being on 10 April. While none of this is conclusive, it does tend to show that Calvert was still active in the government until his departure.[12]

The evidence from his personal estate is more ambiguous. Sometime in 1642, Governor Calvert sold his house, several servants, and his plantation at St. Mary's to Nathaniel Pope. This occurred as early as August 1642, when Pope was assessed 180 pounds of tobacco for the charges of the recent Assembly. Since the assessment for individuals in St. Mary's Hundred was only thirty pounds of tobacco, Pope paid for himself and five other people. Nathaniel Pope never claimed any land rights for servants during this period, and later records show that some of his servants originally belonged to Leonard Calvert. Therefore, it seems likely that Pope was already in possession of the Governor's Field property at St. Mary's. In support of this contention, evidence shows hat Calvert evicted a tenant from the area of the old St. Mary's fort in 1642. He may have done so in order to convey a clear title to the property.[13] Calvert sold the rest of his patented land on 7 March 1643. This transaction involved three thousand acres divided into three manors located south of St. Mary's. He sold the land to John Skinner, a merchant or ship's captain, in exchange for fourteen male and three female slaves to be delivered by 1 March 1644 at St. Mary's. If the slaves were not delivered, Calvert was to receive 24,000 pounds of tobacco.[14]

Taken together, these land sales seem to indicate that Calvert was liquidating his Maryland holdings in preparation for leaving the colony. That would be the only explanation if the sale of his manor land had been for cash or tobacco. However, the provision concerning slaves suggests that Calvert assumed he would be in the colony to receive them. Nor would he be lacking land on which to seat them. He had more than two thousand acres due him that had not been patented and, if that were not enough, he could easily get a grant from his brother for more land.

The best evidence that Calvert made his decision hastily comes from a document recorded after he left for England. On 15 April a new commission for the council was recorded. This was necessary because Thomas Cornwaleys had earlier refused to serve, and Calvert wanted to add Giles Brent and James Neale. The document refers to Calvert as lieutenant governor and lists Brent fourth in a list of six councilors. It was prepared on 25 March 1643, a little less than a month before Calvert's declaration in favor of Brent as deputy governor. If Calvert knew that he was going to England, why did he not acknowledge Brent as deputy governor in this document or, at least place him first on the list? This was not simply an issue of vanity but an important political reality. In the Maryland government, precedence of authority depended on one's place in the commission. For example, in two court cases the next year, defendants were to be brought before the lieutenant general or the "next of Counsell in Commission." Again the evidence is ambiguous but argues that Calvert's plans had not been made by the beginning of April.[15]

If the timing of Calvert's decision is not entirely explainable, the motive is certainly obscure. Maryland records contain not so much as a hint why he chose to return to England. Traditionally, his trip has been explained by an imagined need to consult with Lord Baltimore about the civil war and the position that the Calverts would maintain in it. While the brothers undoubtedly talked about this upon Calvert's arrival, it hardly seems like a suitable reason for him to cross the Atlantic. His letters of November 1642 clearly indicate that Lord Baltimore expected Leonard Calvert to stay in Maryland, and the war was already well underway by that time. If the troubles in England required a shift in policy, that could have been done by letter. It did not require Leonard Calvert's personal appearance. In his instructions to Giles Brent, about six months after Calvert left Maryland, Lord Baltimore commented that he had expected his brother to conclude his affairs in England so that he could return with this year's shipping but was now aware that that would not be the case. Does the reference to "his affairs" reflect the personal nature of Leonard Calvert's trip?[16]

There is little information on where Leonard Calvert was or what he did while in England, but one thing does stand out—Calvert fathered two children during his visit. This is remarkable given the short length of his stay. With the best possible weather and no other delays, Calvert spent at most twelve months in England. Even assuming that he and his new wife put their first child out to a wet-nurse, a common practice to avoid breaking the proscription against intercourse while breast feeding, this did not leave much time to conceive a second child. Given natural time constraints, we have to assume that Calvert met and married his wife almost as soon as he arrived in England, otherwise there would not be time to complete one pregnancy and begin another. Perhaps, Calvert's motive in going to England was to seek a wife or to complete arrangements that had been made for him. This would account for such a swift courtship and conception.[17]

The question of who was the mother of Calvert's children bears directly on this point but is not easily settled. A tradition of long standing, dating at least to the 1840s, holds that Leonard Calvert married Ann, sister of Margaret and Giles Brent. This tradition was questioned in the 1920s based on English records that seemed to contradict the relationship. Evidence included a baptismal record for an Ann Brent dating to 1637 and a listing of an Ann Brent as a non-juring spinster in 1651. Other researchers pointed to the absence of a marriage record of any kind.[18]

There are problems with all three of these lines of argument. An Ann Brent was baptized in 1637 at Ilmington Church, but which one? If she was the sister of Margaret Brent, who was born about 1601, her mother was an amazing woman. There is also a birth record for an Ann Brent dated 1612. The Brent genealogy lists her as the daughter of Richard and Mary (Huggerford) Brent. This would make her the aunt of the Maryland Brents. Yet, her supposed father died in 1591. More likely she was the daughter of Richard and Elizabeth (Reed) Brent, the parents of the Maryland Brents. This would make her only two years younger than Leonard Calvert. Part of the confusion stems from the Brent habit of using the same names generation after generation, whence they become hard to distinguish.[19]

The second piece of evidence cited as contradicting a Calvert-Brent match is the listing of Ann Brent as a non-juring spinster in 1651. In this reference, she is specifically identified as the daughter of Richard Brent and is listed with other siblings that identify her as the sister of Margaret and Giles Brent. This terminology is misleading and includes an assumption on the part of the author who reported it. A non-juring person was one who would not swear an oath to uphold the Parliamentary government and the Protestant religion. In the 1650s most of the Brents were non-juring simply because they were Catholics. This became important because their estates had been sequestered by Parliament in 1644 and the only way to get them back was to petition for their return. In a series of petitions, the children of Richard Brent Sr., specifically, Fulke, Richard Jr., Edward, George, Ann, and Jane Brent, attempted to free various parts of the seized lands. The records do not call Ann Brent a spinster. Based on these records, the genealogist assumed that Ann Brent was a spinster since she was thirty-nine years old and still listed under her maiden name, but in this regard it is important to look at her sister Jane. Although Jane Brent was listed three times in the same set of records, only once did they mention that she was married and never did they list her by her married name but always as Jane Brent. What is important in this record is that these women were the daughters of Richard Brent, not whether they were married. This evidence is not the conclusive proof against a Calvert-Brent relationship that it was thought to be.[20]

Finally, there is the question of a marriage record. It should surprise no one that individuals from such active Catholic backgrounds would want to be married by a priest and that the chance of a marriage record would be slight. A search of the published marriage registers for the counties associated with the two families (Wiltshire, Dorset, Warwickshire, Gloucestershire, and Worcestershire), reveals nothing. Most of the parish registers do not go back that far, and those that do contain a consistent gap in the records associated with the Civil War, from 1639 to 1653. Even if Leonard Calvert and Ann Brent had been staunch members of the Church of England, there would still be little possibility of finding a record of their marriage because of the disruptions of civil war.

But both families were strongly Catholic, not Protestant, and to have been married in a Protestant church by a Protestant minister would have been unthinkable. Nonetheless, one of the problems of English Catholic genealogy is the lack of vital records. If a record was kept at all, it was held by a mission priest and subject to the extreme vagaries of preservation. More often than not, no record was made. The ceremony was performed by a priest in front of witnesses and the memories of the witnesses provided the record.[21]

If all of the evidence against the marriage of Leonard Calvert and Ann Brent seems so ephemeral, is there any real evidence supporting such a relationship? No hard evidence has come to light. One can point to an early and consistent tradition that some kind of family relationship existed between Margaret Brent and Leonard Calvert, but that remains an assumption. One other suggestion that a relationship existed is the rapid change in the fortunes of Giles Brent. In late 1642 he was off the council and being sued, civilly and criminally, by the government. Only a few months later he was not only back on the council but was appointed to govern in Calvert's absence. Such a reversal could have happened naturally, but a pending family relationship would certainly provide a better explanation.

Whether Calvert was leaving Maryland for politics or love remains an open question, but he had preparations to make before he sailed. On the same day he appointed Giles Brent, Calvert exempted Nathaniel Pope and his nine servants from attendance at musters or being called out of his house to go on any march. This was the same exemption that the governor had claimed for himself the previous summer when the Assembly was debating a response to the Indian raids. The granting of this exemption has been misinterpreted many times and can only be understood in the context of recent archaeological discoveries at the site of Governor Calvert's house, which date its construction between August 1641 and August 1642.[22]

Calvert's motivation for building it was less clear. Apparently he lived at the fort for eight years without feeling the need for a large house. Within a year, he had patented the land and built what was likely the largest house in Maryland. One could argue that Calvert sought a house worthy of his status as governor, but this does not seem to fit his personality. His purpose was twofold: to provide a suitable meeting space for the Assembly and assure the safekeeping of provincial records, and to provide lodging for the legislators. The Assembly had voted for the first in 1639, when they authorized the building of a town house, though whether any of the six thousand pounds of tobacco voted by the Assembly for its construction were actually used in building Calvert's house remains uncertain. Whatever the case, the northern section of the house fulfilled the functions of the town house well into the late seventeenth century. Calvert's other purpose in building such a large house may have been to provide an ordinary or inn in which the Assemblymen and other travelers could stay while visiting St. Mary's. Given the dispersed nature of settlement in early St. Mary's, accommodating the first Assemblies must have been quite a task. Calvert's house, later known as the Country's House, filled both of these roles during most of its history and was built with these dual roles in mind. The exemption granted to Pope and his servants recognized the need to keep the government house open and safe.[23]

It is probable that governmental functions continued there after Calvert sold the house and land to Pope in 1642 or 1643. The Assembly continued to meet there; the location of the 1645 session was identified as at "Mr. Pope's house." It is likely that other government records, symbols, and supplies were kept there as well. By exempting Pope and his servants, as he had earlier done for himself, Calvert sought to provide protection for these items.[24]

With his public and personal responsibilities arranged, Calvert sailed for England. He left the province between 12 April, when the bargain for the Jesuit property was made, and 15 April, when Brent was sworn in as governor. One of his last recorded acts was to take a deposition from Richard Ingle concerning a debt owed by Margaret Brent. Although the deposition was written on 11 April, it was not recorded until five days later when Peter Draper, Calvert's attorney, brought it into court. Since Calvert and Ingle both left Maryland at about the same time, it is possible that Calvert took passage on Ingle's ship. If they were not friends, they at least were business associates, and Calvert could be certain that Ingle would continue that relationship.[25] It would be interesting to know if Ingle took Calvert to London, the hotbed of Parliamentary activity, or put in somewhere along England's southern coast to allow him to join his brother in Wiltshire. Given the situation, Calvert probably would not have risked going to London since he was known to be a Catholic and therefore presumed to be a Royalist. While the two men may have parted on friendly terms, the next time they met would be as enemies.

When Leonard Calvert sailed away from Maryland, he left a government that seemed paralyzed and unable to perform basic functions. The proclamation appointing Giles Brent deputy governor conferred on him the full range of powers that Calvert had used, but Brent never exercised those powers. Whether this was because of his own lack of initiative or some private understanding with Calvert will never be known. A flurry of activity lasting through late April followed Brent's taking the oath of deputy governor, then nothing much occurred for the rest of the year.

Maryland government virtually shut down. Brent made no attempt to call an Assembly. After 24 April, no executive documents such as commissions or proclamations are recorded until late in December. While the provincial court continued to meet, Brent was conspicuous by his absence. He sat on the bench in April and except for one possible appearance in July stayed away from the court until January. The same lack of activity is evident in the land records. Warrants and surveys are recorded through January 1643. Some planters continued to submit claims for land throughout the year, but there is no record of any being granted until May 1644.[26]

Several things contributed to the lack of activity. Certainly Brent's residence on Kent Island, far from the seat of government, was one. If Calvert expected Brent to neglect his own business to run the government, he was disappointed. But it is possible that Calvert did not actually give Brent the unrestricted powers that appear in his appointment. In July 1643, Lord Baltimore wrote a letter of confirmation to Giles Brent as deputy governor but restricted his authority in three specific areas: Brent could not call an Assembly, grant land, or meddle in the dispute between Lord Baltimore and the Jesuits. Although the letter was written in July it did not arrive in Maryland until late in December 1643. That Brent was already conforming to the restrictions long before the letter arrived suggests that Leonard Calvert had made those arrangements before he left and that, like Brent's appointment, Lord Baltimore was only confirming them.[27]

Brent's authority may have been limited in some areas, but he still had to face a nagging problem that Calvert had left unresolved. The continued threat from the Susquehannocks prompted Brent to issue on 17 April a commission to Thomas Cornwalyes to lead an expedition against the Indians. Cornwalyes was authorized to press every third man in the colony and to make sure they were equipped and supplied by their communities. Like all previous attempts, this commission was withdrawn under protest.[28] Instead of an expedition, Brent then proposed to fortify Palmer's Island at the mouth of the Susquehanna River and to garrison it with a company of ten "choice shott." They would guard the head of the bay, presumably slowing or stopping the Indian raids. The garrison was to be supplied with thirty pounds of powder, one hundred pounds of shot, twenty barrels of corn, two iron pots, an iron pestle, swords or half pikes, and a small boat. They were also to receive enough nails to build a house. This establishment was optimistically named Fort Conquest.[29]

Brent intended Fort Conquest to be a permanent solution to the Indian problem. The twenty barrels of corn were enough to support the company for almost a year. The proposal does not list any guns or cannon for the fort. Presumably the soldiers either had their own or were supplied from provincial stocks. Although they were given nails to build a house, there is no mention of axes or other tools to cut the wood. Again these may have been supplied by the soldiers. The money to pay for the garrison was raised by an assessment on the colony and by donations of supplies. Ample evidence indicates that the garrison was actually sent to Palmer's Island and, since April was the beginning of the raiding season, the troops moved swiftly.

But a defensive posture did not suit Captain Cornwalyes, who was eager to carry the war to the Indians' home ground. He sought, and was granted, permission to raise a company of volunteers and to lead them against the Susquehannocks. Brent gave him the power to accept volunteers on whatever terms they would accept and to dispose of any captured goods as Cornwalyes saw fit. It is a testament both to the charisma of the captain and to the seriousness of the threat that more than fifty men volunteered to go with him.[30]

Since it was to be an all-volunteer expedition and not chargeable to the colony, little in the official records addresses it. However, enough evidence exists in different sources to suggest what happened on the march. Numerous scholars have contended that there were two expeditions against the Susquehannock between early 1643 and mid-1644, a supposition based on contradictory accounts in English and Swedish sources. It is more likely that Maryland made one thrust into Susquehannock territory, because close reading of both sets of accounts discloses remarkable similarities in the narratives.[31]

The expedition probably sailed from St. Mary's early in the summer. After Brent granted permission for the march in April, Cornwalyes appeared regularly in the court records until early June, then disappeared in those records until early November. Since the court continued to meet through the summer and Cornwalyes, a major creditor, does not appear, it is likely that he led the expedition within this period. The purpose of the march was to stop the Indians from raiding Maryland, making an early departure necessary.

Cornwalyes and his men sailed up the bay, probably stopping on Kent Island to confer with Brent. They also might have picked up additional men and supplies at this point. They may well have stopped again at Palmer's Island to check on the fort and to hear news of Indian movements. After Palmer's Island, as the Marylanders sailed up the Susquehanna River, they were in enemy territory and had to be on their guard. Their object was the main Susquehannock village, located some sixty miles upriver on Conestoga Creek. The town, protected by a palisade and containing an estimated nine hundred people, was situated on a naturally fortified point of land north of the creek. It sat on a rise, about ninety feet above the water, with steep sides on all but the north slope, which rose gradually. The Susquehannocks could reasonably muster about 250 warriors to oppose Captain Cornwalyes and his fifty or so militiamen.[32]

The village was two miles from the Susquehanna River, and Cornwalyes may have disembarked his men and marched overland, hoping to catch the Indians by surprise. He did not. The militia arrived before the town and set up two small cannon. After firing a number of rounds into the village they awaited the Indian response, unaware that most of the warriors had slipped out unseen and now surrounded them. A small party of Susquehannocks attacked the boats, killing three of the men left to guard them.[33]

The attack on the boats is probably recorded in a court case that has been interpreted as a failed trading voyage, when in fact the timing and circumstances argue that it took place during Cornwalyes's expedition. John Hollis testified that he was on deck when Thomas Boys called on him to help Roger Oliver in the ship's hold. Although not stated in the account, it is implied that the ship was under attack. Hollis leapt into the hold and saw Oliver struggling with an Indian. Using his gun as a club, Hollis struck the Indian on the head with the barrel. He saw Oliver fall to the floor, but because he was fighting other Indians he did not examine him. When he did Oliver was dead. John Nuttall also testified to Roger Oliver's death, though Nuttall did not witness the struggle and did not see the body until six hours after the attack, suggesting that he was not in the boat at the time. Perhaps he was with Cornwalyes on land. When he examined the body, he found one wound in the throat and a gash on the chin. Next to the body was a blood-stained Dutch knife broken at the handle. The English account of this battle reported that the Indians surprised some of the Marylanders in the reeds, killing three while losing only one of their own.[34]

The main body of the militia soon came under attack, and Cornwalyes ordered his men to retreat to the boats. A desperate fight ensued, and without someone like Cornwalyes to hold them together, the Marylanders might have been wiped out. As it was, in fighting their way free the militia reportedly killed twenty-nine of the Indians while losing only one of their own. The cannon and other supplies were left behind.[35]

On the basis of surviving evidence, the battle can only be described inconclusively. The single English account emphasizes the valor of the militia fighting against overwhelming odds; it does not mention losing the cannons and having to retreat. On the other side, Swedish governor Johan Printz, writing in June of the next year, reported that the Marylanders had lost two cannon and some men. A much later report, written in 1654 by Swedish geographer Peter Lindeström, provides details that he later heard of the battle on a much exaggerated scale. He claimed that the Maryland force numbered between two and three hundred men and that a number of them were killed and fifteen captured. Lindeström went on to describe the cruel tortures that the prisoners suffered. The editor of this translation of Lindeström's account refers to it as an atrocity story and relegates it to the same category as Lindeström's description of mermaids. Surely if Maryland had lost twenty or thirty men as the story implies, there would be probate or other court records dealing with the legal ramifications. Yet Lindeström's mention of the cannons identifies this story with Cornwalyes's expedition.[36]

Some results are clear. The Indians had surprised and driven off the militia, captured cannons and other spoils of war abandoned during the retreat, and protected their village—all marks of a victory. The Marylanders claimed to have inflicted heavy casualties on the Susquehannocks while losing only four men. Further, they had penetrated deep into Susquehannock territory, proving that the village was within their reach. The Susquehannocks took this threat seriously. Almost ten years earlier, they had told William Claiborne that they did not like to fight close to home. Most importantly, neither the attack on the village nor the presence of Fort Conquest kept the Indians from raiding the settlements in the summer of 1643. The Susquehannocks continued to slip down the bay, terrorizing settlers and Piscataway alike. They looted the Jesuit plantation at Mattapany a second time and threatened all of the Patuxent River settlements. There is little information on where or when the raids occurred but Governor Brent later reported that Patuxent River "received an assault to their very neare cutting off one of their plantations." Apparently the eastern shore Indians, perhaps sensing a weakness in Maryland, joined in the war. The Patuxent frontier was in danger all year long.[37]

In preparing for the next summer and the raids that were sure to come, Brent in December 1643 issued two commissions. One authorized James Neale to raise a volunteer company and patrol the area of the Patuxent River looking for eastern shore Indians. This was to be a small operation and organized around those who were willing to go. In contrast, Brent gave command of the colony's major expedition against the Susquehannocks to Captain Thomas Cornwalyes. The captain was authorized to levy men and press supplies and equipment from the colony as he saw fit. The fact that Brent was willing to trust the provincial defense once again to Cornwalyes is either testimony to the perceived success of the previous expedition or a sign of resignation that no one could do better. With luck, this new expedition might have kept the province safe in the next year, but other events would soon intervene, alienating Cornwalyes from the government and ensuring that no expedition would be conducted.[38]

CHAPTER SIX

"Which bills . . . I have thought fit not to accept"

In late fall 1643, merchant ships began arriving in the Chesapeake, carrying with them the manufactured goods so important to the settlements and, once again, bringing news of renewed fighting in England. During the previous winter, king and Parliament had tried to negotiate a peaceful settlement. The talks had broken down in March, and both sides prepared for another year of conflict. In July, Royalists took the port of Bristol, giving them desperately needed access to the sea. Munitions and other supplies waiting on the Continent needed a safe landing place, and soon troops from Ireland would arrive to support the king. Despite this success, the larger campaign stalled, and by fall each side was cautiously probing the other.[1]

Though major battles decided the course of the nation, many smaller actions determined the fate of individual families. Lord Baltimore, his family, and relatives were in the line of several armies' march during this period. Their lives changed as the result of these large and small events. Sir Thomas Arundel, Baron of Wardour and brother-in-law of Cecil Calvert, was with his regiment at the Battle of Stratton on 16 May when he received two pistol wounds to the thigh. He was taken to Oxford, where he died on 19 May 1643. The news of Baron Arundel's death was overshadowed by the dislocations his family suffered at the same time. While he was off fighting with his regiment, the County of Wiltshire erupted in a localized version of the Civil War. The lines of conflict were clearly drawn according to long-standing rivalries and allegiances. In Wiltshire were two prominent families, represented by the earls of Hertford and Pembroke. Hertford became a Royalist and an important military leader. Pembroke sat in Parliament and later became its governor of the Isle of Wight. Families that had supported Hertford or Pembroke before the war carried those loyalties into the conflict. It is not hard to imagine which side the Arundels supported. If their natural tendency toward Royalism was not enough, they knew the Earl of Pembroke was virulently anti-Catholic.[2]

Early in 1643 it became known that Hertford would be coming to Wiltshire from Oxford to raise troops for the king. In anticipation of that move, a number of local houses were turned into Royalist garrisons. The history of these garrisons reflects the local nature of the conflict in Wiltshire and holds implications for Lord Baltimore's actions during these months. Leading the Parliamentary forces in the county was Sir Edward Hungerford. He was from an old county family and had served as lord lieutenant and sheriff of the county in the 1620s. In 1640 he served as a member of Parliament, and in 1642 he was sent to execute the militia ordinance in Wiltshire. Through late 1642 and early 1643 he attempted to reduce the Royalist garrisons in the county and to raise money for Parliament from Royalists and from papists.

Wardour Castle, home of the Arundels, proved difficult to reduce. The massive fortification had been built in 1392 when sieges were common, and it had been designed to withstand such assaults. The castle was a large, hexagonal tower with two smaller, rectangular towers flanking the entrance. It was built of stone and had walls that were eight feet thick and able to withstand any field cannon that might be brought against it. Although physically strong, the castle was held only by Lady Blanche Arundel, her daughter-in-law, three of her grandchildren, twenty-five soldiers, and about as many servants, many of them women.[3]

On 2 May, Sir Edward Hungerford and Colonel William Strode brought their combined force of about 1,300 men to reduce the castle. They sent a messenger to Lady Blanche telling her that since the castle was a well-known resort for Royalists and malignants (i.e., papists), they had been authorized by Parliament to search the house and if they found any arms or plate, to seize them for the war effort. She denied them entrance, saying that her husband had ordered her to keep the castle for the king and she would obey him. Hungerford brought up two cannon and began pounding the walls, a bombardment he continued for five days with little effect other than rattling the nerves of the defenders. The attackers repeatedly offered the women and children the opportunity to leave, but they refused.

The presence of women and children in the castle placed the Parliamentarians in an awkward position. This was a local conflict, despite its national overtones. Attackers and defenders both were related to numerous families in the neighborhood. The slaughter of prominent women and children would cause consternation in the county and reprisals on their own families, and the attackers hesitated to storm the castle while these non-combatants were still inside. Antonia Fraser has neatly summarized the formal rules governing a siege during the Civil War. The attacker had to first ask for a surrender. If the defenders "promptly surrendered," non-combatants were "generally allowed to depart peacefully," leaving the soldiers to negotiate the details of surrender. "If on the other hand, there was no surrender, then according to the rules of war, the besieged civilians were equally at risk with the military when and if the stronghold was taken by force; there need be no quarter given."[4]

The end of the siege of Wardour Castle came quickly after the arrival of Edmund Ludlow and his troop. Ludlow, also from Wiltshire, would eventually become Lieutenant General of Horse under Cromwell in Ireland. He discovered two vaults under the castle, part of a 1578 remodeling, that were used to store supplies and carry waste out of the structure. Hungerford's men put barrels of gunpowder into these vaults and set them off. The first explosion caused little damage, but the second shook the castle and damaged the understructure. Hungerford next brought up a petard to force the door of the castle. This was a generally bell-shaped device with a strong explosive charge that was attached to a door or wall so as to direct the force of the explosion against the target. He also secured materials for fireballs to throw in the windows. With a flourish, Hungerford turned over an hourglass and informed the defenders that if they had not surrendered by the time the sand ran out, the castle would be stormed. Knowing that they could not hold out once the door was blown, Lady Blanche asked for terms. The articles of surrender specified that all were to be given quarter, that the ladies could pick six servants to accompany them, and that the castle and goods were to be safe from plunder.[5]

Lady Blanche surrendered, but the terms were not kept, and she and her family were carried as prisoners to Shaftsbury. The castle was thoroughly plundered with five cartloads of goods and furniture sent to Dorchester. Inside the castle, the soldiers reportedly destroyed a "chimney piece" valued at £2,000 and a large number of pictures. Although it cannot be proved, it is often assumed that the "chimney piece" was an altar and the pictures were Catholic in nature. Soldiers also damaged the estate by burning houses, destroying fences, cutting timber, breaking dams, and selling off anything they could move. It was estimated that the damage totaled £100,000.[6] The castle was entrusted to Edmund Ludlow, who commanded his own troop and a company of foot. The victors took down their siege works and filled the trenches. They broke down the vaults under the castle and filled them as well to prevent the placing of new mines. Many of the windows on the lower floor were bricked up and a well dug in the castle courtyard, a necessity since the lead pipe that used to carry water to the castle had been dug up and sold. Ludlow began to stockpile food and other supplies in anticipation of a Royalist siege. In order to get a sufficient supply of ammunition, he had to send to Southampton on the southern coast, which had a strong garrison. Despite these preparations, the castle was soon retaken by the Royalists.[7]

While this fighting was taking place in Wiltshire, where was Lord Baltimore? His home, Hook House, was only a mile and a half from Wardour Castle. If he stayed in Wiltshire during the summer of 1643, he must have suffered the same confiscations and troubles that other Catholics, Royalist or not, endured. It may have been particularly hard for Lady Baltimore, Ann Arundel, to see her family home destroyed by the war, but there is no way to know where the Calverts were staying. They may have fled to Oxford with the king, or to some other location beyond the reach of the fighting.[8]

The only specific evidence concerning Baltimore's whereabouts or plans is contained within the commissions and other documents he sent to Giles Brent during this time. The first of these, already discussed, was written on 14 July 1643. There is no indication of where it was written or how it was sent to Maryland. All of Cecil Calvert's earlier, and later, proclamations and commissions end with a standard phrase including the date and the place it was written For example, part of the 1636 Conditions of Plantation end with the phrase, "Given under my hand & Seale at Warder castle in the Realm of England, the 29th August 1636." Of all such documents, only that of 14 July 1643 lacks a place name. Was this simply a slip of the pen, or does it mean that Lord Baltimore did not want others to know where he was? In the commission he expressed his plans to be in Maryland by January. This is perhaps a reflection of his desire to escape the war. In any case, one wonders how he planned to get to Maryland. At the time the document was written, Parliament controlled all of the ports and shipping. In part, that may explain why it took so long for the commission to reach Maryland. It was written in July but did not reach Maryland until late in December. In the last paragraph, Baltimore made a point of emphasizing that the document should be speedily proclaimed in Maryland, but that did not happen for twenty-two weeks. Even with the worst weather and wind, no crossing of the Atlantic should have taken so long. Perhaps the letter had to wait for the Royalist capture of Bristol to open a sea link to Maryland.[9]

The second set of documents dated to this period was written on 17 and 18 November 1643 at Bristol. The closing phrase changed back to its original form but included one new element, exemplified in the appointment of Thomas Gerard as a member of the council: "Given under my hand & seale at armes at Bristol the 17th November 1643." The phrase "at armes" at first suggests active participation by Lord Baltimore in the war, but that is how he would end commissions well into the 1660s, making that explanation less probable. More likely it reflects a new seal which would later become the Great Seal of Maryland. The front depicted Calvert mounted and in full armor with his sword drawn. The phrase "at armes" thus possibly refers to this image of Lord Baltimore.[10]

Even this is speculation, as there is little evidence of what Lord Baltimore's seal looked like until 1648. Although the seals were made of silver, the impressions they left were in wax, and only one small fragment of a wax impression of the Maryland seal on a document before 1648 has so far been discovered. Unfortunately it shows what would be the reverse side of the 1648 seal and contains a portion of Lord Baltimore's family crest. Until a more complete specimen is discovered, we cannot be certain that the knight in armor motif did not occur on the earlier seal.[11]

Yet the language describing the seal changes so abruptly and permanently in 1643—and later the same language is used to describe the 1648 seal—that we must conclude that Lord Baltimore created a new one. If that is the case, we must consider the context in which this change occurred. It was created at a time when the Royalist cause was at its height and, with a little more luck, might have triumphed. It shows Lord Baltimore in what would be the archetypical Cavalier pose of a knight in armor. It was first used in Bristol, a city only recently stormed and currently garrisoned by victorious Royalist forces. If the new seal does not indicate Baltimore's involvement with the Royalist cause, it at least shows his sympathy for it.

The commissions themselves also contain valuable information on a number of topics important to our story. The restrictions that the 14 July commission placed on Giles Brent have been mentioned. It is in this commission that one first hears of a dispute over the Chapel Land purchase. Lord Baltimore did not accept the bills of exchange drawn up by his agents for the purchase. He declared they contained some mistakes and refused to pay them. Father Hughes believed Baltimore rejected these bills because he wanted the Jesuits to give up the land for free. He linked this to the draft of a surrender written by Baltimore in 1642. That document, though, refers specifically to the Patuxent River lands that were never passed under the Great Seal. The Chapel Land was actually granted and could not be taken away in the same manner.[12]

A more likely explanation of why Lord Baltimore objected to the bills is that no matter what was conveyed in the purchase, two hundred pounds sterling was a large sum in the best of times, and quite possibly Lord Baltimore did not have the money to pay it. Several of his communications to Maryland at this time indicate a concern over expenses. With the disruptions of the war, confiscations by Parliament, and other dislocations, Cecil Calvert may have had a hard time raising money on which to live. The addition of £200 of extra debt would be a great burden. By rejecting the bills, he gained some time to sort out his finances and, in July 1643, he may have thought the war almost over.[13]

The Chapel Land purchase was not made in isolation. The Chesapeake economy was based on credit and the £200 was tied into that network. Thomas Cornwaleys, one of the most prominent merchants in the Chesapeake, had signed the bills for the Jesuits. When his accounts with English suppliers came up £200 short, repercussions were bound to follow. Lord Baltimore reported that £40 of bills owing to Leonard Calvert from Cornwaleys were rejected. Possibly this was in retaliation for Lord Baltimore's rejection of the earlier bills, but it is also possible that Cornwaleys did not have the money. We know of these bills to Leonard Calvert only because he objected to his brother, but there might have been others as well. In a credit economy, when one card falls the whole house may be threatened. Cornwaleys's reputation with his creditors may have been damaged by this incident. If true, it would become one of the irritants that would drive Cornwaleys away from Maryland.[14]

Knowing that a Maryland court might not deliver a verdict he liked, Baltimore forbade Brent from granting process in the case. Believing that he and his brother would be in Maryland by January, he was certain they could work out the problems with the Jesuits and Cornwaleys. He went so far as to promise the payment of appropriate damages. Until then, Brent was to take no action in the case.[15]

By 18 November, Cecil Calvert was aware that neither of the Calverts would be going to Maryland that year. In order that the government could continue to function, he granted Brent the power to call assemblies, to ratify laws in his name, and to grant land. He sent a commission naming Brent, Lewgar, and three others as his commissioners of the treasury in Maryland. They were to make an inventory of his property and the rents due to him. An indication of his financial situation was his instruction that his servants be sold. He believed that it would be cheaper to hire servants on a yearly basis than to supply them from England. Baltimore mentions the chapel and the secular priests in several places. He directed that the goods he ordered to be delivered to Father Gilmett be left with him but that he sign a note for them. He also told his commissioners to pay four cattle and twenty barrels of corn to Gilmett for his salary.[16]

The salary provided for Gilmett (and Father Territt) was only the beginning of these expenses. Lord Baltimore was about to realize how expensive it would be to maintain his own priests. In May of the next year, as required by Baltimore's instructions, John Lewgar filed an account with the court of all Lord Baltimore's goods, rents, and debts for 1643. The account shows a large and growing estate, with most of the wealth in cattle. There were 149 head of cattle of various ages, including fifty-six calves. Lewgar was careful to note where the estate had been increased during the year. The increase came in the form of rents, fines, and in the natural increase of the livestock. If we calculate the value of this increase, it totals almost twenty thousand pounds of tobacco or approximately £166. This is a healthy addition for one year but was it enough?[17]

Expenses related to the secular priests figured prominently on the debit side of the account. Lord Baltimore paid almost three thousand pounds tobacco to hire servants for Gilmett and 4,900 pounds for goods for him. A number of lesser bills were also charged to the account for the benefit of the secular priests. In total, 11,511 pounds of tobacco were charged to the account for the support of Gilmett and Territt. This represents over half of the increase in the estate in 1643 and, when we consider the salaries to be paid to Lord Baltimore's officers, there can have been no real increase in the estate. This is particularly important when we look at the overall financial picture. Although rich in cattle and other livestock, Lord Baltimore's estate began the year almost twelve thousand pounds of tobacco in debt. Were it not for the expenses of the secular priests, Baltimore might have made up much of it. Keeping his own priests in Maryland would prove a very expensive luxury.

Given his many expenses and the troubled state of England, Baltimore realized that he could not afford to pay for the Chapel Land and its improvements. Therefore, he required his commissioners to seek a way out of the bargain. He suggested giving the house and land back to Copley. The Jesuits would be paid a reasonable sum for the time that Gilmett had spent at the Chapel. Payment of this rent was to come from Lord Baltimore's estate in Maryland. Further, he desired that they attempt to rent the premises for Gilmett until mid-summer 1645 and again that it be paid for out of his revenues in the province. The diet of the secular priests should be supplied from Baltimore's plantation at West St. Mary's. If any of these conditions could not be met, the commissioners were to find suitable lodging and provisions for the priests, "with the best accomodation for them & the least charge" to Lord Baltimore. Throughout this entire article there was an emphasis on containing expenses and paying for necessary costs from the estate in Maryland without asking for or charging anything to Lord Baltimore in England. It is clear that Lord Baltimore was in financial difficulty and that Maryland would have to pay for itself. At the end of this paragraph, Baltimore neatly summarized his economic woes:

> And I would have them contrive the business (if possibly they can) that Mr. Gilmett and Mr. Territt may by all means be continued in that Province till that time: when I doubt not (by the grace of God) to be able to provide better for them then by reason of the extremity of the present troubles in England I could doe this year which I hope they well consider & have a little patience till then.[18]

This statement illustrates the difficult financial straits in which Lord

Baltimore found himself, but it also reflects an optimism about the future. He expected to be in better financial shape by mid-summer 1645. What was the source of this optimism, and was it justified? Possibly, after the Royalist success in 1643, he thought the war would soon end. A return to peace would make collecting rents, debts, and other assets much easier. However, if this was the cause for his optimism, why wait until mid-1645? If from his perspective the end of the war was so near, why not place the date sometime in 1644?

Father Thomas Hughes suggested that Baltimore was hinting at the voluntary transfer of the Chapel Land from the Jesuits to himself and that Calvert was still pressing for the release of this land. No evidence supports his claim. In all of the documents dealing with the land issue, Baltimore focused on Indian lands and in particular on the Patuxent River properties. The Chapel Land, having passed the Great Seal, was already granted, and the Jesuits had a legal right to it. Even if the land were given outright to Lord Baltimore, he would still have the problem of supporting the priests, and it does not explain why mid-summer 1645 would be important.[19]

A more plausible explanation exists for where Baltimore expected to find more revenues and why mid-summer 1645 was important. By the time these instructions were written, the Calvert brothers must have been deeply involved in negotiations with King Charles and his ministers over a proposed commission for seizing London ships trading to Virginia. This commission would be granted at Oxford on 26 January 1644 and would give broad powers to Leonard Calvert for taking ships, cargoes, and debts, on sea or on land, that belonged to residents of London or other ports then in rebellion against the crown. Because of the importance of this commission, we must look closely at what the king expected and allowed Leonard Calvert to do.[20]

Charles authorized Leonard Calvert to go to Virginia and, with the assistance of the governor, seize any London ships, their cargoes, and anything belonging to them. Having taken a ship, Calvert could sell it, trade it away, or have the captain agree to pay a fine rather than lose the vessel. In addition he could discharge or compound with any Virginian who owed a debt to a Londoner or other person from a port in rebellion. Any of the seized goods or cargoes that Calvert did not dispose of in the Chesapeake could be imported into England without customs duties, taxes, or other payments.

Since Cecil Calvert would hire a ship and crew for the voyage, secure ordnance, and provide a stock of provisions, all of which would be expensive, the king stated that any profit derived from this venture would be split evenly between himself and Baltimore. Leonard Calvert was authorized to dispose of Baltimore's share in any way that his brother directed without having to account for it to the king. The other half of the booty was specifically assigned to three purposes. First, any expenses Leonard Calvert incurred in Virginia were to paid out of the king's share. Second, Calvert was to recruit men in Virginia to sail to England and fight for the Royalist cause. The cost of transporting them also was to be paid out of Charles's half of the profits. Finally, if enough money was left over, Calvert would pay Sir William Berkeley, governor of Virginia, the equivalent in tobacco of £2,000, for two payments of his yearly salary. Were this commission to be put into effect, it would provide a major windfall profit for Lord Baltimore and his brother.

To see how much revenue this commission potentially represented, it is necessary to look at the state of the tobacco trade in the 1640s. The average London ship trading to Virginia during this period carried between 200 and 250 tons of cargo. At a standard average of four hogsheads of tobacco to the ton, this represented a cargo of 800–1,000 hogsheads. Each hogshead held about 350 pounds of tobacco, the other 100–150 pounds being the wooden cask itself. Based on these figures, the average London ship, fully loaded, carried about 300,000 pounds of tobacco. At two pence per pound, this cargo would be valued at £2,500–£3,000. In addition to the value of the cargo, the ship itself was a valuable resource. A newly built and outfitted ship of this size cost about £2,000–£2,500, almost as much as the cargo she carried. The seizure of even one such ship and cargo would add significantly to Lord Baltimore's treasury.[21]

The potential was even greater given the extent of the tobacco trade and London's participation in it. By 1639 more than 1.5 million pounds of tobacco were being exported annually from the Chesapeake to England, and two-thirds of that trade went to London. Through the 1630s, an average of thirty-five ships carried this tobacco, but it is uncertain how many of them were from London. A 1649 pamphlet listed thirty-one ships in the trade, ten of which were from London. If the same proportion held five years earlier, there would have been ten London ships in the Chesapeake. Taken together, these ships and their cargoes would have been valued at £45,000–£55,000, a princely sum by any standard.[22]

To be most effective, Calvert would have to catch the tobacco fleet after it was loaded and ready to sail for England. That would not be possible in 1644, since the commission had not been granted by November 1643. By the time Calvert received the commission and other preparations were made, the tobacco fleet would already be sailing homeward. However, he could be in place and ready to put the commission into effect early in 1645. If all went according to plan, by mid-summer 1645, Lord Baltimore would be in a much better financial situation.

King Charles and Lord Baltimore were not the only ones looking at commercial vessels as potential sources of revenue. Parliament framed its own ordinance for dealing with enemy merchants. On 1 December 1643, almost two months before Leonard Calvert's commission was approved, Parliament passed an act for seizing ships found trading with ports hostile to the Parliament. It was from this act that Ingle derived much of the legal basis for his actions, and the provisions of this act molded testimony in the court cases that followed. As with Leonard Calvert's commission, this act had a profound effect on later events and so must be examined.[23]

Briefly, the act authorized persons approved by the Lord High Admiral to equip vessels as warships and to seize any ship that was trading with the king's supporters. If a ship would not yield peacefully, it could be taken by force. Any booty taken under this act was divided into thirds with shares going to the ship's owner, the provisioner, and the crew. The only exceptions were custom duties and a tenth part that was due to the Admiralty. Parliament agreed to provision the ship while at sea and therefore received a third of the profits. Thus far, the act was similar to Calvert's commission. Parliament, however, was much more concerned with the legal ramifications of this policy. It required an official hearing before the High Court of Admiralty before any ship could be claimed as prize. Those seeking such a designation had to produce documents relating to the voyage and cargo of the ship as well as requiring several of the captured ship's officers to testify before the court. They were not supposed to dispose of the ship or any of the goods until the court had passed on the legality of the seizure. Such proceedings ensured that Parliament got its share of the prize. While this act was mostly aimed at ships trading to Ireland and the Continent, it could be and was applied to vessels trading to the Chesapeake.

The saga of Thomas Weston's voyage from Maryland in 1643 reveals the multiple dangers faced by merchants and captains sailing from the Chesapeake. Weston had been an ironmonger in London and since 1638 had been trading to the Chesapeake. He first appears in the Maryland records in 1640, and by 1642 he was a resident of the province. Apparently he made regular trips back to England in his ship, the *John of Maryland*, a vessel described as a barque of twenty-five tons burden. In preparing for his trip to England, he had collected over twenty thousand pounds of tobacco, which was stored in the hold in bulk rather than in hogsheads. (On such a small ship, it was more efficient to pack the tobacco in the hold than to carry it in hogsheads.)[24]

The *John of Maryland* left the Chesapeake near the end of June. Weston told the crew that he did not feel safe sailing to London because it was in rebellion against the king. Rather, they would find some place under Royalist control to make port. He proposed to stop in Ireland to gather news about the conflict, but bad winds forced them onto the coast of Cornwall. From a local fishing boat they discovered that the area was still in royal control, and they decided to make land there. Accordingly they sailed into Padstow on 2 September 1643. Despite Weston's care to end up in a Royalist port, the ship and its cargo were seized by the Royalist vice-admiral of Cornwall. Over the next few months, four thousand pounds of tobacco were ruined in the hold, and the ship itself was damaged. Eventually Weston secured an order from the king for the release of the ship and cargo, but by that time he could not get back to Cornwall and had to hire a ship to take him back to Maryland. It was in this atmosphere of legally sanctioned piracy that the tobacco ships sailed back to the Chesapeake in late 1643.[25]

CHAPTER SEVEN

"The highest fine that . . . can or ought to be assessed"

Richard Ingle was one of the captains who sailed back to the Chesapeake in 1643. For the first time since he initially appeared in the records, he was master of the same ship two years in a row. From this point on, Ingle would be associated with the *Reformation,* and the stability of this association suggests that he had become part owner of the vessel. There is no record of when the *Reformation* sailed or where she first made land in the Chesapeake. Accomac court records do not record Ingle's arrival as they had in years past. Indeed, that port may not have been safe for the *Reformation.* Despite his apology to the Yeardleys after the altercation of the previous year, Ingle might not have felt safe making landfall there. His fear was well-grounded, for Argall Yeardley had begun collecting testimony on the event in August 1643 in expectation of Ingle's arrival in the fall. Although her route to Maryland remains uncertain, the *Reformation* was anchored in St. Inigoes Creek by early January 1644, unloading cargo and collecting tobacco for the return trip to England.[1]

As was normal on any trading ship, the crew also began trading and collecting their own debts. On 12 January 1644, Thomas Greene, the *Reformation*'s boatswain, sued William Hardige, a tailor, for a debt due by bill and account. Edward Packer, sheriff of St. Mary's County and Greene's lawyer, claimed that Hardige owed the mariner fifty pounds of tobacco and two pounds of beaver skins. Greene also sued Hardige for fifty pounds of tobacco owed to Francis Ottoway, who might have been the surgeon of the *Reformation.* These suits, no different than many others filed during that court session, may have been the first sparks set to the fuse that ignited Maryland's "troubled times." Hardige sued Packer, on the same day, for seven hundred pounds of tobacco due to him for work performed, probably tailoring. Packer admitted the debt to be due but claimed that he was holding the tobacco to satisfy Hardige's debts to Greene. No record of the settlement of these cases survives, but it is obvious from later testimony that William Hardige felt considerable resentment toward the *Reformation* and her crew. The haggling over these suits undoubtedly influenced Hardige's later actions. Debts totaling less than 150 pounds of tobacco may have set in motion a chain of events that almost destroyed Maryland.[2]

What happened during the next week is uncertain, but on 18 January, Hardige went before Governor Brent and accused Richard Ingle of treason, claiming that he had boasted of resisting arrest in Virginia in February 1643. According to Hardige, a sheriff at Accomac had commanded Ingle in the name of the king to come ashore. Also according to Hardige, Ingle stood on the deck of the *Reformation*, drew his cutlass, and refused in the name of Parliament. He then reportedly threatened to cut the head off anyone who attempted to board the ship. Hardige had heard Ingle say this himself. He further testified that he had heard Ingle, both on Kent Island and at St. Mary's, say that he was a Captain of Gravesend for the Parliament against the king. To strengthen the case, Hardige claimed others could testify that Ingle had said King Charles was no king.

These were serious charges that would have had significant consequences for all parties involved were Ingle tried and convicted. Ingle could lose the *Reformation* and all her goods, and worse, he could be executed. The province of Maryland would be placed clearly on the side of the Royalists in a civil war whose outcome was in doubt. Ingle and his ship were a major part of the lifeline connecting the colony to England, from whence came all the luxuries and most of the necessities of life. If that line were severed, there was no assurance that another would be quickly found, especially in these troubled times. Given the possible consequences of these charges, one must ask if the alleged events actually took place and what motives the various individuals had for pursuing them.

As for the incident at Accomac and its aftermath, Ingle had clearly refused to surrender in the king's name and had threatened one of the king's officers. The other statements attributed to him cannot be proven, but they were well in character for a man passionately devoted to the cause of Parliament and never one to watch his tongue in public. As already reported, several of the Virginians who had been unexpectedly transported to Maryland testified that Ingle had regaled the Marylanders with stories of his exploit. If Maryland authorities were looking for a way to demonstrate support for the king, the prosecution of Ingle would do nicely.[3]

That may have constituted a clear motive for prosecution, but it neglects several important points. By January 1644 the Accomac incident was old news in Maryland. It had to have been common knowledge as early as April 1643, when Ingle kidnapped the Virginians and bragged about it. Yet no one in Maryland arrested him or accused him of treason at that time. The incident did not occur in Maryland waters but was entirely a Virginia affair, and Maryland had little cause to prosecute the case when Virginia authorities had already made peace with Ingle. What had changed in the course of nine months that made it advantageous to arrest Ingle? Hardige's accusations can be dismissed—as his contemporaries did dismiss them—as having arisen out of personal malice. A more likely reason is that the government had changed hands. In April 1643, Leonard Calvert was still governor but was planning to sail for England. As mentioned, he may even have sailed aboard Ingle's ship. Before he left, Calvert appointed Giles Brent governor pro tem, and it was Brent who set in motion the events of the Plundering Time.

Hardige found Governor Brent a ready and willing listener. Brent's motives in this action can only be guessed, but the evidence suggests several possible political and personal reasons. Brent was clearly a Royalist, just as Ingle vigorously supported Parliament. Ingle might have appeared as an easy target that could satisfy Brent's need to show support for the Crown. It is also possible that although Leonard Calvert's commission to seize London ships was not granted until 26 January 1644, word of its drafting might have been sent over with the shipping of 1643. Brent might simply have been overeager in putting the plan into action.

The governor also had several on-going financial problems with Ingle. In February 1643, Ingle had sued Brent for eight thousand pounds of tobacco due him and which Brent refused to pay. A month later, Ingle protested a bill of £16 that Margaret Brent had drawn on a London factor the year before. Neither of these issues had been settled in 1643, and they lingered to cloud relations between Ingle and the Brents. By seizing the ship, Brent could strike a blow against Parliament, remove the problem of the debts owed to Ingle, and possibly even make a profit from the ship when it was brought to Bristol.[4]

Ingle later claimed, in answer to a suit by Brent, that the governor had "tampered" with Hardige to get him to make the accusations but that Hardige had refused. Given the prominent role Hardige and his in-laws played in helping Ingle during the rebellion, there may be some truth in this charge. Certainly Thomas Cornwalyes thought that Hardige brought the charges out of spite, and several juries agreed with him. Such charges against Brent were not new. In October 1642 several inhabitants of Kent Island had accused him of bending the law to suit his own profit. Ultimately he was cleared of this charge, but it fits the general image of Brent as a man jealous of his own power and authority.[5]

Having decided to arrest Ingle, Brent had to proceed with care. A heavily armed merchant ship with a loyal crew was a dangerous enemy. Brent devised a plan that would isolate Ingle and make the ship vulnerable. The governor, together with Thomas Cornwaleys, went on board the *Reformation* early in the morning of 18 January to invite Ingle to have dinner at Brent's house later in the day. Brent then issued a warrant for his arrest when he stepped ashore. Brent was clearly aware of the significance of the action he was planning and took steps to protect himself if things went awry. This warrant, and all others having to do with Ingle on that day, have an additional note that they were "issued by & with the advise of Mr Secretary." None of Brent's warrants dealing with other people have that subscription.[6]

Brent ordered William Hardige, with the assistance of Cornwalyes, to arrest Ingle. The inclusion of Cornwalyes in this plan is curious, since he and Ingle were known to be close friends. It may be, as he later stated, that Cornwalyes was convinced that the charges would not be upheld in court, and he simply wanted to see that the volatile Ingle would not do anything to give credit to the prosecution. It is hard to imagine any other motivation for Cornwalyes's voluntary participation. Brent cautioned Hardige and Cornwalyes to keep Ingle's arrest secret and to meet the governor on board the *Reformation* at one o'clock that afternoon. Brent did not want to alert the crew, most of whom he expected to be ashore on ship's business.

Significantly, he did not entrust this job to Edward Packer, the sheriff who would normally be expected to serve the warrant but whose close ties to the *Reformation* rendered him untrustworthy in the governor's eyes. Brent had a warrant drawn up authorizing Packer to seize the *Reformation* and all her goods. The sheriff was to make an inventory in the presence of two seamen and two planters, but a marginal note in the records claims this warrant was neither signed nor served. It may be that Secretary Lewgar had prepared the document without fully understanding the governor's plan of action, but it is more likely that Packer never received the warrant because Brent did not trust him to carry out his orders. There is no record that Packer was ever informed of the plot until Ingle was arrested and turned over to his custody. Since Brent was set to meet Cornwalyes and Hardige aboard the ship, he set in motion a different plan.[7]

Sometime that morning, Ingle was ashore at St. Inigoes Point in the company of Richard Garrett, the *Reformation*'s gunner, and William Durford, a planter and brother of John Durford, the ship's mate. Intending to return to the ship, they were intercepted by Brent, Cornwalyes, and a party of Marylanders. All three were taken peacefully and escorted to the governor's house. Cornwalyes probably assured Ingle that he knew the charges would not stand up in court. After his arrest, Ingle was turned over to the sheriff who was instructed not to let him return to his ship. Since Maryland had no jail, Packer or a deputy had to stay with Ingle as long as he was under arrest. The angry captain was held for about nine hours before being released.[8]

The *Reformation* was riding at anchor in the St. Mary's River at the mouth of St. Inigoes Creek with her captain and most of her crew on shore. According to later testimony only four of the ship's company were aboard at the time of the seizure. By one o'clock in the afternoon, a party of thirty Marylanders led by John Hampton had come aboard to trade. Soon, Governor Brent and Captain Cornwalyes arrived and ordered the ship seized. The Marylanders easily overpowered the few crew members on board and appropriated the ship's weapons. Brent then addressed the crew and the guards. He said that the ship was from London, which was in rebellion, and should not return there. It should go to Bristol which was under the king's control.[9] A paper was then nailed to the main mast listing the charge against Ingle:

> These are to publish and proclayme to all persons as well seamen as others that Richard Ingle Mr. of this ship is arrested upon highe treason to his Majesty & therefore to require all persons to be aiding & assisting to his Lordship's officer in seising of this ship, & not to offer any resistance or contempt therunto nor be any otherwise aiding or assisting to the said R. Ingle, upon peril of highe treason to his Majesty. [10]

With the ship secured, Brent sent ashore for John Durford, the *Reformation*'s mate. When Durford arrived, he was ushered into the Great Cabin where Brent, Cornwalyes, Hampton, and Hardige were waiting. Brent proposed that if Durford would agree to be captain and take the ship to Bristol, he would be given double wages. Durford agreed to this proposal, and Brent then offered the company an oath to support the king without Parliament and to take up arms against Parliament. Hampton and Hardige swore the oath readily, but Durford pleaded for more time to convince the rest of the crew. Brent told the crew that anyone who agreed to sail the ship to Bristol would receive double wages while those who refused would be detained in Maryland. Thomas Eves, the cooper, was sent for beer, and Brent drank a health to the king without Parliament.[11]

Although he briefly may have enjoyed the thought of being captain, Durford was really playing for time. His evasion should have signaled

Brent that the matter was not settled, but the governor chose to ignore it. He appointed John Hampton commander of the guard and expressly told him not to let Ingle back on the ship without a special warrant from him. Having thus carried the ship and secured it, Brent and Cornwalyes went ashore to deal with Ingle.[12]

The day's events had gone well for the governor. Ingle had been arrested without apparent incident. The *Reformation* had been seized and part of her crew had already agreed to sail her to Bristol. Perhaps more importantly for Brent, Cornwalyes, Lewgar, and others of the council had supported him, despite their own reservations. When he convened the council that evening, probably at Margaret Brent's house in St. Mary's, he must have been full of optimism about the venture.[13]

There is no record of what happened at this meeting and very little later testimony about it. We know that Brent, Cornwalyes, Lewgar, and James Neale among others were present. Ingle was brought before the council and the charges read. The session must have been a stormy one, for each of the participants had a different recollection of what was agreed upon. James Neale later testified that he had asked Brent to release Ingle into his custody but the governor had refused. Cornwalyes then offered to be bound "bodye for bodye" for Ingle which was accepted. Brent apparently assumed that Cornwalyes would take Ingle to his house and keep him there until the trial. Cornwalyes, on the other hand, thought Ingle had been given bail and could freely return to his ship.[14]

When the meeting ended, Ingle, in the company of Cornwalyes and Neale, left the house. Outside they met the sheriff, Edward Packer, who was ready to take Ingle back into custody. Secretary Lewgar, also leaving the meeting, assured Packer that the prisoner had been turned over to Cornwalyes and was free to go with him.[15]

The three men—Cornwalyes, Neale and Packer—accompanied Ingle to the *Reformation,* where Cornwalyes told John Hampton to return his rapier to the ship's gunner. He ordered the rest of the guard to return the seized weapons and told them "go every man to his rest." Contrary to most accounts of the incident, Cornwalyes did not disperse the guard and set Ingle free. Cornwalyes knew that the charges would not stand up in court and fully expected Ingle to stay in the area to answer them. He believed that the situation had sufficiently cooled that the night would be quiet. Cornwaleys had no authority to send the guard away, and when he told them to rest, he meant on the ship. He intended to stay with Ingle and was in the *Reformation*'s Great Cabin with him when the ship was retaken.

By this time, all of the crew had returned aboard, but the atmosphere seemed relaxed. Most of the guard had gone below deck to sleep. Under the leadership of John Durford, Thomas Greene, and Frederick Johnson, the crew suddenly overpowered the few guards who remained on deck, then lashed and nailed the hatches to trap the sleeping Marylanders below. Cornwalyes and some others they locked in the Great Cabin. The struggle was short but violent. Several crew members were later indicted for "beating, wounding and abusing the guard." Except for those in the cabin, the Marylanders were put over the side and sent ashore. Ingle had his ship back—and he had hostages.[16]

After regaining his ship, Ingle could have sailed away, but he did not. He remained at St. Inigoes through 19 January. Perhaps he hoped to salvage his trading connections or the debts owed to him. One can imagine the tense negotiations between the Marylanders and the *Reformation* that went on that day. A compromise was not reached, and the next day, 20 January 1644, Ingle set sail down the St. George's River. Along the way he seized several boats and weapons from various people, including Henry Bishop, and reportedly threatened to "beat down the dwelling houses of divers inhabitants" including that of the governor.[17]

It would make a much better story had Ingle sailed back to England immediately after his escape and returned the next year to take his revenge on Maryland, but there is ample evidence that the *Reformation* stayed in Maryland waters for a long time in the spring of 1644. Ingle eventually made an uneasy peace with Brent and the Marylanders, probably because both sides were economically dependent on the other. Cornwalyes testified that for "sixe years now last past . . . [Ingle] was and became the chiefe man that was ymployed and whose shipp from tyme to tyme was fraighted by your Orator and others the Merchants Adventurers for transporting their goods and Merchadizes to and from the said Province of Maryland . . . whereby the said Richard Ingle did much benefitt and enrich himselfe and the Owners of his Shipp."[18] Henry Stockton later testified that the *Looking Glass* went to Maryland in 1645 because Ingle had not come back and was not expected. For this reason, the province was in need of many things and had much tobacco to trade. These statements imply that Ingle had most of the Maryland trade to himself. Certainly he was connected to the major landowners in St. Mary's. Because of their reliance on him, Maryland needed the *Reformation,* whatever the political opinions of her master.[19]

Yet this was a two-way relationship. Despite John Durford's assertion that the Marylanders "stood in more need of their Commerce with the said shipp the Reformation and her Commodities than the said Captain Ingle doe of the Country," the success of the voyage depended on bringing the ship back to England full of tobacco. Without the cooperation of the Marylanders, the *Reformation* faced financial disaster. By late January and early February it was too late to try to pick up a new cargo of tobacco in Virginia. Thus it was in the interest of both parties to settle their differences, but the road to compromise was anything but smooth.[20]

Ingle sailed down the St. George's River on 20 January 1644, headed for Kent Island and leaving Governor Brent sadly disappointed. Instead of having a ship ready to send to Bristol, complete with crew and cargo, Brent was left with a grapnell of "uncertain title" that he seized from Henry Bishop. The governor was not amused. On the nineteenth, even before Ingle had left, he removed Packer from the office of sheriff and replaced him with Robert Ellyson. After negotiations broke down and Ingle sailed for Kent Island, he entered charges in the provincial court against Cornwalyes, Neale, Packer, and Hampton for aiding Ingle's escape. Brent also decided to pursue the case against Ingle despite his absence.[21]

Whatever Brent's motivation was in this incident, the disruptions of the Civil War were beginning to polarize Maryland. About this time a case of slander was brought before the court that reveals the disturbed nature of Maryland society. On 31 January 1644, Thomas Bushell complained against Micol Harker, "spinster," for reporting that Bushell had said he hoped there would be "nere a Papist left in Maryland by may day." The case, dismissed for lack of evidence, reveals how divided Maryland was and foreshadowed attitudes that would sweep across Maryland in the next year.[22]

On 1 February 1644 an inquest was held at St. Mary's with Giles Brent and John Lewgar sitting as judges and a jury of twelve freemen sworn to investigate the bills presented to them "to the best of their conscience according to their evidence." John Lewgar, acting as His Lordship's attorney, declared that the court had the authority to investigate charges of treason even if the events occurred outside the province. He declared the purpose of the inquest was not to convict anyone of treason but to determine whether the person charged with treason should be bound over and sent to England for trial or to the location where the events were said to have occurred.[23]

Having answered the question about jurisdiction, Lewgar submitted three indictments against Ingle to the jury. The first charged that on 22 February 1643, Ingle resisted arrest in Virginia and in so doing invoked the name of Parliament. Further, Ingle had threatened the king's representative, the commander of Accomac, with a cutlass. This incident must have been known to every person on the jury. The second bill claimed that on 20 November 1642, at the port of Gravesend in England, Ingle had accepted a commission from Parliament against the king. The third bill accused Ingle, on 5 April 1643, of uttering slanderous words against Prince Rupert, a cousin of the king and a general in the Royalist army. This incident took place aboard the *Reformation* while she was riding in the Potomac River near St. Clements Island.

William Hardige was the first witness called, but Cornwalyes objected to him as "infamous" and, as he later testified, knowing the allegations proceeded from a personal grudge. Governor Brent not surprisingly found nothing wrong with Hardige's testimony and accepted it. The jury disagreed with the governor and returned all three bills as "Ignoramus," meaning literally "unknown to us" and indicating that the jury thought there was not enough evidence to determine the truth of the matter. Interestingly, a secondary meaning of this phrase in Latin is to "overlook or excuse." Given that Ingle was not shy in expressing his opinions and that the incident at Accomac must have been well known to the jurors, it is possible that this secondary meaning expressed their intent.

The trial had not found Ingle guilty of any of the charges, but neither had it fully cleared him. It was only a matter of time before Brent would try again and, with a little luck and a new jury, he might make the charges stick. Thomas Cornwaleys knew that the case would be harder to prove if there were no direct accusations against Ingle. He and several others, convinced William Hardige that it would be in his best interest to drop his charge and leave the province. Accordingly, Hardige went to Virginia and was not mentioned in the Maryland records for more than a year. In an unlikely about face, Hardige came back to Maryland the next year as one of Ingle's men.[24]

Undaunted by this defection, Brent and Lewgar decided to try again. They impaneled a new jury and submitted three new bills against Ingle. The first charge was one that Brent and Lewgar were sure they could prove. They accused Ingle of breaking out of Sheriff Packer's custody on 18 January against his will and by force of arms. Ingle was also accused of slandering Prince Rupert by calling him "Prince Rogue" at Mattapanian in St. Clements Hundred on some day in April 1643. Further he was accused of saying the king was no king unless he joined with Parliament. This incident was said to have occurred on 30 March 1643 on the *Reformation* in St. Georges River. The jury heard testimony from five witnesses and returned the first two of the bills "Ignoramus." They had not reached a verdict on the third bill by seven that night and were dismissed. On 3 February 1644 a new jury took up this bill and again returned the verdict as "Ignoramus." A final inquest was held on 5 February and the jury was given the same bill to consider. The jury could not reach a verdict and was dismissed. Clearly the planters of Maryland realized the economic importance of the ship and the political consequences of arresting Ingle, even if the governor did not.

Having failed to convince four juries, Brent should have given up at this point, but he did not. On 8 February, Lewgar acting as His Lordship's attorney, filed charges against nine people including Edward Packer, Thomas Cornwaleys, and James Neale. All of the charges related to the events of 18 and 20 January and seem never to have been submitted to a jury. Cornwaleys came into the court, insisted that the charges against Ingle were of no consequence, pointed to the four jury verdicts as proof, and asked to be cleared of any charges against him in this unfortunate incident. Brent did not dismiss the charges but was willing to put them on hold until Ingle returned from Kent Island. This was not enough for Cornwaleys, who returned the next day and again demanded a dismissal of the charges or a trial. A hearing was held, and Brent fined Cornwaleys a thousand pounds of tobacco for his part in the rescue—the only fine or punishment ever meted out by the government for any part of Ingle's arrest or escape. Cornwaleys had expected to be cleared and requested that the fine be respited. Brent agreed to wait for its collection.

Despite the fine against Cornwaleys, a compromise was reached. At a hearing held at St. Inigoes house on 8 February, Cornwaleys promised that Ingle or his attorney would appear in court to answer the charges against him within a year. As security, Ingle would deposit a barrel of powder and four hundred pounds of lead shot before leaving the province. Cornwaleys posted a bond of four thousand pounds of tobacco that the powder and shot would be delivered. Ingle received a certificate that allowed him free and unmolested trade in Maryland, and the compromise ended open hostility between Ingle and the Maryland authorities. Thomas Eves, cooper of the *Reformation,* testified later that the ship had been on its guard for three weeks until the agreement was reached. From Ingle's arrest on 18 January to the bail certificate on 8 February is exactly three weeks. Charges against all of the other parties were eventually dropped, Robert Ellyson was discharged from being sheriff, and Edward Packer was reappointed. Cornwaleys's fine was allowed to stand.[25]

Relations between the Marylanders and Ingle became civil if not cordial. Ingle collected an outstanding debt of eight thousand pounds of tobacco from Governor Brent and a smaller one from Secretary Lewgar.

Brent went so far as to lend Ingle a pinnace so the captain could more easily collect his debts in the province. Sometime in late February, Ingle transported the governor himself to his plantation on Kent Island. While at Kent Island, Brent granted Ingle what was to be known as Ingle's Island, and the captain bought a stock of hogs and set them to roam there. Clearly it was his intention to trade to Maryland in the future.[26]

With a calmer political situation, the *Reformation* returned to St. Mary's sometime in early March, as is demonstrated by a pair of suits filed that month. In the first of these, Thomas Hebden sued Francis Ottaway on 1 March for certain drugs that were supposed to have been delivered with that year's shipping. Ottaway may have been the ship's surgeon on the *Reformation*. The drugs were not delivered, and Hebden sued for £3. Ottaway appeared to defend himself against the charge. In the second suit, filed 16 March, Robert Ellyson sued Ingle for 650 pounds of tobacco for sheriff's fees. The tobacco in question was found to have already been deposited with Secretary Lewgar. Since Ellyson became sheriff following Packer's dismissal on 19 January and most of Ellyson's duties as sheriff were in early February, Ingle must have deposited the tobacco sometime between then and the day the suit was filed. It is unlikely that Ingle would have risked coming to St. Mary's before his bail certificate was granted in mid-February and, because of the earlier case, we know there was a crew member in court at the beginning of March, so a late February or early March date must be assumed.[27]

Whether or not Ellyson's news about Ingle being out of the province was a surprise, Brent chose this time to move against Ingle in absentia. On the same day, 16 March, Lewgar, as attorney for Lord Baltimore, complained to the court that Ingle had left the province without depositing the powder and shot, had not paid custom duties, and was heading for London, a port in rebellion against the king. Secretary Lewgar requested that Ingle's estate in Maryland be seized and held until Ingle appeared to clear himself. The governor agreed and an inventory was made of all of the debts owed to Ingle. His estate was valued at 1,123 pounds of tobacco. Ingle had not yet sailed for England but was in Accomac boasting to the Virginians about his escape from the Marylanders. On 31 March, Ingle, who described himself as, "master of the *Recovery* formerly called the *Reformation*," appointed Captain William Roper as his attorney to collect his debts at Accomack and in Maryland. There is no indication in the records that Ingle came back to Maryland that year, but both Secretary Lewgar and John Durford later testified that the *Reformation* "departed in a peaceable manner" from Maryland.[28]

While Ingle was safely away from Maryland, Cornwaleys still had to deal with the after effects of his arrest and escape. Governor Brent held Cornwaleys personally responsible for thwarting his plan to seize the *Reformation.* The governor's animosity was an added burden that the captain did not need. His relationship with the government had been strained since his quarrel with Leonard Calvert in 1642, and the events of 1644 were to test the limits of this relationship.

If the problem of Ingle's escape was not bad enough, Cornwaleys was increasingly involved in another dispute with Lord Baltimore's representatives. Just before Ingle's arrest, the dispute over the Chapel Land purchase began heating up and reached the boiling point soon after Ingle's flight to Virginia. When Lord Baltimore refused to accept the bills of exchange addressed to him, he set in motion a series of events that would have disastrous results for Maryland.

In the transatlantic economy, where bills of exchange were the main currency, means had to be found to ensure that they would be paid. These safeguards were traditionally part of a special body of rules and customs called the law merchant. An important part of this was how a bill was paid if the person it was addressed to refused to honor it. In that case, the merchant was entitled to "protest" the bill. To initiate a protest, the merchant took the bill that had been refused to a notary public and swore out a statement that payment had been refused. The notary then took the bill and presented it for a second time for payment. If the bill was still refused, the notary issued a "notice of dishonor" that gave the holder of the bill the right to sue the party that had drafted it for the principal and damages, sometimes as much as twice the value of the original bill. This process legally fixed the liability for payment on the person who wrote the bill.[29]

In this case, Lord Baltimore refused to pay the bills for £200 and allowed the burden to revert to his commissioners—Leonard Calvert, John Lewgar, and John Langford. Recognizing the unfairness of this action, Baltimore sought to protect his loyal officers by restricting the Maryland government's right to judge the case. This was a temporary stay, and he would seek a suitable compromise, even promising to pay costs and damages. Lord Baltimore may have felt the conflicting claims could wait six months to a year, but other participants were less patient.[30]

On 28 December 1643, Peter Draper, Leonard Calvert's attorney in the province, went to Thomas Cornwaleys and asked for payment of £80 for two bills of exchange written by the captain to Calvert. These were the bills that Lord Baltimore had reported as protested in England. Calvert's attorney sought not only the original £40 but an additional £40 in damages. Surprised and indignant at this request, Cornwaleys replied that he would give no answer except to say that much more was owed to him. Draper then went to John Lewgar and swore out a statement repeating these facts, the first step in seeking a notice of dishonor.[31]

This action by Calvert's attorney, combined with the arrival of Lord Baltimore's instructions to relinquish the Chapel Land, prompted Thomas Cornwaleys to seek his own relief in court. From his instructions to the commissioners, it seems as though Lord Baltimore believed that by returning the building and land, all parties would be satisfied, but the money promised for the purchase had already entered the economy in the form of bills of exchange and could not be recalled. As a private agreement between Lord Baltimore and Cornwaleys this might have solved the problem, but trusting in the word of Lord Baltimore's commissioners, Cornwaleys had used the purchase money to his own and the Jesuits' advantage by writing other bills of exchange. These were now being called, and there was no money to pay them. Cornwaleys's creditors were probably suing him in England and now, in Maryland, Leonard Calvert's attorney was badgering him. On 2 January 1644, very soon after Lord Baltimore's instructions arrived, Cornwaleys went to court seeking the right to sue the original commissioners.[32]

This suit presented Governor Brent with several serious problems.

Lord Baltimore had specifically revoked his power to grant process in this case, yet the new instructions, ordering Brent to return the Chapel Land, left the possibility that the case was now to be settled. The actions of Leonard Calvert's attorney certainly seemed to point in that direction. On a practical level, if Cornwaleys sued and won, the verdict would virtually bankrupt three of the most prominent settlers and make others question the value of being an officer in the government. If the case were not recognized by the government, Maryland justice would appear flawed, and immigrants would think twice before settling under such arbitrary jurisdiction.

To solve this dilemma, Brent sought the opinion of the other members of the court: John Lewgar and James Neale. Lewgar protested that as a potential defendant in the case, he ought not to express an opinion, but Brent reminded him of his oath as a councilor to offer counsel to the lieutenant general. To his credit, Lewgar gave an impartial opinion and one that could have cost him dearly. He said that the office of lieutenant general, which Leonard Calvert had passed on to Brent and which Lord Baltimore had confirmed, was indivisible and that it was not legal to restrict any specific powers. The secretary added that Cornwaleys should be allowed to sue. James Neale, on the other hand, pointed out that any authority they had was derived from Lord Baltimore, and it was in his power to revoke or restrict that authority as he saw fit. Neale said that Baltimore had clearly not wished the suit to be granted and had not signified any change in that wish. The decision was once again in Brent's hands.

The governor reviewed his commission and the other documents and came to a decision, stating that, "according to his cunning and skill, he found himself bound to grant process." As a result of this decision, Brent issued a writ to the sheriff authorizing him to assist Cornwaleys. If Cornwaleys sought to prosecute the suit in the court to be held on 1 February, the sheriff could seize an appropriate amount of property from the estates of the commissioners. This property could be held as security until the suit was settled.

At first glance, the modern reader is struck by the fairness and impartial nature of this judgment. John Lewgar argued for granting the suit even though it could destroy him. Giles Brent has been portrayed as striking out at Lord Baltimore's arbitrary, feudal jurisdiction. However, there was more "cunning" in this decision than first appears. Cornwaleys could not sue until the next court, which was a month away. In that time, more instructions might be received from Lord Baltimore and tempers might cool enough that a compromise could be reached. It also provided Brent with time to try several legal and extra-legal maneuvers.

The first of these occurred on 12 January when Brent tried to seize Leonard Calvert's estate. In 1640, Calvert had granted Kent Fort Manor to Brent. This was Claiborne's settlement that had been forfeited to Lord Baltimore. As part of the grant, Calvert had promised Brent a bond that would defend his title against all claims. Brent now said that he had not received that bond and asked for the right to sue Calvert's estate. This entry was never finished, so it had no effect on later actions. Nevertheless, it is possible, in light of later allegations, that this was an attempt by Brent to shield Calvert's estate from seizure by Cornwaleys.[33]

There is no indication of activity in this case until the court held on 1 February. Possibly the principals were trying to work out a compromise, but they left no record. In any case, Cornwaleys made no attempt to prosecute the suit, which he could have done. No warrant was issued to the sheriff for seizing property in anticipation of the case coming to trial. Whether an agreement was being forged or Cornwaleys was simply too busy defending Ingle and himself, he took no action.

Once again, Peter Draper, Calvert's attorney, stirred the waters. He came into court on 1 February and sued Cornwaleys for 296 pounds of tobacco owed to Calvert. Cornwaleys complained that he had paid it by discount and showed his account book to prove it. The court agreed with Cornwaleys and dismissed the action. Several days later, Cornwaleys was back in court and offered to discount the £40 he owed to Leonard Calvert from the £200 that was owed to him. There is nothing in the records to indicate how this offer was received, but shortly thereafter, Cornwaleys sued the commissioners for the full amount of the bills and damages.[34]

John Lewgar, the only one of the defendants in court, answered that when Lord Baltimore had refused to accept the purchase, the buildings and land were returned to Cornwaleys as they had been before. Lewgar complained it was not fair to make him pay when he had received nothing of value from the bargain. Brent asked Lewgar if the bargain had included any clause regarding Lord Baltimore's refusal of the price or terms. Apparently there was not, and Brent had to decide in Cornwaleys's favor. He asked Cornwaleys to make an oath to prove his damages. The captain was not ready to swear to the damages and asked that he be given time to assemble his proof. Brent was happy to agree to this and deferred judgment.

By 14 March, Cornwaleys must have been getting ready to make his oath. On that day, Brent issued a warrant to the sheriff ordering him to seize seven thousand pounds of tobacco belonging to Leonard Calvert. This was not in security for Cornwaleys's suit, rather it was for a suit filed by Margaret Brent as guardian of Mary Kittomaquand, the Piscataway princess. The suit claimed that the amount owed was part of her estate that remained in Calvert's hands.[35]

The next court was held at John Lewgar's house on 16 March, and Brent was ready to make life difficult for Cornwaleys. To begin with, Brent sued the captain for seven thousand pounds of tobacco. This involved a bill of exchange valued at £24 that had been protested in England. Cornwaleys complained that the damages claimed were excessive. For a bill worth 2,880 pounds of tobacco, Brent wanted 4,120 pounds in damages. When he made his oath for damages, Brent lowered the total to 6,000 pounds and the court, that is Secretary Lewgar, decided in his favor. Next, Brent and Lewgar officially offered Cornwaleys the Chapel Land back in exchange for the protested bills. Cornwaleys refused to accept it and asked to be allowed to make his oath for damages. He swore that he was injured to the value of £400 or 48,000 pounds of tobacco. Since he made his oath, Brent had no choice but to allow a judgment in the case. He set the date for the execution of the judgment against Lewgar and the estates of Leonard Calvert and John Langford as 18 March.[36]

After Brent set this date, he introduced Margaret Brent's suit and the warrant that he had signed two days earlier. The priority of the document effectively denied this tobacco to Cornwaleys. Since Calvert had sold all of his land the previous year, this may have been all of his estate left in Maryland. Cornwaleys was incensed by the move and said some impolitic things about the court and the government. On 18 March, Lewgar indicted Cornwaleys for slandering the government. According to testimony presented, Cornwaleys had complained that Margaret Brent's petition was intended to defraud him of his right to Calvert's tobacco and that she intended to send it to Calvert in England. He implied that Giles Brent and Lewgar were conspiring to assist her. The governor, acting as judge in the case, found Cornwaleys guilty and sentenced him to three weeks in prison with no bail.

There is sufficient evidence to suggest that Cornwaleys was correct in his allegation. The central question in this issue revolves around the cattle demanded by Margaret Brent and whether the seven thousand pounds of tobacco was compensation for them. John Lewgar's account of cattle, dated May 1644, shows that Leonard Calvert had the cattle but left them with Margaret Brent when he sailed to England. They were referred to as part of Lord Baltimore's stock. There is no indication in the account of any payment to Calvert for these cattle, although every other payment is carefully noted. Because of this, it seems unlikely that the seven thousand pounds of tobacco was Calvert's compensation for the cattle. Later, on 8 May, Mary Kittomaquand purchased these cattle out of Lord Baltimore's stock for 5,700 pounds of tobacco. Curiously, the difference between the two prices, 1,300 pounds, is almost exactly the total of court judgments delivered against Leonard Calvert's estate that spring, which was 1,285 pounds. It must be remembered that Margaret Brent was in possession of the cattle all during the controversy. That only makes sense if the Brents were shielding Calvert's tobacco from Cornwaleys.[37]

Even if it were true, Cornwaleys had overstepped his bounds in saying so in open court and provided Brent the club he needed to beat Cornwaleys into dropping the suit in Maryland. Brent, like everyone else in the small community, was aware that Cornwaleys intended shortly to sail for England. Were he to be imprisoned for three weeks, he would miss the ships returning to England. A marginal note entered next to the £400 judgment rendered on 16 March reports the vacating of the decision with the consent of the plaintiff on 19 March. Cornwaleys, deciding to pursue the matter in England, collected certified copies of the details of the purchase and his discounting of Leonard Calvert's bills of exchange. Sometime after 28 March, Thomas Cornwaleys sailed down the Chesapeake to join Richard Ingle at Accomac for the voyage to England. His decision to leave Maryland was only partly based on economic reasons. He later testified:

> Which doings and proceedings of your said Orator in that behalfe [i.e., for Ingle] occaisoned divers persons of the said plantacon to be much offended with your Orator. And did not only threaten to take away your Orator's life and to plunder and make spoile of his house and goods but did also so farr incense the said Governor of the Province against him as that your said Orator was . . . fined . . . a thousand weight of tobacco which is the highest fine that by the laws of the Province can or ought to be assessed . . . And your said Orator observing divers persons of the said plantacon to be discontented with your said Orator and to utter threatening speeches against him . . . did resolve . . . to absent himself from the said Province until such tyme as the said business might be forgotten.[38]

When Cornwaleys sailed away in April 1644, Maryland's last hope of avoiding the Plundering Time was gone. Cornwaleys's leadership would be keenly missed during the crisis. Had he been in Maryland in 1645 when Ingle arrived, there might never have been an invasion or a rebellion. Relying on his friendship with Ingle, he could have soothed over the minor incidents and misunderstandings that led to the conflagration. But Cornwaleys was in England then and had his own problems.

CHAPTER EIGHT

"Our Rebellious subjects . . . drive a great trade . . . in Virginia"

The events in the harbor at St. Inigoes, while unique in some ways, were merely an extension of what was going on in England and in the other colonies. In 1644, in Boston harbor, two separate incidents led to the seizure of ships. The first was a Bristol ship seized by a ship out of London, an action the authorities made no move to stop. The second incident was more complicated. English Royalists had captured a ship in Dartmouth harbor in England and forced the master, a strong Parliamentarian, to join a Royalist fleet under the Duke of Marlborough. Eventually the master managed to escape the fleet and, after a period of trading, turned up with his ship in Boston harbor. There he encountered two ships sailing for Parliament who attacked him as a Royalist. The colonial government stepped in and retook his ship, but they did not let the poor master continue on his way. The Massachusetts court decided that since the vessel hailed from a Royalist port, it should be seized to compensate Massachusetts merchants who had recently lost two ships to the Royalists in Wales. Such legalized piracy was having an effect on trade, and the following year the Massachusetts court proclaimed that all ships in the harbor would be protected, and that no ship was to fire on or attack another.[1]

The same hunger for plunder had swept into Virginia. Sailing along the James River were two London ships in search of trade and a cargo of tobacco. According to their own testimony, they had tried to conduct business but the planters, being strong Royalists, had refused to trade with them. Unable to vend their goods and not having a hold full of tobacco to take home, they faced financial ruin. Whether this was true or the two captains simply were seeking a sure way to increase their profits, they hatched a bold plan to seize a Bristol ship riding at anchor near Blanck Point.[2] As the tide began to flow up the river on 10 April 1644, the pair approached the Bristolman, giving no sign of their intentions. They glided in to anchor on either side of their target, then without warning raised the ensign of Parliament and let fly broadsides into the unsuspecting ship. The fusillade destroyed some of the rigging and resulted in several casualties, including a Virginia planter who had been on board to trade.

Reacting quickly to the attack, the captain of the Bristol ship cut his cables and, with the help of the incoming tide, poled into a nearby creek, where, much smaller than her attackers, she could easily glide over the shallow bottom. The two Londoners had to stay on the river and were reduced to firing cannon. Larger and carrying more men, the London ships could have sent their small boats after the Bristolman and boarded her except that her captain, probably using a swivel gun, kept them from entering the mouth of the creek. Faced with an aggressive opponent and with word of the attack spreading through the countryside, the Londoners broke off their attempt and sailed downstream.

This battle, perhaps the first engagement of the English Civil War in the Chesapeake, was important in ways that the participants could not have imagined at the time. Word of the attack spread quickly among the Indians of the lower bay, who harbored a long list of grievances against the English. They had heard rumors of a war in England and now saw for themselves a fight between English ships. Knowing that there was no better time to strike than when the enemy was divided, Opechancanough, the Powhatan chief, sent out messengers to raise the Indians against the English. Much as they had some twenty-two years earlier, the Indians caught the Virginians by surprise and in attacks on 18 April killed more than five hundred along the James and York rivers. But times had changed. Virginia was no longer a struggling foothold on the Atlantic shore. The population was much larger and was already encroaching on the Indian villages. Their vengeance would be swift and brutal.[3]

Early in 1644, the Indian threat was also much on the mind of Maryland's administrative leader, who was less concerned with how to combat it than how to pay for last year's efforts. When Governor Brent decided in April 1643 that the colony would not support a march against the Susquehannocks, he had hit on the plan to establish Fort Conquest on Palmer's Island, convincing the planters to pay for it by promising that no more taxes would be levied that year. Some of the militiamen who later marched as volunteers with Cornwaleys viewed their service as equivalent to paying their levy and refused to pay their assessments.

Beginning on 1 February 1644, Brent sued eight people for amounts varying between one hundred and five hundred pounds of tobacco in connection with Fort Conquest. Thomas Sturman, who was assessed the latter amount, argued that the additional service violated the agreement made with Brent and that he should not have to pay. Brent countered that the covenant specified only new taxes, not service. The tobacco Brent sought in these cases appears to have been voluntary pledges toward the expenses related to Fort Conquest or to the march, and to cover them Brent levied taxes on those who did not voluntarily contribute. On 7 February, the sheriff was instructed to collect. The list of fifty-six householders did not include anyone who had already contributed. At the top was merchant Thomas Weston, assessed a thousand pounds of tobacco. As late as 18 July this assessment was not collected. By that time, Weston was in England, and his servant or factor refused to pay or even open the door to talk with the sheriff. Secretary Lewgar authorized the sheriff to demand payment and, if it was not forthcoming, to break down the door and seize the necessary goods.[4]

Throughout this period, it was difficult for the government to persuade the planters to support any effective campaign against the Susquehannocks. One reason was that most planters regarded the threat of Indian attacks as remote. Susquehannocks concentrated their raids against the Patuxent River settlements, while most of the settlers lived in the Potomac River area. It is important to remember that all of the proclamations warning Indians to avoid the settlements or authorizing settlers to shoot them were restricted in scope. They specified the area near the mouth of the Patuxent River and were never intended to be general.

Outside the Patuxent area, the government had a very different view of the Indians. During these years when tensions were high along the frontier, the government tried two cases concerning the murder of Indians. On 6 February 1643, John Elkin was tried for killing the king of Yaocomoco. The jury agonized over the verdict, trying not to convict him. At first, despite a signed confession, they judged Elkin not guilty, reasoning that the Indian was a pagan not covered by the law. The governor replied that these Indians were at peace with Lord Baltimore and under his protection and sent the jury back to reconsider. They then found Elkin guilty of murder in his own defense. The governor pointed out that one cannot be guilty of murder while defending oneself and sent them off again. Finally, they found that Elkin had killed the Indian in his own defense. The governor refused to let that verdict be entered and sent for a new jury to hear the evidence. The new jury found Elkin guilty of manslaughter. Members of the first jury were later fined for misconduct. In this case, Leonard Calvert went to extraordinary lengths to deliver a guilty verdict of some kind. It is clear that he saw no difference in this case than if an Englishman had been killed.[5]

The second case occurred a year later, in February 1644. John Dandy was accused of shooting an Indian at Snowhill Manor, near St. Mary's City. He was tried by a jury and convicted of murder. Governor Brent sentenced him to be executed. The only thing that saved Dandy was a petition from many of the freemen. Dandy was a gunsmith by trade and vital to the colony. Brent suspended his sentence on the condition that he serve seven years as a servant to the Lord Proprietor.[6]

These cases demonstrate that the government was willing to extend the protection of its laws to Indians who were at peace with the province. Maryland's government did not condone the indiscriminate killing of Indians and made a strong effort to punish those who did. The threat of

Indian attack was specifically perceived to be along the Patuxent and from the Susquehannocks. If the government did not consider the Potomac area to be threatened, the planters certainly would not. Consequently, they were reluctant to bear the expenses necessary to defeat the Susquehannocks.

Another factor in the reluctance of most of the settlers to support an effective defense was the nature of the Patuxent settlements. The largest and hardest hit settlement was the Jesuit plantation at Mattapany. Most other settlers in the area were either Catholics or allied in some way to the Jesuits. The man who had been most eager to lead the expeditions was Thomas Cornwaleys, well known for championing the Jesuit cause. On the other hand, most of the planters who would have to pay for this policy were Protestants. They probably did not view the raids in the same light as the government.

But the reluctant attitude of the government and the planters began to change with the news of the massacre in Virginia. Reports soon arrived from other settlements reporting additional Indian attacks. The Dutch were fighting near Manhattan, the Swedes suffered casualties along the Delaware, and the Susquehannock threat was still very real in Maryland. It appeared as though the Indian tribes were working in confederation against the Europeans. In fact, one of the prisoners captured by Virginians boasted that the tribes within six hundred miles of Virginia were joined together to drive the English into the sea. These reports increased tensions in Maryland and made the settlers look more suspiciously at their native allies.[7]

Even before the Virginia massacre, one can detect increasing anxiety among the Marylanders. Early in January, the governor issued a proclamation requiring a license before anyone could give a gun or ammunition to an Indian. This measure was specifically aimed at those Indians hired by the colonists to hunt for them, since the trading of arms to the Indians was already prohibited. Apparently the practice was widespread as the proclamation referred to the great number of guns given to the Indians. The only person actually charged with violation of this proclamation was Thomas Cornwaleys. Henry Lee disarmed an Indian he met in the forest who was doing the captain's hunting, and Lee got to keep the gun for his trouble. Since this occurred in March, when Cornwaleys was embroiled with the government. it seems likely to have been part of the harassment Brent aimed at him.[8]

Affairs were still very unsettled along the Patuxent, with expectations of more raids in the summer. In addition, the danger of hostilities between the settlers and the Patuxent Indians began to rise. The settlers had long complained that the Indians were killing their hogs in the forest. Apparently some of them, despairing of government action, decided to compensate themselves. In April, the provincial court warned a number of Patuxent settlers to return corn and other goods seized from the Indians. In June, a letter circulated reminding the settlers that the Patuxent Indians were under the protection of Lord Baltimore and were "to be treated & used with all humanity as our friends and confederates." But the area was still under threat of attack, and in May the governor issued another proclamation warning the Indians, friendly or not, to avoid the settlements along the Patuxent.[9]

It was in this atmosphere of stress that word reached John Lewgar of an embassy from the Susquehannocks to the Piscataways. The reported purpose of the mission was to negotiate a peace treaty between the Susquehannocks and the combination of the Piscataways and the English. Lewgar was anxious to conclude such a treaty if possible but was worried that the real purpose was to lure the Piscataways away from their alliance with the Marylanders. Since this was an unexpected development and Governor Brent was away at Kent Island, Lewgar took it upon himself to send a commission, under Brent's signature, to Captain Henry Fleet, who was to go to Piscataway with a score of armed men and represent the province in the treaty negotiations. Lewgar gave Fleet detailed instructions regarding Maryland's conditions for peace, the first of which was that the Susquehannocks cease all hostile acts and stay out of Maryland territory. Lewgar then sought restitution for the various acts of plundering, including the two raids on the Jesuit settlement. He also demanded the return of the two cannon lost on the previous expedition. Finally, he wanted a present to the governor as a token of respect from the Indians. If Captain Fleet thought that peace was not possible, he was authorized to capture or kill the ambassadors or any of the Piscataways who were vocal against the English.[10]

The results of this commission, if any, are unknown. No change in relations between the English and the Piscataways or the Susquehannocks can be traced to these events. Maryland was still at war with the Susquehannocks in the late 1640s, and the two cannon were still on display in their village throughout the period. The notion that the Piscataways might be enticed into war against the Marylanders caused the government to view them with deep suspicion. To protect them from Susquehannock raids, and probably to watch them more carefully, the government established a garrison at Piscataway in early August.[11]

News of these events did not reach Governor Brent until late in August. Why Secretary Lewgar never bothered to tell him earlier remains a mystery. When he did find out, he was incensed that Lewgar had usurped his authority. He sent a letter to St. Mary's suspending Lewgar from the council and all other offices and stating that his acts were a "highe misdemeanor & offense." To provide for a court in Lewgar's absence, Brent appointed William Brainthwaite, Thomas Greene, and Cuthbert Fenwick to be judges and county commissioners. There is no record that this court ever met. The future may have looked bleak for John Lewgar, but his fortunes would soon abruptly turn.[12]

While Lewgar was trying to deal with the Indians, two Marylanders were on opposite courses in England. Leonard Calvert was preparing to return to the Chesapeake as Thomas Cornwaleys was arriving in London. There is no specific information on Calvert's voyage, but he must have left England after 2 July and was in Maryland by 6 September, a remarkably short voyage of nine weeks. We can assume that he sailed from Bristol since he was carrying commissions from the king. It is possible that Calvert sailed on the *Trewlove*, the ship Thomas Weston hired for his return to Maryland. Weston sailed from Bristol about the same time and is first recorded back in Maryland in early October, though possibly he arrived earlier. There is no indication that Lord Baltimore hired a ship for privateering as called for in the king's commission to Leonard Calvert.[13]

Calvert brought a number of important documents with him. He had a new commission for the government, a new commission for Lewgar as secretary, and a new commission for the council. All were published in Maryland between 6 and 18 September 1644, a period when Calvert reasserted his authority over the government and reappointed John Lewgar to his offices and prerogatives. The commission for the council gave evidence that Giles Brent had moved up in the list from fourth to first, but that did not reflect recent events. Lewgar most likely complained to Calvert about his recent dispute with Brent, who was still on Kent Island, and Calvert apparently took Lewgar's part. This would partially explain why Calvert, as he was preparing for a trip to Virginia in late September, chose William Brainthwaite to be deputy governor in his absence.

Brainthwaite was an unusual choice since he was not on the council and held no major office in the province. The most logical choice for deputy governor would have been Giles Brent. Not only was he listed first in the council commission but until barely a month earlier he had been deputy governor. Brent was now out of favor with Calvert because of his recent dispute with Lewgar. Brainthwaite was a relative and his choice was almost certainly calculated to embarrass and anger Brent. In 1642, Brainthwaite's selection as temporary commander of Kent while Brent was away had caused Brent to give up his leadership of an expedition against the Susquehannocks. His selection as deputy governor so soon after Brent had held the office probably inflamed Brent's jealousy.

Whatever the reason, Brainthwaite was appointed deputy governor on 30 September and Calvert hurried to Virginia to be there for the Assembly scheduled to begin on 1 October. His interest in the Virginia government resulted from other documents that he brought with him from England, a pair of royal commissions to be proclaimed in Virginia. The first, already mentioned, was dated 26 January and authorized the seizing of London ships. The second, dated 28 February, also struck at London and Parliament.[14]

Custom duties on tobacco had been a major source of revenue for the Crown before the war, but now the collectors and most of the trade were in London and the profits were going to support Parliament. The Crown's only hope of securing this income was to have it collected in the Chesapeake. The king authorized Leonard Calvert to negotiate with the Virginia House of Burgesses to pass an act for these duties to be paid in Virginia. Lord Baltimore and his agents would collect the revenue and pay a set contract price to the Crown, keeping any profit above the price for themselves.[15]

When Calvert arrived at Jamestown, he found the situation unfavorable. Sir William Berkeley, who would have been a natural and valuable ally, had gone to England after the April massacre. In his place was Richard Kemp, a long-time Calvert friend but lacking the forceful personality to command the Assembly. In the Assembly were several burgesses who were related to or closely aligned with the London merchants whom Calvert was threatening. Further, William Claiborne, Calvert's old enemy, had just returned from a successful march against the Indians and was riding high in the opinion of his fellow colonists. Given these circumstances, no act for custom duties could be pushed through the Assembly.[16]

That body was also unwilling to allow the seizure of London ships. They sent a letter to King Charles expressing their loyalty to him but declining to interrupt their trade with London because of their acute need for ammunition to defend themselves against the Indians. They also wrote to Parliament, assuring them of their continued friendship. Unlike the custom duties, however, the commission for seizing London ships did not require the approval of the Assembly. It only required the acquiescence of the governor, and Kemp was willing to grant that to his old friends. Calvert had his commission recorded, probably at the quarter session held 8 October. There is no evidence that he tried to seize any ships. Without an armed ship of his own, his luck would have been no better than Giles Brent's earlier that year. But there is evidence that he tried to compound with the Virginians for the debts that they owed to London merchants. Several members of the *Reformation*'s crew later testified that Argall Yeardley told them of Calvert's attempts to seize the debts of Richard Ingle. According to the testimony, Calvert warned Yeardley not to pay Ingle because he had a commission from the king to seize all Londoners' debts. When Yeardley demurred and said that Ingle was soon to come there, Calvert reportedly replied that if Ingle or any other Londoner should come there, he would hang him.[17]

One must remember the atmosphere in which this testimony was given. It was part of the justification for seizing a ship in Maryland, and it was important to prove that the colony was hostile to the Parliament. In that context, there is no way to know how embellished this testimony might be. Whether Calvert tried to put his commission into effect must remain uncertain, but in a larger sense that is relatively unimportant. Of greater import is that many Virginians knew of the commission and believed that it was to be put into action. Evidence of that belief was recorded in the Northampton County Court. William Mumms testified that he was about to load tobacco aboard the *Reformation* in settlement of a debt he owed to Captain Ingle when Richard Lemon advised him against it, warning that there was a proclamation against paying tobacco to London ships. Mumms, uncertain what to do, went to see Obedience Robbins, a member of the County Court. Robbins told him to pay what he owed, saying "God forbid we should refuse to pay Turks or Jew for what we have received."[18]

The Calverts' attempt at helping the Royalist cause and profiting by it came to nothing. There is no testimony or record showing any debts seized or any ships stopped by these commissions. The Virginia colonists may have had strong Royalist sympathies, but they had too many commercial ties to the London merchants to prove that loyalty. Less than four months after Calvert's unsuccessful efforts, the House of Burgesses unequivocally declared themselves for free trade. On 17 February they passed an act declaring:

> that there be a free trade and commerce allowed to all his majesties subjects within the kingdom of England. And it is further thought fitt to be explained particularly, because of some questions and doubts that have been made by Londoners this yeare tending to a prohibition of trade with them, that it was never intended but the contrary thereof always assured

> unto them . . . And this Assembly on behalfe of the inhabitants do pledge the faith of the colony for a continuance of a free and peaceable trade to them . . . as demeane themselves in a peaceable manner and be obedient and conformable to the government.[19]

Earlier in the year, as Leonard Calvert was preparing to sail with his commissions, Thomas Cornwaleys was arriving in London to his own set of problems. Late in May the *Reformation* made her way up the Thames bearing her valuable cargo of tobacco, much of it belonging to Thomas Cornwaleys. The captain was an ardent Roman Catholic and a good friend of the Jesuits. It did not take long for this information to spread through town, and before Cornwaleys' goods were unloaded a warrant was issued by the Committee for Sequestrations to seize the tobacco. Cornwaleys, as a papist, was subject to the law allowing two-thirds of a Catholic's estate to be seized even if they were sympathetic to Parliament. Josias Casswell, representing the committee, boarded the *Reformation* to serve the warrant and to see that the goods were secured. Richard Ingle protested vigorously and reported that Cornwaleys had been the only means of his escape from Maryland. He freely admitted how much he owed Cornwaleys and said that he had saved his life. Given these actions, which Ingle pointed to as support for the Parliamentary cause, he felt it highly unfair that Cornwaleys should lose his goods.

A hearing was scheduled at Camden House before the Committee for Sequestrations in June. Ingle again declared his loyalty to his friend and proclaimed Cornwaleys's virtue in defending the cause of Parliament. Because of Ingle's testimony, Cornwaleys's goods were freed and he was set at liberty. In Casswell's opinion, "Ingle knew Cornwallis to be a verye honest man and soe much alsoe hee did divers times express and say that the said Cornwallis was a good friend to him and his."[20]

As the two friends celebrated in London, the Civil War raged around them. Unlike previous years, the winter had seen little or no cessation of operations. In January a Scottish army had crossed the border and entered England to assist Parliament. This army, combined with local forces, was threatening to wrest control of the north from the Royalists. In the south, numerous armies and smaller bodies of troops marched and counter-marched across the landscape without securing any advantage. A number of smaller actions resulted in victories for both sides. By the time the *Reformation* sailed into the Thames, the campaign was focusing on two fronts. Prince Rupert was marching north to lift the siege of York, and the Earl of Essex was marching southwest to relieve Parliamentary garrisons along the southern coast.[21]

On 2 July, Prince Rupert led his army, some twenty thousand, against the combined Parliamentary forces at Marston Moor. By the time the two armies faced each other, it was late in the day and the Royalists believed that the battle would not begin until the morning. They were settling in for supper when the enemy advanced on their position. Despite being caught off guard, the Royalists fought fiercely and pushed the center back. They fought so well, that the Scottish commander thought the battle lost and fled the field. But a flanking attack by Cromwell's cavalry scattered the Royalist horse. The "ironsides," as Rupert later named them, next attacked the Royalist infantry from the rear, crushing them and causing heavy casualties. Before midnight the battle was over. With the defeat of Prince Rupert's army at Marston Moor, the north was lost to the king, and many scholars see this battle as the turning point of the conflict. Combined with successes in the south, it made a Parliamentary victory seem, for a short time, inevitable.

The Earl of Essex, who was part of that success in the south, began his campaign with the same purpose that drove Rupert north. The Earl intended to relieve a number of cities that were holding out against Royalist sieges. Like the Prince, he led his small force deep into enemy territory, relieving first Lyme and then Plymouth. These relatively easy victories induced him to try more daring plans. He expected that the countryside, freed of its fear of Royalists, would rise up and support him. The countryside did rise, but not as expected. Essex realized he was in serious trouble as he continued his march into Cornwall. He was deep in enemy territory with a Royalist army under Sir Richard Grenville retreating before him and an army under King Charles coming up rapidly behind. His only option and hope was to make for the coast and a scheduled meeting with the fleet under the Earl of Warwick. Though Essex made it to the coast, the fleet never came. With the enemy closing in and no relief in sight, Essex escaped in a fishing boat to Plymouth. His army, some six thousand strong, surrendered on 2 September 1644.

Both campaigns had begun with similar intentions. Rupert and Essex had set out to relieve friendly strongholds in enemy territory, and their efforts turned to disaster when they attempted to extend their means too far. In retrospect, Rupert's loss before York was much more serious. Essex could and did recruit another army, but the Royalists would never again control the north. Still, when it spread through London the news of Essex's defeat cast a pall over the earlier Parliamentary successes. As the campaigning season came to a close, the outcome of the war was again in doubt.

The bad news from Cornwall reached London just as the tobacco fleet was completing its preparations for the annual voyage to the Chesapeake. Among the ships preparing for the trip was the *Reformation.* This would be her third trip to the bay under the command of Richard Ingle, but this particular voyage would forever link her name with the history of Maryland. As a result of the actions of her master and crew, Maryland's society and the course of her future development would be forever changed. Since the consequences of this voyage were so great, we must ask if they were intended from the beginning. What were Ingle's intentions and expectations as he prepared the *Reformation* for the trip?

The evidence is overwhelming that Ingle thought of this passage as just another trading voyage. By October he was loading cargo to be delivered in Maryland and Virginia. When Ingle informed him of the coming voyage, Thomas Cornwaleys freighted £160 of trading goods as well as food, clothing, and supplies for his servants and plantation. The total came to between £200 and £250. George Horsfall, who supervised the lading of the cargo for Cornwaleys, later testified concerning what was shipped. Among other things, he reported four quarter casks of sack, a package of linen and woolen cloth, a large piece of silk, a barrel of pitch, and a rundlett of vinegar. These goods were to be delivered to Cuthbert Fenwick, Cornwaleys's factor in Maryland. The fact that Cornwaleys was willing to trust Ingle with this large, expensive cargo is an indication that their friendship was still strong. To suggest that Ingle accepted the cargo while harboring the intention of plundering Maryland would require the assumption of a character flaw much deeper than the available evidence would support. Ingle may have had a problem with his temper, but there is nothing to suggest that he was capable of such deceit.[22]

Thomas Cornwaleys was probably the major freighter for this trip, but other Marylanders were shipping goods with Ingle as well. Ralph Crouch, a Maryland planter, had ordered some goods from Thomas Clark in London. Valued at £10 10s these goods were loaded aboard the *Reformation* in October 1644. These details imply normal preparations for a trading voyage.[23]

Another line of evidence comes directly from the *Reformation*'s crew. In their later testimony, they were asked what conditions were offered to sail on this voyage. Consistently they stated that they were hired for wages only. Before leaving London, they were not offered shares in any plunder that might be collected. As this would have been a major inducement, had it been possible Ingle would have offered it. However, the only conditions he offered the crew were those associated with a normal trading expedition.[24]

But these were extraordinary times and required more than ordinary preparations. It was at this time that Richard Ingle applied for and was granted a letter of marque from the Lord High Admiral. This commission or letter is often confused with an Act of Parliament passed in August 1644 which names the *Reformation* as one of eight vessels granted special privileges. However, they are very different in intent and execution. Since they form the basis of Ingle's later defense, their provisions must be made clear.

The letter of marque was authorized under an act of Parliament for privateering, passed on 1 December 1643 and authorizing the seizure of vessels trading to ports that were hostile to the Parliament. Several of the *Reformation*'s crew testified that Ingle showed them a commission with the great seal of the Admiralty on it. John Durford, the *Reformation*'s mate, testified that Ingle had been approved by the Admiralty to sail for the purpose of seizing ships trading with hostile ports. From his later actions, it is apparent that Ingle tried to conform or to appear to conform to the provisions of this Parliamentary act.[25]

The intent of letters of marque should not be overestimated. They were not hard to obtain and that given Ingle does not imply any special connection between the captain and the Parliamentary cause. Despite Durford's testimony, a letter of marque did not mean that the ship was sailing primarily as a privateer. It merely provided the legal background should a target of opportunity arise during the course of a regular trading voyage. There was also a practical reason for obtaining such a commission: the act granting them authorized any approved vessel to apply for compensation for food consumed while at sea. This was the ship owners' major expense on any voyage, and having someone else pay for it would certainly help the profit margin. That Ingle had a letter of marque from the Admiralty cannot be doubted. What he intended to do with this power, once at sea, is an open question.

The other act of Parliament associated with the *Reformation* was passed in August 1644 for the defense and relief of the planters. It was proposed by a number of persons trading to the Chesapeake, and it authorized eight ships to transport arms, food, and clothing to Virginia free of export duties. This was not, as has been claimed, an attempt to strengthen Parliamentary sentiment in Virginia. Rather it was a response to the Indian massacre of the previous April. Nor was it a wholly humanitarian gesture. The London merchant community used this occasion to add a provision seeking the right to stop the Dutch from trading in Virginia. Because of the disruptions of the war, the Dutch were capturing a much larger portion of the trade and giving London merchants some difficult competition in an area where they previously had held a virtual monopoly. If the merchants' concerns were truly with the planters, they would not have proposed shutting off this source of vital supplies. In the end, the provision for "interrupting" the Dutch was shelved, but eight ships, including the *Reformation,* were authorized to carry duty-free supplies to Virginia. The ship's master and owners were aware that goods shipped without paying export duties meant larger profits on the other side. Once again, these actions indicate Captain Ingle had a good sense of business and not that he was bent on revenge against Maryland.[26]

By late October, Richard Ingle had completed his preparations for the outward voyage to Virginia. As far as we know, he viewed this as simply another trading voyage. He would have been foolish not to have been on his guard in the Chesapeake, considering his recent experiences at Accomac and St. Mary's and the uncertain nature of the times. But he seems to have been prepared to do business in his regular fashion. If he harbored any ill will, it was toward Giles Brent and not Maryland in general. Sometime late in October, the *Reformation* slipped down the Thames into the Downs to await a favorable wind. With a fair westerly wind, she began a voyage that would forever change the course of Maryland history.

CHAPTER NINE

"If Ingle or any other . . . should come . . . hee would hang them"

As Richard Ingle was preparing to return to Maryland, a ship at Rotterdam was getting ready to sail for Virginia. She was *De Spiegel,* which translates as the *Looking Glass.* She was relatively new and probably built by her owners specifically for the transatlantic trade. The *Looking Glass* was said to be one hundred tons, but that figure is probably low. In the seventeenth century, ships were commonly registered below their actual tonnage. Using a standard figure of four hogsheads of tobacco to the ton, based on the 300–400 casks she was to load for the freighters, were she a hundred tons that would have filled the hold. Yet the owners also sent a cargo for trade and, while in Maryland, the *Looking Glass* picked up a large amount of tobacco from Leonard Calvert and others on consignment. All of this indicates that she must have been in the 150–200 ton range and was comparable to the London tobacco ships. She probably had three masts and would have been square-rigged on the foremast and main but with a lateen mizzen mast.[1]

The size of her crew on the outbound voyage is unknown. At the time she was seized in Maryland, eighteen men were reportedly on board, but it is not clear whether these were all crew members or some were

Marylanders caught on board. Eleven men on the outward voyage can be accounted for in later testimony. The ship's master was Hatrick Cornelius Cocke. Henry Brooks Jr. went along as factor for the freighters. Robert Reeves was the English pilot whom Brooks hired to guide them when they arrived in Virginia. The crew included Gabrant Ouckerson, the steersman, Peter Salmonson, the boatswain, Jacob Johnson, the carpenter, Michael Albertson, the gunner, and Peter Albertson, the sailmaker. All were Dutch. In addition the *Looking Glass* carried several Englishmen in her crew: Henry Williams, Henry Stockton, and Dionisius Corbin. The fact that almost half of the crew and passengers on this Dutch ship were English did not escape the attention of Ingle and his men.[2]

It was customary to allow each member of the crew to bring his own "adventure," and most of the Dutch crew members seem to have taken advantage of this as did the pilot, Reeves. Since the three English crew members are not listed as having an "adventure," it may be that they were picked up at the last minute. The extent of these private cargoes is unknown, but Gabrant Ouckerson may be typical. He claimed an investment of a hundred guilders in trade goods.[3]

No contemporary description of the *Looking Glass* has survived, but we can make an educated guess as to how she was built. In the seventeenth century the Dutch built two kinds of ships. The most famous was the *fluit* or flyboat, developed in 1594. This was a lightly built ship, about four times as long as it was wide. What distinguished the *fluit* from other ships was that it was rounded at the stern rather than squared off. The *fluit* was well-known for its larger carrying capacity while requiring a smaller crew. The second type of Dutch ship was a more conventional, armed merchantman. The latter were built for trade or war and were used on voyages that were expected to be dangerous. Unlike the *fluit,* these ships had a flat stern or transom, a feature that distinguished this type of ship for the Dutch, who called them *spiegel* ships. Given this classification, it is certain that the *Looking Glass* was not a *fluit* but was a square-sterned vessel.[4]

That a Dutch ship was preparing to sail to an English colony is not unusual. The Dutch were the greatest commercial power of the time, and Rotterdam was one of the leaders in the transatlantic trade. Rotterdam had become an important port during the Middle Ages and had sent its own ships to the East Indies by 1598. The Dutch had been trading for tobacco in Virginia possibly as early as 1612 but certainly by 1620. Most of their early Chesapeake voyages were opportunistic, with ships sailing around the bay until they found a cargo. It is no surprise that the commercially astute Dutch found this to be a less-than-satisfactory way to conduct business. In 1635 and 1636, for example, Daniel DeVries, a frustrated Dutch captain, reported spending eight months vainly searching for a cargo. The Dutch sought permanent trading partners in Virginia who could collect the tobacco when it was ready, making trade more economical and leading to increasing Dutch activity in the Chesapeake. Their trade grew in the 1630s and peaked in the 1640s, when the Civil War in England disrupted normal trading patterns. Before the Civil War, Dutch ships had made up a small proportion of the traders; by 1648 they reportedly accounted for half of the ships in Virginia waters.[5]

Virginia planters eagerly encouraged the Dutch to trade with them for a number of reasons. Dutch captains not only bought tobacco at prices higher than the English merchants, they also provided a greater variety of goods at lower prices for the planters. During the Civil War, the Dutch supplied vitally needed powder and shot for the defense of the colony against the Indians. An indication of the importance of the Dutch trade can be seen in Governor Berkeley's reaction to Parliament's ban on trade with foreign nations in 1650:

> We can onely feare the Londoners, who would faine bring us to the same poverty, wherein the Dutch found and relieved us; would take away the liberty of our consciences, and tongues, and our right of giving and selling our goods to whom we please.[6]

The merchants of Rotterdam were active in this tobacco trade. Records are incomplete, but in 1643 the ship *Mary* sailed from Rotterdam to Virginia, and in 1644 three ships, the *Looking Glass,* the *Water Duck,* and *t'Moorhoofd,* are reported to have been there as well. At least six Rotterdam merchants traded to Virginia in the 1640s and imported several thousand hogsheads of tobacco.[7]

The *Looking Glass* was owned by a company headed by Cornelius Conincke and Peter Sonemans, prominent merchants who held positions as civil magistrates in Rotterdam. Other owners included the master of the vessel, Hatrick Cornelius Cocke and his brother Albert, both of whom are described as merchants of Rotterdam. Albert Cocke had had previous contacts with Virginia. In 1643 he had sent eight servants there to be sold, some of whom were purchased by Francis Yeardley.[8]

The owners loaded her with a cargo of strong waters, linen cloth and shifts, hats, shoes, stockings, sugar, frying pans, and other trade goods with a value of 2,338 guilders, but the owners' cargo was only a small portion of the goods the *Looking Glass* carried to Maryland in 1645. Most of the cargo space had been leased to John Glover and Henry Brooks Jr., a pair of English merchants living in Rotterdam. On 11 November 1644, they signed a contract with Hatrick Cocke, master of the ship, to sail from Rotterdam to Virginia or "to another locality if they be not allowed to land in Virginia." They had obviously heard of the London merchants' petition to stop the Dutch trade. The master was to provide the vessel with eight guns, and Brooks was to find four more. They were to stay in Virginia for three and a half months, during which time the ship's crew would load 300–400 hogsheads of tobacco. The master agreed to provide sufficient ammunition and victuals for the round trip, but the freighters were responsible for feeding the crew during the time that the ship was in Virginia. If the full cargo of 300–400 casks were loaded and brought back, the freighters—Brooks and Glover—were to pay thirty-five guilders per cask, but if less tobacco was obtained, the freight would be seventy guilders per cask. The value of the cargo Brooks loaded in the *Looking Glass* is not stated. The fact that she was primarily freighted by English merchants and not Dutch was to be an important point in the court cases surrounding later events in Maryland.[9]

The English merchant community was well-established in Rotterdam and Amsterdam by the mid-1640s. At least thirteen English merchants traded in Virginia from bases in Holland. The advantage of this system was the low import duty charged by the Dutch. The disruptions of the English Civil War also led some merchants to seek more peaceful locations. Henry Brooks, John Glover, and their families were well connected with this group and had been heavily involved in the Virginia tobacco trade for at least five years. The Brooks family was from London and had trading interests in Virginia that had begun before 1640. At that time the brothers, Nicholas Brooks Sr. and Henry Brooks Sr., described as grocers of London, had a joint investment in the trade. Henry Brooks Sr. bought out his brother and became the sole owner. Nicholas Brooks Jr. was the resident agent in Virginia through 1643 but was not as thrifty as his uncle thought he should be. Henry Brooks Jr. went to Virginia in 1643 aboard the *Mary* and brought back the firm's account for the year. The results did not please Henry Brooks Sr., who on 10 September 1644 dismissed his nephew from service. Henry Brooks Jr. was to carry this letter to his cousin and collect all of the assets of the firm. The Brooks and Glover trading concern seems to have been centered in York County, Virginia. Not only did they collect debts there, but they purchased land, gave depositions, acted as attorneys, and contracted to deliver servants.[10]

The previous voyage to Virginia had been eventful for Brooks. He had loaded 748 casks in the *Mary,* commanded by Francis Hurdidge, with the understanding that the ship would sail from Virginia to Holland. Instead, Hurdidge took the *Mary* to the Downs in England. Although the ship arrived in England by June, it was August before Brooks was able to get her to Holland. At that time, Brooks appointed John Glover to handle the tobacco for him. There were problems with the tobacco though, and Glover had testimony recorded that the ship leaked and was in bad repair during the voyage. The crew, it was said, had to pump continuously to keep her from sinking. Brooks appears to have begun trading from Holland very recently, since he was consistently referred to as "of London" in 1644. He was reportedly a Catholic and may well have found the atmosphere of London during the Civil War dangerous. The Brooks and Glover families were also related through marriage because Richard Glover, brother of John, had married Elizabeth Brooks, the sister of Henry before 1644. They had a daughter, Anna Glover, who was baptized at the English Church at Amsterdam on 8 May 1644.[11]

The Glover family, though English, had been living in Holland for a long time. Richard Glover, the father of John, had been in Holland since 1619. He had baptized a daughter at the English Church in Amsterdam on 30 October that year. In addition to the daughter, whose name was Elizabeth, he had three sons, Richard, Robert, and John. All three became merchants in the tobacco trade. Robert Glover came to Maryland, probably in the fall of 1642. By the end of July 1643 he was involved in a lawsuit with Nicholas Cawsin to the value of one thousand pounds of tobacco. Cawsin sued Glover for seven weeks' food, for the use of his boat, and for other promises that Glover had not fulfilled. By December 1643, Robert Glover had died in Maryland. In preparation for his next trip to Virginia, John Glover issued a certificate to Henry Brooks Jr. on 14 October 1644, authorizing him to recover whatever estates Glover's brother had left in Maryland and to find out what cattle were owed to him at Accomack in Virginia. John Glover continued to be involved in the Virginia trade into the 1650s and is recorded as owner, freighter, or insurer of a dozen vessels during the period.[12]

Preparation for the voyage of the *Looking Glass* began in the summer of 1644. In September, Henry Brooks Jr. was looking for an experienced pilot for Virginia and sent a letter to Robert Reeves of Sutcliffe in County Middlesex, England. Reeves agreed to go as pilot and soon came over to Holland. On 12 October 1644, Henry Brooks Jr. borrowed 10,057 guilders from Glover. The reason for the loan was not stated but it may have been for a one-twelfth share of the ship, which Brooks had purchased by early November. Brooks and Glover loaded a mixed cargo similar to that of the owners but also listed several additional items. The freighters' cargo included shoes, hats, strong waters, linen cloth, stockings, frying pans, sugar, and other necessary commodities.[13]

Although Brooks and Cocke had been preparing for the trip as early as September, the contract for the voyage was not signed until 11 November 1644, and it called for the ship to "sail with the first good wind." The departure must have been very soon thereafter. As the *Looking Glass* slipped down the Maas River and into the North Sea, Henry Brooks Jr., standing on the deck with the master of the vessel, never suspected that this was the last time that he would see home or family.[14]

The *Reformation,* meanwhile had raised the Virginia Capes in early December. It is not known whether she made land first at Accomack on the eastern shore or if Ingle made directly for the more settled areas on the James River. Whatever the case, Ingle quickly learned of Leonard Calvert's commission from the king at Oxford. Historians have often speculated on the role William Claiborne played during Ingle's raid on Maryland. Some believe that Ingle and Claiborne acted together while others state that they simply took advantage of one another's actions. While much of this relationship remains clouded, it is now clear that they not only knew one another but had discussed their joint problems with the Maryland government. Robert Rawlins, surgeon of the *Reformation,* later testified "that the . . . schedule is a copie of a certaine paper delivered unto Capt. Ingle by Mr. Claibourne one of the Council of Virginia as a copie of a Commission registered in the courte there."[15]

That certain paper was Governor Calvert's commission. Such news must have been disturbing to a Parliamentary captain like Ingle. William Claiborne undoubtedly acquainted Ingle with Calvert's attempts to put the commission into effect the previous fall. It is easy to imagine these two arch-enemies of the proprietary government sitting down to plot the overthrow of their common foe. Other Virginians had been talking to Ingle as well. While at Accomack, Ingle met with a "Squire Argoll Yarly," the same person with whom he had argued two years before. In the county records, he is referred to as "Esquire Commander," and Ingle would certainly have regarded him as a reliable source. Several of the *Reformation*'s crew, including John Durford and Robert Rawlins, gave testimony concerning a conversation between Ingle and the squire. Thomas Eves, the Cooper of the *Reformation* testified:

> That hee this deponent hath heard one Squire Erlye of Virginia there say and relate unto the said Capt. Ingle that the articulate Calvert had beene with him the said Erlye to forwarne him not to pay unto the said Ingle any debts that hee the said Erlye owed unto him for that hee had a Commission to seize on all debts belonging to any Londoners but hee the said Erlye replying that hee durst not doe it in regard that hee the said Ingle as hee heard was shortly to come thither, the said Calvert

> replyed that if Ingle or any other should come from London thither hee would hang them.[16]

How much of Calvert's bluster as reported by the crew of the *Reformation* can actually be attributed to him? Several of the crew repeated this testimony in detail. Given this evidence, it is likely that Yeardley did relate Calvert's actions in these terms. But did Calvert actually seek out Ingle's debtors and try to stop payment on the debts? Whatever estate or bills Ingle left in Maryland in 1644 had been sequestered by Giles Brent because of Ingle's failure to fulfill the conditions of his bail. His estate totaled only 1,123 pounds of tobacco, while the bail was equivalent to four thousand pounds. Cornwaleys had promised to be security for the bail, but he too had left the province. Thomas Greene, the boatswain, testified that, according to some of the Protestants, Leonard Calvert ordered them not to pay their debts to Ingle. These debts were all in Maryland and Calvert was within his right to try to collect the rest of the bail. However, if Calvert went to Virginia and attempted to stop Ingle's debts as Yeardley reported, that implies a larger purpose. Calvert did have his commission entered into the court records at Jamestown. He seems, at least at the beginning, to have actively tried to carry out the commission. There is no way to know if he actually threatened to arrest or hang Ingle. If he did say these things, it was the biggest blunder he ever made, and it almost led to the destruction of Maryland.[17]

Another possibility cannot be discounted. Argall Yeardley and his brother, Captain Francis Yeardley, were intimately connected with William Claiborne. When Claiborne came back to the Chesapeake in 1652 as a commissioner from the Lord Protector, Oliver Cromwell, he placed Francis Yeardley on the new governor's council. One of the requirements for membership on this new council was that the councilors had to take the "Ingagement" or oath to support Parliament. Despite earlier scruples, both of the brothers were in sympathy with the English Parliamentarians. Calvert's commission was common knowledge in Virginia and Argall Yeardley may have felt that by stirring up the *Reformation*'s captain he could aid the cause of Parliament and help Claiborne.

There is no certain evidence describing the immediate effect of these revelations on Ingle's intention to trade in Maryland. He must have felt that Maryland had declared itself for the king and that to go there was to risk the loss of his ship, if not his life. Some of the *Reformation*'s delay in Virginia may be due to Ingle's concern over this news. A good case can be made that Ingle now decided peace with the Marylanders was not possible. It was probably at this point that he proposed to turn his trading voyage into a man-o'-war cruise. John Durford said that Ingle showed the crew his commission from Parliament, read them a line or two of it, and contracted with them for a sixth part of all of the pillage that came their way. By way of confirming this, Pascho Panton, a second cooper on the *Reformation*, said, "That hee was hired to serve in the said shippe the *Reformation* for wages & not shares but after they came to Virginia this voyage, Capt. Ingle promised his Company a sixth part of what they should take to goe along with him uppon a man of warr voyage for Mariland."[18]

Further, it is likely that Ingle and Claiborne decided to act together in surprising the colony and plundering it in the name of Parliament. For lack of hard evidence this must remain conjecture, but the plan may have been as follows: Claiborne and a small force of men would sail up to Kent Island, where they would seize control of the fort. Ingle would sail to St. Mary's and pretend to deliver Cornwaleys's goods and trade with the inhabitants. Meanwhile, Claiborne, using his connections on the island, would raise the Kent Islanders against Lord Baltimore's government and sail down to join Ingle with a large fighting force. Together, they would plunder the Catholics and establish a Protestant government sympathetic to Parliament.

If Ingle and Claiborne were not working together, their timing was remarkably well coordinated. Why else, for example, would Claiborne choose this time to make another try for Kent Island? It is reported that Claiborne landed on the island shortly before Christmas 1644. He had two ships, his own vessel and that of his cousin, Richard Thompson. From these he landed a force of ten or eleven men. They were joined by seven or eight men who soon arrived from Chicacoan in Northumberland County, Virginia, a settlement founded, in part, by William Claiborne. The locality was inhabited by of many of Claiborne's supporters from Kent Island and fugitives from St. Mary's who refused to live under Lord

Baltimore's government. Throughout this period, it was a good recruiting ground for anyone wishing to cause trouble in Maryland. One indication that Ingle and Claiborne were working closely together is that men from this settlement, possibly the same ones, were with Claiborne at Kent and later with Ingle at St. Mary's.[19]

Relying on the loyalty of his former employees, Claiborne began to stir up Kent Island against the proprietorship, claiming he had a commission and letter from the king to seize the island's government. The rebels gathered at the plantation of Edward Commins before setting off to take Giles Brent's house "by force of armes." Had he succeeded in seizing Kent Island, Claiborne probably intended to take his force to St. Mary's and join Ingle in the final destruction of the Maryland government. Interestingly, two years later he did propose this to a force of men mustered in Kent Field and almost succeeded in persuading them to go.

This part of the plan was not destined to succeed. Despite their personal loyalty to Claiborne, the Kent Islanders were practical men. They undoubtedly remembered Governor Calvert's previous invasions of their island and were in no mood to lose their plantations or their lives. After going about three miles, calmer heads prevailed. When the rebel party reached the house of John Abbotts, someone asked to see Claiborne's commission. He showed them a piece of parchment and a letter, but these did not convince them. In fact, "the sd parties, or the greatest number of them (as it should seeme) doubting the validity of his Authority, to justify them in the sd accon there gaue ouer the designe & left him." Having failed to capture the island, Claiborne and his men got in their boats and sailed away.

Rumors of these events soon reached Governor Calvert at St. Mary's. He issued instructions for a secret mission to Kent Island on 22 December. Mark Pheypo and John Genellas were authorized to recruit eight men as crew for the trip. They were either provided with a shallop or were to press one into service. After passing the Patuxent River, they were to make for the eastern shore of the Chesapeake and sail north "in as secret a manner" as possible with the object of determining if a vessel was at anchor off the southern end of the island. The governor warned them to avoid being seen at Kent and to keep away from all other ships. This concern over the presence of a ship at Kent may simply have been a reflection of Calvert's larger worry about the vessels that Claiborne had brought with him. It may also indicate that Calvert had heard rumors of Ingle's conversations with Claiborne and Yeardley, and that he was worried about the large, well-gunned *Reformation*.[20]

The Marylanders were to proceed farther up the island where they could find an isolated plantation. From there they were to discover if Claiborne was on the island and if so learn his plans and how long he intended to stay. Calvert specifically warned them not to go ashore at Kent Fort until they knew the situation. If they could, they were to deliver a letter to Giles Brent and to bring back his answer.

A marginal note recorded with the governor's instructions provides even more specific details on how the information was to be obtained on Claiborne's whereabouts. The governor told them to land four men near the plantation of Edward Commins on the western side of the island. (It is interesting that both sides chose this plantation for the beginning of their operations.) One of the landing party was to "hollow the house" while the other three hid nearby. When someone came out to answer the call, they were to surprise him and bring him back to the boat for questioning.

These instructions were never carried out. The marginal note includes a Latin phrase *vacant per allias* that roughly translates as "made empty by other means." What these other means might have been can only be conjectured. However, Giles Brent, who should have been on Kent Island according to the instructions, appears in the court records at St. Mary's on the twenty-third of December 1644 and is frequently mentioned thereafter. Apparently Brent, believing that he could not hold the island against this force, had sailed to St. Mary's to inform the governor.[21]

On 1 January 1645, Leonard Calvert issued a proclamation that prohibited ships from going to Kent before first registering at St. Mary's and receiving permission to trade. William Claiborne and Richard Thompson, his cousin, were declared enemies of the province, and the inhabitants were warned not to trade or communicate with them. At the same time, Calvert appointed William Brainthwaite commander of Kent, and he led an expedition to Kent that reasserted proprietary authority over the island. Brainthwaite's arrival on Kent early in January with an armed force may have been one of the factors contributing to the Kent Islanders' hesitation to follow Claiborne. It is worth noting that although Brent was in St. Mary's as early as 23 December 1644, it was not until 7 January 1645 that he filed a suit against Leonard Calvert claiming that Claiborne was planning to dispossess him of his house and lands on Kent Island. It may be that Brainthwaite sent information on Claiborne's plans back to the governor at St. Mary's and that the collapse of the rebel coalition took place soon thereafter.[22]

William Claiborne's incursion on Kent Island could not have come at a worse time for the province. Early in January 1645 the government was facing an internal crisis that threatened to split it apart. On the seventh, Leonard Calvert came into the provincial court to renew his claim against Thomas Cornwaleys for the two bills of exchange that were protested in England. For these two bills, originally valued at £40, Calvert was now seeking twenty thousand pounds of tobacco, a little over £160 or four times the original value.[23]

To Giles Brent and John Lewgar, both sitting on the court that day, this case must have seemed like a recurring nightmare. The previous spring, they had tried very hard to protect Calvert's estate from Cornwaleys and to defuse the Chapel controversy. Now, seemingly without warning, the question loomed before them again. They could do little at this point but grant Calvert a writ of attachment, much as they had done for Cornwaleys previously. They set a date of 1 February for the writ to be returned.

Perhaps because of Calvert's slight against him in October or the appointment of William Brainthwaite as commander of Kent in January, Giles Brent decided to switch sides in this controversy. After Calvert's demand had been filed, Brent prepared two petitions to the council. One asked them to force Calvert to pay the 5,700 pounds owed to Brent's wife for cattle. The other sought security, amounting to twenty-five thousand pounds of tobacco, for the Kent Island properties that Claiborne was threatening. These petitions were submitted to John Lewgar who, on the ninth of the month, sent them to the governor. In a cover letter, Lewgar requested Calvert to pay the sums asked for or to set a time when he could meet with the council to explain why he would not pay them.[24]

Once the controversy was reopened, all of the former litigants joined in with gusto. On the ninth, Calvert sued Cuthbert Fenwick for ten thousand pounds of tobacco due on account. The next day, Fenwick, attorney for Thomas Cornwaleys, submitted a petition to Giles Brent, as a member of the council, repeating the circumstances of the Chapel purchase and demanding 100,000 pounds of tobacco from Calvert, Lewgar, and Langford. Brent sent this petition along to the governor again asking him to pay it or explain why he refused to do so. On the eleventh, Governor Calvert replied to both Brent and Lewgar, saying that he was, "not bound to shew cause nor will shew any upon the day, or within the time uppointed, on Monday next." On the same day, Calvert entered a demand against Giles Brent for thirty thousand pounds of tobacco as satisfaction of an unspecified trespass done by Brent. The writ was again to be returned by 1 February. Cuthbert Fenwick and Thomas Copley put up a bond of thirty thousand pounds of tobacco for Giles Brent in this case. Brent then sent a warrant to the sheriff of St. Mary's County requiring him to attach and keep 100,000 pounds of tobacco or goods from Leonard Calvert to answer the suit of Cuthbert Fenwick. John Lewgar, at the same time, sent a similar warrant to the sheriff, at the request of Giles Brent, ordering him to sequester thirty thousand pounds of tobacco or goods from the governor. On the fourteenth, Fenwick was again in front of Judge Brent complaining that Edward Packer, the sheriff, refused to serve the warrants on Leonard Calvert. Brent appointed Thomas Matthews, a close ally of the Jesuits, to present the warrants to the governor.[25]

Finally, on 25 January, the governor had had enough of this legal wrangling. He issued a warrant to the sheriff for the arrest of Giles Brent. He was to be held under arrest until the governor called him to answer for "several crimes against the dignity and dominion" of Lord Baltimore. This was a serious escalation in the dispute, and the outcome was uncertain. As time moved toward the provincial court scheduled for 1 February 1645, both sides began to reconsider their options. The fateful day came and went with none of the writs or warrants returned. Nor was there any indication of this dispute recorded again. By 4 February, Giles Brent, who should have been under arrest, was sitting in the court as a judge. On 12 February, Calvert, Brent, and Lewgar were all sitting on the provincial court in apparent harmony. Evidently, some kind of accommodation had been made of which we have no record.[26]

Early in February 1645, the Maryland government was not on the brink of collapse as has been suggested. It had faced an invasion by William Claiborne and, through swift action, had defused that crisis and sent him packing. Kent Island was still under proprietary control. The quarrel between the governor and council had been settled without any loss. The government was working as it should have been. A measure of this is the Assembly held on 11 February. Most of the records of this Assembly have not survived, but scattered references provide an insight on the concerns of the government and the freemen at this time. Meeting at Nathaniel Pope's house in St. Mary's, the same house that Leonard Calvert had sold to Pope in 1643, the Assembly was as raucous and divided as its predecessors had been. The civil war in England and the Indian threat in Maryland were heavy on the minds of the delegates. Sometime during the session, Thomas Sturman, a freeman living in St. Michael's Hundred, stood up and asked the governor if his commission for seizing London ships applied to Maryland as it did to Virginia. This was no idle question, for Sturman would soon be one of the chief rebels against the government and was undoubtedly one of the Protestants to whom Ingle addressed his letter. Governor Calvert replied that his commission was restricted to Virginia and did not extend to Maryland.[27] As the Virginia Assembly would soon do, the Maryland Assembly declared itself for free trade. Giles Brent would later testify that "it was the general sense and determination of the Governor and Assembly at Maryland . . . that there should be no stop or interruption used against any ship or ships that came thither from London or anywhere else under the obedience of the Parliament but that they should have peaceable and free trade."[28]

Only one piece of legislation is preserved from this Assembly, but it reveals the scope of the questions covered in this session. An act entitled "For the defence of the Province" authorized Governor Calvert to station a garrison at Piscataway to watch and protect the Indians. This would be paid for by a levy of fifty pounds of tobacco or one barrel of corn. Out of the levy, the governor could pay for the garrison, for the cost of the expedition to Kent Island, and the costs of the Assembly. The government was functioning as it should, addressing the major concerns of defense and administration. However, this apparent harmony was simply a calm before the real storm that within days would strike St. Mary's.[29]

CHAPTER TEN

"A most pitifull ruines, spoiled and defaced . . ."

Between late December 1644 and early January 1645, after an apparently uneventful and speedy voyage, the *Looking Glass,* arrived at Kecoughton in Virginia. While the ship lay at anchor, Henry Brooks went ashore and contacted the local sheriff to see what the trading situation was like. The sheriff told him there was little tobacco to be had, but in Maryland the trading would be good. He related that Ingle had been the chief trader to that area but, because of troubles the year before, had not returned. As a result, the planters were in need of many things. Some Marylanders who were at Kecoughton on business heard of the ship's arrival and eagerly invited Brooks to come to the province. One of those attempting to persuade Brooks was John Rabley, a Virginian who claimed to have been Ingle's pilot in Maryland waters for several years. Rabley agreed to take the *Looking Glass* to Maryland in exchange for £15 of trading goods, a pair of new shoes, and a new sail for his shallop. The agreement probably included the use of the shallop for trading purposes.[1]

This situation must have seemed an unparalleled stroke of luck to Brooks and the crew of the *Looking Glass.* Not only were they invited to come and trade in Maryland, but the planters were in real need of their goods. Moreover, with no sign that Ingle was coming back, there appeared to be no competition for the trade. Brooks had to go to Maryland anyway, for he had promised his partner he would collect the estate of

Robert Glover. Prospects for a successful and profitable voyage had increased dramatically.

The *Looking Glass* probably spent a day or two in Virginia to take on water and make repairs before weighing anchor and setting course for Maryland. Rabley seems not to have been so capable a pilot as he had led Brooks to believe. On the voyage northward, the ship missed the mouth of the Potomac River, sailed past St. Michael's Point (modern day Point Lookout) and came aground near James Point on the eastern shore. After the crew got the ship floating again, they sailed back, found the correct passage, and arrived safely at the mouth of St. Inigoes Creek.[2]

Exactly when the *Looking Glass* arrived at St. Inigoes is not clear from the records. The date is important to understanding the sequence of events in the early days of Ingle's Rebellion and must be fixed as accurately as possible. There is some direct testimony on this point. Hatrick Cocke, the captain of the *Looking Glass,* and Michael Albertson, the gunner, both testified that the ship arrived sometime in January 1645. Gabrant Ouckerson, the steersman, was more specific, saying that the *Looking Glass* came to anchor at St. Inigoes on the eighth or ninth of January. John Lewgar, secretary of the province, testified that he heard the *Looking Glass* was in port when Ingle first arrived on 29 December 1644, but Lewgar's date is based on what others told him and not first hand information.[3]

The only way to evaluate the difference between the testimony of the crew of the *Looking Glass* and Secretary Lewgar is to examine some of the more indirect evidence. The *Looking Glass* was in Holland as late as 11 November and was scheduled to sail with the first good wind. Assuming that a fair wind was immediately available, that the *Looking Glass* spent no time in Virginia and arrived in Maryland on 29 December, the voyage would have lasted forty-seven days, or about six and a half weeks. That would have been an extremely swift passage, particularly for the more difficult westward segment of the transatlantic route. Such a voyage commonly took eight weeks. If the ship arrived on 8 January, on the other hand, the voyage could have taken eight weeks and still have allowed some time for a stop in Virginia.

The first indication of the arrival of the *Looking Glass* in Maryland records does not appear in the records until 17 January 1645, when Henry Brooks entered a record of the account of Nicholas Brooks in Virginia for 1643. This may have been entered in anticipation of lawsuits for the collection of debts. Although this is the earliest reference, a more pertinent one is a lawsuit initiated by John Rabley, the pilot, against Henry Brooks on 7 February. Brooks was understandably unhappy with Rabley's performance and had refused to pay him. The value of the goods Rabley demanded totaled 4,130 pounds of tobacco. On the twelfth, Brooks answered Rabley and had a witness describe the circumstances of the voyage. The court awarded Rabley only 750 pounds of tobacco, for one month's rent of his shallop, indicating that the agreement between Brooks and Rabley had been made a month before the filing of the suit. That would place the *Looking Glass* in Virginia around 7 January and supports the testimony of her crew that she did not reach Maryland until January.[4]

After the ship's arrival in Maryland, trading was brisk and profitable, as expected. Brooks, Cocke, and various members of the crew traded with the planters and were expecting profits on their investments of between three to six times their cost once the tobacco was sold in Holland. Most of the large landowners in St. Mary's are reported to have traded with the ship. Cuthbert Fenwick, as agent for Thomas Cornwaleys, was one of the leading traders. Leonard Calvert, John Lewgar, Thomas Copley, and Giles Brent also bought goods out of the *Looking Glass,* for themselves and to supply other planters and tenants throughout the year. Calvert even loaded tobacco on the ship to be sold on his own account in Holland. Clearly, Henry Brooks had found a market worth exploiting.[5]

By 14 February, the *Looking Glass* was near the halfway mark of her contracted three-and-a-half month stay in America. In the hold were 140 hogsheads of tobacco with another sixty waiting on shore to be brought aboard. The homeward-bound cargo was divided into eleven separate accounts, each with its own marks and each dutifully recorded in the steersman's book. These marks were listed on a schedule entered as evidence, but that document has not survived. The first two marks were for goods that belonged to Brooks and Glover, the freighters of the ship. The third was for Governor Leonard Calvert, and the fourth was for the ship's owners. Hatrick Cornelius Cocke, master of the *Looking Glass,* had the fifth mark for his personal adventure. Marks six through eleven were for Robert Reeves, the pilot, Gabrant Ouckerson, the steersman, Peter Salmonson, the boatswain, Jacob Johnson, the carpenter, Michael Albertson, the gunner, and Peter Albertson, the sailmaker. Trading was still brisk even though much of her outward lading had been traded away and there was every expectation that the freighters' cargo of between three and four hundred hogsheads would be stowed before the contracted time expired. For all involved, this voyage would bring a nice return on their investments.[6]

What was Ingle doing at this time? Several witnesses, all of them Marylanders, report that Ingle also arrived at St. Mary's in January 1645. Fenwick and Lewgar testified that when Ingle came into port, the *Looking Glass* was already there. Since the *Looking Glass* did not arrive until at least 8 January, Ingle must have come soon thereafter. Cuthbert Fenwick, the factor in charge of Cornwaleys's estate, said that after his arrival Ingle sent an invoice listing the goods that Cornwaleys had laded on the *Reformation.* He even delivered some of those goods, including two white boxes, ten pairs of shoes and stockings, and a dozen ells of Dowlas, a type of heavy cloth. Before he had finished delivering the rest of the goods, Ingle reportedly became enraged and sailed back to Virginia. The Marylanders supposed that Ingle's anger was occasioned by the competition of the Dutch ship for the Maryland trade.[7] There was some uncertainty on this point, which Lewgar addressed in his testimony. Ingle, he said, "hearing of a Dutch ship there trading in the port then did in a rage and fury without license of the Governor thereupon presently sail back to Virginia, but why he does not know."[8]

During his brief stay at St. Inigoes, Ingle secretly sent letters to the chief Protestants in the colony, reportedly informing them that he had a commission from Parliament to plunder all the papists and to root them out like vermin. Nor would he confine his plundering to the papists but would attack all those who would not take up arms with him. Finally, he told them that two other ships with similar commissions had gone up into other parts of the country. Historians have assumed that this last claim was simply Ingle's bluster, intended to incite the Protestants to join him, but there were two ships—at Kent Island under the command of William Claiborne and Richard Tompson. This evidence strongly suggests that Ingle and Claiborne were working together.[9]

Ingle's arrival was conveniently close to Claiborne's attempt on Kent Island. If Claiborne had succeeded in capturing the island, he might have raised a force of men and sailed to St. Mary's in time to join Ingle in an attack. That plan fell though when Claiborne sailed away from Kent. It may be that Ingle learned of Claiborne's failure and decided that without Claiborne's force, he was not strong enough to take St. Mary's. Governor Calvert's proclamation against Claiborne issued on 1 January or William Brainthwaite's expedition to the island may have been what sent Ingle into a rage and back to Virginia. It is interesting that Ingle is reported to have sailed away from St. Mary's without receiving the governor's permission to trade. It was this proclamation of 1 January that required ships to register at St. Mary's and it was this permit that Fenwick eventually obtained from Calvert. All who testified to Ingle's first trip to Maryland in 1645 indicate that he went back to Virginia to get more men, strength he needed not to take the *Looking Glass* but to overthrow Calvert's government.[10]

Ingle's sudden departure left Maryland authorities confused and apprehensive. Although several reasons have been suggested after the fact, it is clear that the council had no idea why Ingle left. Perhaps they believed the governor's proclamation scared Ingle away, or that Ingle was incensed about having to share the Maryland trade with the *Looking Glass*. In any case, Fenwick began preparing for a voyage to Virginia to bring Ingle back. He applied to Governor Calvert for a permit so that Ingle could be assured of free trade, which was granted. He also had Calvert and Thomas Copley, the head of the Jesuit mission, write letters assuring Ingle of a friendly reception and inviting him to come up to Maryland. Bad weather set in, and Fenwick could not deliver the letters to Ingle.[11]

The *Reformation* sailed down the St. Mary's to the Potomac, then up the Potomac to anchor at Chicacoan. Ingle complained loudly to the settlers about the papists in Maryland and said that he would offer a share of the plunder to anyone who would sail there with him. He recruited twelve or fifteen men, described by Lewgar as "the most rascally fellows of desperate fortunes he could get in Virginia, most of them being seen to be such by the [deponent] and the rest were generally reported to be of the same condition."[12] One of the most frequently mentioned of these plunderers was William Hardige, the same tailor who, just a year before, had testified against Ingle. Others mentioned in the records include, William Durford, brother of the *Reformation*'s mate and formerly a planter in St. Michael's Hundred, and Thomas and John Sturman, a father and son who had been on Kent Island with William Claiborne.

Ingle may have been eager to get back to Maryland and carry out his plan, but the same bad weather that was delaying Fenwick probably kept him in Virginia. By mid-February, the weather broke and the *Reformation,* accompanied by at least one ship from Chicacoan, sailed up the St. Mary's on 14 February 1645.

That morning the *Looking Glass* was still riding at anchor in the mouth of St. Inigoes Creek. She flew the Prince of Orange's colors on her topmast and a white flag with a red cross from her stern. The latter flag was the cross of St. George and the symbol of an English merchant ship. It was the custom of Dutch ships trading to Virginia to carry both sets of colors as a sign of friendship. Most of the crew seem to have been on the ship as well as Captain Cocke and Brooks, the merchant. Several Marylanders and Virginians, including Giles Brent, were aboard as well.[13]

In the distance they sighted a ship cruising up the river. Though they may not have known it was the *Reformation,* both the ship's crew and the Marylanders must have suspected that it was. Ingle's intention to return to Maryland was no secret. Cuthbert Fenwick had heard about it two or three days earlier and was preparing to meet the ship. They had probably also heard about his letter to the Protestants and the bragging he had done in Virginia. Given these circumstances, they could not have been certain of his plans. Possibly he was coming simply to trade, but he might also be intent on plunder. Much of the testimony presented later was clearly hearsay evidence but nevertheless reflected the uncertainty of the moment.[14]

Several of the *Reformation*'s crew later testified that they were told the governor of Maryland was about to disarm all of the Protestants and also that they were told not to pay their debts to Ingle. It was also said that Calvert had been on board the *Looking Glass* before the *Reformation* came into view. According to this testimony, he tried to convince the master and crew of the ship to fight the *Reformation* when it came. When the master refused, saying that he was at peace with both the king and Parliament, Calvert reportedly called them all cowards. Robert Popely, a Virginian with ties to Claiborne who just happened to be on the scene, testified that Calvert had left the *Looking Glass* in order to raise men to fight Ingle. In the light of this partisan testimony, Governor Calvert would seem to have been a fanatic spoiling for a fight.[15]

This picture must be balanced by the fact that the Assembly, of which he was the presiding officer, had recently voted itself in favor of free trade. Further, Cuthbert Fenwick had just procured a license from Governor Calvert granting Ingle the right to trade in Maryland. The governor had even written a personal letter to Ingle assuring him of his safety while he traded. These are not the actions of a man looking for a confrontation.[16]

Yet Calvert's actions do make sense in a more impartial light. If he knew of Ingle's letter, and it is likely that by this time he did, the idea of disarming the Protestants may have come up but just as quickly been dropped. Beyond the obvious uproar that it would have caused, the Catholics were simply not strong enough to do it. As to his attempt to induce the *Looking Glass* to fight, he would certainly have warned them of the possibility of a fight and asked for their help if it happened. None of the *Looking Glass*'s crew or officers testified to this request. If he had made the request and they turned him down, that would have strengthened their case for regaining the ship. The fact that they did not is suggestive. It is also possible that Calvert left the *Looking Glass* to raise the countryside when he saw the *Reformation* coming. That would have been a prudent move given Ingle's temper and the uncertainty of his plans.

Meanwhile, the *Looking Glass* cleared the decks for a fight. Not knowing what the intentions of the approaching ship were, Captain Cocke had his cannons loaded and primed, and fires were made to provide ignition for the ordnance. With her armament ready and her crew and visitors alerted, the *Looking Glass* was ready. As the unknown ship drew closer, it was seen to have the English colors out and to be carrying a white flag. This symbol, then as now, was a universal sign of peace and a desire to talk. Hatricke Cocke, master of the *Looking Glass* gave orders to stand down, believing the ship to be friendly.[17]

The *Reformation* hailed the *Looking Glass* and asked where they were from and where they were bound. Cocke replied that they were from Rotterdam and that once they had finished trading they were to return there. The *Looking Glass* then asked the same of the *Reformation,* who replied of London and then "cried a main for the King and Parliament of England." This was a demand for the *Looking Glass* to lower her colors and allow boarders. The *Reformation* informed them that it had a commission from Parliament to inspect them and that Ingle intended to do so.[18]

At this juncture, testimony concerning these events splits along very clear lines. The crews of the *Looking Glass* and the *Reformation* viewed their actions and motives very differently, and sorting out the truth may never be possible. The *Reformation's* crew claimed that the Dutch ship refused to strike its colors or to be visited. Because of this, the *Reformation* fired three "great and smale shott" at her with whatever effect the records do not indicate. The *Looking Glass* crew testified that they had not refused to strike and were taking down the flags when the *Reformation* fired.[19]

Whatever the sequence, the *Looking Glass* did strike her colors and, according to custom, the master of the striking ship was to go aboard the other ship and present his charter, bills of lading, and other papers to the opposing captain for inspection. Captain Cocke, still believing that everything could be settled peacefully, took three of the crew, two of whom were English, and rowed the *Looking Glass*'s wherry over to the *Reformation* to speak to Ingle. Upon reaching the *Reformation* they were seized and held prisoner. Cocke informed Ingle that he was from Rotterdam and had no quarrel with either the king or Parliament. Furthermore, when he finished trading, he was going back to Holland not England.[20]

Cocke then presented his papers to Ingle, as was the custom, and the *Reformation*'s captain briefly reviewed them. Several of the *Looking Glass*'s crew testified that Ingle tore up the charter and several other papers and threw them overboard. (The *Reformation* crew later testified that they were told by some of the seamen on the *Looking Glass* that their steersman, Gabrant Ouckerson, had also destroyed a number of papers while Cocke was on his way to meet with Ingle.) A ship's papers were important because the Parliamentary ordinance dealing with prize ships required that all of the ship's papers be presented to the prize court. If Ingle could prove that the *Looking Glass* had traded or was bound to trade with Ireland or Bristol or any place under control of the Royalists, the ship would be his. No such evidence existed, and so he may have destroyed some of the papers to create uncertainty on this point and strengthen his case.[21]

Ingle then informed Cocke that he was seizing the ship because he feared that the Marylanders would use it against him. He promised to return it after he had finished trading. Some of the *Reformation*'s crew, under the direction of boatwain Thomas Greene, got into the wherry and rowed across to the *Looking Glass*. As they approached, they noticed her guns were loaded and her match lit. William Little, a member of the boarding party, testified that he called back to the *Reformation* to, "look to themselves for that they in the *Looking Glass* were ready to fire." But they did not fire. Instead, the *Reformation* fired again into the Dutch ship and those in the wherry boarded her without resistance. The *Looking Glass*'s crew had retreated to the forecastle and when boarded immediately surrendered and came on deck. One of the boarding party claimed to have seen Giles Brent scurrying into the hold with a sword in his hand.[22]

The only resistance the boarding party met was when they tried to enter the cuddy, as the passengers' cabin was known. Finding the door barred and those inside refusing to surrender, they began to break down the door with axes. The only recorded injury in the whole attack occurred when someone thrust a sword out of the cuddy and wounded Thomas Greene on the hand. It could not have been serious since Greene did not mention it in his own testimony. Once they had broken inside the cuddy, the boarding party found Henry Brooks with two primed and loaded brass guns. Brooks chose not to fire and was forced to surrender. Later, as they searched the ship, Ingle's men found Giles Brent hiding in the hold.

One of the search party testified that Brent had a naked sword beside him while another claimed that Brent had thrown the sword one way and the scabbard the other in his haste to find a hiding place. One of the *Reformation*'s crew would later testify that he was told by unnamed members of the *Looking Glass*'s crew that they had planned to catch the boarding party in a crossfire between the cuddy and the forecastle. Given the alacrity with which the crew surrendered, that does not seem likely.[23]

After Ingle seized the *Looking Glass,* he turned his attention to other potential threats or prizes. Lying in a creek about three miles away was a pinnace whose home port was Bristol. This ship is not further identified in later testimony, but there is a good chance that it was the *Trewlove,* the ship Thomas Weston chartered in 1644 and on which Governor Calvert may have returned to Maryland. Weston's ship was at St. Mary's as late as 22 January when one of the crewmen sued another for slander. The court set a date of 1 February for the hearing, but there is no further record of the case. The records are not specific as to where the pinnace was, but we can make a guess that it was at Thomas Weston's plantation. Weston had 1,200 acres granted to him and erected into Westbury Manor on 10 January 1643. The manor was located on the east side of St. George's Creek, and part of the boundary description refers to Weston's branch. This would be either modern-day Schoolhouse Branch or some smaller creek flowing into it. The spot is about three miles from the mouth of St. Inigoes Creek, where the other two ships were anchored. The *Trewlove*'s home port was Bristol, and although there is no description of her size, the records imply she was small enough to be called a pinnace. The *Trewlove* sailed from Virginia sometime in February or early March and arrived in Bristol in June 1645. Given these circumstances and the reported lack of shipping to Maryland in 1645, it is likely that Thomas Weston's troubles in the Civil War continued.[24]

Ingle summoned the master of the Bristol ship on board the *Reformation* and tried the same tactics that had won the *Looking Glass,* but, alerted by the earlier fight, the Bristol ship had moved farther up the creek where the *Reformation* could not go. Her master had taken the precaution of landing a gun at the mouth of the creek where it could be brought to bear on any vessel sent to seize his ship. Since he could not capture the *Trewlove* directly, Ingle made the captain promise to take her to London instead of Bristol, then let him return to his ship. That night under the cover of darkness, the Bristolman slipped out of the creek and sailed home, avoiding the fate of the *Looking Glass.*

The loss of the Bristol ship did not trouble Ingle very much. He had secured the only ship that could threaten his design and was now free to carry out the rest of his plan. The next step was to secure a land base from which to begin rooting out papists.

A perfect place for such a base was a little farther up St. Inigoes Creek and well known to Ingle from past voyages. He decided to seize Cross House, the manorial home of his friend Thomas Cornwaleys. Cornwaleys lived in a style befitting an international tobacco merchant, that is to say a cut above everyone else in Maryland. Cross House was the centerpiece of the captain's manor of Cornwaleys Cross and was designed as a showplace. Earlier, Cornwaleys had described it as built "of sawn timber, framed a storey and half hygh with a seller and chimnies of brick." It probably had a foundation of stone or brick and was strongly built, unlike most houses in Maryland. It was also surrounded by a stout palisade. Given Cornwaleys's interest in military matters, the palisade may have been intended as a fortification. Certainly the three cannon posted around the house were formidable enough. Cross House was not only a defensible strong point but the richest prize in Maryland.[25]

One has to wonder how Ingle could think about seizing and plundering this house. He and Cornwaleys were not only business partners but good friends as well. Even members of the *Reformation*'s crew testified to the closeness of their friendship and how much Ingle owed to Cornwaleys, both in establishing himself in the tobacco trade and in his recent scrape with the Maryland authorities. There is no way Ingle could ignore Cornwaleys's support of Parliament. He had defended Cornwaleys in England against charges of being a Royalist and a papist. Many times he had enjoyed the hospitality of the house, and it is likely that he had even delivered many of the goods and furniture that filled it. There was no question that this action would destroy his friendship with Cornwaleys forever. All of these things he must have known as he planned the assault. Yet there are really two issues involved with Ingle's attempt on Cross House. Its seizure must be viewed as a separate act from its plundering. Although the latter might destroy a friendship; the former was a military necessity. Strategically, Ingle had little choice. He could not leave this strongpoint unoccupied while he plundered the rest of Maryland, for it easily could be turned into a garrison from which the governor's party could mount an organized defense. The house had to be taken and placed under Protestant control.

Occupying the house was Cuthbert Fenwick, his family, and as many as twelve servants. With the force at his command and some help from the Maryland Protestants, Ingle probably could have taken it by storm, but that would have been dangerous. He decided instead to rely on the friendship and trust he had built up over the years, hoping that Fenwick would surrender the house to him with the promise that it would not be plundered. As he had told the master of the *Looking Glass* earlier, he simply wanted to make certain the house was not used against him.[26]

About this time, Fenwick, having either heard the commotion around the *Looking Glass* or seen the *Reformation* coming into St. Inigoes Creek, sent three of the servants, Andrew Monroe, Thomas Harrison, and Edward Matthews, to bring Cornwaleys's new pinnace, then riding in the mouth of St. Inigoes Creek, up into the creek near Cross Manor house. Ingle's men overtook them and brought them on board the *Reformation*. The servants were offered a choice of joining the rebels or being held prisoner. Monroe and Harrison joined immediately and were active in the plundering that followed. Matthews declined and was kept aboard ship.[27]

Ingle then sent some of his own men to Fenwick, asking him to come on board the *Reformation*. Cornwaleys's factor hurried out to the ship, carrying with him the letters from Governor Calvert and Thomas Copley and hoping that this was simply a misunderstanding. Ingle read the letters, put them in his pocket, and told Fenwick that they had come too late. Ingle wanted to avoid a fight if he could, so he put on a good face and entertained Fenwick in the great cabin. He asked Fenwick to write a note authorizing the surrender of the house, the guns, and the other arms, saying that he only wanted to make sure this strongpoint would not be used against him. Ingle promised that everything would be returned untouched. Fenwick resisted, replying that if he did sign such a warrant, Ingle would not let him return to shore. Ingle promised that he would let him go, reportedly saying, "Nay, if I have promised, I will be as good as my word." When Fenwick still would not agree, Ingle had him put in the round house under guard for the night. The next morning the note was written and Fenwick was put ashore. Either by chance or prearrangement, as Fenwick stepped ashore he was seized again by John Sturman and other Marylanders and conveyed back to the ship.[28]

Early on the morning of 15 February, Ingle sent John Durford and sixteen men—sailors, Maryland Protestants, and Virginians—to demand the surrender of Cross House. Carrying Fenwick's note to his wife, the rebels approached the house and called for the defenders to yield in the name of the king and Parliament. According to Fenwick's later testimony, few were left in the house to oppose them. He stated that, "he had not in the house of the said Thomas Cornwaleys any of his servants Except Negroes and one Richard Harvy a Taylor all the rest being either prisoners with Ingle, fled to the Governor or in Arms as Associates to the said Ingle."[29] With their leader captured, their numbers reduced, and a strong force on the doorstep, the defenders asked for quarter, which was granted, and surrendered the house. Over the next few days, it became the collection point for plundered goods and captured Catholics.[30]

Whether Ingle, despite his promises to the contrary, intended to plunder Cross House from the beginning is not known. The plundering did not start immediately after the surrender. It may be that Ingle had more important things to do. He installed a garrison in Cornwaleys's house and with his crew went in search of the governor. William Little, a crewman, was one of those assigned to stay at Cross House. He later testified that he spent two hours there before going back to the ship. In that time, the house and its contents were untouched.[31] Yet when Ingle returned to Cross

House, he discovered that its garrison had found Cornwaleys's silver and had already divided it into eight shares. Fenwick had hidden the silver in the woods at the beginning of the troubles, but whether by accident or information from one of the servants, Ingle's men had discovered its hiding place and brought the silver back to the house. Whatever his original intentions, Ingle now gave orders to plunder the house and made sure that he had a share of the silver. Henry Williams, an English member of the *Looking Glass*'s crew, testified that Cross House was plundered three times. The first time the plunderers took Cornwaleys's merchandise, tobacco, and trading goods. The second time they came back for all of the household items including the furniture, linen, and even the hardware from the doors and windows. All that was left in the house were Fenwick's personal goods, which Ingle had given assurances would not be taken. Needless to say these disappeared next, leaving the house virtually empty.[32]

The site of Thomas Cornwalyes's house remains a mystery, but Cuthbert Fenwick's later testimony provides a glimpse of what was, without doubt, the finest house built in Maryland before the 1660s. Fenwick had been with Cornwaleys since 1634 and was in charge of the plantation after Cornwalyes sailed to England in 1644. He was intimately familiar with the house, its furnishings and the rest of the plantation. In response to the questions concerning what was plundered, Fenwick gave a room-by-room inventory of the house and what was missing from the rest of the manor.[33] Fenwick's testimony begins with a passage that has been repeatedly mistranscribed. Most transcriptions suggest that Ingle seized two hundred iron guns worth £20. Were this true, Cornwalyes would have been keeping an arsenal nearly large enough to outfit the entire male population of St. Mary's. It cannot be true, for guns were worth about £1 each and two hundred of them would be worth considerably more than £20. The problem is that the word "hundred" is actually "hammered" and refers to cannons not hand guns. Cornwalyes had two "hammered" iron cannon, made by welding bar iron together, and one cast-iron cannon, all of which were mounted on wooden carriages. These, plus several hand guns were worth £20. These cannon were probably located in the yard outside the house.

Cross House, as Cornwaleys's manor house was called, was a large and impressive structure. While only a story and a half, it had at least six and possibly eight rooms, along with storage space in the double lofts. Garry Wheeler Stone, who analyzed the evidence of early Maryland architecture and set it within its English context, believes that the house was built in the shape of an H, with the hall forming the center bar. While the plan of the house was not new, the way Cornwaleys adapted the functions was ahead of his time. The house became a reflection of a growing desire to separate the owner from his servants and tenants. Unlike medieval houses, where the hall served as the main living space, Stone views the hall at Cross Manor more as a hall-vestibule in the Renaissance tradition. The lack of a fireplace and any treatment of the windows is one piece of evidence that separated this hall from the traditional function. Stone suggests that this was a formal space where Cornwaleys would meet his guests or tenants. The presence of large pieces of furniture in this room may have added to the appearance of wealth in a society where most planters barely had a table.[34] For more details of the inventory, see the Appendix.

Cornwaleys's estate is impressive in its listing. There can be no doubt that he was a rich man—the total value of the plundered goods amounted to £2,623—though without something to compare it with this fact loses much of its meaning. It is hard to accurately picture the distribution of wealth in the earliest decades of Maryland's history, but by the 1650s, probate inventories become common and allow us to assess questions of relative worth. These marvelous documents list all the personal property owned by an individual at the time of his death. In a credit economy where repayment had to wait until the next crop, an unexpected death could cause severe problems for creditors. To protect this relationship, the courts commissioned an inventory of the dead man's property that could be used to pay his debts. Gloria Main completed an intensive study of these documents from six counties in Maryland over the period 1656–1720. Her analysis set up a temporal division ranging from 1656 to 1683, and this group of estates provides a useful base against which to compare Cornwaleys's losses.[36]

Between 1656 and 1683 only two inventories were made with personal estate values over £800. These two estates represented a minuscule

TABLE 1: COMPARISON OF CROSS MANOR TO LATER ESTATES

CATEGORY	CROSS MANOR %	ESTATES > £800[35] %
Livestock	35	19
Bound Labor	8	34
Crops	10.5	9
New Goods	17.5	12
Other Capital	13	4
Total Capital	84	78
Cash	0	2
Consumption	16	20

Source: Examination of Cuthbert Fenwick, answer 19, 20 October 1646 in Cornwaleys *vs.* Ingle, Chancery, Examinations, C24 690/14, PRO.

0.3 percent of the population. Not until the eighteenth century did the average of Maryland's richest estates even approach what Cornwaleys lost. Even though the period surveyed was twenty to forty years later, Cornwaleys's estate was three times as large as the average wealthy estate.

Fenwick's detailed listing provides us with insight into Cornwaleys's view of his Maryland investment and his priorities. Using the categories proposed by Main, we can again compare Cross Manor to the richest estates in Maryland (Table 1). The largest differences are in the first two categories, livestock and bound labor. Many of the later estates had numerous slaves, representing a large investment in bound labor that was not present in early Maryland. Cornwaleys was one of the earliest slave owners in the province, but he reportedly had only three slaves. The accumulation of livestock, on the other hand, was viewed almost as a savings account by early Marylanders. Cornwaleys was clearly tied into the cattle economy as his herd of 120 was the most valuable item in the inventory.

Cross Manor was an agricultural enterprise; more than half of the estate's value and 63 percent of the capital was invested in livestock, bound labor, and crops. But this was significantly less than the average of later estates, where agriculture accounted for 80 percent of the capital invested. The difference is in Cornwaleys' attempts to diversify his investments. While his estate had an agricultural base, he was invested in many other enterprises. Cornwaleys was a merchant with fully 20 percent of his capital invested in new goods for resale to other planters. This total might have been even higher if we could more accurately separate those goods in the house that were meant for resale. His investment in other capital equipment included several boats, goods for the fur trade, blacksmith tools, carpenter and joiner tools, and milling equipment. From the beginning, Cornwaleys never intended simply to farm. In 1638, he wrote to Lord Baltimore, "If therefore your Lordship nor your country well afford me no other way to support the great expenses that I have been and daily am at for my subsistans here, but what I must fetch out of the ground by planting this stinking weed of America, I must desert this place and business."[37] Some seven years later Cornwaleys was still seeking his living in other ways. He may have become accustomed to growing "the stinking weed of America," but he kept his interest in other areas as well. Over a third of his capital investment was in non-agricultural tools and supplies, in contrast to later estates, where barely a fifth of capital was so invested.

Fenwick's inventory of Cross House allows us to look at Cornwaleys's estate in another way as well. Since it is a room-by-room description, we can compare this house to other, later houses in Maryland. How does Cross House, the largest and most complex of the early manor houses, compare with those built later in the century? Again, Main's data provide a baseline for comparison. In a survey of the most wealthy houses in the six counties during the period 1660–1719, she listed an average of 6.3 rooms in the main house. Cross Manor House had six to nine rooms, depending on the inclusion of various closets and lofts. It also had a cellar, which Fenwick failed to mention. In terms of overall space, Cross House was probably as complex as any of the houses built in seventeenth-century Maryland. In addition to the main house, Cornwaleys had at least six other buildings on the site, which compares well with Main's figure of 5.1 "other places" for this group. Even by the standards of a much later time, Cross Manor was an impressive estate.[38]

When Ingle and his men had finished with Cross Manor, little remained. In short order, the rebels had emptied the house of anything of value, had taken the hardware from the doors and windows, and had killed or driven off all of the livestock. Near the end, Ingle gave an order to burn the house to the ground. This order was later retracted, perhaps in deference to Fenwick's wife, but the rebels did pull up and burn all of the pales from the fences surrounding the house, possibly to eliminate its potential as a fort.[39] Michael Albertson, the gunner of the *Looking Glass,* left a melancholy picture of the once proud estate, now ruined:

> after the said Cornwallis his house had been pillaged and plundered as aforesaid, which before he heard was a very fair house and very well furnished with all manner of necessaries, he went to the said house to see the same and then saw and found it a most pitifull ruines, spoiled and defaced . . . both within and without and found nothing at all in it but a bed for the woman of the house and her children to lie in.[40]

Having secured the house, Ingle turned his attention to the rest of the St. Mary's. He sent armed parties out to capture specific Marylanders, including John Lewgar, Thomas Copley, Nicholas Causin, George Binks, and others. Most importantly, Ingle wanted to capture Governor Calvert and carry him back to England to stand trial. The search parties had some success. John Lewgar was surprised, apparently while he was asleep. He later testified that when he was brought down to Cornwaleys's house he had no shoes or stockings. One of the guards gave him some from the plundered goods that were accumulating there. Lewgar eventually joined Fenwick and Brent as prisoners aboard the *Reformation.*[41]

Ingle now had two heavily armed ships and a secure base from which to operate, all accomplished with little opposition. It began to look as though the proprietary government would simply dissolve without a fight.

CHAPTER ELEVEN

"Burn them Papists Divells"

With the attacks on the *Looking Glass* and Cross Manor, Ingle seemed to be in complete control of the military situation. Most historians believe that he completely routed Maryland forces. Governor Calvert is reported either not to have been in the province or to have fled to Virginia at the first sign of trouble. The provincial government offered no resistance to Ingle but simply faded away.[1] According to Russell Menard, "Baltimore's supporters apparently surrendered without a fight; Leonard Calvert abandoned the province for refuge in Virginia; Ingle and his men . . . burned some houses, looted others, sent several priests to England in chains, and returned to London with Giles Brent and other Catholics as prisoners, leaving the settlement in the hands of a small group of mercenaries recruited in Virginia."[2] Despite this commonly held view, there is evidence of organized resistance to Ingle during the spring and into the summer of 1645. It is not surprising that a period so violent and unsettled would leave few records, yet in those that survive, we see brief glimpses of this resistance. Taken together, they give us a picture of a small force trying to hold out against long odds. A review of the evidence will make this picture clearer.

In his testimony concerning the surrender of Cross Manor House, Cuthbert Fenwick reported that Cornwaleys's servants were captured by Ingle, joined with the rebels or "fled to the Governor." This raises the question of Governor Calvert's whereabouts when Ingle began plundering Maryland[3] Whether or not he knew of the secret letters Ingle sent to some of the Protestants, Leonard Calvert must have been expecting trouble from the *Reformation.* Several unreliable witnesses place Calvert on the *Looking Glass* when Ingle's ship hove into view. A member of the *Reformation*'s crew testified he was told by the crew of the *Looking Glass* that Calvert had asked the master of the ship if he would fight, and Cocke gave him the same answer that he would later give to Ingle. He and his ship were at peace with the English and would not fight. This is consistent with the fact that the crew of the *Looking Glass* was found in the forecastle and surrendered without a fight. It was then reported that Calvert called them cowards and went ashore to bring men on board to fight. However it happened, Calvert was soon aware that Ingle had not returned with peaceful intentions. If he did leave, as was reported, to find men for a fight, he probably intended to raise the militia in defense of the province.[4]

Calvert was about to discover what had become painfully obvious to both sides in the English Civil War: A citizen militia might be effective against a foreign enemy but in the case of civil war it is torn by the same forces that caused the conflict. Maryland's militia was built on an English model that dated back to the reign of Queen Elizabeth. In several key areas, the model was changed to fit the time and place. Under Elizabeth, every able-bodied man was required to defend the realm in case of attack, but some of the more prosperous and better recruits were singled out for special training. These became known as the trained bands. In theory, they were better trained and better armed than the mass of the militia and were to provide the bedrock foundation of national defense should England be invaded. In reality they were poorly trained, poorly armed, and viewed more as social clubs. Before the Civil War the reputation of the trained bands was quite low, and, except for those of London, they demonstrated why during the war.[5]

The ideal of specially trained bands was carried over to Maryland. There are references to the trained bands of St. Mary's and of Kent Island but no evidence that the trained band was anything other than the total male population able to bear arms. Every householder was required to have a gun for every man in his house and to allow them to be trained during musters. In Maryland, where the population was small and the danger real, the entire male population had to be drafted. By the 1640s the militia seems to have been organized on the basis of the hundred. We hear of the trained bands of St. Mary's and St. George's Hundreds. These were probably groups of neighbors who got together to train on muster days. A sergeant was appointed over each band, and at least two lieutenants were commissioned. A captain led the St. Mary's militia, while Kent Island's trained band was headed by the commander of the island.[6]

Although this hierarchy existed on paper, it seems to have been ignored in times of crisis. The aborted expedition that Giles Brent was supposed to lead against the Indians in 1642 reveals how the province mobilized. At the time, William Blount was the captain of the St. Mary's militia, but he was out of the country. It would seem that one of the lieutenants might have been a logical choice to take his place, but instead William Brainthwaite was appointed to captain the expedition. In fact, neither of the commissioned lieutenants were part of the expedition. The only officer of the militia to participate was Sergeant William MacFenning. The bulk of the soldiers were pressed into service by the sheriff, indicating that they were not specially trained soldiers. The rank and file of this troop were a mixed lot, including a gentleman, several small planters, and a number of servants. What all of this suggests is that Maryland met the crisis not by calling well-trained men to arms but on an ad hoc basis. If this was the response to an outside threat that everyone agreed was real, how much more confused would it be in a civil war?[7]

The governor, on becoming aware of Ingle's attack on the *Looking Glass,* tried to raise a force for defense. Ralph Bean testified that Calvert told him and another man to take up arms and resist Ingle. The testimony does not indicate whether they did so. Later records show that several prominent members of the St. Mary's militia, particularly Lieutenant Thomas Baldridge, not only failed to support the government but actively led the plundering that followed. At this date it is impossible to see the full extent of the division, but it seems that most Protestants either fully supported the rebels or did not resist them while the Catholics sided with the proprietary government. Since there were many more Protestants than Catholics, the situation was grim for Lord Baltimore's forces.[8]

Despite the odds, Calvert soon had a band of men under his command numerous enough that Ingle did not feel he could easily overwhelm them. Calvert and his men gathered at St. Thomas fort, which played an important but little known role in the defense of the province. There is no reference to it before Ingle's rebellion and only a few mentions of it in the court cases resulting from the rebellion. Where was it and when was it built can only be guessed, for the historical record is too sparse to allow any conclusion. In 1639, Margaret and Mary Brent patented seventy acres of town land in St. Mary's, lying about "the house where they now dwell commonly known by the name of St. Thomas's." The similarity of names suggests that the fort was built around Margaret Brent's house or on her property. The remains of an old fort were mentioned in a 1705 deed for this property, but it is hard to imagine that traces of the fort lasted that long. Only a detailed archaeological survey and excavation will answer these questions. Though we cannot say how long it stood, we can be fairly certain as to when it was built. The lack of any reference to fortifications on this property before the rebellion suggests that it was built in response to the actions of Ingle and his associates.[9]

St. Thomas's fort was one of two forts built in the St. Mary's area during this period. While Calvert and the Catholics built this one, Nathaniel Pope and the Protestants built the other around Calvert's old house in St. Mary's. Both forts were constructed in anticipation of further trouble between the two parties and each represented a large amount of work for the soldiers. Given the apparent need for defensive fortifications by both sides, it is strange that St. Inigoes fort, the only place in the vicinity that was fortified before this period, seems to have played no part in the events of the Plundering Time.[10]

St. Inigoes fort is another site that is known to have existed from a few historical references but which has become entwined with legends and misinterpretations through the ages. The fort may have been the one authorized by the Assembly in 1638 and about which Father Copley complained to Lord Baltimore. It was certainly built by 1642, when Governor Calvert issued his instructions in case of Indian alarm. The householders between St. Inigoes Creek and Trinity Creek were to send their women and children to St. Inigoes fort. The sheriff would appoint six men to guard it and the rest would respond to the alarm.[11]

This single reference provides all of the information we possess on the location of the fort and its size. The name and geographical range listed in the instructions indicated the fort was located on the Jesuit manor of St. Inigoes but do not allow any more specific placement. Traditionally the location was thought to be at Fort Point, on the St. Mary's River midway between the two creeks mentioned in the instructions. In 1823, Father Joseph Carberry and his brother recovered five cannon from the waters off Fort Point. Several of the guns were six hundred feet offshore in as much as twenty feet of water. The Carberrys assumed that the guns had been in St. Inigoes fort when the point eroded away and ended up in the water. The earliest reference to this spot as Fort Point occurred the next year in the sketch map made of the St. Mary's River by Majors Abert and Kearney of the U.S. Army. Until an earlier reference to this area as Fort Point is revealed, there is no way to know if this was indeed the site.[12]

The question of erosion massive enough to wash away six hundred feet of shoreline is one that can be addressed. As a test of the question, the 1824 map was scaled to the size of a modern topographic quadrangle and the Fort Point area copied onto tracing paper. Overlaying this on the modern map revealed no significant difference in the shoreline between 1824 and now. Is it possible that in the 170 years prior to 1824 six hundred feet of shoreline eroded and then stopped during the following 170 years? That does not seem likely, and there really is no natural way to account for the guns being in twenty feet of water. It would seem more likely that they were dumped off a ship in water that deep.

Circumstantial evidence does suggest a location for St. Inigoes fort. After Ingle's rebellion and into the 1650s, the Assembly passed various acts concerning shipping and customs duties. A significant part of many of these acts included the provision that the ships had to ride under command of the fort for a specified time before they left the province. There is deep water off Fort Point but no protection from winds in that area. The mouth of St. Inigoes Creek would have been a much better mooring area and was already established as one well before the Plundering Time. A fort located in the Priest Point area would have commanded both the river and this mooring site.[13]

The size of the St. Inigoes fort has been subject to much speculation. Some have thought it to have been as large as 360 feet on a side with as many as twelve large guns mounted on the walls. This cannot have been true. In his instructions, Leonard Calvert told the householders to send their women and children to the fort to be defended by six men. A garrison that small could not have been expected to defend a large fortification. At best, St. Inigoes fort was a small, defensive fortification, perhaps with a guard inside but not intended to hold large numbers of soldiers.[14]

Since Ingle and his men began their attack at the mouth of St. Inigoes Creek, the fort was probably one of the first structures captured. That would explain why Calvert and his men did not occupy it, but why did the Protestants not use it for their headquarters? St. Inigoes fort is not mentioned in any of the court cases after the rebellion nor in any of the testimony given in England. Several of the *Looking Glass* crew testified that Maryland was not fortified before Ingle came, and this assertion was not challenged by Ingle nor any of his men. If the fort was still in existence in 1645, it cannot have been very large or well built. The Protestants chose to build a new fort at Pope's house rather than occupy the one at St. Inigoes.

No matter where or how big St. Inigoes fort may have been, it was not a resource available to the governor's party. They probably built their fort around Margaret Brent's house and prepared to resist as long as they could. The records do not permit us to state how long this garrison held out against the rebels, but the scattered references do give us a clue. Nicholas Gwyther, who had been a servant to Thomas Cornwaleys when Ingle attacked, sued for his freedom after the rebellion. The Assembly required that he submit an account of the product of his labor after the war was over. His account, entered into the Assembly records, lists the product of his labor from "the taking of St. Thomas' fort until the last of November 1646." The surrender of St. Thomas's fort was seen as the end of effective resistance to the rebellion. However, all that we can say from Gwyther's account is that he made one tobacco crop after the taking of the fort, and that probably in 1646, by which time, the rebels long had been in control of the province.[15]

We can say the fort was garrisoned at least into the spring of 1645. During the rebellion, Leonard Calvert killed a steer belonging to Blanche Oliver for use in the fort. That occurred before he was forced to leave the province and indicates some resistance was planned. The only sure evidence of the length of time the garrison of St. Thomas's fort held out is presented in a 1648 court case regarding the ownership of a cow. John Sturman sued Thomas Copley for detaining a cow that belonged to his father, Thomas Sturman. John Greenhold testified that while he was being held prisoner at Sturman's house after the taking of St. Thomas's fort, Sturman pointed out the cow to him and said that it had been mismarked by some of the governor's party. During that summer, when the cow wandered into Pope's fort, Sturman seized it and remarked it. John Sturman, son of Thomas, and Robert Smith both testified that Sturman had remarked the cow in the summer of 1645. This testimony clearly indicates that the cow had been remarked and brought back to Sturman's house before Greenhold saw it. Either Greenhold was held prisoner for a long time or St. Thomas's fort held out through the spring of 1645.[16]

A final piece of evidence, though circumstantial, also suggests that the fort held out for a number of months. It is clear from the documents that Richard Ingle's priority was to capture Leonard Calvert. When he left Maryland in April 1645, he took a number of Marylanders with him but not the governor. Had St. Thomas's fort fallen before Ingle departed, he would have insisted that the governor be his prisoner. This suggests that the fort was garrisoned through April and supports the testimony of John Greenhold.[17]

But the taking of St. Thomas's fort was in the future, and both sides had more immediate problems. With the proprietary forces at St. Thomas's and the rebels at Pope's fort, the conflict settled into a pattern of raiding and counter-raiding. Both sides began foraging to support their garrisons and plundering their opponents. The people who suffered most in this situation were those who had no part in it. For example, Blanche Oliver, widow of Roger, lost an ox to the garrison at St. Thomas's fort and a cow to Pope's fort. For a widow raising two children by herself, the loss of two cattle was as devastating as the loss of all of Cornwaleys's estate. Both parties began remarking cattle into their own marks and pressing corn from the planters for their use. If there are more references to the rebels' plundering activities, it is simply because they were more numerous and the eventual losers.[18]

The extent and type of plundering that took place depended on the individual estate. When it belonged to a member of the Catholic gentry, the entire estate was plundered. Ingle took all of the tobacco and a major portion of the valuables, while the household goods, livestock, and tools went to the rebels. Ingle was keenly interested in tobacco. He sent parties to all of the planters in search of tobacco owed to Catholics and declared that any that had been marked to Calvert, Lewgar, Cornwaleys, Fenwick, or Copley was now his. He had seized most of their debt books and probably used them as a guide. A planter refusing to yield this tobacco to the rebels lost all of his crop and sometimes had his tobacco house burned. Walter Bean lost six hogsheads of tobacco, Francis Pope lost five, John Medley three, Richard Banks two, and Walter Waterlin and John Mansell one each. Thomas Gerard may have lost as many as seventeen hogsheads of tobacco that had been marked to other creditors.[19]

In addition to their tobacco and silver plate, Ingle wanted to capture a number of the gentry themselves to transport back to England, for he needed them to prove that Maryland was hostile to Parliament and governed by Catholics. Allegations of both would justify his actions under the Parliamentary ordinances and assure that prize money was awarded to his ship and her crew. He had captured Giles Brent, John Lewgar, and Cuthbert Fenwick. For the moment the focus of his anger, Governor Leonard Calvert, was out of reach, but Father Thomas Copley remained at large, and Ingle set out to find him. In a month, Ingle accomplished what Lord

Baltimore had tried but failed to do for seven years: he almost wiped out the Jesuit mission to Maryland.

Despite the problems with Lord Baltimore, the Maryland mission in 1645 was finally beginning to flourish. There were now five Jesuits in the province, a number that would not be equaled until the 1660s. The mission possessed several large, developed plantations, two well-furnished houses, and a number of smaller mission stations. The Jesuit home plantation at St. Inigoes must have been one of the places plundered early in the rebellion, as it was located near Thomas Cornwaleys's plantation on St. Inigoes Creek. Father Copley appears to have been away at the Portobacco plantation when Ingle struck. He gathered together some of the Jesuit tenants and supporters and began fortifying that house in anticipation of an assault. The *Reformation* crew referred to Copley's house as a garrison, and several people were held prisoner at Pope's fort after "the taking of Mr. Copley's house at Portobacco." How long the garrison held out and the events that led to its surrender are unknown, but all five Jesuits were soon captured and brought to St. Mary's.[20]

Fathers Copley and White were integral to Ingle's plan to justify his actions and so were put aboard the *Reformation* in chains. The other Jesuits, Fathers Bernard Hartwell, John Cooper, and Roger Rigby, were not needed in England but could not simply be left in Maryland. According to the English Provincial records, all three died in 1645 or 1646 in Maryland or Virginia. The records conflict as to their date of death, the circumstances under which they met their fate, or where the events occurred, suggesting that no one in England knew what happened to them except that they died. In his history of the English Province, Henry Foley appears to have quoted from an annual letter of 1645: "This year the colony was attacked by a party of 'rowdies' or marauders and the missionarers were carried off to Virginia, among others, Father Fisher [Copley] and a companion." Even if quoted, this sheds no more light on the fate of the other Jesuits.[21]

One piece of evidence offers a clue as to the fate of the priests. Henry Stockton, testifying before the High Court of Admiralty in August 1645, blurted out a curious revelation. Stockton was recounting how Ingle's men seized Cornwaleys's pinnace, which Ingle then gave to some of the rebels. The reason the ship was given away, according to Stockton, was to "carry away some [illegible] men of the Country out from there and to put them ashore upon some place or other among the heathans and there to leave them." Based on the grouping of the letters, the illegible writing could represent the word "church," "young," or something else. When Stockton referred to the heathens, he meant the Indians, implying that these men were turned out to suffer captivity and possible death at the hands of the savages.[22]

Regardless of the specific adjective, who in Maryland would warrant such cruel punishment? All of the planters and servants captured by the rebels at St. Thomas's fort, Thomas Copley's house, and other places were eventually released, and many left the province. No evidence of executions or any serious harm beyond the plundering of estates survives. When a member of the Catholic gentry came into his hands, Ingle took him to England as evidence in his defense. There is no indication that any of the gentry disappeared during this period. The only group who left a record of mysterious deaths were the Jesuits. If Stockton's testimony refers to the missing priests, it is likely that they were put ashore in the Susquehannock country to suffer death by exposure or at the hands of the Indians and ought to be receive consideration for being Maryland's first martyrs.

The destruction of the Maryland mission went beyond the removal of the priests. Mission property was plundered, a house burned, and other houses turned over to the rebels. Typical of the events of the day is the story of Robert Percy, the Jesuit overseer. Percy became a prisoner at Portobacco when Ingle's men took Copley's house. They transported him down to St. Mary's and held him at Pope's fort. Sometime before the house was taken, Percy had hidden the Jesuit silver in the woods. John Hilliard came to him and offered to forgive a debt of five hundred pounds of tobacco if Percy would tell him the location of the treasure. Hilliard also admitted that in plundering the house, he had taken a number of objects from Percy's chamber. Apparently Percy did not tell Hilliard what he wanted to know. Later, after the rebellion had ended, Hilliard attempted to sue Percy for the tobacco, but Percy countered that the items stolen from him were worth more than the debt and so the case was dismissed.[23]

The case is important, for it demonstrates the Jesuits had a substantial estate to be plundered. Jesuit holdings in Maryland yielded a vast amount of wealth to the rebels but in a different form from that possessed by Cornwaleys or Calvert. Father Copley filed a claim in England against Richard Ingle for over £1,800. Included in this total were the usual goods, livestock, and miscellaneous items necessary for supporting agricultural enterprises in colonial Maryland. Father Copley claimed household items "sufficient to furnish plentifully 2 large houses" and valued it at £200. There were sixty head of cattle valued at £360, twenty-one servants at £210, six hundred bushels of corn worth £60, an unspecified amount of English wheat, peas, oats, and barley at £20 and thirty-six guns valued at £36.[24]

The Jesuits, as gentlemen planters, were tied into the credit system in Maryland and lived a gentleman's life. Father Copley reported the loss of indentures, bills, and account books with a value of £500, a very large extension of credit in a small economy. In their role as gentlemen, they had a number of luxury items including twenty-two pieces of silver and five gilt bowls valued at over £44, clothing worth £55 and five hanging tapestries, one with gold and silk embroidery, valued at £80. They claimed eight feather beds and two flock beds complete with bedsteads and linens worth £70. That the Jesuits were highly educated was evident in their library of books valued at £150. The library was worth almost as much as the household furnishings of the two large houses. Except for the library, none of these items would have been out of place in any of the manor lords' estates.

However, it is the rest of the list that sets the Jesuits apart. They claimed a number of items made of gold and silver and containing diamonds, a ruby, and a sapphire. Topping the list was a "great diamond" valued at £200. We should carefully consider the value of this item. In a society where a servant could annually produce 800–1,000 pounds of tobacco, this single diamond was worth more than the labor of thirty servants for an entire year, a remarkably expensive piece of jewelry. In addition, they listed two pieces, each containing eight diamonds and valued at £32, a jewel with a diamond and a ruby worth £20, five diamond rings at £10, a ring with a great sapphire at £5 and engraved agates worth £1. They also listed two gold chains, two gold bracelets, two silver chains, and other items valued at £65. What were they doing with precious stones and gold ornaments? There is no indication that anyone else, including Thomas Cornwaleys, had anything like them. Their total value was £333 and represented almost 20 percent of their claim. It has long been suspected that these items were altar vessels and other religious symbols. If they were, their actual purpose could not be stated because of English laws. The Jesuits might have brought some of these things with them, but others may be the result of pious bequests over the previous decade.

All of it was swept away. The cattle and household goods probably stayed in the hands of Maryland rebels. In all likelihood the jewels, gold, and silver found their way aboard the *Reformation* and became part of the spoils that Ingle took back to England. The Jesuit mission in Maryland, begun with hope and continued through tribulation, was all but destroyed in a short time. It would be three years before a Jesuit returned to Maryland, and almost two decades before the mission would be back on a solid foundation.

The victory of the rebels in St. Mary's was extensive but not total. They had broken the control of the Catholic manor lords and destroyed the economic basis for that control. The government was crippled, and several of Lord Baltimore's officers had been captured. But the victory was not complete while the governor and his men still held St. Thomas's fort. Ingle was apparently not strong enough to break this stalemate and went in search of easier pickings. Strangely, the only part of Maryland not in open rebellion was Kent Island, and it was there that Ingle sailed.

Events on Kent Island are even more obscure than those at St. Mary's. We know that William Claiborne made an attempt on the island in December or January. When it was discovered that he had no legitimate authority, the planters abandoned him, and he sailed back to Virginia. News of events at St. Mary's must have reached the island fairly quickly, but it is uncertain whether the this was enough to incite rebellion or if it was Ingle's arrival that emboldened the rebels. Whatever the timing, Giles Brent's property at Kent Fort was soon plundered. One of the principals in this action seems to have been Edward Cummins, at whose house

Claiborne had earlier called together the planters. Cummins became an active participant in the rebellion. During the plundering he was seen to go "up into Mr. Brent's loft & throw down the books, saying 'Burn them Papists Divells' or words to that effect," and the books were taken outside and burned. Another prominent rebel was Thomas Bradnox, described as a "captain of the rebels," who set up a garrison in Brent's house. Others may have been plundered on Kent Island, but only Brent left any evidence.[25]

Giles Brent's claims against Ingle reveal a significant difference between the scope of his enterprises and those of Thomas Cornwaleys. In his suit, Brent reported the value of his estate as £2,000, but this figure was very much inflated. To begin with, Brent alleged that his capture and involuntary transport to England cost his estate £1,000 in losses due to the lack of his care and oversight. That was half the estate he claimed to possess. In specific damages, Brent only listed £1,254 for goods belonging to him and to his sister, Margaret Brent. The documents in this case illustrate the nature of the Brent lineage family but make it difficult to separate Giles Brent's property on Kent Island from his sister's property at St. Mary's.

> . . . for the last 4, 5, 6, or 7 years last Giles and Margaret Brent have resided in Maryland and the said Giles hath kept a house, wife, and family at a place called Kent and Margaret is sister to Giles and did at divers times come and reside with Giles Brent at his house at Kent aforesaid and did keep or leave in her brother's said house divers goods, and chattells and household stuff. And Margaret Brent had likewise a house in Maryland at a place called St. Maries and Giles did at divers times reside for part of the year with his sister at her house in St. Maries where he had certain goods, etc.[26]

Throughout the suit runs the same ambiguity about who owned what property. Although cattle and other goods were said to be at Giles's farm or Margaret's plantation, the ownership is left open to question. This was a clear indication of the operation of the lineage family in Maryland. Based on the lack of a claim for household goods for Margaret Brent's house, we can assume that most of the loss was claimed for Giles Brent's property. Some of the cattle could have been from the St. Mary's farm.

The total of Brent claims included £500 for livestock, £200 for bills and accounts, £160 for eight servants, £120 for tobacco, and £100 for household goods from Kent Island. Without delving too deeply into these claims, we can spot two obviously inflated values. Brent said he lost 6,157 pounds of tobacco and valued this loss at £120. At this price, each pound of tobacco would be worth five pence. While that may have been a price for tobacco in the 1630s, by the time of the plundering the price of tobacco was down to two pence per pound. Assuming that the weight was not inflated as well, the tobacco would have been worth only £52, less than half the claimed value.[27]

A second overpriced item in the account was the value of the eight servants priced at £160. That price assigns a value of £20 to each servant. The cost of transporting a new servant from England may have reached £20, but these were clearly not worth that amount. Of the eight listed, three had begun their service in 1639, two in 1641, and one in 1642. Most were near the end of their indenture and would have been worth considerably less than the cost of a new servant. The Jesuits, who lost twenty-one servants, valued them at only £10 per servant. A more accurate price, based on contemporary inventories, would place their value at £6 or less. The loss of servants, to both Giles and Margaret Brent would have been £48 rather than £160.

More interesting is not that Brent inflated his losses but how small they were, even in their inflated state, when compared with other estates. Brent valued the loss of household goods at £100. Though this amount was equal to what the Jesuits claimed, it was four times less than that of Thomas Cornwaleys. Brent claimed to have lost accounts valued at £200, but the Jesuits claimed accounts totaling £500. Servants lost numbered twenty-one for the Jesuits, fifteen for Cornwaleys, and only eight for the Brents. The total loss claimed by Cornwaleys was over £2,600, for the Jesuits more than £1,800, but the Brent claim was closer to £1,000.

Compared to most planters in Maryland, Brent's estate was large, but on the social level, where he wanted to be acknowledged, it was relatively small. Trying to compete with the other manor lords undoubtedly created economic problems for Giles Brent. Some of his insecurity and jealousy

TABLE 2: COMPARISON OF CORNWALEYS AND BRENT'S ESTATES

CATEGORY	CORNWALEYS %	BRENT %
Livestock	35.0	47.4
Bound Labor	8.0	15.2
Crops	10.5	15.2
New Goods	17.5	3.8
Other Capital	13.0	5.7
Total Capital	84.0	87.3
Consumption	16.0	12.7

Source: Examination of Cuthbert Fenwick, answer 19, 20 October 1646 in Cornwaleys *vs.* Ingle, Chancery, Examinations, C24 690/14, PRO.; "Ingle in Maryland," *Maryland Historical Magazine,* 1 (1906): 136–40.

over positions may have been the result of a perceived inferiority to the others. The lineage family aided Brent in overcoming these difficulties. While this type of family organization was declining in England, it was adaptive and successful for the Brents in Maryland.

The other major difference evident in Brent's claim was its strict focus on agriculture (Table 2). While Cornwaleys was invested in a number of other enterprises besides agriculture, almost four-fifths of Brent's investment was in livestock, labor, and crops. He had very few goods for resale and, except for the pinnace *Phoenix,* very little in what is described as "other capital." In fact, if the ship were considered transportation and not a capital investment, Brent would have claimed less than 1 percent in this category.

These two characteristics, lineage-based family and a concentration on agriculture, were important to Lord Baltimore's attempt to transplant a conservative, manorial system to Maryland. The Brents, more than any other early Marylanders, conformed to Baltimore's plan. Their claim against Ingle showed both of these factors in operation. They were conducting an almost exclusively agricultural enterprise, and the family controlled the assets of the individual members. The remarkable vitality of this family organization was demonstrated by its persistence through the rebellion despite the loss of its leader and half of its assets. When Lord Baltimore's forces regained control, the Brents were in the forefront of the political and economic establishment.

But in the spring of 1645, those events could not be predicted, and Giles Brent was a prisoner in the great cabin of the *Reformation* along with several others. Ingle's capture of Brent, Lewgar, Copley, and White has been viewed as an act of vengeance, and that might well have been true. It was also a practical response to the requirements of the Parliamentary Ordinance under which Ingle was operating. That law stipulated that he was to bring into court several of the "principle officers" to testify. Parliament hoped to discourage outright piracy, particularly against its own merchants, and to make sure it received its share of captured goods.[28]

While these four captives would certainly aid his case, Ingle did not take several other significant individuals. Leonard Calvert was beyond his grasp. Had Ingle captured Calvert, his arguments would have been more believable. Calvert was mentioned by name in the king's commission and had actually taken up arms to oppose Ingle. These actions would have supported the claim that Maryland was hostile to Parliament. But Ingle was never able to capture the governor.

The choice of who to keep prisoner and who to let go was not totally driven by vengeance. While all of the captives were Catholics, not all Catholics were taken prisoner. Cuthbert Fenwick, the Catholic overseer for Thomas Cornwaleys, became Ingle's prisoner but was later released. Apparently he was not important enough to bring back to England. Thomas Gerard and Nicholas Harvey, other Catholic manor lords, were not taken prisoner. Instead, Ingle kept only those members of the council against whom he could make a case. Both Brent and Lewgar were part of the government that had seized his ship in 1644, and that act could easily be construed as hostile to Parliament. In like manner, he was selective in the Jesuits he took back to England. Fathers Copley and White could demonstrate that Lord Baltimore had allowed Catholics and Jesuits to thrive in Maryland since its founding. The other three Jesuits were not essential for this proof and were assigned a different (and probably worse) fate. In these choices, Ingle was fulfilling the requirements of his letter of marque and strengthening his legal claims to the *Looking Glass* and the plundered goods.

The one exception to this plan was Henry Brooks Jr., the merchant of the *Looking Glass*. More than any other person, the merchant of the ship could have demonstrated whether the ship was trading with the Royalists or had traded to Royalist ports. His presence would have been required by the High Court of Admiralty in assessing the validity of Ingle's prize claim. Yet Brooks was not one of the captives taken back to England. Several people testified that Brooks was a Catholic, which only could have helped Ingle's case. We have to assume that Brooks would have been taken back to England had Ingle been able to do so.

What happened to Henry Brooks? He was Ingle's prisoner in February 1645 when the *Looking Glass* was seized. The earliest reference to Brooks after the rebellion indicated that he was dead. That he was alive when the ship was captured yet was not transported back to England suggests that he died in captivity during February or March 1645. The cause of his death is uncertain. Perhaps he died of injuries suffered when the *Looking Glass* was seized, although there was no testimony to indicate that he was hurt. He could have died because of the conditions of his captivity or some unknown illness. If it was the latter, his condition may have been made worse by his treatment as a prisoner. Whatever the cause, Brooks, like the Jesuits, was a victim of the rebellion.[29]

By late March, Ingle had both ships loaded with full cargoes of tobacco and plundered goods. It was time to return to England, and he began to make preparations for the voyage. One of his first actions was to appoint John Durford, his faithful mate, to be master of the *Looking Glass* for the return trip. Ingle asked the crew of the *Looking Glass* if they would help sail the ship and, if they encountered any Royalist shipping, would they fight for him. The crew agreed to help sail the ship because they had little choice. Had they refused, Ingle would have left them in Maryland and they would have lost everything. But in the matter of fighting Royalists, Ingle received the same answer the crew had given Leonard Calvert. The *Looking Glass* was a neutral ship, friendly to both sides, and the crew would fight only against "Dunkirkers or French," whose piracy was common in the English Channel, not English Royalists. Ingle could not trust the Dutch crew and reportedly told Durford that if a fight threatened, he should confine the Dutch in the hold.[30]

To insure his control of the *Looking Glass,* Ingle transferred some of the crew from the *Reformation* and hired a number of men from Maryland and Virginia. Robert Popely was hired as chirurgeon of the *Looking Glass*. Popely described himself as being of York River, Virginia, and said that he was in Maryland "on his own occasions." In later testimony, he claimed to have been with Ingle in Maryland before the seizure of the *Looking Glass* and to have been on the *Looking Glass* with Leonard Calvert before the fight. Another individual probably hired by Ingle was Ralph Bean of Maryland. Several witnesses testified that the new mate of the *Looking Glass* was named "Been." Certainly Ralph Bean was involved with Ingle while he was plundering Maryland. He was reportedly the one who demanded five hogsheads of tobacco from Francis Pope and had his party load them on Ingle's ship. The testimony implies that Bean was in charge of the men who took the tobacco and suggests the kind of role the mate of a ship might have.[31]

When Ralph Bean of Maryland gave testimony in the High Court of Admiralty in August 1645 he must have had a change of heart. In his testimony, Bean said that he was aware of what was going on in Maryland but tried to stay neutral amidst all of it. He blamed Ingle and his crew for attacking Maryland for no cause. Ingle, he told the court, "did plunder divers houses and plantations and burnt some but this he did not see then although he was there in the Country, because he resisted and would not be near when and where such things were committed, abhorring such strange acts and misdemeanors or outrages done to those whom this examinant conceiveth wished no hurt at all to them."[32] Bean further testified concerning the tobacco that was taken. He mentioned the five hogsheads seized from the house of Francis Pope without mentioning his involvement in the action. In fact, the responsibility for these acts is never fully explained in his testimony. Bean said only that they occurred as a result of Ingle's direction, not who carried out any of the orders.

Other colonists may have served on the *Looking Glass* for the return voyage, but they remain nameless. We can assume there were others because Ingle did not have enough men on the *Reformation* to sail both ships and could not trust the Dutch crew. The hiring of Ralph Bean as mate of the *Looking Glass* also implies that Ingle was short of experienced sailors.

Once back in England, they may have shared Bean's doubts about their culpability. In any case, no other colonist who testified in England can be associated with the *Looking Glass* crew.

With full crews and almost full holds, the *Reformation* and the *Looking Glass* sailed out of the Potomac and into the Chesapeake sometime in late March or early April 1645. As was his normal practice, Ingle made for Accomac before leaving the Chesapeake. On 10 April, Ingle signed a receipt for seventy hogsheads of tobacco loaded on his ship by William Stone and others at Accomac. This receipt marks the earliest possible date for Ingle's presence at Accomac after the rebellion. A number of other transactions were entered for Ingle as early as 1 March, but these could have been presented by William Stone, Ingle's agent, and do not prove his presence. However, he was there on 10 April to sign the receipt. Thus, Ingle's participation in the rebellion lasted at most two months and may have been shorter. Coincidentally, the receipt also marked the last reference to Ingle's presence in the New World.[33]

One looks in vain in the Virginia court records for any mention of the troubles in Maryland, the presence of the *Looking Glass,* or petitions from the prisoners. Reports of the rebellion in Maryland must have reached Accomac by this time, and the presence of the *Looking Glass* was a rather blatant announcement of Ingle's part in them. Yet the Virginians made no mention of these events and traded with Ingle as though nothing had happened. It may be that, whatever their loyalties to the parties in England, they were sympathetic to the Maryland Protestants against the Catholics. One should also not lose sight of the fact that two heavily armed ships in the harbor would be an important deterrent to any rash, Royalist inspired actions. Ingle, with the captive *Looking Glass* following, was allowed to sail unmolested out of the Chesapeake.

The voyage home was swift but not uneventful. The two ships traveled together, constantly on guard for enemies on the horizon or within. Ingle believed that Brent and Copley were trying to turn the crew against him, and later testified that they had attempted to cut his throat during the voyage. Whether or not this was true, they and the other prisoners represented a danger that had to be carefully watched. As the ships neared

Plymouth, lookouts spotted sails on the horizon. Ingle summoned Durford and Bean to the *Reformation* for a discussion what to do. He suggested that if the ships were Royalist warships, Brent and Copley would try to betray them. His solution was to throw them overboard before the ships got close enough to pose a threat. Bean objected to this cruel treatment, and the prisoners were spared. The unknown ships sailed below the horizon and the crisis was averted. The *Reformation* and the *Looking Glass* reached London early in June after a voyage of only eight weeks.[34]

Ingle expected to have little trouble having his actions justified by the Admiralty and Parliament. He was sailing with their letter of marque and believed that he had found Maryland in hostility to the king and Parliament. There was no denying that Maryland was governed by Catholics, and that made it suspect from the beginning. He had two captured Jesuits to prove how subversive the province had become. His strongest argument was that Leonard Calvert and Lord Baltimore had accepted a royalist commission and had actively tried to carry it out. With all this evidence, he must have been confident that the *Looking Glass* and the plundered goods would be judged forfeit and that this trip to the Chesapeake would be his most profitable ever.

CHAPTER TWELVE

"These had protection in a certain fortified citadel . . ."

The Plundering Time began with Richard Ingle's attack on the *Looking Glass,* but he was only one actor in a much larger drama. One could argue that without Ingle there would have been no rebellion, but it is also true that Ingle and his ship were not powerful enough to overwhelm the province by themselves, as Ingle himself was keenly aware when he went back to Virginia to hire more men for the assault. He also knew that he needed local support. That was the point of the letters he secretly sent to leading Protestants. Clearly this was not an isolated raid on Maryland or simply vengeance for an earlier incident. Ingle hoped for a complete change in the government of the province, and that required the active participation of Maryland Protestants.

The plan for a change in government fell on fertile ground among Protestant planters. There had always been tensions between the Catholic manor lords and Protestant freemen. Not only was the government run by Catholics but Jesuits were allowed to practice their "superstitions" openly. That was a heavy yoke for many Protestants to bear. These tensions could only have been aggravated by a cavernous split between Royalist Catholics and Parliamentary Protestants. The colony had survived and flourished for nearly a decade without these differences seriously threatening its stability. The potential for conflict was present but no overt moves were made by either party requiring individuals to choose one side or the other. Ingle's actions forced the colonists to make those decisions.

The role of the Maryland Protestants in this conflict is the least understood or appreciated aspect of "Ingle's rebellion." This is the result, at least in part, of Leonard Calvert's attempt to heal the wounds after the rebellion. Those who swore the oath of fealty to Lord Baltimore and behaved themselves were pardoned, including most of the Protestants in Maryland. For the sake of harmony, they would not be persecuted for the rebellion. Various political and economic reasons dictated that Ingle and his crew, who certainly were culpable, would bear full responsibility.

But who were the rebels who swept the proprietary government out of power and destroyed the manorial system in 1645? A wide variety of individuals participated in the rebellion, but they can be attributed to three general groups. The first was the *Reformation* crew, whose participation is well known. The second group requires more attention. Ingle reportedly went back to Virginia and hired a number of the "most rascally fellows" to aid him in overthrowing the proprietary government. They were recruited at the frontier settlement of Chicacoan in Northumberland County. Because of its location, Chicacoan was long a convenient rallying point for any who fled Lord Baltimore's government. The assumption has been that these men were Virginians who saw in this an opportunity for quick plunder. Cuthbert Fenwick reported that Ingle brought twelve of these men with him. Only four of the twelve can be identified by name, and three of those had been settled in Maryland the year before. It is likely that most of Ingle's hired force were men like these, and they were not Virginians but Marylanders who for political reasons had found living in the province difficult. They still had estates there and were tied into economic and kinship networks. This was a chance for them to come back and reestablish themselves under more favorable circumstances.[1]

It is perhaps ironic that the only Virginian specifically identified as an active participant in the plundering did not come to Maryland with Ingle. That was John Rabley, who had been hired by Henry Brooks to serve as pilot on the *Looking Glass* on the trip from Virginia to Maryland. He was in Maryland when the rebellion began and eagerly joined in to acquire some of the loot. If Rabley, who was there by chance, is mentioned so prominently as a plunderer, why are the other so-called Virginians who came to Maryland with Ingle not mentioned? It is likely that many of the men in this group had lived in Maryland or had ties to someone there.[2]

Together, these first two groups numbered at most thirty or thirty-five men, an imposing force, given the population, but not one sufficient to take and hold the province if the residents had been unified in opposition. But the residents were not unified, and many of the Protestants quickly offered their support to the rebellion. Some of these were servants happy to gain their freedom sooner than expected. Thomas Harrison and Andrew Munroe, servants of Thomas Cornwaleys, were sent at the beginning of the troubles to secure Cornwaleys's pinnace. As soon as they could, they surrendered the ship and joined the rebellion. This was to be expected, since servants had no stake in Maryland and Ingle offered them a chance to escape their indentures. Yet the rebellion was not led or even fully supported by servants. No servants of Protestant planters were freed as part of the conflict. Only those indentured to Catholics were allowed to free themselves. This fact belies the idea that the Plundering Time was a period of anarchy and indicates that there was some control over events.[3]

That control was exerted by the third group, Protestant freemen who organized to expel the governor and to govern themselves. One of Ingle's justifications presented to the court in England was that he helped settle the government of the province in Protestant hands. The details of this organization are obscure but several of the leaders can be identified. Thomas Sturman, who in the recent Assembly had pointedly questioned Governor Calvert about his commission, played a significant role in the rebellion. Sturman had come to Maryland as a cooper working for Cloberry & Company on Kent Island and later settled in St. Michaels Hundred. He was becoming an important leader of the freemen in the Assembly and held a number of important posts in the 1640s. Sturman played a prominent role in the plunder of Cornwaleys's house and commanded a garrison established in the house during the early phase of the rebellion. Later, after the taking of St. Thomas's fort, a number of prisoners were held at his house in St. Michaels Hundred. Despite his active and obvious part in the events of the Plundering Time, Sturman did not seem to hold any official position in the rebellion. This may be due to a lack of surviving records or it may be that his role was more opportunistic. Although we cannot fully assess Sturman's position in the rebellion, he was clearly recognized as a leader by his peers.[4]

Another prominent rebel was Thomas Baldridge. Like Sturman, Baldridge, also from St. Michaels Hundred, was becoming well established in Maryland. He had represented the hundred in the Assembly of 1640, and in the early 1640s had served as sheriff and coroner of St. Mary's County. As early as 1642 he was a lieutenant in the county militia responsible for the southern part of St. Michaels Hundred below Trinity Creek. In the early days of the rebellion, Baldridge, calling himself "Captain and Commander" of the rebels, led a party to take the house of Nicholas Harvey on the Patuxent River. After the house was surrendered and plundered, Baldridge had it burned to the ground. Baldridge and his wife, Dorothy, moved into the Jesuit manor house at St. Inigoes during the rebellion, and she was still living there early in 1647. Captain Baldridge fled the province after the rebellion and by 1649 was serving as a justice in Virginia. Unlike Sturman, Baldridge seems to have had a command position and was recognized as one of the leaders of the rebellion.[5]

The third and perhaps the most important of the Protestant leaders was Nathaniel Pope. The role Pope played in the rebellion has been consistently misunderstood by scholars looking into this period. One recent biography claimed that he fled to Virginia during the rebellion and did not return until Calvert had retaken the province in 1646. Not only did Nathaniel Pope not flee to Virginia, the available evidence strongly suggests that he was one of the most prominent leaders of the Protestant party. Because of Pope's pivotal role in the events of the Plundering Time, we must explore his actions up to and during the rebellion.[6]

Nathaniel Pope's story is unusual for early Maryland. He was one of the few men who transported himself into the province and arrived as a freeman, not as a servant. Whether he came directly from England or had been in Virginia first has not been determined, but he was already his own man when he arrived by 1638. He came by himself and transported no servants. These circumstances suggest that Pope did not have much money when he arrived. Within a year he had patented Pope's Freehold, a hundred-acre tract due him for transporting himself, and seemed to be following the same course that many new immigrants did.[7]

Over the next three years, Nathaniel Pope does not often appear in the records. He was occasionally called as a juror and was present at a number of Assemblies, but his participation in the government was minimal. Nor did he engage in extensive merchant activity. He was listed only once in the court records as a creditor and then only for thirty pounds of tobacco.

This profile suddenly changes in 1642, when Pope begins to appear more frequently in the records as a creditor and as an agent for others. The abrupt transition may be exaggerated by the loss of most court records between 1638 and 1642, but Pope was not listed in the estate accounts, which often include a list of creditors. If he had been engaged in any widespread economic activity before 1642, he would have been listed in those records.[8] The change in Nathaniel Pope's economic fortunes appears to coincide with his agreement to purchase Leonard Calvert's house, land, and servants at St. Mary's. This agreement was probably made before August 1642, in which month Pope's tax assessment was 180 pounds of tobacco when it should have been only thirty. Barely a year and a half later, Pope was claiming to have paid off a bond of fifteen thousand pounds of tobacco owed to Leonard Calvert for the purchase. Where did he get tobacco sufficient to pay off such a large debt?[9]

To answer this question, we must gauge how much time he had to raise it and what resources were available to him. It would be helpful to know the exact date of his purchase from Calvert, but that information is not preserved. At best we can provide limits within which the deal was completed. At least one of the servants Calvert sold to Pope had not been brought to Maryland until late 1641 or early 1642. By February 1642, Calvert was still referring to him as his servant. This dating becomes important when one considers the growing season for tobacco. If Pope were going to use his purchased servants to grow tobacco in 1642, he should have already been starting the crop. If the purchase was not made early in the year, he would not have the growing season of 1642 to help pay off the bond to Calvert. Only the crop of 1643 would be available to him for paying off the debt. Pope purchased nine servants from Calvert and, if they all worked in the fields in 1643 and were all experienced hands, Pope would still have been six thousand pounds short.[10]

The other unusual aspect of this transaction was that Pope was paying off the debt in May. Had he been growing his own tobacco, the traditional time for paying off debts would have been November or December, but if he had to collect this tobacco from other people his payment would have been delayed. This would imply that he was engaged in some activity other than simply growing tobacco. He does not appear to have had enough time and resources to raise this amount of tobacco by himself, so we must look beyond agriculture for Pope's source of wealth.

The answer to this question may lie in the property purchased from Calvert. Nathaniel Pope bought what was probably the largest house in early Maryland. He had no personal need for so much space and was not part of the class that had to make a proud showing. We can only assume that he used the house, as would later be customary, as an ordinary or inn, but this ordinary had the advantage of being the center of the government. The Assembly met in part of the house and the provincial court probably sat there as well. The Assembly of July 1642 assessed the province 6,520 pounds of tobacco for the expenses of the burgesses, money that went to pay for their lodging, meat, and drink during the session. If Pope was running an ordinary at the house, most of this tobacco came to him. Another Assembly was held in September, and a third may have been held in April 1643. Each of these would have brought large quantities of tobacco to the owner of the ordinary. The provincial court met frequently in St. Mary's during this period and always brought with it people needing food and lodging. Even the normal daily business of government could be counted upon to produce lodgers at the ordinary.

This source of revenue alone would probably have allowed him to pay off the bond on the property, but his position in the center of things brought him additional lucrative opportunities. He began to act as attorney for a number of people, including Marmaduke Snow, Philip White, James Neale, and William Stone. Pope also began to sue as a creditor on his own account. As part of his increasing status, in 1643 he purchased the rights to two thousand acres of land, enough for a manor. Having started out with very little, Pope had begun to prosper.[11]

Along with this prosperity came a more prominent political role. Pope was elected as one of two representatives from St. Mary's Hundred to the Assembly of August 1642. He began serving on juries with regularity. In fact, he served on two of the juries that found Ingle innocent of the charge of treason in 1644. Pope was one of three planters chosen to advise Henry Fleet in his aborted negotiations with the Susquehannock Indians in June 1644. Although the Maryland records do not record it, Pope had achieved the title of "Mr." by 1645. He was the most prominent Protestant in St. Mary's just before the rebellion.[12]

In many ways, this meant that Pope had the most to lose in any rebellion. If he supported the wrong side, everything he had accumulated would be gone. That may be why his role has been so difficult to assess. He had to make the same decision that all Englishmen faced at this difficult time. The evidence clearly indicates which side he chose. In February 1647, Pope was sued by both Robert Kedger and Nicholas Gwyther for work or services performed sometime in 1645–46. In both cases, Pope claimed that the work was done for the party then in rebellion and was "cut off." The importance here is that both plaintiffs looked upon Pope as financially responsible for the debts of the rebellion. In another case, Thomas Bushrod sued Giles Brent in an action on a bill of five thousand pounds of tobacco. John Lewgar was to have paid this bill to Pope in May 1645. Brent testified that the plundering of Lewgar's house gave Pope bills of greater value than what was owed to Bushrod. Brent eventually lost the case, but it demonstrates that Pope benefited from the plundering of John Lewgar's house. Finally, Blanch Oliver lost a cow to the garrison at the fort, and Pope promised to replace it. In this case, Pope freely admitted his responsibility for the actions of the garrison. All of these incidents show a clear pattern indicating Pope's association with the rebellion.[13]

Pope's leadership was evident in several ways. From the evidence in the cases above, Pope was clearly viewed as a leader, and he acknowledged his own responsibility to Blanch Oliver. Yet no evidence was more telling than that associated with the rebel fort. The center of the rebellion was in the fort constructed around Pope's house in St. Mary's, consistently referred to in later testimony as "Mr. Pope's fort." Since Pope willingly participated in the rebellion and the fort was built around his house, it is reasonable to conclude that he played an important part in the troubles. It is possible that Pope continued to play the same middleman role under the Protestant government that he had under Lord Baltimore's. An Assembly was held in 1646 under Captain Edward Hill, probably in this house, and Pope was responsible for collecting 4,000 pounds of tobacco levied by that Assembly. In every way, Pope was at the center of the rebellion, not as a hostage but as a leader of the Protestant community.[14]

Like the other rebel leaders, Nathaniel Pope was not an anarchist. The Protestants were not out to destroy Maryland but to replace the government with one sympathetic to Parliament and anti-Catholic in sentiment. Plundering occurred during this time, but it was no different than what was going on in England during the Civil War, where it was common practice to plunder one's enemies both to support the government and for personal gain. Maryland Englishmen were no different from those they left behind. The picture usually presented of the Plundering Time is one of total lawlessness, but this does not seem to be true. If the plundering in Maryland looks like an outbreak of anarchic lawlessness, it is only because it is separated by an ocean from England. Similar events there are recognized as part of a pattern relating to the Civil War, and that is how events in Maryland should be viewed.

There were many practical reasons for choosing Mr. Pope's house as the Protestant strongpoint, but the most important might have been symbolic. Ingle's stated purpose was to place the government in Protestant hands, not to destroy it. When he returned to England, he and others strove to gain recognition for this new government. As part of the effort, the Protestants had to show that they were indeed in control of the government. The northern half of Pope's house had probably been built in 1642 with provincial funds as the first statehouse of Maryland. It was the only physical expression of the government, and by controlling it the Protestants gained a measure of legitimacy for their claim on the government.

To protect this asset, a fort was built around the house. Few historical records relate to the fortification. It is identified as "Mr. Pope's fort," but when it was built, who designed it, and what it looked like remain uncertain. The earliest reference to the fort shows that it was in existence by the summer of 1645. It is difficult to believe the fort was not built at the beginning of the rebellion. Several of the *Reformation* crew testified that many of the plundered household goods were unloaded "at the fort" for Protestant use. This could refer to Pope's fort or to some other strongpoint during the early stages of the rebellion, as for example the garrison established at Cornwaleys's house after it was taken but abandoned by April 1645. Since the governor's party had established themselves in St. Thomas's fort at the start of the troubles, we can assume that Pope's fort dates to the same time period.[15]

The fort was garrisoned through the summer of 1645, and a number of Catholics were held prisoner there. How long this lasted is uncertain. There is no evidence that the fort was garrisoned after the summer. It may be that the taking of St. Thomas's fort, the Catholic stronghold, effectively eliminated any resistance in Maryland and with it the need for a fortified position. Whether or not that is true, Pope's fort soon faded into history.

Beginning in 1982 and continuing sporadically through 1987, archaeological investigations around the Calvert house (Pope's house) revealed the design of the fortifications and provided much information on its construction. The fort consisted of a ditch and an interior palisade. The ditch is generally between five and six feet wide and four to five feet deep. It was dug with a gentle slope or step on the exterior and an almost vertical interior edge. Inward of the ditch, generally five to six feet, is a palisade trench one and a half feet wide that in some areas contained rounded molds of the pales that were four to six inches wide. These molds, when found, are always against the exterior edge of the trench. It is believed that the dirt from the ditch was thrown up against the palisade to form a parapet for the protection of those inside. The evidence for this embankment is twofold. Early in the excavation it was noted that the outside edge of the ditch had been subject to considerable erosion and that a number of large gullies had eaten away at the edge. The interior of the ditch, despite being more vertical, was straight and not eroded. A parapet above this edge is believed to have protected the edge from erosion. Excavation of two sections of the ditch provided confirming evidence of the parapet. Massive redeposition of subsoil along the interior of the ditch was noted. This reddish yellow clay looked just like the natural subsoil but lay on top of a thin wash of dark silt and cow bones. Evidently the clay had been cast out of the ditch during construction but had slumped back in some time later. This was only found along the inside edge of the ditch.[16]

The use of a ditch, palisade, and parapet reflect a familiarity with European fortifications that is also evident in the design of the fort. Pope's fort, by anyone's standards, was an unusual fortification. It displayed some sophistication in its design but also a certain lack of precision in carrying out that design. The fort was neither rectangular nor triangular but a combination of both forms. On the west side, the fort was basically rectangular with two small, oblong bastions defending against attack from the river. In contrast, on the east side, the walls narrowed to a point where they joined a single, large, circular bastion centered on the east wall. At first glance, this arrangement seems quite strange, but it had historical precedents. A similar fort was built on the Blackwater River in Northern Ireland in 1601. While some of the details vary, the general shape and concept were the same. Blackwater fort had two small bastions on the river side and a large, centered bastion on the land side. The illustration showed this fort with precise walls but the description revealed that it was "made by excavating ditches and throwing up the soil to form parapets." Blackwater Fort was a timber and earth construction just as was Pope's fort.[17]

Because the object was to protect Mr. Pope's house, it is not surprising that the orientation and size of the fort reflected the floor plan of the house. Both house and fort were set at an angle of 8 degrees off cardinal directions. The large bastion on the east side is centered on the middle of the house, and the corner of the northwest bastion is in line with the west wall of the house. The inner edge of the ditch on the northern side of the

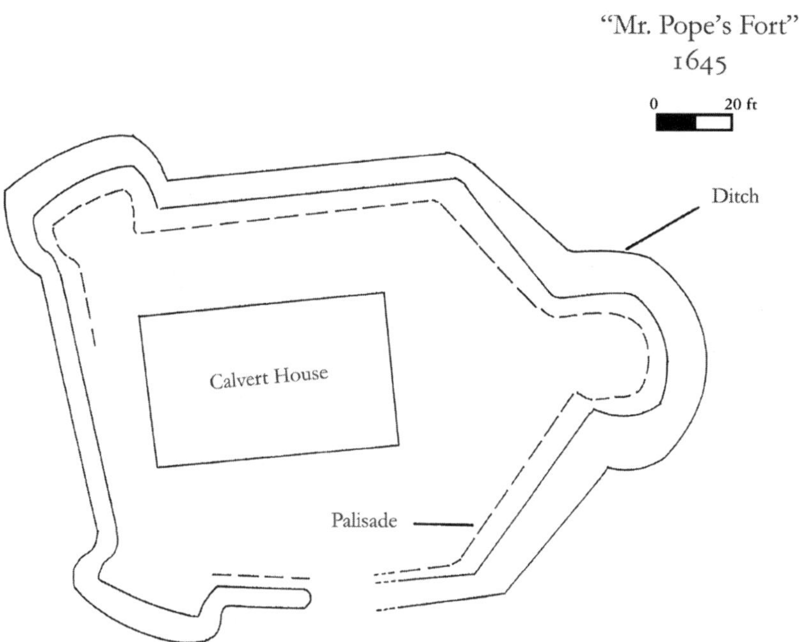

Author's sketch based on a summary of archaeological excavation, 1982–1987.

fort is a remarkably consistent twenty-seven feet from the northern wall of the house. If only the northern and eastern sections of the fort are considered, the fortifications were precisely laid out in relation to the house.

On the southern and western sides of the fort, this correlation falls apart. The west wall ditch, which should be parallel with the west wall of the house actually angles toward it. While the house is set at 8 degrees, the ditch runs at 14 degrees and is only fifteen feet away from the house at its southwest corner. This same lack of precision can be seen in the layout of the southwest bastion. Compared with the regular shape of the northwest bastion, the southwest bastion seems ill-formed and stretched out of proportion. The misshapen bastion may be the result of trying to match two ditches set at different angles. There is clear evidence of a gate in the south wall of the fort, and this feature divides the wall into segments. The eastern segment of this wall, coming out of the precisely laid out eastern bastion, is set at 8 degrees and is exactly twenty-seven feet from the wall of the house. However, the western segment of this wall runs due east and averages thirty-six feet from the wall of the house. This section of ditch is significantly out of alignment with anything else in the fort.

Two more unusual characteristics mark this corner of the fort. First, the palisade trench, an important part of the defensive works over the rest of the area, disappears. The whole area has not been uncovered, but the palisade can be traced for ten feet as it comes out of the northwest bastion. By the time the next excavation area is reached, at fifteen feet from the bastion, the palisade trench is not present. It is replaced by a series of small postholes, spaced four feet apart, that run where the palisade should have been found. The line of postholes even appears to turn into the southwest bastion. It seems that the palisade was replaced by some type of breastwork in this area. The other unusual feature of this corner of the fort is the depth, or lack thereof, of the fort ditch. A twenty-five-foot long section of ditch was excavated in the middle of the west wall in 1987. Much to our surprise, the ditch was very shallow. On the northern edge it was three and one-half feet deep, but by the southern edge it had sloped upward and was barely two feet deep. This can hardly be considered an effective defensive feature.

This evidence suggests that the fort was never fully completed according to plan. It was begun by someone with surveying experience and/or military training. Under his guidance the northern and eastern sections were completed. For some reason, both the precision and execution of the design faltered when it came to the southwest corner. The fortifications did not run where they were supposed to, the ditch was never completed to a proper depth, and a flimsy breastwork replaced the palisade. What looks like a professional fortification on one side degenerates to a haphazard, half-hearted attempt on the other.

The lack of precision evident in the west section of the fort is not indicative of waning enthusiasm on the part of the defenders or the absence of a threat to the fort. Remarkably, the eastern end of the fort was expanded and changed with the same lack of military knowledge. The carefully aligned and well-built eastern bastion was filled in and the fort wall moved about thirty feet to the east. In constructing the new eastern wall of the fort, the large centered bastion with converging walls was abandoned for a rounded end with little evidence of a bastion. The new construction lengthened the fort by only thirty feet but added an area roughly seventy by one hundred feet within the palisade by straightening the walls. This addition almost doubled the space within the palisade. The expansion of the eastern end of the fort was done with no understanding of the military importance of a bastion but simply to provide more space.

The archaeological investigation presents a problem of interpretation. The earliest part of the fort, on the north and east, was laid out and built with military precision by someone familiar with the European science of fortification. Before the fort was completed, this knowledge was removed from the site. The west side of the fort and its eastern expansion were finished by someone unfamiliar with the principles of fortification. What could have caused such a change in the character of the fort?

To answer that question, one must consider who designed it. Nathaniel Pope must have played some part in the work. The fort was built around his house and was identified with him. However, neither Pope, nor any of the other rebels, had previously shown any special knowledge of military matters. Thomas Baldridge was a lieutenant in the militia, a position that required no special knowledge. In fact, all those Marylanders who might have had the training to build such a fort were either captured or safely behind their own palisade at St. Thomas's fort.

More likely, the design was provided by an outside source. Richard Ingle had just arrived from a nation deep in the midst of a civil war where every city, town, and most residences were fortified. Contemporary maps show many small fortifications. Most are of a more typical star shape, but some triangular forts have been noted. Ingle and his crew would have been familiar with those, while the Marylanders might never have seen one. If Ingle were responsible for the design of the fort, it would help to explain the apparent differences. The north and east sections would have been completed under his direction between February and March 1645. When the *Reformation* sailed away from St. Mary's, the plan for the completion of the fort was left behind but not the skill in design or the understanding of the principles. The rebels finished the southwest corner and expanded the fort without really comprehending the reasons behind the plan.

Though Pope's fort might not have been as well built as its European counterparts, it was strong enough for its purpose and was described by one contemporary commentator as a "fortified citadel." Part of the strength of the fort must have been the cannon that defended it. There are no historical references to cannon in the fort, but archaeology yielded two cannon balls and a piece of gun barrel. The association of ball size to cannon type is problematic but does offer some insight on the kind of guns in question. One of the cannon balls would be appropriate for a type of gun known as a saker, typically about 9.5 feet long and weighing around 2,500 pounds. The second ball was appropriate for a demi-culverin, which was ten feet long and weighed three thousand pounds. The cannon barrel, although partial, had a bore diameter consistent with a demi-culverin. The saker and the demi-culverin were the most common types of cannon in use during the seventeenth century.[18]

It would be safe to assume that the cannon used in Pope's fort were captured from proprietary control. Such weapons were not easily imported and were not in the possession of the average planter. Richard Ingle had twelve guns aboard the *Reformation,* but it is highly doubtful that he would have volunteered any of his ordnance. Given the rarity of such weapons, how many cannon were there in Maryland at the time of the rebellion? On the original voyage to Maryland, Lord Baltimore sent over eight guns, described as four sakers and four demi-culverins. These descriptions conveniently fit the archaeological evidence from Pope's fort. Other possibilities exist. Ingle reportedly seized three cannon from Thomas Cornwaleys. One was made of cast-iron while the other two were described as "hammered iron." No description of their size survives, but they were all big enough to require carriages. Together, the three guns were valued at £20. They were not part of Lord Baltimore's ordnance, since Cornwaleys claimed their value as part of his estate.[19]

If we can rely on Lord Baltimore's guns as a guide, we can estimate what kind of weapons Cornwaleys had at his house. Both the sakers and the demi-culverins that Lord Baltimore sent to Maryland were valued at 14 shillings per hundredweight. Each of the sakers weighed 24.8 hundredweight and was worth a little more than £17, and each demi-culverin weighed 29.5 hundredweight and was valued at about £20.5. Since all three of Cornwaleys's guns together were only worth £20, it is clear that they were much smaller than those evident in Pope's fort. Cast-iron guns were both bigger and more expensive than hammered iron guns. If we assume that the cast-iron gun represented half of the total value, then Cornwaleys would have had one gun weighing about sixteen hundred pounds and two weighing about eight hundred pounds. The cast-iron gun would be called a minion and the two smaller guns would be classed as falcons. Though these guns might have been used at the fort, they have not, as yet, been found archaeologically.[20]

Another interesting aspect of the military nature of this site was the discovery of body armor used by the defenders. Three fragments, each representing a different set, were found in the fill levels of the fort ditch. In the seventeenth century, a complete set of armor consisted of a breast plate, a back plate, tassets to cover the hips, a gorget for the neck, and some type of helmet. Remarkably, all three fragments found at Pope's fort relate to the tassets and their hangers. Why should this part be so well represented? It is likely that the defenders felt the other parts were still useful but the tassets were more of a burden.[21]

Finding any body armor in Maryland in a context as late as 1645 is a surprise. Armor was common in Virginia into the 1620s, but it was thought to be too heavy and cumbersome for wilderness fighting, and its use is thought to have decreased rapidly in the late 1620s and 1630s. This is indeed reflected in the historical record as well. In 1623, John Smith advised potential Virginia settlers to issue armor to each man if possible. Lord Baltimore, in his recommendation to settlers published in 1635, copied Smith's list of supplies with the notable exception of armor. Each man was still to be issued a musket, a sword, and other military supplies, with no mention of armor.[22]

It is clear from the historical record that armor played a very small part in the settlement of Maryland. The cost of a common grade of body armor was set by statute in the 1630s at £1 2s. This was not an overly expensive piece of equipment, yet no armor is evident in the inventories of Marylanders who died before 1645. Several of the deceased were wealthy enough to import many servants but not one of them had armor. Even Thomas Cornwaleys, a man noted for his military experience and possessed of his own cannon, did not claim the loss of armor in his suit against Ingle. Leonard Calvert, whose inventory was taken barely six months after he regained the province by force of arms, had no armor listed. If anyone should have possessed body armor, it was the Lieutenant General of Maryland.[23]

Since armor was so rare in early Maryland, how did parts of three sets end up in the ditch of Pope's fort? There are several possible sources. When Leonard Calvert declared war on the eastern shore Indians in 1639, he ordered a boat to go to Virginia and pick up supplies. The first item on his list was "20 corsletts" which was the term used to describe a full set of body armor. There is no record of this purchase being made, but if it was, the armor could have been captured, along with the cannon, from provincial stores. This seems like the best explanation for the use and disposal of the armor. It is unlikely that the rebels or Calvert's forces would buy their own armor in Virginia, carry it to Maryland, and only then dispose of the tassets. On the other hand, if it was not their armor in the first place, throwing away an inconvenient part would make sense.[24]

The armor tells us something about the shadowy history of Pope's fort during and after the summer of 1645. The complete tasset was found in the fill of the north ditch, along with numerous bones, oyster shells, and other domestic debris. About a foot of fill had accumulated in the ditch before the tasset was deposited. The accumulated fill below the armor represents an uncertain length of time, but it is clear that the rebels did not dispose of the tasset right away. Perhaps they kept them until proprietary resistance ended. This would imply that the fill below the armor had accumulated in the spring and early summer of 1645. It would seem that the ditch was not long completed before it began to fill up.

Although such a sequence is highly speculative, excavations in other parts of the fort reveal much the same story. A segment of ditch along the south wall was excavated in 1986 and is typical of this sequence. The exterior edge of the ditch was dug at a relatively low angle and had a pronounced step about halfway down the side. During excavation, the interior edge was thought to be sloped as well and the ditch narrowed to only two feet wide at the base. The interior edge looked like undisturbed subsoil. During a final clean-up of the profile, the author noticed what looked like a small fragment of bone sticking out of this subsoil. The small fragment turned out to be a complete cow jaw that ran into and under this supposed subsoil. This jaw, along with several other bones, was found lying directly on the bottom of the ditch. By following out the bones, the original profile of the interior edge was seen to be almost vertical and the base of the ditch was seen to be four feet wide.

Like the discovery of the armor, the presence of these cow bones is significant because of their context. Normally, if a ditch is open for any length of time, a dark layer of silt will wash into it from the surrounding soil, filling the bottom. There was only a minimal amount of silt under these bones, indicating that they were deposited soon after the ditch was dug. On top of the bones was a massive redeposition of subsoil that most likely came from the fort parapet. Thus, shortly after it was completed, the ditch was partially refilled by the slumping of a portion of the defenses. This is another indication that the threat that initially caused the fort to be built had abated very soon after it was completed.

All of the archaeological evidence suggests that Pope's fort did not function very long. Construction appears to have begun with great enthusiasm and careful planning, both of which disappeared quickly. Almost as soon as the ditch was completed, the rebels began throwing trash into it. Before very long, large portions of the defensive works slumped into the ditch, and no attempt was made to repair the damage. The defenders clearly were not worried about a siege or attack, and this suggests that St. Thomas's fort had been taken by that point.

Again one arrives at the question of when the proprietary forces surrendered and the circumstances under which that occurred. Leonard Calvert was probably still in Maryland until at least early June. This is supported by very fragmentary notes copied from the Virginia Council records before they were destroyed in the Civil War. The notes refer to Calvert's appeal to Governor Berkeley and the council for aid in opposing the rebels. Mention of his appeal occurs in a segment that covers events from 7 June to 9 August 1645. Governor Berkeley did not return from England until 7 June, so that is the earliest Calvert could have made it. This dating also suggests that Calvert could not have been in Virginia prior to that date. Richard Kemp, a longtime ally of the Calverts, was acting governor until Berkeley returned and Calvert would have made his appeal to Kemp had he been able to do so. The notes refer to a number of chronological events related to the ongoing Indian war in Virginia and end with a discussion of a council meeting on 9 August. After that is the mention of Calvert's appeal. Without seeing the original document, it is impossible to know if the copyist followed a strict chronological order or added the Maryland passage after going through all of the Indian war material. The impression given by the notes is that Calvert did not attend the council until 9 August. If true, this would support the idea that St. Thomas's fort held out through the summer of 1645.[25]

How St. Thomas's fort came to be taken will probably never be known. Both John Greenold and Nicholas Gwyther, soldiers in the fort, imply that the end was violent. Greenold was held prisoner after the fort was subdued. It seems unlikely that Governor Calvert was taken prisoner in the fort, for had he been captured, the rebels surely would have placed him on the next ship bound for London. Perhaps Calvert, seeing the situation in Maryland resolving into a stalemate, went to Virginia to seek aid from the Royalist government. In his absence, the rebels might have seen an opportunity to eliminate the opposition.

However it happened, by late summer 1645 there is no further evidence of resistance to the rebels in Maryland. In part this is because there is no further evidence at all concerning what was going on in Maryland. Our main source of information on this period is the governmental records, and the proprietary government had ceased to exist. The governor was in Virginia trying to raise an invasion force. Council members, with the exception of Thomas Gerard, were either prisoners in London or had fled to Virginia. The lack of records following the intense plundering of the gentry has led many to suggest that this was a period of complete lawlessness. As we have seen, such was not Ingle's intention, nor was it that of the Maryland Protestants, who made up the bulk of the rebels. They wanted a government controlled by Protestants and loyal to Parliament.

It is likely that the Protestants set up a provisional government, as evidenced by testimony from both Protestants and Catholics. In England, Captain Ingle was proclaiming that he had settled the government into the hands of the Protestants, implying that this was a lawful government that had been established to rule the province for Parliament. Ingle believed that the situation was stable and the economy would continue as it had in past years. Before he left for England, he deposited receipts and bills with Nathaniel Pope totaling between 30,000 and 40,000 pounds of tobacco. Ingle expected Pope to act as his agent and to collect this tobacco for him in anticipation of his next voyage to Maryland. This was not something he could have expected if the province had degenerated into anarchy.[26]

Another view of events of this period is provided in a letter from the Maryland Assembly of 1649 to Lord Baltimore. Members complained of being plundered and banished by the rebels. They did not say that the rebels had destroyed or eliminated the government but that they had "assumed the Government of your Lordship's Province unto themselves." The rebels proposed an oath in support of Parliament that all inhabitants were to take and collected taxes to support the new government. The only Catholic to take that oath was John Thompson, and he reportedly gave a third of his cattle to the government. The promulgation of oaths and the collection of taxes are functions of a government.[27]

But this was a provisional government at best. It functioned to hold the province for Parliament but does not seem to have performed the daily tasks expected of a government. There is no evidence that land was surveyed or granted during this period. Nor is there any indication that a governor or council was appointed. The most important task of all, the holding of courts, did not take place. If courts had been held, their decisions would have been repudiated later and would have left a record. No such record exists. The Protestant government could not perform any of these tasks for a simple reason—there was no legal basis for its jurisdiction.

Protestants may have had de facto control of Maryland, but legally they were rebels against an authorized government. Ingle at least had his letter of marque to justify his actions, but Maryland Protestants were on their own. To remedy this situation, it is likely that they sent James Baldridge, brother of one of the rebel leaders, to England with Ingle. He probably had a hand in preparing a "Petition of diverse Inhabitants of Maryland" that was presented to the Committee of Foreign Plantations sometime before 28 November 1645. The petition complained about the Calverts' tyrannical government and reported that they were trying to convert Protestants to the Catholic faith. It also listed Calvert's commission from the king and claimed that Brent had seized the *Reformation* solely because she was in the service of Parliament. Because of these outrages, the petitioners asked that Lord Baltimore be deprived of his province and that the government be settled in the hands of Protestants by an act of Parliament. Finally, it asked for immunity from prosecution for Richard Ingle and all those who took part in the rebellion. This petition was favorably received, and on 25 December 1645, the House of Lords asked the committee to draw up an ordinance like the one requested. It would provide the Protestant government with the jurisdiction it needed and would end proprietary rule in Maryland. With his province held by rebels and Parliament about to deprive him of his sovereignty, Lord Baltimore did not pass a cheerful Christmas season.

CHAPTER THIRTEEN

"To hold yourself upright and hang from the gibbet at Tyburn"

As the *Reformation* and the *Looking Glass* made their way up the Thames in early June, Richard Ingle was probably readying his case against the Dutch ship and against Maryland. A successful conclusion to both of these issues depended on his ability to show that the province was hostile to Parliament. If he could do that, his actions would be legal and he and his crew would receive their prize money. Given Leonard Calvert's commission from the king and other circumstances, he had little doubt the courts would find in his favor.

Deep within the ships were a number of captives whose future was less certain. Fathers Copley and White would be eligible for a death sentence as soon as they stepped on English soil. No Catholic priests, especially known Jesuits, coming to London could have been confident of surviving the experience. As recently as February, Father Henry Morse had been hanged at Tyburn for returning to England after banishment. It was Father Morse who had replaced Father White in England when the latter made the first voyage to Maryland in 1633.[1]

The worries of the other captives might not have been so severe, but they were still very real. Giles Brent and John Lewgar were Catholics and well aware of the sentiments of Parliament and the courts toward their coreligionists. Both also had been deeply involved in the attempt to seize the *Reformation* in 1644. Whatever the ultimate merits of that case, in the London of 1645 their motives would be questioned. Their forced return to England could mean loss of property and possibly a jail sentence.

Others in England and Holland would soon find their lives changed by recent events in Maryland as well. Thomas Cornwaleys, still living in London, was probably aware of these developments as soon as the ships arrived. He must have been shocked to find that his friend and trading partner had destroyed his estate. Cornwaleys was not the sort of man to accept the news easily. Having demonstrated his loyalty to Parliament, he probably thought the law would protect him, and he was ready to use it.

Somewhere in the west of England, Lord Baltimore received news of the loss of the province. Whether it came by messenger from London or from Thomas Weston, who arrived in Bristol about the same time, the burden must have lain on shoulders already heavily weighted with cares. Maryland was Cecil Calvert's life's work, and in an instant, it was gone. Nor did it seem likely that the loss could be reversed. Soon after word of rebellion in Maryland came reports of the terrible loss the Royalists suffered at Naseby on 14 June 1645, a battle often seen as the beginning of the end for the king's cause. Although there is no way to prove it, the combination of these two events might have led Lord Baltimore to review his loyalties and consider the future. Bleak as it appeared, to have done nothing would only have made matters worse. Baltimore had to find a way to defend himself before Parliament.

Across the North Sea in Rotterdam, merchant John Glover waited anxiously for Henry Brooks and his cargo of Chesapeake tobacco. Much could go wrong on a transatlantic voyage, and many ships had never returned. As the days passed without word, Glover may have begun to despair. How and when the news reached him is uncertain. We can expect that the captain of the *Looking Glass* sent word to him as soon as he arrived in London. The news that the ship had safely reached England was a mixed blessing. It meant that all was not lost at the bottom of the ocean, but it also forced him into a legal battle over the ownership of ship and cargo. Glover had to be present in England to direct the defense and began to make travel plans.

All of these people would soon be engaged in a heated legal dispute brought on by the troubles in Maryland. The charges, countercharges, and testimony associated with their court cases provides much of the information for understanding the Plundering Time. The sequence of events over the next few months followed a well-established legal pattern defined by custom and Parliamentary ordinance.

The legal battle began with the ships' arrival in the Thames. The exact date cannot be determined, but they were definitely in England by 13 June and had probably reached Gravesend the week before. Gravesend, an important jumping-off point for the *Reformation* when she left London, was just as important on her return. It was the first landing point for any ship going to London, and here custom duties were first assessed. The captain was required to provide the collection agent with a detailed itinerary showing the ports he had visited and the people with whom he had traded. He also had to turn over a list of all the cargo detailed by individually numbered package and listing the contents of each.[2]

These requirements were normal for any trading voyage, but Ingle would have to provide a second list of all goods seized as a result of his letter of marque. The ordinance authorizing the seizures was quite specific in this regard. The captain who seized a ship under a letter of marque "shall not break bulke, sell, spoil, waste or diminish any of the said ships or goods until they shall be adjudged in the High Court of Admiralty to have been lawfully taken according to the true intent and meaning of this Ordinance, and a true and just inventory and appraisement shall be taken and made of the same."[3]

The need for this inventory arose from two separate requirements. Parliament was worried that the ordinance would become an excuse for open piracy and wanted to make sure that if one of their supporters were plundered, the goods could be returned. Secondly, the goods had to be assessed for customs duties and divided among three interested parties.

Only one of these, the captain and crew of the capturing ship, were present at the time of seizure, and they had control of the goods for a relatively long period. Some of the expensive and easily portable items often disappeared before the government or the other parties could claim their share. That this was a serious concern is shown by another ordinance passed by Parliament in June 1644:

> The parliament has received divers complaints of the abuses of several Captains . . . of their embezzling the moneys and other goods of value, under pretense of pillage, so soon as they take any ship. . . . It is ordered . . . that if any Captain . . . embezzle or purloin any moneys, goods or lading whatsoever taken in any ship or prize or shall presume to break open any trunks or chests . . . unless it be to visit and search them and to carefully lock or make them up again . . . shall not only lose their share of such prizes but shall suffer other punishment as their offenses shall demerit.[4]

To search for hidden goods, either embezzled or smuggled, a number of "tidesmen" or searchers were put aboard at Gravesend. They kept their own set of detailed records on the cargo and accompanied the goods, load by load, as they were sent ashore. The tidesmen's job was to make sure that the goods stayed together until the duties were paid. No one could go ashore until they were questioned and searched by the tidesmen.[5]

Ingle probably completed his inventories and other paperwork as the ships made their way up the river from Gravesend to London. Upon arriving in the capital, he made arrangements with customs officials for guaranteeing payment of the duties, unloading the cargo, and securing the *Looking Glass*. The crew of the Dutch ship was released and allowed to fend for themselves. Only the officers of the ship were needed to testify and, since their livelihood and wages were tied up in the ship, they could be counted upon to attend any hearing.

The two Maryland officials held prisoner, Giles Brent and John Lewgar, were probably released at this time as well. Although Ingle accused them of hostility to Parliament, no charges seem to have been filed against them. The Committee for Sequestrations probably talked to them soon after their arrival, trying to pick clean anything that Ingle had not already taken. Both Marylanders were still in London as late as September 1645. John Lewgar was staying at the house of John Weber, a hosier, near the Fleet Conduit, while Brent's residence is unknown. They certainly would want to tell their side of the story and could be expected to be available to give testimony.[6]

The only prisoners not released in London were the Jesuits, Copley and White. Being Catholic priests and returning to England, they were in violation of English law and were put in prison to await trial. If found guilty they could be sentenced to hang and then to be drawn and quartered. How long they had to await their trial is uncertain but, given later events it could not have been long. They were called to the bar, charged with their crime, and asked how they pleaded. They answered not guilty to the charge because they had not returned to England of their own free will. They had been captured in another place and forced to return unwillingly. The judges could not argue this point and freed the Jesuits with a warning to leave the kingdom within a specified time.[7]

Apparently they did not leave in time. Father White was again arrested, sent to prison, and this time sentenced to death. Remarkably, Father Copley does not appear to have been further troubled. This may be because he could claim not to be an Englishman at all, having been born in Madrid of English parents. Later in Maryland, Copley would register a certificate from King Charles, dated 1635, which called him an alien. This defense may have been enough to save him from going to jail a second time. Copley was soon allowed to pursue his own business in London and was there at least until January 1648. Father White was held in prison for three years under the threat of execution for not leaving the country.

An often repeated story about Father White's imprisonment reveals much about the man and provides an insight to his life and work. At the time he was put in jail, he was sixty-six years old, ancient by contemporary standards, and by all accounts weak and infirm. He had spent the last eleven years under difficult frontier conditions that had seriously affected his health. Nevertheless, he continued to fast two days a week, taking only water and bread. This dedication amazed his jailer, who reportedly told him that if he did not eat more he would not have enough strength to "hold yourself upright and hang from the gibbet at Tyburn." Father White assured him that "It is this very fasting which gives me strength enough to bear all for the sake of Christ." Eventually he was released, possibly as part of the army's flirtation with English Catholics after the war, and arrived in Antwerp in 1648. But in 1645 he remained in Newgate prison, awaiting a martyr's death.[8]

Meanwhile, Ingle had begun proceedings against the *Looking Glass* in the High Court of the Admiralty. This court, which met at Westminster, was the normal venue for trying cases under maritime or commercial law and was specifically designated by Parliament to handle claims for prize ships. The admiralty court was different from a Court of Common Law. It was called a prerogative court because, unlike other courts, it was not based on the traditions of common law and was not established by statute. Courts like the High Court of the Admiralty either grew out of medieval governmental policies or were established by a royal commission. They had evolved their own body of civil law distinct from the common law. The admiralty court had been established to handle piracy cases but had expanded to cover all aspects of maritime law.[9]

The admiralty court differed from other courts in a number of important ways. Cases were not tried by juries but by a commission of appointed judges. During the Civil War, these judges were appointed by Parliament. This was the court designated to handle civil or criminal actions involving Englishmen outside England or in association with foreigners. Because the court often dealt with mariners who would go to sea for months at a time, it was one of the few courts that would accept testimony by deposition. Finally, because so much of its business was commercial law, it allowed plaintiffs not only to sue individuals but also to sue things as well. This meant that ships and goods could be secured under admiralty jurisdiction until the action was determined.[10]

It was under this provision that Captain Ingle sued the *Looking Glass*. He filed a libel against the ship for trading with a port hostile to Parliament. A libel was the plaintiff's formal, written document listing his allegations and reasons for the suit. The modern sense of the word libel is derived from the often slanderous allegations that plaintiffs made in public versions of these documents.

The court began taking depositions on 13 June 1645. The first group of witnesses included the chief officers of the *Looking Glass,* who testified in detail about the owners of the ship, the freighters, and where the ship had sailed in her voyage. The latter point was important to establish whether the ship had traded with any ports hostile to Parliament. The witnesses were asked questions about the encounter with the *Reformation* and, in their answers, all stressed that they had obeyed Ingle's commands as soon as they learned who he was. According to them, they were in the process of striking their colors when the *Reformation* began firing. They emphasized that they had seen no signs that Maryland was hostile to Parliament or that it did not welcome trade with Londoners.[11]

The issue of religion came up because Ingle wanted to demonstrate that Maryland was run by Catholics and that the *Looking Glass* was freighted by a Catholic, Henry Brooks. By pursuing this aspect, even if the judges decided that Maryland was not hostile to Parliament, many of the plundered goods could be retained under the ordinance for the seizure of papists' estates. All of the *Looking Glass*'s crew agreed that Leonard Calvert was a Catholic but not Henry Brooks. Brooks might well have been a Catholic, but to admit this in court would have jeopardized any hope of getting the ship and its cargo back.

The captain of the *Looking Glass* also testified that his crew had not thrown papers overboard at the taking of the ship, and accused Ingle of tearing up his account book. The loss of papers was important, because they were the only record of where the ship had been and what goods were on her. In claiming the *Looking Glass*'s crew had destroyed the papers, Ingle could argue that the ship had traded with or was bound to a port loyal to the king—reasonable justification for her seizure. By claiming that Ingle had destroyed papers, Captain Cocke cast doubt on Ingle's other claims and could suggest that Ingle had embezzled some of the goods before an inventory was taken. Moreover, since the law required that all papers be preserved, their willful destruction could subject Ingle to fines or other forfeiture.[12] The *Looking Glass*'s crew finished their testimony on 23 June.

The next group of witnesses included a Virginian, whom Ingle had hired to be surgeon on the *Looking Glass,* and a number of the *Reformation*'s crew. Robert Popeley, the surgeon, claimed to be a resident of York River in Virginia visiting Maryland on his own affairs at the time Ingle arrived. Ingle, he told the court, had showed him his letter of marque in Maryland before the seizure of the *Looking Glass*. Popeley was a convenient witness for Ingle. He had seen Calvert's commission when it was published in Virginia, had been with Ingle before the seizure, and had been on the *Looking Glass* with Calvert as the *Reformation* came up the St. Mary's River. He claimed to have heard Brooks tell the captain of the *Looking Glass* to fight Ingle, to which the captain supposedly replied that he would fight Ingle and never yield his ship. This statement is so remarkably contrary to what actually happened that we must question its validity.[13]

Surgeon Popeley seems to have had the ability to be in just the right place at the right time to bolster Ingle's claims. Given the importance of his testimony, an inquiry into his background is in order. He termed himself a resident of York River, but no records of a Robert Popeley there have surfaced. The name Popeley is well known in Virginia. A Richard Popeley came to the Chesapeake in 1620 and was one of the freemen who accompanied Claiborne in the initial settlement of Kent Island. In fact, Poplar Island, located a few miles south of Kent, was originally named Popeley's Island after him. In June 1644, as William Claiborne was preparing to march against the Indians in retaliation for the April massacre, he asked that Captain Richard Popeley be appointed an officer of the York County militia. The Popeleys of York River were intimately involved with Claiborne, and it is reasonable to imagine that Robert Popeley was part of this family.[14]

Even if he was not related to this group, Surgeon Popeley blatantly lied in one aspect of his testimony. In speaking of the religious issue in Maryland, he attempted to portray the Catholics as the majority in the province and the Protestants as an oppressed minority:

> most of the persons resident at Maryland were papists and of the papist religion and it was generally reported at Maryland in this deponents hearing by such protestants as were there at

> Maryland that if Captain Ingle had not come thither, those of the popish religion there would have disarmed all of the protestants of that country there.[15]

After Popeley's testimony on 26 June, we have the first evidence, in the deposition of John Durford, that Thomas Cornwaleys had instituted a suit against Ingle and the *Reformation.* It is likely that Cornwaleys's suit was begun about this time because several of the *Looking Glass's* crew, who had already given their depositions, were later called to give others bearing on this suit. Had Cornwaleys's suit been active at the time they had been first called, their testimony would have included more detail on Ingle's actions after the seizure of the *Looking Glass.*[16]

Beginning with John Durford, the mate of the *Reformation,* a string of crew members testified concerning the *Looking Glass* and Maryland. These included the gunner, surgeon, cooper, a servant to Ingle, and a common sailor. Those who had been with Ingle on his earlier voyage in 1644 testified on the seizure of the *Reformation* and Cornwaleys's part in it, claiming that the crew had regained the ship without his help. Although they admitted that the ship had remained in Maryland to trade for tobacco after the rescue, they attributed that to the protection of their cannon and not to an agreement between themselves and the country.

The important point for these witnesses was that Maryland in 1645 was openly hostile to Parliament. Several had been present when William Claiborne gave Ingle a copy of Leonard Calvert's commission. Others had heard Argall Yeardley tell Ingle that Calvert had threatened to hang him. They tried to link the seizure of the *Reformation* in 1644 to the commission and reported that Brent had forced them to take a loyalty oath and had urged them to take the ship to Bristol for the king. The apparent refusal of the *Looking Glass* to strike her colors and be visited was to them but another indication of provincial hostility. Ingle, they said, had sent them ashore to capture Leonard Calvert, and they had only plundered those who were Catholics or who would not join with them. They made a strong case that Maryland was indeed hostile to Parliament.[17]

Beginning on 7 July, the court took three depositions from English members of the *Looking Glass's* crew. These men repeated much of the testimony given by the Dutch crew but expanded on certain points. According to them, Maryland had not been fortified before Ingle came, and other London ships had traded there without any trouble. These witnesses were aware of Calvert's commission but reported that the country would not allow it to be read or enforced. In significantly damaging testimony, they reported seeing Ingle or some of the men under his command cut out the marks on a number of tobacco hogsheads and replace them with Ingle's own mark. Such actions were contrary to Parliament's directions and amounted to open embezzling of plundered goods. All three testified that the Dutch ship and crew wanted to remain neutral and had offered no resistance when Ingle boarded it.[18]

The court now called the boatswain of the *Reformation* and two other crew members. Although they testified to the same set of questions, there was a distinct change in the tenor of their depositions, which laid a much stronger emphasis on the religious aspects of this dispute. They reported that the Protestants in Maryland had told them about a number of Leonard Calvert's misdeeds. He had supposedly instructed them not to pay their debts to Ingle because they were forfeit to him. It was their belief that had Ingle not come to Maryland, the papists would have disarmed all of the Protestants. They further stated that Calvert had imposed heavy taxes on the Protestants to be used in support of the king. So important was it to demonstrate the evildoings of Maryland Catholics that one of the sailors, Pascho Panton, entangled himself in a lie. In testifying about the unjust taxation he claimed that most of Maryland's colonists were papists. Less than a page later, he reversed himself and testified that the majority were Protestants. We can only speculate on why religion suddenly became more important in the case. Perhaps the accusations concerning Ingle's destruction of papers and embezzling goods were beginning to have an effect on the court. It might be too that religion was only a secondary issue and that the real point was to emphasize that the Catholic-controlled government of Maryland was hostile to Parliament. If that assertion could not be demonstrated, Ingle would not only lose the prize money but also would be liable in a number of suits already or yet to be filed against him.[19]

Up to this point, every witness had been asked about his financial relationship to the case and what he expected to get out of it. All previous testimony from the *Reformation*'s crew simply indicated that they had been hired for wages and shares. These three now testified more directly to Ingle's purpose. Their original bargain was for wages on a merchant voyage, but in Virginia, Ingle had proposed that they go on a man-o'-war voyage to Maryland to "root out the Papists" and had promised them a sixth part of any plunder. Two of the three swore that the decision to make such a warlike voyage was made after the ship arrived in the Chesapeake and after Ingle had talked to William Claiborne and Argall Yeardley. It was probably at this point that Ingle decided to establish a Protestant government in Maryland. The question of the Maryland government was soon to come before Parliament, and it may be that Ingle needed this testimony to support that effort.

The evidence presented in Ingle's suit apparently did not convince the judges of the admiralty court. They decided against the claim that the *Looking Glass* should be considered a prize and presumably ordered that it be returned to her owners. This was a major victory not only for the owners but for Lord Baltimore and the Marylanders. By implication the judges of the High Court of Admiralty had declared that Maryland was not in opposition to Parliament before Ingle raised rebellion there. Had it been otherwise, the mere fact that the *Looking Glass* had traded there would have been cause for her seizure. This court decision cast doubt on the legitimacy of all of Ingle's actions in Maryland.

When the judges of the admiralty court decided against him, Ingle had only one recourse. Because of the nature of this court, there was no higher court in which to appeal for redress. In common law, if a litigant felt that a judgment was wrong or unfair, he could ask for a writ of error, causing the case to be reheard in a higher court. The only appeal from the admiralty court was to an appointed body called the Court of Delegates. Their primary purpose was to hear appeals from ecclesiastical courts, but their jurisdiction had been extended to cover many of the prerogative courts. No new testimony was taken in this process, but two of the judicial delegates were appointed to review the existing evidence.[20]

The delegates appointed in this case, Sir Nathaniel Brent and Doctor

Robert Aylett, were strongly associated with Parliament and could be expected to look favorably on Ingle's claims. Sir Nathaniel Brent, no relation to the Maryland Brents, had been associated with Merton College at Oxford since 1589. Through the years he held various offices in the college until in 1622 he became warden of the institution. In 1636, during a royal visit, he presented both Prince Charles and Prince Rupert for degrees. At the beginning of the Civil War, Brent fled Oxford before the king occupied it and went to London to join the new government. In January 1645, King Charles deposed Brent from his position at Merton for, among other reasons, accepting the post of judge marshal in the High Court of Admiralty. Dr. Aylett was a cleric and poet educated at Cambridge University. Like Brent he accepted a position with the Parliamentary government early in the war. Eventually, he would become one of the masters in the High Court of Chancery under the Protectorate. These men could, if they saw fit, reverse the decision of the admiralty court. A complete transcript of the proceeding was made for them, but no decision has been found. Perhaps their judgment was superseded by other events in the case.[21]

Soon after the *Reformation* crewmen finished their testimony, Richard Ingle submitted his answer to the libel of Thomas Cornwaleys. On 31 July, Ingle responded to the twenty-eight points that Cornwaleys had charged against him. Typical of his answers was this: "To the seventh position he answereth and accepteth of the same so far forth as it maketh for him and not otherwise." The only new information we can glean from these answers was in regard to the goods Cornwaleys had sent to Maryland. Ingle claimed to have delivered much of the shipment to Cuthbert Fenwick when he first arrived. However, finding that Fenwick was "in Armes & opposition & hostility against the King and Parliament, did deliver the remainder of the same to one Nathaniel Pope & Thomas Baldridge to be kept by him and delivered as the Parliament of England should appoint."[22]

This is independent confirmation of the roles these men played in the rebellion. It is more likely that Ingle left the goods with them to be traded on his own account. Ingle also argued that Maryland was part of Virginia and that Calvert's commission was equally applicable there as in Jamestown. He argued that the pinnace which Cornwaleys claimed was lost was jointly owned by Cornwaleys and the Jesuits. Ingle claimed that Calvert had used that ship in Virginia against Londoners and other supporters of Parliament. Though he could have brought this ship to England as a prize, Ingle had given it to the Protestants to support their government.

The next group of witnesses, who began giving testimony in August, were more detailed and more focused on events on shore at Maryland. This was inevitable since the group included three major Catholic leaders: John Lewgar, Giles Brent, and Thomas Cornwaleys. Their testimony provides the first real sense of the violence and disruption of the Plundering Time and constitutes the only testimony to present any details on the physical reality of the rebellion. Their testimony must be carefully reviewed.[23]

John Lewgar was the first of the Maryland leaders to testify, on 6 August 1645. First to come up was the question of Maryland's sympathies in the Civil War. Lewgar reported that he was aware of Calvert's commission but that the governor had told him that it only applied to Virginia. He stated that Calvert had been asked about this in an Assembly at St. Mary's, and the governor had publicly proclaimed that his commission was not for Maryland. Lewgar was asked several questions about Ingle's arrest in 1644, and he strongly denied that it was linked with Calvert's commission. The only reason for Ingle's arrest was that he had slandered the king, which was still an offense, even in Civil War London. Lewgar went on in detail about Cornwaleys's efforts to have Ingle and his ship freed. Cornwaleys got Ingle's accuser to drop the charge. Lewgar pointed out that after Ingle was freed, he had traded with both Lewgar and Brent. Ingle had received a grant of an island in the Chesapeake from Brent at this time. As far as Lewgar was aware, Ingle had left Maryland in peace in 1644.[24]

When discussing the events of 1645, Lewgar emphasized that the Marylanders had made no resistance to Ingle until he began to plunder them. They had rallied in defense of their lives and estates, not in opposition to Parliament. Lewgar reported seeing one of Thomas Copley's houses after it had been plundered and was present as Ingle broke open various chests and trunks belonging to Copley. Ingle had freely distributed the contents without first making an inventory of them. Lewgar had seen one house that Ingle's men had burned and had heard of two others. He had also seen the burning of Copley's library, which Lewgar estimated to be worth £100. Finally, Lewgar said that he and the other Marylanders had all been brought to England as prisoners by Ingle.[25]

The next day, Giles Brent testified and essentially repeated what Lewgar had reported. Brent provided more details about the Assembly held in January–February 1645, saying that the Assembly had been held at Mr. Pope's house in St. Mary's. It was Thomas Sturman, soon to be a leading rebel, who had questioned Governor Calvert about his commission. Brent testified that it was "the general sense and determination of the Governor and Assembly at Maryland . . . that there should be no stop or interruption used against any ship or ships that came thither to trade either from London or anywhere else under obedience of the Parliament."[26] Brent also emphasized that Ingle had been arrested for treasonous words against the king's majesty not because he had come from London.

The testimony of Thomas Cornwaleys was necessarily brief since he had been away from Maryland since 1644. Cornwaleys provided support for Brent's and Copley's claims to their plundered goods. He testified about his role in the release of Ingle and claimed that he had sent William Hardidge, Ingle's accuser, away to Virginia. Cornwaleys reported that after Ingle was freed, he had traded without hindrance in Maryland so long as he was there. Cornwaleys's most startling testimony regarded the period after Ingle's release. According to Cornwaleys, Richard Ingle transported then-Governor Giles Brent from St. Mary's to Kent Island. That Governor Brent would trust himself with Ingle on the *Reformation* barely a month after he had tried to seize the ship is a clear indication of conditions in Maryland in early March 1644. It was on this voyage that Brent had granted Ingle an island in the Chesapeake to be known as Ingle's Island.[27]

Asked about Thomas Copley and his politics, Cornwaleys provided a description of Copley that is a marvel of understatement. He did not mention that Copley was a Catholic, let alone a Jesuit, but testified that Copley had:

> two fair mansion houses fitted and furnished with all manner of necessaries and other provisions of household stuff fit for any gentleman of quality to live in and for all the time of his

> abode there . . . the said Copley was generally accounted, reputed and taken to be a sober, quiet and peaceable man and one that lived without . . . sedition and was no way opposed or in hostility against the King and Parliament.[28]

Following Cornwaleys's testimony, a number of the *Looking Glass's* crew gave new depositions in the cases of Cornwaleys *vs.* Ingle and Copley, et al. *vs.* Ingle. Most of this testimony repeated their earlier depositions, but their understanding of events in Maryland was limited. They were all in general agreement that Maryland had not been fortified before Ingle arrived and that no resistance had been offered until the plundering began.[29]

The most significant testimony in Cornwaleys's case was that given by Josias Casswell on 15 August. Casswell was a searcher working for the Committee of Sequestrations, whose job it was to seek out and seize the estates and goods of Royalists and Catholics who slipped into London. In 1644 he had had a warrant to seize the goods of Thomas Cornwaleys who had just arrived in London aboard the *Reformation.* Ingle, he said, had been quite vocal in protesting this action, claiming that Cornwaleys had saved his life and his ship. Ingle had even gone before the committee to testify on Cornwaleys's behalf, and his report had persuaded the committee to release Cornwaleys and his goods. The importance of this testimony was that it contradicted everything Ingle and his crew had tried to prove about Cornwaleys's part in the seizure of the *Reformation.* This testimony, coming from someone well known to the judges and who had nothing to gain by it, must have seriously damaged Ingle's defense.[30]

It is likely that the admiralty judges found Ingle liable for his actions in Maryland, at least for his actions against Cornwaleys. Captain Cornwaleys later reported that the court had left him free to seek justice in the courts of common law. In this regard, a petition was filed in Chancery Court on 22 August seeking the right to take depositions of witnesses in Maryland and of seamen who were likely to be out of the country by the time the case came to trial. In the petition, Cornwaleys carefully summarized the facts of the case and claimed damages as high as £4,000. As part of this process, John Lewgar was examined on 20 September and repeated the testimony given in the admiralty court.[31]

It was something of a gamble for Cornwaleys to pursue his case in the court of common law. This institution was fundamentally different from the admiralty court. Under common law, Cornwaleys could sue only Ingle and not his ship, as was permissible in the admiralty court. He ran the risk that Ingle might divest himself of his significant assets before judgment was rendered, a problem because the common law courts were notoriously slow in reaching a judgment. Also, because the offense had been committed in Maryland and involved breaches of maritime and civil law, technically the common law court had no jurisdiction in the case. Beginning in the sixteenth century, the common law lawyers made up a convenient fiction that such alleged actions occurred in a parish of London rather than overseas, a practice still commonly accepted in the seventeenth century. Ingle complained about it in a petition to Parliament wherein he reported that Cornwaleys had charged him with a trespass in the Parish of St. Christophers, London, when the actions had occurred in Maryland.[32]

Given that the common law courts had significant disadvantages for Cornwaleys why would he chose to continue his case there? Perhaps the simplest answer is that it was more politically expedient to do so. From the beginning of the seventeenth century, prerogative courts, like the Admiralty, had been under attack by lawyers of the common law as tools of royal oppression. Whether or not they actually were, they had the appearance of it. All of their officers were appointed by the Crown, and many were not trained in English common law. Instead, they were familiar with civil law, which was the law of merchants and of Europe. James I fostered prerogative courts because they were easier to control and supported his claim to authority by Divine Right. On occasion he went so far as to sit on the admiralty court. While this was his right, it did not look very good to a growing body of dissenters. By the time of the Civil War, prerogative courts, such as the Star Chamber, were looked on suspiciously as Royalist institutions. In London in 1645 the common law court was probably a safer place for Cornwaleys to continue his case. However, he may have had a more practical reason. The admiralty court, being a prerogative court, could not attach real property. According to English law, land could only be seized by a writ issued by a common law court. It may be that Ingle and his wife had a house or other property that Cornwaleys sought to claim.[33]

About the same time that Cornwaleys was bringing his suit in common law court, Ingle filed his response to the suit of Giles Brent and Thomas Copley in the admiralty court. His answers in this response were more detailed than those he gave to Cornwaleys and provide details on Maryland and Ingle's view of the events. He had some interesting things to say about Thomas Copley. Ingle never came out and said that Copley was a Jesuit, and we can only speculate why. What he did do was leave the distinct impression that Copley associated with Jesuits. Ingle reported that Copley's usual abode was in a house called "St. Ignatius Loyolas Colledges" and that he lived there with Jesuits and papists.[34]

This was not a college in the sense of an institution of higher learning but a company or association of priests and brothers living together for religious purposes and supported by a landed foundation. This meaning of the word college can be traced back to medieval England and was one that had been suggested for Maryland as early as 1640. In that year, the General of the Society complimented Father Poulton in Maryland on his desire to establish a college. That was just after Leonard Calvert had granted the Jesuits their property rights. But Jesuit title to the land was never secure enough to fully implement the plan. Nevertheless, the idea must still have been current in 1645 for Ingle to have mentioned it.[35]

Ingle went on to charge Copley with trying to raise the Indians against the Protestants. Copley, while in a garrison at Portobacco, reportedly tried to have the Indians "cut the throats of the Protestants." This language was not to be taken literally but rather was an indication that Copley was trying to involve the Indians in the conflict. Some of the Protestants seized Copley and brought him to Ingle for punishment. This is apparently the same incident referred to in the Maryland archives as the "taking of Mr. Copley's House" at Portobacco. That raid was led by John Durford, Ingle's mate on the *Reformation.* Copley and Giles Brent were also charged with trying to cut Ingle's throat on the voyage to England, which is why he threatened to throw them overboard. Again, Ingle used language meant to indicate that they had tried to foment a mutiny against him while at sea.[36]

Ingle reserved special venom for Giles Brent, in part because Brent's actions provided Ingle's best chance to prove that Maryland was in opposition to Parliament. Ingle stated that he had twice found Brent openly hostile to Parliament, and the second time, Brent had drawn his sword against him. Ingle understandably had thought it his responsibility to take Brent prisoner and bring him to England for punishment. He had considered it to be his duty "by virtue of his Commission and was bound into by the solemn national vows and covenant." According to Ingle, none of the Catholics had protested Leonard Calvert's commission, and both Copley and Brent had actively assisted Calvert in trying to enforce it. He admitted receiving letters from Calvert and Copley promising him free trade and safe passage if he came to Maryland, but he had assumed that they were meant to "enveagle & deceive him."[37]

The testimony in these cases and another brought by John Glover, the freighter of the *Looking Glass,* would drag on through November, but Ingle must have known that he had already lost in the admiralty court. He decided to pursue the legal battle in another venue, and filed a suit against Cornwaleys and possibly other Marylanders, claiming £5,000 loss and damages for the seizure of his ship in 1644. In addition, he persuaded William Cloberry to file a suit against Cornwaleys for the sum of £10,000 in relation to the loss of goods and possessions on Kent Island. Cloberry had been one of the leading backers of William Claiborne's trading venture and was anxious to gain any compensation for his lost property. On the basis of these suits, Thomas Cornwaleys was arrested and thrown into prison. Only through the help of his friends, probably by posting a large bond, was Cornwaleys released. He apparently went into hiding to avoid a recurrence of these events.[38]

As part of his answer to these suits, Cornwaleys estimated that Ingle and his partners had lost the grand sum of £6 by the temporary seizure of his ship, far less than the £5,000 Ingle was claiming. He went on to state how it was through his, Cornwaleys's, efforts that the ship was set free and how, because of this, Cornwaleys was forced to flee the country. Cornwaleys also collected testimony about the naval fight that had occurred in the Pocomoke River in 1635. It was during this battle that three

Kent Islanders and one St. Mary's resident were killed. Cornwaleys had been in charge of the Maryland boat and apparently Cloberry was trying to charge him with murder. Both suits were soon dismissed, but they served Ingle's purpose by delaying and distracting Cornwaleys from his other cases.[39]

Things had gone terribly wrong for Richard Ingle. Rather than being hailed as a hero and reaping the benefits of his plunder, he now stood to lose everything. He had apparently lost the prize money for the *Looking Glass,* was under suspicion in the admiralty court for stealing or embezzling goods, and a number of people were suing him for goods and damages that could ruin him. His efforts on behalf of Parliament were not only unappreciated but had got him into serious trouble. The only solution was to change the rules of the game.

CHAPTER FOURTEEN

"The Soldiers were to expect no pillage . . ."

After the plundering in 1645, there is little in the way of evidence to indicate what was happening in Maryland. Presumably the Protestants continued to occupy Pope's Fort, supporting the garrison on cattle once owned by the plundered Catholic lords. In all probability little corn or tobacco was grown in Maryland in 1645, since the disruption and plundering took place during the planting season. The economy would have been at a standstill. Those who supported the tobacco economy by extending credit and supplying goods to the planters had been driven off and their holdings dispersed. Maryland's prospects were bleak. Somehow, despite these troubles, Maryland began to revive. Under very clouded circumstances a government formed, courts opened, and an Assembly convened. The evidence for this transformation is slim, but what exists encourages speculation as to how Maryland came back from the brink of disaster.

The first sign of revival is the presence of Captain Edward Hill in St. Mary's during the summer of 1646. Hill was a prominent member of the Virginia House of Burgesses, where he represented Charles City County several times and on a number of occasions had served as Speaker of the Assembly. During the session held in March 1646, Hill was one of two members authorized to go to Maryland and demand the return of several men who had secretly fled Virginia. When he arrived in St. Mary's, there may have been no one in authority to whom he could present his demands.[1]

While in St. Mary's, Captain Hill accepted the position of governor—from whom remains a mystery—and held that position from July to December 1646. Under his leadership an Assembly was held and much of the governmental fabric refurbished. The most ironic twist to this affair is that Hill derived his authority not from the rebels of the previous year but from Lord Baltimore's charter. How and why Edward Hill became governor of Maryland is a question that has vexed Maryland historians.

The first mention of Hill appears in a commission in which Leonard Calvert appointed him to be governor while he was out of the province. As compensation for this position, Calvert granted Hill one-half of the rents and customs due to Lord Baltimore for that year. The commission ended with the phrase, "Given under my hand and Seale this 30th July 1646 in Virginia." It would seem to have been a simple arrangement and not one likely to cause any controversy, but the document's origin has never been adequately explained. If Leonard Calvert wrote it, why did he find it necessary by the end of the year to hire soldiers to invade and subdue Maryland? On the other hand, if the document was not legitimate, why did a later Maryland court award Captain Hill his salary for the year as specified in the commission?[2]

Following Calvert's death a year later, a number of letters were recorded that shed light on the episode. Captain Hill, unaware of Calvert's recent death, wrote on 18 June 1647 asking for his salary and some valuables that he had left in St. Mary's. Thomas Greene, who succeeded Calvert as governor, answered the next day and informed Hill of the change in government. Greene reported that he was unaware of what was owed to Hill but assured the captain that if he sent an attorney, he would get a fair hearing. The news of Calvert's death raised Captain Hill's hopes, and he believed that he was now the only legal governor until Lord Baltimore should decide otherwise. He immediately replied to Governor Greene and argued that the invasion that replaced him, even though led by Leonard Calvert, had been illegal. For the first time a true sense of conditions in 1646 becomes apparent. Captain Hill wrote that Calvert, being out of the province, had no right to appoint anyone. Hill claimed that the authority to appoint a governor lay with the Council of Maryland, and that body had elected him governor. He went on to complain about the arbitrary abuse of power by Calvert in his invasion of Maryland, and in a significant phrase, stated, "When the single power of the Governor [Calvert] should disanull his own and the country's Act, by a Countermand, his owne, I say though acted by another person." The last part of this statement casts serious doubt upon the validity of the July commission.[3]

Governor Greene argued in reply that Hill was not a legal representative of Lord Baltimore, even if he had been appointed by the council, and referred to Lord Baltimore's commission to Leonard Calvert dated 18 September 1644. In it, the council was given the right to appoint a governor if Calvert died or left the province without doing so himself, but with an important restriction. The appointee had to be a member of the council. Obviously, Hill was not and so could not claim to be governor.[4]

Interestingly, Greene did not deny that Hill had been elected by the council. Instead he argued that Hill's not being a member of the council rendered his appointment invalid. This implies that in the summer of 1646 conditions were sufficiently peaceful in St. Mary's that Lord Baltimore's council could meet. Could this be true, and who would have been there to meet? Before Ingle came to Maryland, the council consisted of seven men: Leonard Calvert, John Lewgar, Giles Brent, Thomas Greene, William Brainthwaite, James Neale, and Thomas Gerard. In the summer of 1646, Calvert was in Virginia. Ingle had carried Lewgar and Brent to England in 1645, and both were still there in the fall. Lewgar, though, was in Virginia by mid-1646 and may have gone back to Maryland. At the time of the troubles, James Neale fled Maryland, and his attorney, Nathaniel Pope, gave his house and plantation to a Virginian. Thomas Greene could not have participated in such an election, since he later told Hill he did not know what was due for his salary. The whereabouts of William Brainthwaite remain unknown. Of the pre-rebellion councilors, the only one who stayed in Maryland was Thomas Gerard. If the council that Greene and Hill both mentioned was Lord Baltimore's, then it was a sadly depleted one.

Yet both correspondents in 1647 stated that Lord Baltimore's council elected Captain Hill. Some historians have suggested that he was actually elected by a Protestant Assembly. Hill himself wrote: "His Lps Council had then the immediate power, in the Election & choice of a Governor . . . they supposed it absolutely necessary for the safety of the Province to confirme mee." Governor Greene took the same position, arguing that Hill was wrong to assume that "the Counsell residing in the Province had full power & authority to elect & chuse you, which is evident they had not." Nevertheless, some of the council must have been in Maryland to elect Hill, and it is not hard to see why they would choose him over one of their own. They were all Catholics, and anti-Catholic feeling was still running high. Captain Hill, a Protestant not connected with the previous regime, would have been acceptable to the Protestants. But one important problem still remained. The council must have known that the person appointed had to be a member of the council. They also knew that if Leonard Calvert appointed the governor, this restriction would not apply. That may explain the origin of the July commission from Calvert to Hill. It is important in this regard to keep in mind the controversy John Lewgar started by signing Giles Brent's name to a commission in 1644. That would explain Hill's assertion that the appointment was made by Calvert even though "acted by another person."[5]

As strange as this episode was, there is an even greater mystery related to Hill's appointment: How did he come to be elected as *Lord Baltimore's* governor? The whole point of the rebellion in 1645 was to overthrow the proprietary government and replace it with one controlled by Protestants and sympathetic to Parliament. In London an ordinance was before Parliament to sanction this very thing. It called for the repeal of Baltimore's charter and the establishment of a Protestant government. Lord Baltimore would fight the ordinance, but in 1646 the outlook could not have been promising. To Maryland Protestants, who must have been aware of events in England, there could have seemed no reason to allow the restoration of proprietary rule. With no pressure from England, none from Virginia, and the rout of Lord Baltimore's forces the previous year, there is no logical explanation for this change in attitude. We can only wonder if the Maryland colonists had become so disgusted with the unsettled conditions that a government of any kind was preferable to anarchy. Perhaps they were willing to acknowledge Baltimore's property rights if the government was in the hands of a Protestant.[6]

However it came about, in the summer of 1646 a government based on proprietary authority existed in St. Mary's County, fulfilling most of the functions of the old government. Under Hill at least one court was held. No record of its deliberations survives, but reference is made in later court papers to one case involving the ownership of cattle. Significantly, that later court upheld the validity of the judgment in the case. Captain Hill also restored much of the county government. He appointed John Hatch to be sheriff, an office Hatch continued to hold after Leonard Calvert returned to Maryland. An Assembly of the freemen was called in the fall of 1646. The only evidence of this meeting also is derived from later references. There is no indication of how long the Assembly met or what business was discussed. It adjourned by December 1646.[7]

Captain Hill's Assembly, whatever its claim to legitimacy, faced several serious problems. One of the most important was that its jurisdiction extended only to St. Mary's County. The rebels on Kent Island never submitted to its authority. The island would remain in rebellion until it was subdued by Leonard Calvert the following year. Even more important than the hostility of the Kent Islanders were the intentions of Leonard Calvert. If Calvert had issued the July commission or given it his approval, he must have regarded it only as an interim measure. It was always his intention to retake the governorship for himself.

At the same time that Hill was calling the Assembly, Calvert was making arrangements for his return to Maryland. These preparations by their very nature have left us little evidence, yet we can see shadowy reflections of them in the records as Calvert gathered supporters and supplies. As part of his preparations, Calvert sent a pardon to the inhabitants of St. Mary's, stating that if they would submit to Lord Baltimore's authority their former crime of rebellion would be forgiven. The date of the pardon is not certain, but it may have been issued on 5 August 1646. In the Act of Oblivion, passed in 1650 to end most of the disputes arising from the time of troubles, the rebellion is said to have lasted from 15

February 1645 until 5 August 1646. The only possible event that could have occurred on that date was the proclamation of pardon at St. Mary's. It is likely that Calvert had heard of the government formed under Captain Hill and used the pardon to capitalize on this sudden change of fortune. That does not imply that Calvert recognized the validity of Hill's appointment or commission. He was uncertain, until his actual arrival in Maryland, whether the pardon had been accepted, but he knew all along that Hill was acting as governor. It is quite likely that Calvert refused to accept any government for Maryland in which he was not the head.[8]

As part of his policy of reconciliation, he was also making peace with old enemies. One example of this process is preserved in Calvert's message to Thomas Thorneborough. While he was at Kecoughtan, Calvert sent a messenger to Thorneborough asking to meet him at York. Thorneborough had taken some part in the rebellion of the previous year and Calvert, before his entire company, forgave Thorneborough and confirmed to him whatever estate he had acquired in Maryland. Thorneborough was soon to accompany Calvert in the invasion of Maryland. At least in this case, the policy of reconciliation worked.[9]

The military force Calvert raised for the reduction of Maryland seems to have consisted, in equal parts, of Marylanders who had fled the province in 1645 and Virginians who were promised rewards for their help. While a number of the Virginians may have been Puritans associated with Richard Bennett, they certainly were not the Puritan mercenary force that some have suggested. No specific number of soldiers is listed in any of the sources, but a careful review of the documents suggests twenty-eight men formed the core of this expeditionary force. They were mostly men who later sued Calvert or his estate for soldier's wages. The troop was led by Captain John Price and Lieutenants William Lewis and William Evans. The company also included two sergeants, Mark Pheypo and Thomas Jackson. In addition to the officers and sergeants, twenty-three private soldiers left records of their service.[10]

We can be fairly certain that this number includes all of the soldiers raised by Calvert. On 6 October 1647, Captain Price sued for 45,600 pounds of tobacco and one hundred barrels of corn due to the soldiers

TABLE 3: ESTIMATED SALARY OF THE SOLDIERS AT ST. INIGOES FORT

RANK	TOBACCO (LB)	CORN (BBL)
Captain Price	3,100	11
Lt. Evans	2,500	5
Lt. Lewis	2,500	5
Sgt. Pheypo	1,500	5
Sgt. Jackson	1,500	5
Privates (23)	34,500	69
Totals	45,600	100

Source: Archives of Maryland, 4:338, 362, 469.

in St. Inigoes Fort for their wages. From November 1647 through June 1649 individual soldiers recorded their demands for wages. Based on these records, we know that each private soldier was entitled to 1,500 pounds of tobacco and three barrels of corn as his salary for the year. Sergeant Mark Pheypo filed a combined claim with Nicholas Keytin, a private soldier, for 3,000 pounds of tobacco, suggesting that sergeants were paid the same amount of tobacco as private soldiers. They may have been entitled to more corn, but there is no way to prove it. Lieutenant Evans filed a joint claim with John Jarboe for 4,000 pounds of tobacco and eight barrels of corn. If we subtract Jarboe's salary as a private soldier, the lieutenant's salary was 2,500 pounds of tobacco and five barrels of corn. We have no evidence concerning the salary of Captain Price, but we can estimate it from the total demand made on 6 October. These figures are shown on Table 3. The corn ration for Captain Price and the two sergeants is conjectural and is based on subtracting known obligations from the total demand. Nevertheless, it is clear that this "budget" does not have room for more than twenty-three private soldiers, and that this must have been the company that Leonard Calvert led to Maryland.[11]

Who were the men who accompanied Calvert in the reduction of Maryland? Of the twenty-eight identified, thirteen definitely had been established in Maryland before the Plundering Time and must have fled to Virginia. Three of the others seem to have been living in Virginia before 1645 but were Catholics. Thus, more than half of the soldiers were already associated with Maryland or were sympathetic to the Catholic proprietor. The remaining dozen seem to have been Virginia Protestants, but were they Puritans associated with Richard Bennett? Three disappear from the records almost immediately, one died in 1648, and the other eight became settlers in Maryland. Not one played a significant role in the settling of Providence, nor were they associated with the Puritan regime of the 1650s. It seems unlikely that Richard Bennett's Puritans had much of a part in this company. More importantly, all of the officers and sergeants were either Marylanders or Catholics. To claim that this force was recruited and led by "Colonel" Richard Bennett is not only misleading but gives Bennett a military importance that he did not have in 1646. Later, Bennett would hold offices in the Virginia militia, but in this period he is referred to as "Mr." Bennett while many others use their military titles. It is clear that this military force was raised by Leonard Calvert, commanded by men of his choosing, and acted under his authority alone.[12]

Because of Richard Bennett's later importance in Maryland affairs, there has been a tendency to overemphasize his contribution to the expedition. It is not unusual that Bennett, a confirmed Puritan, would support the proprietary Catholic forces. Nor is it necessary to assume that he already had the idea of a Puritan refuge in Maryland as a reason for his help. Bennett was also a merchant and, before the Plundering Time, had close ties to several of the Catholic leaders. Before Ingle's invasion, Bennett had financial dealings with Leonard Calvert and Thomas Cornwaleys. Even after the rebellion, Bennett's conscience was not troubled by trading with Thomas Copley, the Superior of the Jesuit mission. Bennett may have been "one of the Chesapeake's most intense Puritan ideologues and Parliamentary supporters," but he was not averse to a good investment. Apparently helping Leonard Calvert was just such an opportunity.[13]

How much did Bennett invest in the retaking of Maryland? He may have had a hand in recruiting some of the Virginians, although this is by no means certaint. If the surviving records are any indication, his contribution was small, yet he expected ample payment for it. Bennett sued Calvert's estate for three pounds of gunpowder, thirty pounds of shot, thirteen hens, one cock, a peck of salt, one hundred pounds of beef, and four and a half barrels of corn used during the voyage. Much of this list was confirmed by the testimony of Robert Sharpe, one of the soldiers. If these were all of the supplies for the expedition, it would have been a short foray by a small number of men.[14] For a sense of the scale of this bill, we can compare it to John Lewgar's supply bill for the aborted march against the Susquehannocks in 1642. That expedition involved a sergeant and twenty men for twenty-three days. The total for their supplies ran to 3,427 pounds of tobacco. Using the prices listed in this bill as well as those from contemporary accounts as a gauge, Bennett's bill amounts to only 898 pounds of tobacco. Lewgar's supply bill lists three times as much powder and shot, and its total is more than three times Bennett's. That these supplies could have sustained an extended campaign in Maryland is doubtful. It is more likely that the items in Bennett's bill were last-minute additions to the provisions Calvert had already assembled.[15]

Based on the surviving evidence, it is clear that the "company" that invaded Maryland late in 1646 was raised and supplied by Leonard Calvert. There is no evidence of anyone else's hand in these actions. Richard Bennett played a part in this drama, but a supporting role not a leading one. Any other conclusion overestimates his importance to Maryland.

Although there is no specific evidence pertaining to where or when Governor Calvert gathered his forces, circumstantial evidence may allow us to get close to the event. When Calvert, at Kecoughtan, sent his message to Thorneborough asking to meet at York River, he may have been gathering his force. At York, according to later testimony, Calvert addressed Thorneborough before his (Calvert's) company. These were the soldiers recruited for the expedition, assembled there because York River was the most northern Virginia settlement of any consequence. Beyond was unsettled Indian country. The only English settlements to the north were around Chicacoan on the Potomac, a center of anti-Catholic, anti-Calvert feeling. York River was the settlement closest to Maryland where Calvert could expect a civilized reception and was probably the location from which the expedition to reduce Maryland sailed.[16]

With final preparations complete, Calvert brought his men aboard the pinnace and addressed them concerning the voyage. He reminded them of his pardon to the inhabitants of St. Mary's and declared before the assembled company that if the people of St. Mary's accepted the pardon and submitted themselves to Lord Baltimore's authority he would receive them in peace and there would be no pillage. This statement is consistent with Calvert's policy of reconciliation rather than revenge. It also indicates uncertainty about the kind of reception he might find at St. Mary's. Yet he must have known that Hill was already governing in Lord Baltimore's name. The speech is another indication that Calvert did not recognize Hill's authority. Clearly, the point of this expedition was to restore Lord Baltimore's legal and appointed governor to his rightful place.[17]

Exactly when the governor and his company sailed from Virginia is difficult to determine. The earliest surviving record is the meeting of the Assembly on 29 December 1646 at St. Inigoes Fort. By that date, Calvert had secured St. Mary's and sent a summons to those who had been at Hill's Assembly earlier in the fall. There is a tradition that Calvert surprised this Assembly while it was in session and arrested its members, but that is not plausible. A letter to Lord Baltimore from the Assembly in 1649 recounted these events and implied that the invasion and the summoning of the Assembly were separate actions. It stated that Hill's Assembly had been under adjournment but that it was called back "a very short time" after the invasion, suggesting that Calvert entered Maryland late in December.[18]

Very little evidence survives concerning the first days of Leonard Calvert's return to Maryland. The only document bearing on this important and critical moment is the letter of the Assembly to Lord Baltimore mentioned above. In describing these events, the Assembly reported that Calvert, "surprised all those who had Combined themselves against him and cast them in Prison." The context of this statement indicates that it was not the Assembly that Calvert surprised but other, unnamed persons. We can guess that they were members of Hill's government and the soldiers holding Pope's Fort. Despite this nebulous action, the taking of St. Mary's must have been generally without opposition. No evidence is left to suggest organized resistance to Calvert's resumption of the government nor any indication that the soldiers were allowed to pillage.[19]

Recognizing the tension and wishing not to offend the Protestants,

Calvert quickly came to an agreement with Captain Hill and guaranteed him the salary that the council had promised as soon as it was available. Hill was not happy about having to give up the government, but he had little choice in the matter and probably left Maryland soon after Calvert's return. By 26 January 1647, Hill issued a power of attorney certificate to John Hollis to sue and recover the salary and other debts. The certificate refers to the debts as due "heere in Mary-Land," but it was sworn and recorded before Samuel Taylor, a resident of Chicacoan. A copy of the original was made for the Maryland records by Robert Clarke. The haste with which Captain Hill left St. Mary's is apparent in that he left behind a number of valuable items, including 146 arm-lengths of roanoke which Calvert had in his possession. With Hill gone back to Virginia, there was no one to lay claim to the government but Calvert.[20]

As one of his first official acts, the governor summoned the burgesses who had been elected to Captain Hill's Assembly. Calvert met them at St. Inigoes Fort on 29 December 1646 and declared that they should be as free to speak and debate as they had been at any other Assembly. Next he called six of his soldiers and questioned them about what he had told them prior to the invasion. The soldiers testified that Calvert had promised no pillage would be allowed if the pardon was accepted.[21]

The summoning of the burgesses from Captain Hill's Assembly, though much maligned by later Maryland Assemblies and wondered at by generations of historians, was a brilliant stroke on Calvert's part and should be evaluated within the political context of Maryland at the time. Putting aside the legality of his actions, Captain Hill had established a government under Lord Baltimore's authority. Governor Calvert did not want to wreck that fragile structure, merely to place himself at its head. The burgesses had been popularly elected by the planters still resident in Maryland and represented their choices for leaders. Rather than rejecting these men as rebels, Calvert accepted their election and sought to bring them over to his side. This was a technique he had used since the earliest disputes with the Kent Islanders and is important to understanding his policy in this critical period. Assuring the burgesses that they could speak freely and having the soldiers testify were parts of his strategy. The burgesses, for their part, were surrounded by an armed force, had just recently been pardoned of rebellion, and were likely to be quite agreeable to Calvert's agenda. The summoning of the burgesses was also typical of Calvert's policy on his return to Maryland. He consistently denied the validity of Hill's government while ratifying and confirming its actions.

The record of this Assembly is woefully short. Apparently John Lewgar made a complete copy of the laws passed and sent them to Lord Baltimore. Unfortunately, that record has not survived. From later references we know that several acts were passed by the Assembly but, for the most part, we have no idea what they concerned. A single piece of legislation is preserved from this session, an act giving the governor the right, if there was a defect in the laws of the province, to use his discretion in judging cases. While the language of this act is somewhat different, the sense of it is similar to one passed in 1642.[22] Another act, hinted at by later references, apparently declared that debts incurred by the Hill government were invalid and not collectible. Thus, when Robert Kedger and Nicholas Gwyther both sued Nathaniel Pope for services rendered to the previous government, Pope could claim that those debts were "cut off" by act of the Assembly. The act did not extend to cattle. Blanch Oliver sued Pope for a cow killed at his fort and was granted a cow and a calf by the court.[23]

Only one other act passed by this Assembly left enough evidence to speculate on its subject and intent, and it was by far the most important piece of legislation passed. It imposed a custom duty on exported tobacco and was probably the reason Calvert called the Assembly so soon after his return to Maryland. The intention was to provide revenue to pay Calvert's soldiers. Gathering, supporting, and paying an armed force was an expensive proposition. Calvert must have had a hard time securing the financial resources necessary to begin the expedition. Most of his resources and those of Lord Baltimore had been left in Maryland in 1645. He counted on forcing support from the planters. No copy of this act has survived, but it called for a duty of sixty pounds of tobacco on every hogshead exported from Maryland. Later this would be amended to only that tobacco shipped on Dutch vessels.[24] Lord Baltimore, who had a copy of the act, was clear in his response to a later Assembly: "and this injustice to us was also much aggravated by the rejection of the payment of those Customes due unto us uppon all Tobacco exported from thence."[25]

The Assembly debated at length the measure and the cost of paying the soldiers. Several planters were concerned that the duty might not be enough to cover the costs and worried that they would have additional taxes to pay. Elias Beach told Calvert that he was thinking of abandoning Maryland because he feared how much the soldiers might cost. To soothe these fears and see the act passed, Calvert promised that sixty pounds per hogshead was all the province would pay for the government and, if that was not enough, he freely pledged his estate and that of Lord Baltimore. It was a pledge made out of political expedience but one that would have great consequences in the future, cause hard feelings between Lord Baltimore and his colonists, and make the crisis more difficult. In the end, the act effectively specified that Lord Baltimore would be responsible for the whole cost of the government in exchange for a duty paid on all tobacco exported from Maryland. Calvert seems to have thought that the sixty pounds duty would be enough if it were diligently collected. His pledge calmed the Assembly and the act passed. The Assembly having accomplished the main task he set for it, Governor Calvert adjourned it on 2 January 1647.[26]

The invasion of Maryland had been carried off with remarkable ease. Leonard Calvert had regained the government and pushed his legislative agenda through an Assembly that could and should have been hostile. The custom on tobacco, if properly collected, would defray most of the cost of the venture. None of this would have been possible without Leonard Calvert's leadership and his conciliatory approach.

The key to the success of the entire venture was the custom duty on tobacco. While Calvert was alive, every effort was made to collect it. Barely two weeks after the Assembly adjourned, Calvert sent a warrant to William Bretton authorizing him to investigate what goods Ralph Beane had imported and whether he was attempting to export tobacco without paying the duty. The penalty for doing so was the seizure of all the tobacco. For the shipping of 1647, it is very likely that the duty was paid.[27]

Calvert also had the problem of how to deal with the plunderers who were still resident in Maryland. The ownership of plundered goods and cattle had to be determined. Calvert had pardoned the rebels for their actions, but he was unwilling to let them keep their spoils. The rebels agreed to return any stolen goods they still had in their possession or to pay triple damages. Some of the plundered estates may have been recovered in this fashion, but there is no way to be certain. Under the circumstances, it was the best that Calvert could do.[28]

At the same time, Leonard Calvert began to rebuild his personal estate. Shortly after the Assembly was dismissed, Nathaniel Pope conveyed to Calvert his house and the land belonging to it at St. Mary's. This was the same house Calvert had built about 1641 and sold to Pope in 1642. In exchange for the house and land, Calvert discharged Pope of four thousand pounds of tobacco "due for his present levy and to allow him a room at the end of the house to put his things in till Spring of the yeare that he can remove them."[29]

It is clear that Pope conveyed this property in exchange for a debt of four thousand pounds of tobacco, but how or why Pope came to be indebted for such a great sum is uncertain. Another curiosity is that this obligation is referred to as a levy, a term normally used to indicate a per capita tax collected from the freemen. It seems unlikely that Pope's assessment could have been set at four thousand pounds, since the two highest individual assessments before the rebellion were one thousand and eight hundred pounds levied on Thomas Weston and Thomas Cornwaleys, both prominent merchants. Calvert had promised the Assembly just two days earlier that the province would not be unduly burdened by the cost of the soldiers. Such a large assessment would surely be considered a burden. In the records, two references to levies at this time place this amount in perspective. In January 1648, the administrator of the estate of Richard Cox, in listing amounts paid out of the estate, included the notation "to his levy 30 lbs." This is the same amount levied on Cox in 1642 and shows that the average assessment did not rise greatly. The other reference to a levy was the 150 pounds of tobacco demanded of John Thimbly by the sheriff, John Hatch, in January 1647. Thimbly had announced his intention to go down to Virginia with Captain Hill, and the sheriff wanted the tobacco due for the levy. When he heard of the difficulty, Captain Hill said that the 150 pounds could be deducted from his levy to pay that of Governor Calvert. This suggests that there were two levies and that they were owed to these individuals.[30]

Earlier, levies had been collected to pay for unusual public expenses, such as marches against the Indians, or to pay the costs of the Assembly. Yet both Captain Hill and Governor Calvert seem to have treated these levies as their own personal property. Calvert's inventory, taken on 30 June 1647, listed as an asset of the estate, "by levies paid 1,270 pounds." It is possible that Captain Hill, as an inducement to take the office of governor, was voted a salary to be paid by levy and that Governor Calvert demanded the same when he returned. In this regard, it is interesting that one of the charges later made against Thomas Greene, who became governor after Calvert, was that he tried to arrange a payment of 12,000 pounds of tobacco, thirty barrels of corn, and a house befitting his station from the Assembly of 1648. Whether the levies of 1646–47 were intended as salaries, that is the way both Hill and Calvert treated them, and they were not troubled about dispersing them to their own advantage.[31]

Even if the levy did represent a salary for the governor, it does not explain how Nathaniel Pope came to owe 4,000 pounds of tobacco. This rate was so much greater than any individual assessment before or after this period that we must suspect something else caused it. Is it possible that the sum was due as part of the custom duty on tobacco and not a levy in the traditional sense? If that was that the case, at sixty pounds per hogshead Pope must have exported about sixty-six hogsheads, a total shipment of about 23,100 pounds. That is not an unreasonable figure, since Pope managed to pay off a bond of 15,000 pounds to Calvert in 1644. It is also possible that because of his central location Pope was appointed to collect the levy. Without further evidence, this debt must remain unexplained.

Whatever the cause of the debt, Calvert accepted the house and land at St. Mary's in fulfillment of it. The property at St. Mary's was transferred to Leonard Calvert, who took up residence in the house he had built several years earlier. Once again it was referred to as the Governor's House at St. Mary's. Pope had been in the process of expanding or repairing the house and the deed mentioned a number of sawn boards and loose timber about the property. As part of the transfer, the governor agreed to pay for these repairs.

By the end of January, Governor Calvert had firm control over St. Mary's and its immediate surroundings. Not only had the Assembly met but the provincial court had been in session as early as 5 January. Although St. Mary's had been easily subdued, the province would prove to be more difficult. Kent Island was still in open rebellion, and much of St. Mary's County, officially at peace, was seething with revolt. In two separate instances, men were brought before the court for making threatening or reviling speeches against the government. William Pinley, in referring to the Virginians who accompanied Governor Calvert, said "that rather than he would have come up upon such employment as they did, he would have gathered Oysters for his living." The court sentenced him to twenty lashes.[32]

On 16 January, Calvert issued a proclamation placing an embargo on the county, the purpose of which was to prevent communication with enemies of the province in this "time of war." No one was permitted to leave the province without permission of the governor, nor could they export any cattle or corn. Further, if a planter noticed someone who was not a resident or was from Kent Island, he was to report it to the fort without delay.[33]

Part of the reason for the embargo was Calvert's intention of launching an expedition against the rebels on Kent Island. He had told the soldiers as much before coming up to Maryland. By mid-January, his plans were well enough known that the rebels gathered at Chicacoan were waiting for him to leave so that they could cause trouble in St. Mary's. The expedition to Kent did not leave until April, and it is possible that Calvert did not feel secure enough to attempt that enterprise until the threat from Chicacoan was neutralized.

How serious this threat was became clear two days later when John

Lewgar presented charges against Thomas and John Sturman, Francis Gray, John Hampton, Robert Smith, and Thomas Yewell. All had been prominent in the uprising of 1645 and had already been pardoned twice for crimes of rebellion, but the new indictment charged that they had secretly fled the province on 13 January and gathered in the house of John Mottram at Chicacoan. There they had plotted against the person of Leonard Calvert and made preparations to raid Maryland for cattle and to burn and destroy property. Without specifying whom, the indictment alleged that some of the defendants had come back to Maryland on the seventeenth and spread rumors about impending invasions. One rumor had it that a Captain Wyatt, with several ships, was in the bay with a commission from Parliament for the government of Maryland. Since Parliament had not yet heard arguments concerning the ordinance for Maryland, this was an obvious falsehood. Another rumor concerned an expedition led by William Claiborne, supported by fifty men in several ships. It was said that he, too, was coming up from Virginia with a commission for the government or St. Mary's or to support the rebellion on Kent. At just about this time, Claiborne and twenty men from Chicacoan were on Kent Island trying to raise the planters for just this purpose. The final count in the indictment charged that some of the defendants had come to Maryland in the night, stolen and killed cattle, and taken the meat back to Virginia to share with the other defendants.[34]

The only evidence presented to support these charges was the testimony of Edward Thomson, a resident of Chicacoan. He was told by Samuel Taylor that Francis Gray had threatened to kill those who supported Governor Calvert. He also said that a group at Chicacoan was waiting for the governor to go to Kent so they could, "goe over & would fire and burne and destroy all that they can."[35]

In his summary of the charges, John Lewgar reported that some of the defendants were already in prison. He argued that they should be judged and if found guilty banished from the province with the loss of their land and goods. Those defendants who were not in custody were advised to surrender to the sheriff or risk proceedings against them in their absence. Apparently, Calvert had arrested the Sturmans, John Hampton, and Francis Gray, probably after their return on the seventeenth. This is supported by a bond granted to these men and Robert Sedgrave, who was not included in the indictment, on 19 January. Each pledged a bond of two thousand pounds of tobacco that they would not leave the county without informing the governor, nor would they have secret communication with John Mottram, Thomas Yewell, Thomas Lewis, or Robert Smith.[36]

On the same day, Calvert repeated the indictment against Smith, Lewis, and Yewell, claiming that they "adjoined themselves to persons hostiley affected against this Province and doe hence return into the Province by night as enemies and Robbers, and kill and Carry away the Cattle of the Inhabitants."[37] He called on them to surrender to the sheriff by 4 February or risk being proclaimed rebels. On 27 January, Calvert issued an assurance to Smith and Yewell, promising them a pardon if they submitted by the above date and took the oath of fealty. Perhaps to carry this message, Calvert issued a pass to John Sturman, William Hardidge, and Francis Gray to go to Chicacoan. There is no indication that the rebels submitted, but no further references to night raids or indictments are recorded.

The plans of the rebels may well have been changed by simultaneous events taking place on Kent Island.[38] By spring 1647, Governor Calvert had reasserted his control over St. Mary's and the surrounding area. The government had been rebuilt, an Assembly convened, and courts held. The discontent so evident in January had been quelled. Only one major task remained before the victorious governor—the reduction of rebellious Kent Island.

CHAPTER FIFTEEN

"Catholicks of this nation . . . have deemed it necessary . . ."

While Ingle was in Maryland in the spring of 1645, the decisive campaign of the Civil War was about to begin. Royalists began the year with high expectations. Although the loss of York the previous year had given Parliament control of the north, the king's forces had thoroughly defeated one of Parliament's armies in the west and had humiliated one of its senior generals. In January and February, Royalist cavalry had traveled widely, raiding and causing uneasy murmurs within the halls of Parliament. News from Scotland indicated that the army under Montrose had continued to fight over the winter and had achieved some important victories. As important as these victories were in their own right, more importantly they forced part of the Scots army to move north out of England to protect their homeland. As spring came to England, the Royalists had much cause for optimism.[1]

Parliament, on the other hand, began the year with serious troubles. After the previous campaign, its military leaders began blaming one another and quarreling, which in turn lowered morale and increased the rate of desertion. The remnants of Parliament's three armies were surly and mutinous over issues of bad leadership and back pay. The campaign had clearly demonstrated that locally raised and based troops were not useful for a national struggle—some units had refused to serve outside their local area, and most were unhappy to do so. Parliament had find a way to field a well-led, professional army for the coming season.[2] They succeeded by taking two steps. The first was to create a national army made up of troops from different regions and to guarantee these soldiers regular issues of pay. The New Model Army, as it has come to be called, was made up of veteran soldiers from Parliament's three armies augmented with large numbers of conscripted men. All it needed was a leader.

Parliament's second action provided the right man. On 3 April 1645, they passed the Self-Denying Ordinance, requiring members of Parliament to resign their military commissions. The stated reason for this unusual step was the perception that some members, holding both civil and military positions, were prolonging the war for their own ends. The ordinance prevented the old commanders from leading the New Model Army. The only senior military officer not a member of Parliament was Sir Thomas Fairfax. With Cromwell's strong backing, Fairfax was appointed to lead the New Model army. This turned out to be an important turning point in the war. Through force of personality and a strong dose of military discipline, Fairfax made the New Model the equal of any contemporary fighting force. That was not yet apparent in the spring of 1645, and Royalists, much to their later regret, underestimated its potential.

Fairfax took his army in search of the king's, and the two forces met at the battle of Naseby in June, a decisive victory for Parliament that doomed the Royalist cause. After Naseby, Royalist forces, seemed to fade away, in part because, unlike their foes, they had not been paid. In September the city of Bristol, the only major seaport open to them, fell after only four days. At almost the same time, Montrose's luck ran out in Scotland, and his army scattered. On 10 October, the New Model Army stormed and captured Basing House, long an important and symbolic Royalist stronghold. The tensions of this disastrous year came to a head at Newark in late October. Prince Rupert forced a confrontation with the king after which he and a number of the king's senior officers were dismissed and soon left the country. Charles gathered what was left of his forces and retired to Oxford in November with no real hope of continuing the war. Late in April 1646 he secretly rode north toward Newark. On 6 May he surrendered to the Scottish army there, ending the Civil War.

With their cause in tatters, Royalists began to reassess the future. Over the next few years, many would claim never to have supported the king or to have done so only reluctantly. Parliament turned a trickle of reborn Roundheads into a flood when it passed an ordinance for compounding the estates of "delinquents," or less active Royalists. By swearing allegiance to Parliament and paying a fine, usually equal to one or two years' income from the estate, the property owner could be restored to his sequestered lands. The deadline for compounding was set at 1 May 1646. After the battle of Naseby and subsequent events in the fall of 1645, this prospect looked much more appealing.

Lord Baltimore surely was looking to the future as well, though no evidence survives to give a glimpse of his thoughts or even his whereabouts after the letters from Bristol in November 1643. He was probably at Oxford in January 1644 when Leonard Calvert received his commission. After that, he vanished from history for two years. If he had not already reconsidered his position, the course of events was about to force him to do so.

Sometime before 28 November 1645, a document came before the Committee for Foreign Plantations, headed by the Earl of Warwick, entitled a Petition of Diverse Inhabitants of Maryland. In a serious indictment of Lord Baltimore's government, the petitioners complained of "tyranicall rule" exercised by his officers, all papists, and reported how they tried to convert Protestants away from the Church of England. Citing Calvert's commission from the king and Brent's seizure of the *Reformation* as evidence of the government's hostility to Parliament, along with other outrages, the petitioners asked Parliament to deprive Lord Baltimore of his patent for Maryland and settle the government of the province into the hands of Protestants. Lastly, they asked for immunity from prosecution for all who had taken part in the rebellion, especially Richard Ingle.[3]

There is no indication of who these "diverse inhabitants" were or when the petition was written. All we know is that the committee read it on 28 November. It could have been prepared in Maryland and sent over specifically to ask for recognition of the Protestant government. The date the petition was acted upon bears no significance, for the committee met on an irregular basis and often postponed business for as long as a year. Even if the petition had been presented to the committee in June, when the *Reformation* arrived in London, it would not have been unusual for the committee to wait until November to act upon it. Although we cannot know who wrote the petition, it is potentially significant that the only inhabitant of Maryland called to testify in this matter was James Baldridge, brother of Captain Thomas Baldridge, one of the rebel leaders. Regardless of by whom or when it was written, the petition is another indication that the rebellion was not an outbreak of uncontrolled anarchy but an organized political movement whose goal was to replace the Catholic government with a Protestant one.[4]

The committee recommended that the Earl of Warwick make a report of the Maryland business to the House of Lords. He must have made a convincing case, because the Lords ordered the committee to prepare an ordinance that placed the government under Protestant officers and provided protection for any who "have or shall act" in Parliament's favor. The text of this ordinance echoed that of the petition and ordered that Lord Baltimore's patent be revoked. It required the committee to appoint a Protestant governor and council and authorized these officers to govern the province and to use whatever force necessary to quell any opposition, granting immunity to all who acted under this authority. Here was the legitimacy and protection that the Maryland Protestants had sought for their new government.[5]

The order to draft an Ordinance for Maryland was sent to the committee on 25 December 1645 and was still not finalized by 24 February. That was not fast enough for Richard Ingle, who was facing a losing battle in the courts. He petitioned the Lords for an order to stop all legal proceedings against him until a hearing could be held in the House of Lords. This order was granted and a date of 3 March set to examine witnesses in the case of Cornwaleys *vs.* Ingle. Through all of March and April, Thomas Cornwaleys petitioned Parliament, trying to get this hearing, but other business got in the way. When he secured a date, Ingle failed to appear, and the proceedings had to be postponed. Having gotten a stay of the suits against him, Ingle was in no hurry to have the hearing before the Lords. He was quite willing to wait until the House considered and passed the ordinance, which would grant him immunity. In the course of the year, the hearing of Cornwaleys's case against Ingle saw a dozen postponements, the last in October 1646.[6]

While all this was going on, the Ordinance for Maryland was slowly proceeding. On 28 March 1646, the Earl of Warwick presented a draft to the House of Lords, where it was read twice and then assigned to a committee. The review lasted until 24 November, when the ordinance was read a third time and approved. The Lords recommended that the bill be sent to the House of Commons for enactment. It appeared the Maryland Protestants were going to get their government and Captain Ingle, who had lost his case in the admiralty court and was losing in the common law court, would be permitted to keep his plundered goods.[7]

Just when developments seemed to favor the rebels, Lord Baltimore reappeared. As late as 15 November, Cecil Calvert was at home in Wiltshire, but by 28 November he, or his agent, petitioned the House of Lords to delay sending the ordinance to the House of Commons until he could present a defense. In his petition, Baltimore said he was unfamiliar with the charges against him and needed a written copy to review. He further stated that he would probably need the testimony of witnesses in Maryland, which could not be obtained until the tobacco fleet returned sometime between March and June 1647. In January he further petitioned to use the testimony taken in the admiralty court, and this was granted.[8]

The delay of the ordinance angered a number of individuals. On 8 February, a petition signed by seventeen London merchants trading to the Chesapeake was received by the House of Lords. It repeated the charges against Lord Baltimore and claimed that his request for delay was only a ruse to avoid having to surrender the province. The merchants asked that the ordinance be sent to the House of Commons as approved earlier. The House of Lords took up this issue once more on 4 March 1647, and then nothing more is heard of the Ordinance for Maryland. Richard Ingle would bring up the same charges against Lord Baltimore in 1650 when Parliament was considering the reduction of the Chesapeake plantations, but that was a separate issue. There is no further reference to the ordinance or to a Protestant government for Maryland. With the ordinance died Ingle's chance for immunity.[9]

It is likely that Thomas Cornwaleys had already been given permission to continue his suits against Ingle even before the ordinance was allowed to lapse. On 25 November 1646, Captain Ingle submitted to the court an inventory of goods and debts owed to him in Virginia and Maryland. The list amounted to 30,000–40,000 pounds of tobacco or about £300. Ingle later signed a power of attorney authorizing Cornwaleys to collect any debts owed to him in the Chesapeake. While the £300 was much less than what Cornwaleys claimed to have lost, it is the only part of the settlement that we know about. He undoubtedly recovered at least some of the plundered goods that had been held by the authorities during all of the legal wrangling. He might also have recovered damages from Ingle's estate in England, but there is no record of that. In any case, he probably recovered less than he lost.[10]

The fate of the ordinance remains uncertain. It may be that Lord Baltimore's defense was effective in convincing the House of Lords to table the bill, or the testimony reported from the Admiralty court might have seemed as convincing to the Lords as it was to the judges. It is just as possible that the whole question of Maryland got caught up in the rush of events during 1647 and was defeated by an unusual political alliance between Catholics and Protestant dissenters.

When the war ended with the king's surrender Parliament, and the country as a whole, were bankrupt. It had become increasingly difficult to collect the taxes needed to pay for the war, and with the war's end it became impossible. Taxpayers who had been bled dry by both sides simply had no more to give. Parliament tried to impose a new assessment on the country at a much lower rate in March 1647, yet by December none of the money had been received. This was particularly bad news since Parliament faced massive debts. In addition to all of the bills accumulated for supplies and other expenses, two were in need of immediate attention. In order to get the Scottish army to turn over the king and leave the country, Parliament had promised to pay their expenses, some £400,000. The government made a partial payment and promised the rest when it received more money.[11]

A more immediate and dangerous threat came from Parliament's own armies. The New Model Army had been formed with a guarantee of regular pay for its soldiers. Like every other plan before it, the system broke down and by early 1647 the soldiers and others were owed an incredible £2.8 million. In the past, Parliament had bought off the soldiers it demobilized with several weeks' back pay and promises to pay the rest at an indefinite time after the war was over. This is what it hoped to do with the New Model Army.

But the New Model was undergoing a crisis. When formed, it had been the pride of Parliament. The special treatment they received gave the soldiers a sense of purpose and an identity. Sir Thomas Fairfax's discipline and a string of important victories had provided an esprit de corps not found in any of the other Civil War armies. They had won the war for Parliament and justifiably believed that the civil government, out of simple gratitude, would keep the agreement it had made with them.[12]

After the king surrendered, things rapidly began to change. Far from being England's savior, the army was now regarded as an unnecessary and dangerous burden on a disrupted and over-extended economy, and Parliament threatened to demobilize it without paying back wages. At the same time, with peace restored and the legal system rebuilt, many officers and even common soldiers were being sued for actions taken while in the service of Parliament. The army felt it should be exempt from such prosecution. Finally, many of the soldiers had fought for Parliament because they thought the king was ruling in an arbitrary and despotic fashion. This was particularly true in the area of religion. Charles favored an Episcopal form of church that enforced conformity through heavy fines. Now that he was overthrown, Parliament was threatening to establish a Presbyterian church with the same enforcement powers. The laws against non-conformists had always been applied to Catholics, but they also fell heavily on

Protestant dissenters. These men, called Independents, had fought for Parliament and now felt betrayed.

Through the winter of 1646 discontent bubbled up in the army. Most of the senior officers, including Fairfax and Cromwell, were in London attending Parliament or on personal business and unaware of what was taking place. The first indication of trouble occurred in March at a raucous meeting of the troops. The army presented Parliament with demands for back pay, immunity from prosecution, and for a settlement of the religious question. Parliament made the mistake of ignoring the petition and formed a plan for demobilization. The day before this plan was to go into effect, a mass meeting of the army took place at Newmarket. Fairfax sent an order authorizing it, though historians believe the army had determined to hold the meeting with or without such an order.[13]

At Newmarket, Fairfax argued for a moderate course away from a direct confrontation with the civil government. The army, who still held Sir Thomas in awe, would not embarrass him. On 1 June 1647, it agreed to the Solemn Engagement, promising not to disband until demands for back pay and immunity were met. The question of the religious settlement was put aside for the moment since Fairfax favored the Presbyterian system. A Council of the Army, consisting of an officer and soldier elected from each regiment, was assembled to direct negotiations with Parliament. As an added incentive for Parliament to consider their demands, the army began an ominous march toward London.

As the army was discovering its new power, the Catholic community in England came to understand its own lack of it. Throughout the war, Parliament had been virulently anti-Catholic and Catholics had flocked to the Royalist cause. The phrase "malignants and papists" had become Parliament's description of Royalists. With Parliament now in full control of the country, Catholics, already suffering under heavy fines, feared even worse was in store. They began to look desperately for ways around the coming disaster.[14]

One of the earliest Catholic plans was outlined in a pamphlet entitled *A moderate and safe expedient to remove jealousies and feares of any danger, or prejudice to this state, by the Roman Catholicks of this kingdom,* published by an unknown author sometime in 1646. The writer argued that Parliament's objections to Catholics were political, not religious. Because Catholics could not take the Oath of Allegiance, they were viewed as spies and potential enemies to the civil government. Moreover, the system of fines and sequestrations was not converting Catholics but only making them poorer, resentful, and more dangerous. It would be better to allow them to freely move their estates to one of the colonies where they could become productive citizens and not be a threat to the government. Maryland was mentioned as the best place to settle Catholics because it already allowed them to practice their religion and was sandwiched between Virginia and New England, two larger and solidly Protestant colonies. The writer encouraged Parliament to aid Catholics in emigrating to Maryland.[15]

Had these recommendations been followed, Maryland would have become the Catholic refuge that George Calvert had envisioned. There is no evidence to connect Lord Baltimore with the pamphlet, but obviously he would be the major beneficiary were it followed. Were Maryland to become a Catholic refuge, certainly the rights of Lord Baltimore would have to be respected. When the pamphlet was published, however, Maryland was in the hands of the Protestants, most of her Catholic settlers were in exile, and Parliament was considering recognition of the Protestant government. There is no indication that the proposal outlined in this pamphlet was ever seriously considered, and possibly it was simply part of the overall campaign to defeat the Ordinance for Maryland. It is important to remember that the pamphlet argued for assisted but voluntary emigration, because another, more insidious proposal was being developed.

A group of English secular priests, headed by Father Thomas White, known to history as Blacklow, apparently prepared a petition to Parliament that sought toleration for Catholics under specific conditions. Catholics would take an oath recognizing their allegiance to the civil government and denying the pope's authority in temporal matters. Jesuits and other regular orders would be expelled from England, and a bishop would be appointed, with the approval of Parliament, to oversee the secular priests. Those who subscribed to the oath would have all fines and sequestrations lifted from them. The petitioners knew the proposal would not sit well with some of their community, so they suggested that any Catholic who would not take the oath be transported to Maryland. Although this petition is of uncertain date, it was already common knowledge early in 1647. The Jesuit general wrote a letter on 11 May 1647 condemning the proposal but urging discretion.[16]

Once again, while Maryland figured prominently in this project, Lord Baltimore's association is unknown. His distrust of the Jesuits and his employment of secular priests suggest that he favored at least some parts of the proposal, but a number of other things point to a close relationship between Lord Baltimore and the secular priests at this time as well.

The first of these was the college to which Philip Calvert was sent for his education. George Calvert, their father, had made Cecil Calvert responsible for the education of his youngest brother. For any Catholic this involved difficult decisions since English colleges were closed to them. A number of English Catholic colleges had grown up on the Continent to meet this need, but it was illegal to send English boys to them. Despite that restriction, it was common practice for English Catholics to send their sons or wards to those institutions. Lord Baltimore had at least six to choose from when contemplating his decision. He chose the English College at Lisbon for Philip Calvert.[17]

The English College at Lisbon was the most recent of the Continental establishments, having been founded only in 1628. It was, from its inception, different from the others in that by its constitution it was to have no Jesuits involved as teachers or confessors. The college was staffed entirely by the secular clergy of England. When the first president died within a year of its founding, Father Thomas White was appointed to replace him. He served in this position from 1628 to 1632 and wrote the constitution by which the college was organized. Even after he left, the college maintained many of his opinions and was seen to have a distinctly "political" atmosphere.[18]

The lack of Jesuit participation had a serious effect on the college.

Although the quality of education was comparable that of Jesuit institutions, the Lisbon College could not command the resources that the Jesuits did. Consequently, it was always in financial difficulties and life at the college was frugal. Meat for supper was "a luxury and an event." Never, one scholar has written, "were students better hardened for the rigors of the English mission."[19]

The choice of the English College at Lisbon for the education of his brother reflected Lord Baltimore's religious associations at the time. He was in the middle of his argument with the Jesuits and seeking members of the secular clergy for Maryland. The surest way to keep Philip from Jesuit influence was to send him to Lisbon.

Though Lord Baltimore clearly favored the secular priests over the Jesuits, that is not enough to associate him with the Blacklow faction of that body. However, there is evidence of an even closer relationship. In 1642, when Lord Baltimore was looking around for priests to send to Maryland, he had prepared a list of ten suitable candidates. It is indeed suggestive that out of several hundred secular clergy, all three of the leaders of the Blacklow faction were on the list. The opinions of Fathers White, Holden, and Fitton, are well-known. It is uncertain if the others on the list shared the same opinions. Nevertheless, the inclusion of these three argues for a close association between Lord Baltimore and the Blacklowists. Another possible indication of a continuing association is Lord Baltimore's appointment, in 1664, of Jerome White, nephew of Blacklow, to be Surveyor General of Maryland.[20]

Even more important than these connections was the similarity in outlook between Lord Baltimore and the Blacklow faction. Father Thomas White, leader of this group, believed that the Catholic Church was mired in too many medieval traditions and favored changes that would modernize it. One tradition he challenged was the position of the pope as head of the church. White favored a strong national church, with its own bishop, tied to Rome but not under its control. That idea was echoed in Lord Baltimore's 1642 letter to Leonard Calvert wherein he reported the actions of a number of Italian nobles against the pope. Baltimore made the point that one can be a Catholic but still quarrel with Rome. That line of thought ran through all of his arguments on church property and on faculties for the secular priests he sent to Maryland. Baltimore's contention that the idea of mortmain for church property was a medieval concept out of place in his day would have been applauded by the Blacklowists.[21]

Another similarity between the two was the Blacklowists' recognition of a minority status for English Catholics. The Jesuits and other regular orders still looked for a restoration of the Catholic Church to all of its privileges in England. Father White and his associates concluded that such a restoration was impossible and that the only chance for the Catholics was to urge religious toleration for all sects. From the beginning, this had been Lord Baltimore's vision for Maryland. Certainly there is enough evidence of a connection to suspect Baltimore's involvement with the Blacklowists' proposal.

Regardless of Baltimore's involvement in either of these schemes, both attempts to settle Catholics in Maryland were swept aside by the abrupt shift in power from Parliament to the army in the summer of 1647. The Council of the Army became increasingly frustrated with Parliament's lack of action and with its continuing attempt to establish conformity in religion. Many of the soldiers had already concluded that the only solution to the religious question was the recognition of toleration for all sects, including Catholics. But Catholics were still viewed as potential enemies obedient to a foreign despot, the pope. Early in the summer of 1647, negotiations began between members of the Catholic community and the army to find a way for Catholics to swear allegiance to the government but remain spiritually faithful to their religion. The negotiations went so well that by July, Cromwell and Fairfax could tell the French ambassador that toleration for Catholics would soon be proclaimed.[22]

In preparation for this event, the army outlined six conditions for granting toleration to Catholics. Of these, five could easily be agreed upon. Catholics could not bear arms, hold public office, or negotiate with a foreign state. Catholic worship had to be performed privately in homes and not in churches, and toleration was to apply only to native-born Catholics. These five conditions posed no problem for the Catholic community, who already obeyed them anyway.[23]

It was the last condition that gave some Catholics pause. The army required that Catholics agree to three statements, later termed the Three Propositions. The first denied the pope's authority to absolve Catholics of allegiance to the civil government. The second stated that the pope could not lawfully order Catholics to kill or injure a person because he was considered a heretic. The third proposition held that the pope could not allow Catholics to lawfully break an oath made to a heretic. These propositions had deep roots in the controversy between Rome and the English government. At different times through the sixteenth century, Rome had advised English Catholics that they need not be loyal to the government and that to assassinate a heretical leader was a good deed. The Jesuits had become famous for taking oaths with "mental reservations," and the third proposition denied the validity of that procedure. The propositions amounted to a denial of papal authority and would be later condemned by the Holy Office, but to English Catholics, they seemed a small price to pay for the granting of toleration.[24]

The prospect of religious liberty was enough to temporarily unite all factions of the English Catholic community. The clergy made their assent to the propositions conditional on the granting of religious toleration. They believed that, given freedom of worship for English Catholics, the pope would not interfere with temporal matters anyway. A statement signed by nine priests was issued in support of this proposal. The signers were the superiors, resident in England, of the various groups of clergy and included the main body of the secular clergy, the Jesuits, the Dominicans, the Carmelites and the Franciscans. A representative of the Benedictines also signed the statement. At the same time, a group of lay Catholics consisting of six lords and twenty-seven gentry issued their own statement accepting the army's conditions without qualification.[25]

As with the other schemes, Lord Baltimore's name is absent from the list of subscribers. Nevertheless, he would certainly have gained much by the acceptance of this proposal. While the effort would not result in a mass migration of Catholics to Maryland, the extension of religious toleration to Catholics would make Baltimore secure in his proprietorship in a way that could never have been accomplished before. The most important aspect of this affair is not the proposal itself but the remarkable convergence of Catholic and Independent thought in the last half of 1647. Attempts to find a compromise would continue through 1649 and may have had an effect on Baltimore's Act Concerning Religion, which was proposed in Maryland in April 1649. The close contact between Catholics and Independents in England may have influenced Lord Baltimore to extend an invitation to the Virginia Independents, which led to their immigration and settlement in 1649.

Unfortunately, all attempts to win toleration for Catholics were doomed to failure by the unstable political situation in postwar England. Part of the reason why Catholics might have been included under any toleration law was the army's need for support against Parliament. To get that support, army leaders courted the king and his supporters, including Catholics, in an effort to outmaneuver the Presbyterian-controlled House of Commons. When the Army Council, especially Cromwell, discovered that Charles I had been playing both sides against one another, it fixed the king's fate and that of the Catholics with him. Neither the petition containing the Three Propositions nor the one proposing to transport Catholics to Maryland was ever presented to Parliament. When the House of Commons took up the question of a religious settlement in October, the bill called for an established, Presbyterian Church but provided toleration for all Protestant sects. Catholics were specifically excluded from this toleration.[26]

Although this constituted a serious defeat for every Catholic faction, all hope was not lost. So long as the political situation remained uncertain and the army was not demobilized, there would still be opportunities to reopen negotiations. Nevertheless, religious toleration for Catholics in England would remain unreachable for the foreseeable future. There would be no mass migration, voluntary or involuntary, of Catholics to Maryland as a result of these actions. But conditions in Maryland had already changed, and Lord Baltimore's fortunes were on the rise once again.

CHAPTER SIXTEEN

"The said Mrs. Brent protesteth against all proceedings . . ."

In late 1646, as Governor Calvert's plans for retaking St. Mary's were nearing completion, someone else was readying an expedition to the northern part of the bay. News of Calvert's preparations must have been widespread in Virginia, and William Claiborne was not about to let Calvert snatch Kent Island from him again. Around the same time that Calvert was sailing for St. Mary's, Claiborne and his cousin, Richard Thompson, had turned their ships northward for Kent. They stopped for a time at Chicacoan, where Claiborne found willing volunteers, and when he left for Kent his force had grown by twenty more men.[1]

Claiborne arrived on Kent Island sometime after Christmas. He assumed command of the Kent Fort garrison from Peter Knight, who had been holding the island for him, and announced that he had a commission from the governor of Virginia to seize what had been his estate on the island. He left the impression that the document gave him much broader powers as well. After the news of Calvert's return to St. Mary's reached the island in January, Claiborne mustered the inhabitants in Kent Field and harangued them on Lord Baltimore's tyranny. He proposed to lead them on a "warlike" expedition to take the fort at St. Mary's and to seize the person of the governor. As always, Claiborne was a persuasive speaker, and the Kent Islanders were, in the heat of the moment, ready to follow their old commander along whatever course he chose to lead them. Provisions and supplies to support the venture were gathered and loaded on the ships in the expectation of a timely departure.

His eloquent and effective exhortations notwithstanding, it is clear that many of the islanders did not trust Claiborne. As with his earlier attempt to raise the island in rebellion, after the initial excitement died down questions about his authority arose. Some of the men asked to see his commission. Claiborne refused to show it, which convinced many that he was acting on his own, without the backing of the Virginia government. This made the venture much more risky, and they began to draw back from it.

When they discovered that he did not plan to actually lead them to St. Mary's, the plan fell apart altogether. In an effort to salvage the momentum, Claiborne suggested that he could deliver them to Point Lookout and then seek additional help from Chicacoan. This plan failed to win them over, and the islanders dispersed. Some of Claiborne's reluctance to get deeply involved in this enterprise probably stemmed from the Virginia council's order that he not interfere with the government of the island. Technically, he should not even have been on Kent Island. Within a day of the dispersal, with no other option, Claiborne sailed to Virginia. The best hope of Claiborne and the rebels at Chicacoan had come to naught. Without the expected help from Kent Island, the rebels in Virginia did not have the strength to reverse the gains that Calvert had made.

Governor Calvert probably had little direct knowledge of the events on Kent Island, but the sudden lack of activity by the rebels at Chicacoan may have given him a sign. He continued to prepare his invasion force and to bring order back to St. Mary's County. There is little to document conditions in the county at this time, but two reports give some idea. On 19 January 1647, Calvert authorized Lieutenant William Lewis to search and inventory the Jesuit property at St. Inigoes. The house was occupied by Mrs. Baldridge, wife of one of the rebels, and Calvert wanted to determine what goods in the house still belonged to the Jesuits. The inventory Lewis filed was brief and unimpressive. It included some copper and brass utensils, a few pewter vessels, miscellaneous furniture, and other minor household items. Only the smith's shop seemed to be fairly intact.[2]

The significance of the inventory is clear when considering what the Jesuits had lost, not what was left. In their case against Ingle, the Jesuits claimed £200 of household items, including linen, brass, iron, pewter and silver. The quantity and quality of these goods show that the Jesuits lived as opulently as any of the gentlemen in Maryland. Not all of these items would have been at St. Inigoes before the plundering. Father Copley reported that the goods were sufficient to stock two large houses. As St. Inigoes house was the mission's headquarters, it must have contained the greater portion of these goods. The paltry inventory filed by Lieutenant Lewis cannot have equaled even a tenth of what had once been there and reflects the magnitude of the loss suffered by the Catholic gentry.

Depopulation and displacement as consequences of the rebellion can also be seen in the fragmentary record. On 21 January, Governor Calvert sent a warrant to Lieutenant Lewis to warn the inhabitants of St. Clements Hundred to pay their rent to Lord Baltimore at the fort before 4 February. On the twenty-ninth, Lewis returned a list of ten names from St. Clements, fewer than half the number listed in July 1642. More significantly, only five names appear on both lists. In less than five years, three-quarters of the settlers of this hundred had died or fled. Five other names were on the list, all of whom had been settled somewhere else in St. Mary's County in 1642. At least three of the five claimed land rights for having come back to Maryland in 1646, perhaps with Governor Calvert. Although we have no specific evidence for the other hundreds in the county, St. Clements Hundred was probably typical of the county as a whole. Russell Menard has suggested that the population of St. Mary's County fell to about one hundred in 1645–46, a large drop by any standard, leaving fewer than the original number of settlers.[3]

Maryland may have suffered a "death crisis" during Ingle's rebellion, but under the watchful eye of Leonard Calvert, the patient showed remarkable powers of recuperation. Assuming Menard's figure of one hundred inhabitants to be a correct estimate for the beginning of 1647, by the end of the year that number had doubled. The list of headrights claimed for 1646 and 1647 included at least twenty-four individuals who had been settled in Maryland before the rebellion and seventy-three who appear to have been new immigrants. In addition, a number of planters returned to their homes without claiming new headrights. In 1648, ninety-five new claims were filed with the province. Within a short time after the reestablishment of a settled government at St. Mary's, the province was repopulated as old settlers returned and new ones immigrated.[4]

By February 1647 this process was well underway, but the outcome was far from certain. Despite Claiborne's failure to convince the Kent Islanders to assault St. Mary's, the rebel party was still strong and defiant. Perhaps recognizing that no help was forthcoming from Virginia and nervous over Calvert's none too secret plans, the rebels sent a letter to the governor at St. Mary's seeking peace. Calvert's reply contained the same policy of reconciliation that he had proposed earlier:

> Though your paper sent by Mr. Knight contain many things in it of that fowle nature as deserve to be answered rather by the Sword than by the pen of the magistrate, Yet Soe great is our inclination to See an end to these troubles Soe unfortunately begun amongst us and all things reduced into their Old State again, of peace and quiett, that passing by all the rest of your paper, We give this Answer in brief, to that part of it, which prays for peace, that when you Shall Send this Gentleman or any other agent from you with Sufficient authority under the hands of the greatest part of the Island to treat and conclude fully with us, all things Shall come in question on either part, You Shall find this government ready to Condescend, to giving of all Satisfaction to your demands of quiett and peace as may be reasonable.[5]

Governor Calvert hired Nathaniel Pope to carry this message to Kent Island. The selection of Pope was in keeping with Calvert's desire to integrate former enemies back into the fabric of government, and Pope would certainly have been trusted by the rebels on Kent, but he was an unfortunate choice nonetheless. Pope arrived on the island about 9 March, and what he did there became the subject of two separate investigations. In September 1647, Thomas Bradnox and Edward Commins testified that instead of encouraging the island's inhabitants to submit to Lord Baltimore, Pope suggested they abandon the settlement for Virginia until they could raise a force large enough to seize the whole country. According to Commins, Pope accused the governor of making large promises but never keeping them, adding that if they did not stand together they would all be betrayed. Despite these sworn oaths, the court found little substance in the allegations and reported that Governor Calvert had reached the same conclusion. Whatever the real truth concerning Pope's activities on Kent Island, his mission to extend the olive branch failed. Soon after his arrival, a party of rebels twice assaulted the home of Robert Vaughan, a staunch supporter of Lord Baltimore. The first time they were repulsed, but after killing two of Vaughan's servants, they took the house and made Vaughan a prisoner. He was held at the house of Thomas Bradnox for three weeks.[6]

News of Governor Calvert's expedition to Kent reached the island in late March. Believing he could not hold off the invasion, Peter Knight, captain of the rebels, began making preparations to abandon the island. He had his men kill and butcher a number of cattle, and he looted Brent's house of anything that was left, including the locks on the doors. Finally, they took all of the iron work from the mill at Kent. With this plunder loaded aboard ship, Knight and his company hastily set sail for Virginia.[7]

The arrival of Calvert and his company in April 1647 brought the island back under the Maryland government. There is little to indicate how many men Calvert had with him or what they did when they reached the island. The first evidence of Calvert's arrival is a list of fourteen men who swore the oath of fealty to Lord Baltimore. Eleven of them had been pardoned that same day for crimes of rebellion. Robert Vaughan, Francis Brookes, and Walter King also swore the oath but were not included in the pardon. These three had remained loyal to Lord Baltimore through this difficult time and at least the first two were well rewarded for it later.[8]

There is no way to know if this list encompasses the entire free male population of Kent early in 1647. A pamphlet published in England in 1648 claims that there were fewer than twenty men on the island after the rebellion, which seems to agree with the list of those who swore the oath of fealty. If that is true, we have another example of the cost of the rebellion to Maryland. Of the fourteen names on the list, only five had been free residents in 1642. One other immigrated to the island in 1643. At best then, only six of the individuals who took the oath in 1647 had been freemen before the rebellion. Seventy-three freemen were listed as living on the island in 1642, suggesting a persistence rate of only 8 percent, a figure even lower than that for St. Clements Hundred. Some may not have taken the oath, but Calvert was unlikely to have left any large body of rebels unaccounted for. The composition of the list is significant in that it includes names of some of the leaders of the rebellion but also lists several of Lord Baltimore's supporters. If both groups took the oath, what reason would their followers have for not doing so? It is possible that by the time Calvert came to Kent Island, it was virtually abandoned.[9]

Looking to the future, Calvert set about establishing a government and bringing the population, rebel and loyalist alike, under its control. One of his first acts was to appoint Robert Vaughan as commander of Kent. This gave Vaughan broad powers to do whatever was necessary to defend the island against invasion or mutiny. The same document created commissioners to help him dispense justice—William Cox, Thomas Bradnox, Edward Cummins, Philip Conner, and Francis Brooks. The commission, including Robert Vaughan, was made up of two loyal supporters of Lord Baltimore, two former rebel leaders, and two men who seem not to have been attached to either party. It is likely that Calvert was trying to balance the scales of justice in this fragile political situation. The governor's final act was to seize the estates of rebels who had fled the island, a measure actually less vindictive than an attempt to force compliance to the government. The seized assets were to be accounted for and held only until their owners submitted to the government at St. Mary's. Having now brought the rebellion to an end, Governor Calvert sailed for St. Mary's.[10]

In the space of four months, Leonard Calvert had rebuilt Maryland from its broken pieces. His Lordship's authority was once again recognized throughout the province, even on Kent Island. The population began to recover as old planters returned and new ones immigrated. The economy improved as planting and trade were both restarted. His was a major accomplishment given the violence and passions unleashed by the

Plundering Time, and Leonard Calvert deserves full credit for it. His planning and resourcefulness had organized the invasion, and his political understanding had peacefully brought the rebels back to the government. No other figure combined the authority, leadership, and perseverance necessary to succeed in these circumstances. Calvert had been appointed governor in the 1630s; by mid-1647 he had earned the position.

Having brought Maryland back from the brink and set her on the course to recovery, Leonard Calvert now approached his own end. How or when he became ill, and the illness he contracted, are mysteries. He apparently felt well on his return from Kent in April. On 13 May and 1 June, he held sessions of the provincial court. Sometime after the latter court he was taken sick and never recovered. By 9 June the end was clearly in sight. Calvert lay in his bed at the Governor's House in St. Mary's, surrounded by some of his friends and servants, including Margaret and Mary Brent, Thomas Greene, Mary Bean, James Lindsey, and Francis Anthill.[11]

In later testimony, Calvert was described as being of "perfect memory." He began to order his affairs and those of the province. In front of the assembled witnesses he appointed Thomas Greene to be governor and Margaret Brent to administer his personal estate. Perhaps recognizing that his personal estate and the welfare of the province were intertwined, he told Margaret Brent, "I make you my sole Exequutrix. Take all & pay all." Following these announcements, he asked to be left alone with Margaret Brent. They talked privately for some time, then the rest of the witnesses were called back into the room, and Calvert made several bequests. He gave his servants, James Lindsey and Richard Willan, a suit of clothes each and told them to divide his linen between them. To his godson, Leonard Greene, he gave a mare colt. Finally, to Mrs. Temperance Pippett of Virginia, he also gave a mare colt. Within six hours, after a strenuous life, Leonard Calvert died.[12]

Although we can never ascertain the nature of Calvert's illness, some tantalizing evidence supports speculation. The account of Calvert's estate included a charge of 1,250 pounds of tobacco paid to Dr. Waldron of Virginia. The fee paid to Dr. Waldron is significant, because only a few months earlier Calvert had contracted with Henry Hooper, a chirugeon, to serve him for one year in exchange for food, lodging, and one-third of Hooper's profits. In the seventeenth century, there was an important distinction between doctors and chirugeons. The latter performed minor operations and blood-letting, the former treated patients with medicines and potions. The call for a doctor suggests that Calvert was seriously ill.[13]

Another significant expense was for a substance called mithridate, a medical compound made up of sixty-four different ingredients. It could be taken internally or, mixed with honey, could be used as a salve. Legend held that it had been discovered by King Mithridates of Pontus in the first century B.C.E., who supposedly wanted to find a universal antidote for venoms and poisons. To test potions, he poisoned condemned criminals and tried to cure them. The recipe was repeated in many classical medical texts and was a major export of Venice. In sixteenth-century England, mithridate was the accepted antidote to venomous bites and intentional poisonings. By the seventeenth century, as the threat of intentional poisonings decreased, mithridate began to acquire a reputation as a cure for the plague. Eventually, mithridate would lose its specific association with poison and become a drug thought to be useful for many illnesses.[14]

The use of mithridate to treat Calvert's illness is suggestive, for it had very specific uses in the seventeenth century. Of these, two can be eliminated by historical circumstances. If Calvert's friends thought he had been poisoned, some investigation or prosecution would certainly appear in the records. The use of mithridate for treating the plague was new in the seventeenth century but Dr. Waldron could have known of this use. However, the plague seldom strikes only one person and there is no sign that anyone else in Calvert's immediate circle was sick.

A likely explanation for the mithridate would be to treat venomous snake bites. This is still a danger in Maryland and can only have been more common in the seventeenth century. A snakebite could represent an illness whose onset was sudden, which could kill the patient in a short time, and yet still leave the afflicted person of "perfect memory" up to the time of his death. Snakebite is not often fatal to a healthy adult, but its effects could have been made much worse by blood-letting and other medical treatments. The evidence that Leonard Calvert died of a snakebite is suggestive but cannot be proved.

Leonard Calvert was buried between 10 and 15 June 1647. Margaret Brent, his executrix, probably made the arrangements. As befitting his position as the first governor of Maryland, Calvert had the most elaborate funeral recorded in the early records. His account listed almost 1,700 pounds of tobacco spent on the ceremony, roughly £14, or about seven times more expensive than the average. Jerome Hawley, one of Lord Baltimore's original commissioners of Maryland and later treasurer of Virginia, had funeral expenses of only 640 pounds of tobacco. It is clear that Calvert's was the most impressive Maryland funeral of the decade and for many years to come.[15]

The account is not sufficiently detailed to provide a description of the elaborate ritual but there is enough information to catch a glimpse of it. To begin with, there is no separate listing for a shroud or coffin but it in inconceivable that Calvert would not have had both, given the amount of money spent on the funeral. The expense for these items may have been included with one of the other bills.

The first listed expense was for a hearse cloth or pall to cover the coffin. This was a large piece of black cloth, often edged with white, that was draped over the coffin and, in elaborate burials, often bore the arms of the family. In early seventeenth-century England, an average hearse cloth would cost about 10 shillings while an elaborate one could cost 30–50 shillings. Calvert's estate paid 437 pounds of tobacco for the hearse cloth or about 43 shillings. Even with freight charges included, this was an expensive piece of cloth. The mention of a hearse cloth in Calvert's account is the only such reference to this item in pre-1658 accounts.[16]

Another item related to the funeral was the purchase of wax lights or candles. The burning of candles at seventeenth-century Catholic funerals was considered to be a votive offering in favor of the soul of the deceased and was quite common. Margaret Brent paid 110 pounds of tobacco to Thomas Matthews for a combination of mithridate and wax lights. If we could separate the cost of the two materials, we could estimate how many candles were used at the funeral. There is no contemporary reference to the cost of mithridate in early Maryland, but a doctor's inventory from 1686 listed three pounds of mithridate valued at £1, the equivalent of 80 pence per pound. If the price was the same in the early seventeenth century, then half a pound would have cost 40 pence or twenty pounds of tobacco. Such a quantity would leave ninety pounds for wax lights. A 1639 inventory listed candles at thirty pounds of tobacco per dozen. The remainder of Calvert's account would then be for thirty-six candles, used either at the wake or the funeral itself.[17]

These items were all part of the kind of funeral Calvert could have expected in England. Margaret Brent tried to ensure a traditional Catholic funeral for her friend, but there were some essential things missing from the ceremony that were beyond her control. First, there is no evidence of a Catholic priest in Maryland to oversee the burial. All of the Jesuits and secular priests had been scattered or had died during the rebellion. Father Copley would not return to Maryland until the next year. In addition to the lack of a priest, there may not have been a church in which to hold the funeral. The chapel at St. Mary's had been plundered during the rebellion and may have been burned down. The lack of such services and facilities must have made Calvert's burial even more poignant for his mourners.

The funeral feast to dispel some of the gloom was an important part of traditional ceremonies. In England it often represented half to three quarters of the total funeral expenses. In Calvert's account, the cost of a "Beefe, a veale & other necessaries for his Buriall" was 1,200 pounds of tobacco or about 70 percent of the identifiable burial expenses. This celebration may have temporarily helped to lift the spirits of the mourners, but when the funeral feast was over Calvert's friends still had to face the difficult task of holding Maryland together without his leadership.[18]

This effort began with Thomas Greene and Margaret Brent seeking legal confirmation of the positions assigned to them by Leonard Calvert. We must look at Calvert's chosen successors and wonder why he selected them. The choice of Thomas Greene as governor was and is surprising. Although Greene had come to Maryland with the original settlers, his appointment to the council had been relatively recent, dating only to 1644. Calvert had not shown any particular favor to Greene before this time, nor had he appointed him to any significant office. Others who had held important posts in the government, like Giles Brent, were in the colony and could have served. Calvert's selection of Greene to succeed him was therefore unusual. The two men seem to have shared a strong friendship that grew deeper during the troubled times. Greene's son, who had been born the year before, was named Leonard, probably in honor of Calvert, who was his godfather. Calvert's regard for the boy is shown by the fact that the younger Greene received one of only three individual bequests from Calvert's estate. Greene had been at Calvert's side since the governor's return to Maryland. He was one of three councilors to attend the Assembly of 1647 and the only one to join Calvert on the court bench that year. He was someone that Leonard Calvert had learned to trust.[19]

If the choice of Thomas Greene was a surprise, the selection of Margaret Brent to handle Calvert's estate was a shock. Normally, a man would call upon one or more of his male friends to be his administrator and look after his wife and children. Occasionally, a wife would be granted the administration of her husband's estate. But to ask an unmarried, and possibly unrelated, woman to be an administrator was unheard of before this case. This step is so unusual that we must ask why Calvert chose her.

The traditional explanation is that Calvert and Brent were related through Calvert's marriage to Ann Brent, sister of Margaret, which supposedly took place while Calvert was in England. That connection may or may not have existed. Even if it were true, why Margaret and not Giles Brent, who would have been related to Calvert, too, and a far less unusual choice? However, the argument of a relationship is irrelevant to this case. Margaret Brent had already proven herself a capable administrator of her own and her brothers' estates. When Giles was in trouble with the government in 1642 and in danger of losing everything, he deeded Margaret all of his lands and goods. She continued to administer them through this period, even though Brent was in the province, and regularly appeared in court as her own and her brothers' attorney.[20] In their letter to Lord Baltimore, the Assembly of 1649 clearly explained why Calvert chose her to administer his estate and, by extension, that of Lord Baltimore. The explanation makes sense in the context of the time and there is no reason to doubt its validity:

> we do verily believe and in Conscience report that it was better for the Collonys' safety at that time in her hands then in any mans else in the whole Province after your Brother's death for the Soldiers would never have treated any other with that Civility and respect and though they were even ready at several times to run into mutiny yet she still pacified them.[21]

Calvert knew how great a debt was owed to the soldiers and that the date for payment of their salary was rapidly approaching. His plan for paying the debt was the custom duty on exported tobacco. To benefit from this duty, he had to wait until the first full crop was harvested late in 1647. Until then, he made whatever arrangements were necessary to keep the soldiers supplied and quiet. When he became aware that he was dying, he probably realized that the whole plan could come apart without his guidance. He needed someone to manage this delicate period. A number of men in the province had the experience necessary and under normal circumstances could have managed it quite well, but these were not normal circumstances and someone different was needed.

In choosing Margaret Brent, Calvert was relying on what one historian, referring to the female defenders of such Royalist strongholds as Lathom House and Corfe Castle, called "the pre-war standards of courtesy and respect towards a great lady." Many men in Maryland could have handled the financial aspects, but none could command the respect due to Margaret Brent. That is what Calvert counted on and what the Assembly repeated to Lord Baltimore. Over the next few months, that respect would be tested. As he lay dying, Leonard Calvert knew as much and hoped to provide the time needed for the tobacco custom to become due.[22]

Mrs. Brent's first step was to secure letters of administration for the estate. These were granted to her on 19 June, and on 30 June the estate was appraised by Captain Price, Mr. Nicholas Causin, and Mr. Robert Percy. A number of additions were made to this inventory on 11 March

1648. In the end, the personal estate was appraised at 24,504 pounds of tobacco or approximately £204. Not included in the estate were three books of accounts and bills due to Calvert.[23]

Looking at the inventory recorded in the summer of 1647, one is struck by its spartan nature. Of the total, 11,000 pounds of tobacco represents land and houses, and another 8,400 pounds of tobacco was in horses. When these are subtracted, Calvert had goods valued at only 5,104 pounds of tobacco or a little more than £42. The estate listed but four pieces of silver, the most valuable of which was later subtracted as belonging to someone else. Calvert's household contained few luxuries.

The significance of this inventory is not what it contains but what is missing. No cattle or hogs are listed, although it is hard to overestimate the importance of livestock to early Marylanders. This omission is obvious if we compare Calvert's inventory to two contemporary estates. Robert Tutty's inventory, appraised on 24 June 1647, lists four cattle and fifteen hogs for a combined 1,650 pounds of tobacco. The entire estate was only valued at 4,830 pounds. Almost a year later, Peter Macrill's inventory listed eight cattle and fourteen pigs for a total of 3,650 pounds out of an estate of 4,780 pounds. Both men left estates that placed them in the poorer half of the population, yet each owned cattle and hogs. Calvert should have had livestock comparable to what his peers claimed to have lost during the rebellion. Thomas Cornwaleys reportedly lost 120 head of cattle and a hundred hogs during the troubles. Giles Brent claimed to have lost a hundred head of cattle and a hundred hogs. Governor Calvert had been back in Maryland for more than six months without attempting to find or repossess any cattle. During the same time, he had issued a warrant to Francis Brooks to collect Lord Baltimore's cattle on Kent Island. Perhaps the governor had no cattle of his own at the time of the rebellion.[24]

Other significant omissions from the inventory include bound labor, agricultural tools, or any indication of a tobacco crop. His inventory shows two large houses, a well-developed plantation at St. Mary's, and three manors in St. Michaels Hundred. There is no indication of a work force. The inventory lists three beds belonging to Calvert, presumably his bed and those used by his hired servants, James Lindsey and Richard Willan.

These men, who were with him in his last hours were probably personal servants. There seems to have been no provision for field hands at either St. Mary's or Piney Neck plantations.

The lack of cattle, hogs, bound labor, and tobacco in Calvert's inventory probably resulted from several causes. The first, we must assume, was the plundering associated with the recent rebellion. Calvert was Ingle's target, and whatever estate the governor had in the province would certainly have been confiscated. However, at the time of the rebellion, Leonard Calvert had only recently returned to Maryland. Before he left in 1643, he tried to liquidate his holdings. Since he had only been back for five months before Ingle came, it is likely that he did not reacquire much of the estate that had previously been his. It is important to note that there is no record of any attempt by Leonard Calvert, Margaret Brent, his executrix, or Lord Baltimore to sue Ingle or any of the rebels for losses to his estate.

A little more than a year later, on 6 July 1648, Margaret Brent filed an account for the estate along with a revised and perfected inventory. The difference between this inventory and the previous one was the inclusion of debts owed to Calvert. The new inventory and the account give us a much better picture of the extent of Leonard Calvert's estate. Its total value was 56,232 pounds of tobacco or a little more than £468, placing Calvert in the richest 10 percent of Maryland estates through much of the seventeenth century. He had modest investments in land, horses, and personal goods, but most of his assets were in debts owed by others (Table 4). The largest, owed by Lord Baltimore and amounting to 18,548 pounds of tobacco, represented over half of the total debts owed to the estate and probably reflects the cost of regaining the province. Other major debts included 5,061 pounds due from Captain Henry Fleet, a 2,800-pound judgment against Captain Cornwaleys, and 2,000 pounds due from William Smoote for a pinnace he bought from Calvert before his death.[25]

On the other side of the ledger, Margaret Brent paid out 23,350 pounds in expenses. Once again, the largest amount was related to the cost of regaining the province. In the year after Calvert's death, Brent paid out 9,522 pounds of tobacco to the soldiers at St. Inigoes Fort. The soldiers' pay would become a major point of dispute between Lord Baltimore

TABLE 4: SUMMARY OF GOVERNOR CALVERT'S INVENTORY

DESCRIPTION	TOBACCO (LBS.)	PERCENT
Personal Goods	3,124	5.6
Horses	8,400	14.9
Land & Housing	11,000	19.5
Debts Due	33,708	60.0
Total	56,232	100.0

Source: Archives of Maryland, 4:388–89.

and his colonists. Even at this time, we can see the use of Calvert's estate to defray the cost of the garrison.

After the payment to the soldiers, the largest amount paid was by Margaret Brent to herself as administrator of the estate. The laws of the province allowed the administrator to keep a certain percentage of the total money collected and expended as compensation. Brent retained 5,432 pounds for receiving and laying out a total of 27,160 pounds of tobacco. Her compensation represented 20 percent of the total and is unprecedented in Maryland history. Several times the early Assemblies dealt with this issue and each time set the maximum compensation at 10 percent of the total. Several contemporary accounts do not list any compensation at all, while the account of Thomas Weston's estate, filed about a month after Calvert's, listed the administrator's salary as 10 percent of the total. Since Brent's salary was recorded and accepted by the governor, we must assume that it was a legal charge to the estate. Why she was allowed 20 percent when the law specifically limited administrators to 10 percent, is a question that cannot be answered. Perhaps this arrangement was part of the private conversation between Brent and Calvert before he died.[26]

At the same time that Margaret Brent was organizing Calvert's personal affairs, Thomas Greene was taking steps to secure the government of Maryland. The day after Leonard Calvert died, Margaret Brent and the other witnesses testified before the council concerning Greene's appointment as governor. He was then officially proclaimed governor by virtue of Lord Baltimore's commission to Leonard Calvert in 1644. The proclamation carefully pointed out that Greene was a member of the council and fulfilled the requirements of the commission. The need for quick action on Greene's part is obvious. The province had but recently been in open rebellion, and the only man with the authority and ability to keep the peace was now dead. There was a very real danger of new troubles.[27]

As word of Calvert's death spread, the worst fears of the council were realized. Much of the discontent evident earlier in the spring began to resurface. Walter Broadhurst was accused of saying that there was now "noe Governor in Mary-Land for Capt. Hill was Governor & only him he acknowledgeth." Others began to threaten violence against the government. James Johnson said that all that came up in the Governor's Company were rogues and that he hoped soon to see a confusion of all papistry in Maryland. He threatened to shoot Captain Price and said "he cared noe more for the Governor (meaning Mr. Greene) than he did for any of the rest . . . he wished Captain Hill would come and resume the government." Johnson was fined two thousand pounds of tobacco and sentenced to be given thirty lashes for his outburst. He was probably not the only one thinking in these terms.[28]

At what seemed the worst possible time for Governor Greene and the council, Captain Edward Hill reentered the picture. On 19 June 1647, two letters arrived in St. Mary's. The first, from Sir William Berkeley, governor of Virginia, was in response to a letter Leonard Calvert had written before his death. Calvert was seeking the return of a mare and colt that were being held at Chicacoan. Berkeley assured him that they would be returned and used the opportunity to ask Calvert to see that Captain Hill received whatever was justly due for his service in Maryland. The second letter was addressed to Calvert and was from Captain Hill in Chicacoan on 18 June. Its tone is submissive, almost whining, and in it Hill asked for his salary and the 146 arms-length of roanoke that he had left at St. Mary's. In the end, Hill stated his hope "that fame and suggested rumors, all together false, shall not prejudice my right." These rumors involved an invasion that Hill was supposedly planning and, true or not, such rumors must have been frequent in this tense atmosphere. We can only imagine what effect these letters had on the Maryland leadership. The invasion threat must have seemed very real and immediate action necessary.[29]

Greene answered Hill's letter on the same day that it was recorded and informed him that Leonard Calvert had been "some dayes since layd in his grave and hath appointed mee in his steed." He went on to say that he was unaware of what was due to Hill but if the captain would send an attorney he would receive justice in court. Then, responding to the implied threat in Hill's letter, he warned that the government of Maryland would "give the disturbers of his majesty the King's peace, their due punishment att any time when they shall invade us. And for your good therefore, whatever we heare to the contrary, wee wish you shall be none of them."[30]

This letter was sent on 19 June, and the news it contained changed Captain Hill's attitude. The next day he sent a letter to Thomas Greene and Giles Brent, as his Lordship's council. There was no longer any discussion of a salary owed to him. He argued that the governorship was rightly his and that Calvert's invasion was illegal, arguments based on an incorrect or convenient reading of Leonard Calvert's commission. There was very little chance that Greene or the council would accept them and voluntarily hand over the government. The real purpose of the letter was to deliver a threat to the council in the hope that they would surrender in the face of a possible invasion. Near the end of the letter, Hill stated,

> I am all together unwilling to move the stone violently, what innundation, loss & ruine it will produce to the whole, I am not ignorant of, I had rather some moderate way were taken for the satisfaction on all sides. Occasion (by the death of the late Gentleman) is now bald, all discontents may easily be pacified and brought to good tearmes of qualification. Peace may breath a quiet possession unto them & every one there resident . . . If it faile for all I know yee may be blame worthy. For others of humors different from mine, privately embrace a parliamentary influence, which may prove fatal to the whole.[31]

Thomas Greene had no illusions about what was intended by this letter. He knew of Hill's involvement with the Chicacoan rebels and had heard of plans for an invasion. On 21 June, he answered Hill's letter and, quoting Calvert's commission, stated that he was now the legal governor. As for Hill's threats, he dismissed them and said that the only way he would surrender the government would be on Lord Baltimore's written instruction. Probably on the same day, Greene wrote a letter to Sir William Berkeley informing him of Calvert's death and requesting that Berkeley order Captain Hill not to threaten the Maryland government. Governor Greene referred to rumors of a military force gathering at Chicacoan that would soon invade Maryland. More threats of invasion from that settlement appeared through the next year, but none ever developed. As the government of Maryland became more stable, they gradually decreased.

A greater danger to the government than invasion lay in the demands of its own soldiers for subsistence and pay. Less than a week after Calvert's funeral, Captain Price informed the new governor that there was no corn at the fort and the soldiers were in desperate straits. Sergeant Mark Pheypo was authorized to take five barrels of corn from Cuthbert Fenwick at 120 pounds of tobacco per barrel. This solved the immediate problem but left the larger issue unresolved. In the fall, as the time for paying the soldiers drew nearer, Captain Price sued Margaret Brent, Calvert's administrator, for 45,600 pounds of tobacco and one hundred barrels of corn due to the soldiers. The suit was filed on 6 October 1647, and Governor Greene issued a writ of attachment against Calvert's estate, which was to be returned on 3 January 1648. As far as the soldiers were concerned, they had made a personal bargain with Leonard Calvert, who had pledged his estate to see that they were paid. Had their demands been met, Calvert's entire estate would have been swallowed up by the debt. The writ of attachment gave Margaret Brent and the government breathing room until after the tobacco crop of 1647 was shipped and the custom on exported tobacco paid. It protected the bulk of Calvert's estate from individual suits while the government sought ways to pay the soldiers.[32]

During the latter part of 1647, Margaret Brent attempted to see that the custom was collected. However, the planters were reluctant to pay it because the custom duty represented 15–20 percent of the tobacco in each hogshead. On 13 December, Brent sued Thomas Gerrard for 5,000 pounds of tobacco in damages, claiming that he secretly exported six hogsheads without paying the customs duty. The collection of this tax would prove quite burdensome.[33]

Even if the government had been more efficient in collecting the duty, they would not have raised enough to pay the soldiers. Captain Price's demand including both tobacco and corn totaled 57,000–61,000 pounds of tobacco. Based on a rate of sixty pounds per hogshead, the planters would have had to export 950–1,016 hogsheads or approximately 350,000 pounds of tobacco, requiring a labor force greater than the entire population of Maryland to grow it.[34]

Leonard Calvert probably knew that before he died. At the Assembly of 1646, which voted for the tax on tobacco, Calvert assured the burgesses that his estate and that of Lord Baltimore would pay for any cost that the tax did not cover. He also agreed with the soldiers to accept a cow with calf in lieu of six hundred pounds of tobacco. It is clear from Calvert's later inventory that he had no cattle, so he must have counted on disposing of Lord Baltimore's stock. This may also be the reason for a commission Calvert issued to Francis Brooks on 31 May 1647 to collect all of Lord Baltimore's cattle on Kent Island. When Leonard Calvert died, these preparations were thrown into confusion.[35]

Lord Baltimore's estate, including the cattle, could only be disposed of by someone acting as his attorney. Before the rebellion, that had been John Lewgar's job. Since Lewgar was no longer in the province, it had become Leonard Calvert's responsibility. After his death, there was considerable confusion over who represented Lord Baltimore's personal interest. Early in October, Robert Clarke, Surveyor and Clerk of the Court, was filling the role of Lord Baltimore's attorney in a case against Nathaniel Pope even though no commission was issued for that purpose. Margaret Brent, while administrator of Leonard Calvert's estate, was clearly not Lord Baltimore's attorney. As late as 2 December 1647, when sued for a cow from Lord Baltimore's stock that had been promised by Calvert before his death, Brent could only reply "that shee, not having his Lordship's stock att her disposall, is disinabled to make it good." Thomas Greene, on 12 December, acknowledged the lack of a recognized attorney for Lord Baltimore. He gave away several cattle from Lord Baltimore's stock on the condition that if an attorney for his Lordship should come to the province within a year, he could demand the cattle back in exchange for tobacco.[36]

This confusion could not continue much longer. The deadline for paying the soldiers was again rapidly approaching. In addition, Margaret Brent was being sued not only for Leonard Calvert's personal debts but for actions that he took as governor. Thomas Greene was hesitant to dispose of Lord Baltimore's estate without specific authorization. Together, Brent and Greene found a tentative solution to the problem. They decided that Brent, as administrator for Leonard Calvert's estate, could legally claim to also be Lord Baltimore's attorney until another was appointed. This decision had to have been made on 12 or 13 December. On the earlier day, Governor Greene reported that there was no attorney for Lord Baltimore in the province, but on the next day, Brent was specifically referred to as Lord Baltimore's attorney. Equipped with this new power, Brent was ready to face the impending crisis.[37]

The provincial court met on 3 January 1648 with Thomas Greene and Giles Brent on the bench. The first case to be recorded was that of the soldiers' demands against Calvert's estate, which had been postponed from the October court. Margaret Brent first responded that this demand was not due from the estate and then claimed "the priviledge of an administrator & not to be troubled within a twelvemonth and a day." This custom gave executors time to get all of the bills and accounts in order. No debts had to be paid until a year and a day after the death of the individual. By claiming this privilege, Brent again protected Calvert's estate for a period of six months. This was the first step in Brent's plan.[38]

Next, the governor raised the question, in open court, of who should be Lord Baltimore's attorney in the province. He asked Giles Brent, as the only member of the council present, if Leonard Calvert's administrator should fill this role until another should be appointed. Giles Brent's answer was a foregone conclusion. In fact, this whole episode was staged solely to provide legal recognition for an arrangement that had already been made. The court then ordered that Margaret Brent be recognized as such.

Starting the next day, 4 January 1648, individual soldiers began filing demands for payment of their wages. Over the next several months, claims totaling 13,000 pounds of tobacco and twenty-eight barrels of corn were filed against Margaret Brent as Lord Baltimore's attorney. These totals represent 28 percent of the tobacco and corn demanded by Captain Price and the soldiers in October 1647. Does the absence of further claims indicate that the rest of the debt was paid off by this time? It may be that the custom on exported tobacco was beginning to provide the revenue that Calvert had hoped it would. Nevertheless, it was obvious by January that there would not be enough revenue from that source to pay off all the debts.[39]

It was at this point that Margaret Brent's appointment as Lord Baltimore's attorney became important. By late March she had exchanged six of Lord Baltimore's cattle in partial payment of soldiers' wages and six more cattle for various other expenses related to the soldiers. The six cattle paid for soldiers' wages reduced the amount of tobacco owed to about 9,500 pounds, and by June, Brent had paid that out of Calvert's estate.[40]

That left the troubling question of the twenty-eight barrels of corn. The Assembly, meeting on 24 January, solved the problem by authorizing the governor to press corn at a rate of 150 pounds of tobacco per barrel. Any household that had more than two barrels of corn per adult was subject to this confiscation. The important point about this action was that compensation for the corn did not have to be paid until the next crop was harvested late in 1648. This gave Margaret Brent almost another year to collect the tobacco needed to pay for the corn.[41]

Through the careful management of the governor and his Lordship's attorney the crisis caused by the unpaid soldiers had been settled. They had paid off most of the debt and with a little luck would finish the job at the next crop. However, the political costs had been higher than anyone suspected and would not fully manifest themselves for another year. They would prove detrimental to the people who saved Maryland and would signal a major change in how the province was governed.

One of the first consequences stemming from the settlement was an attempt by Margaret Brent to capitalize on her newly found power and position. She had always been strong-willed and, in a society heavily biased against women, she had established herself as the equal of any man. Her new position as Lord Baltimore's attorney placed her in the middle of the effort to stabilize the government. She must have taken part in the council's deliberations, and these important men listened to her advice.

This new respect gave her the confidence to do something no woman had ever thought to do. On 21 January 1648, Margaret Brent entered the Hall at St. John's, where the Assembly was meeting, and asked, as a land owner, to be given a vote in the Assembly. More than that, she also requested a second vote as Lord Baltimore's attorney. As a land owner, she could justly argue that her personal interest was not being represented in the Assembly and, from our perspective, it was a reasonable request. As Lord Baltimore's personal representative, her need to be involved in the Assembly was even greater. She must have known that the freemen were unhappy with the state of things and would attempt to make decisions that would have a major impact on Baltimore's estate and province. She believed that she not only had a right to be in the Assembly but also had a duty to be involved in these decisions.[42]

The governor and Assembly were unwilling to accommodate her that far, and the governor denied her requests on both counts. Upon his refusal Brent stated that she protested against all actions of this Assembly. Brent's attempt to take a seat in the Assembly and the governor's refusal to let her do so has often been seen as an important step on the road to equal rights between the sexes. It certainly was that, but it may have had another more practical reason as well. Brent and the governor must have known of the freemen's resentment of the custom duty on tobacco. They could not be certain what the outcome of the Assembly would be and needed to protect themselves in case the worst happened. By recording Margaret Brent's unconditional protest against the acts of the Assembly, she and the governor could claim that they had nothing to do with the passage of any act that offended Lord Baltimore. As it turned out, this was an important action.

Margaret Brent's suspicions about this Assembly were well grounded. Almost from the beginning of the session it was one of the most raucous and undisciplined Assemblies held in early Maryland. The freemen were upset over a number of issues and let the governor know about it. On 25 January 1648 the first bill, entitled "An act for the confirmation of the Lordship's patent," was read. The title was innocuous but it must have contained some interesting provisions, for the Assembly not only rejected the bill but ordered that it be "Throwne out of the house."[43]

The next bill read that day was an "Act for the repeale of the present Act of Customes & the Act Touching Trade," and this was the business that really interested the burgesses. These two acts had been passed by the Assembly of 1647 at St. Inigoes Fort under the eye of Leonard Calvert. Together, they formed the basis for paying the soldiers and running the government. The freemen thought the sixty pounds of tobacco per hogshead was too burdensome. The act for repeal was read for the third time on 27 January and was prepared for a vote, but the vote was never held. Instead, on 28 January, the freemen unanimously signed a protest against the laws passed by the Assembly of 1647. They argued that Leonard Calvert had recalled Hill's Assembly, which was not a legitimate Assembly, without issuing a new summons to the province. Because of this oversight, the burgesses stated that the laws were not lawfully passed and should not be recognized. Thomas Greene was unequivocal in his response:

> I, Thomas Greene Esq., his Lordship's Governor for the time being doe absolutely protest against all such undue proceeding, & doe hereby declare the foresaid Assembly held by the Governor aforesaid at the time and place aforesaid to be most lawful . . . And I further declare in the face of this present Assembly that I shall to the uttmost of my power, by vertue of his Lordship's Commission given to mee in that behalfe see the due observance of the same throughout all the parts of the Province until his Lordship's disassent thereunto shall appear under his hand and Seale.[44]

With the governor so vehemently opposed to the repeal of the customs duty, the Assembly was at an impasse. The House met five times between 29 January and 21 February, but the records are brief and nothing seems to have been accomplished. Finally, on the afternoon of the twenty-first, the house voted to draw up a remonstrance concerning the grievances of the province. A remonstrance was a formal statement of facts or grievances and an accepted way for Parliament to address their complaints to their sovereign. The Grand Remonstrance had been one of Parliament's first steps on the road to Civil War in 1641. The House appointed a committee of Giles Brent, Robert Vaughan, and Cuthbert Fenwick to compose the document. Over the next two weeks, the House reviewed the remonstrance and made it the eighth clause of a larger bill to settle the government of the province. The overall bill came up for a vote on 4 March 1648. The first seven clauses passed without comment, and the governor approved them. When the eighth clause, the remonstrance, came up for a vote, there were only three dissenting members who represented only eleven votes. The clause would have become part of the final bill, but the governor refused to enact it, saying that he "neither for his own peculiar voice nor in the Lord Proprietor's name assented to enacting this bill." And with that denial, the remonstrance was allowed to lapse.[45]

Thomas Greene held the settlement together through a very difficult period but he was not the leader that Leonard Calvert had been. He was inexperienced in the use of power and, like Giles Brent before him, insecure and jealous of those he saw as a threat to his position. Greene angered the freemen by submitting a bill entitled "An Act for the Support of the Governor," which requested that the Assembly provide him with 12,000 pounds of tobacco, thirty barrels of corn, and a house suitable to his position. These demands must have seemed like an incredible imposition on burgesses who were already upset at the cost of paying the soldiers. What made it even worse, according to later testimony from Robert Vaughan and Cuthbert Fenwick, was that Greene offered to drop his opposition to the remonstrance in exchange for passage of this bill of support. Greene was also accused of delaying justice for his own gain, showing favoritism in his court decisions, and being too sensitive to imaginary affronts to his dignity as governor. All of these things served to make Greene unpopular and to increase discontent in the province. However, a unique convergence of events, both in the Chesapeake and in England would soon quiet this discontent and effect a major change in the government and society of Maryland.[46]

CHAPTER SEVENTEEN

"I will not . . . trouble . . . any person . . . in respect of his religion"

The tobacco fleet returning to London in the summer of 1648 brought sad and disturbing news to Lord Baltimore. The death of Leonard Calvert was a personal loss and a political disaster to Cecil Calvert. From the first voyage to Maryland, Lord Baltimore had relied on his brother to lead the colony and protect his interests. Though they had had their differences over specific issues, the Calvert brothers had shared a trust and confidence that could only come from a family relationship. With the death of Leonard Calvert, Lord Baltimore was forced to rely on strangers to govern his province and look after his investment.

There is no way of knowing Baltimore's reaction to the appointment of Thomas Greene as governor. The two possibly met before the first expedition to Maryland but were not close friends. In the list of "Gentlemen adventurers that are gone in person to this Plantation," published in 1635, Baltimore was not even certain of Greene's first name, calling him Henry Greene. Through the first decade of settlement, Baltimore did not appoint Greene to any office. He was not appointed to the council until late in 1644, when Leonard Calvert returned from England. It is likely that Calvert recommended Greene and Lord Baltimore simply agreed to the appointment. Now this relative stranger was the chief agent in charge of Lord Baltimore's province in Maryland.[1]

Baltimore must have been pleasantly surprised therefore by the initial reports of Governor Greene's actions. Greene justified the faith that Leonard Calvert had placed in him by loyally and faithfully upholding the interests of the Calvert family. He had blocked the repeal of the custom duty on tobacco, defended the legality of the Assembly of 1647, and stopped the formulation of the remonstrance. He was clearly someone who could be trusted and a good choice for governor.

Baltimore's approval of Thomas Greene was in sharp contrast to his feelings toward the Brents. He saw Giles Brent as an instigator, the prime mover in the Assembly's writing of the remonstrance. Brent had been the first person chosen for the committee, and Baltimore attributed authorship to him. When Baltimore wrote a new commission for the Council of Maryland in August 1648, he did not include Giles Brent, marking the end of Brent's public career in Maryland. In 1649 he left Maryland and settled permanently in Stafford County, Virginia.

As distrustful as he was of Giles Brent, Lord Baltimore was even more upset with his sister Margaret. While her brother had tried and failed to affect Baltimore's interest in the Assembly, Margaret Brent had actually given away part of Baltimore's estate. Cecil Calvert was incensed that she had been appointed his attorney and had made decisions affecting his fortune with no consultation or instructions from him. Brent's actions were tied up with Leonard Calvert's well-attested promise that his estate and Lord Baltimore's would pay the soldiers their due, but Baltimore contended that Calvert had not promised his brother's estate and, even if he had, he had no right to do so.

Lord Baltimore was particularly upset by the dispersal of cattle from his stock. A large portion of Lord Baltimore's investment in Maryland was in cattle. The 1644 account of his estate showed ninety-three cattle and fifty-six calves, worth about £500. After the rebellion, Margaret Brent is recorded approving the sale of twelve cattle from Baltimore's stock. This may not seem like a large number, but it was all of the identifiable cattle left from the herd of 149 head. The others were either dead, transported out of the province, or remarked as someone else's property. Lord Baltimore had once owned the largest herd of cattle in Maryland;

now it was completely gone. That Margaret Brent had taken the remnant and given it away for debts which Baltimore believed were not properly his, made him feel the loss more keenly. He decided he must protest her actions and counter their effects and that he must do so vigorously.[2]

As Lord Baltimore gazed across the Atlantic he saw other problems as well. None was greater than the severe loss of population that Maryland suffered during the Plundering Time. From a pre-rebellion high of 600–800 souls, the population had dropped to fewer than three hundred. In January 1648 only about 160 freemen lived in the province, and few of these had families or large numbers of servants. Baltimore relied on rents and the custom duty to pay for the government, to pay the soldiers, and to provide profit for himself. With so few inhabitants, payments would be difficult and profit nonexistent. Another issue was that Maryland was a small colony adjacent to a large, and ever-growing one. The trouble that had swept over Maryland in 1645 might easily occur again unless the province were more fully populated. One of Lord Baltimore's priorities was and would continue to be encouraging settlement. The attempts of 1646–47 to induce or force English Catholics to immigrate had all failed, prompting Cecil Calvert to cast about for other groups who might be recruited to make their homes in Maryland.[3]

Another important issue facing Lord Baltimore in 1648 was the need to defend and strengthen his hold on the patent for Maryland. Thus far he had been lucky. When Parliament denied the Ordinance for Maryland, it had confirmed Baltimore's control of the province, but there was no guarantee it would do so again. His foes were still active and would not need much to bring the issue once more before Parliament. Cecil Calvert had to answer his critics and strengthen his control over the colony.

Late in 1647 or early in 1648, Lord Baltimore devised a complex plan to change Maryland and to make it more acceptable under the existing political circumstances. With no other choices available, he gambled on several individuals and groups to help him. These were difficult times, and England was changing as a nation. If Maryland were to survive, she would have to change as well.

One of the first things Lord Baltimore had to change was himself.

Early in the Civil War, Cecil Calvert had been a Royalist. He was not a reluctant, half-hearted supporter but willingly and actively sought commissions from King Charles. Now, with the war over and the king decisively defeated Parliament or the army would rule the country in the foreseeable future. In 1648, Lord Baltimore, like many other Royalists, faced an important choice. Some chose to forfeit their estates and live in exile on the Continent in order to maintain their staunch support of their king. Most buried their Royalist feelings and attempted to salvage what they could from the wreckage. They proclaimed that they had been neutral during the war or had only aided the king's forces under duress. Lord Baltimore was not unique among his contemporaries in this regard. He began to make overtures to Parliament and the army for protection.

As he sought ways to strengthen his ties to the winning side, Lord Baltimore must have remembered the previous year's struggle, when he had been repeatedly forced to defend the legality of his patent and his government. The single most damaging charge against Calvert was the religious one. His critics pointed out that Maryland was owned by a Catholic, that it had a Catholic government, and that the Jesuits were allowed to own land and openly preach there. While these things could be excused under a Royalist regime, the likelihood of such tolerance under Parliament was slight. More than anything else, the survival of Maryland depended on Calvert's ability to deal with that charge.

Of course Cecil Calvert had been aware of the issue even before the Civil War. From the late 1630s on, he had attempted to make Maryland conform to English law in regard to religion. Even now he was negotiating with the Society of Jesus for the surrender of their lands and the promise to conform to certain standards. Sometime in 1647 he submitted another draft of a land surrender to the Jesuit Provincial. This one was much more comprehensive in outlining Baltimore's control over the clergy. It first recognized that no land could be acquired from any source other than Lord Baltimore. Even though the Church had supported the Indians' right to give away their own land, Baltimore still insisted that the Jesuits acknowledge his title to the land. Were he to make an exception for the Jesuits on this point, no one would feel compelled to take land under his title and trouble would ensue. The draft surrender also stated that all land in Maryland was subject to the English statutes of mortmain and that clergy were subject to the same laws in Maryland as they were in England. The only exceptions Baltimore made were for those laws that sentenced priests to death for practicing their religion. All these were issues that had arisen before the rebellion.[4]

Baltimore also prohibited Jesuits from going to Maryland without specific permission from himself or his representative. That had been the practice in 1642 and was now to be binding on the Jesuits. He reserved the right to expel any Jesuit from Maryland at any time and promised to pay £20 for any priest so expelled. Each new missionary had to take the oath of fidelity to the proprietor if he were to be accepted into Maryland.

The date of this proposal is uncertain except that it was given to the English Provincial in 1647 and was probably presented between July and December of that year. The Jesuit General, replying to a July letter from the Provincial, authorized sending as many men to Maryland as seemed necessary. By 28 December the General had written that no men were to be sent without Baltimore's consent. Some kind of compromise was soon reached, because on 25 January 1648, less than a month later, the General complimented Father Thomas Copley on his intention to return to Maryland. The importance of this proposed agreement is that it represents Lord Baltimore's continuing effort to make Maryland, and the Jesuits, conform to English law.[5]

Baltimore's next step, taken about a year later in June 1648, was to prepare a new Conditions of Plantation governing the granting of land in Maryland. In general outline, the Conditions of 1648 were similar to the last set published in 1642. Lord Baltimore took the opportunity to refine some of the terms and provide greater specificity in regard to rents. One result of the rebellion was that everyone seeking land in Maryland was now required to take the Oath of Fidelity to the proprietor.[6]

Nonetheless, the clauses added to the end of the document reveal one of its primary purposes. Of the last five items in the Conditions, four related directly to the Jesuits and the land controversy. One prohibited the granting of land to any organized body, spiritual or temporal, without special license from Lord Baltimore. This was certainly aimed at the concept of mortmain and Jesuit landownership. A second prohibited the bequeathing or gift of land to such an organized body. A third denied the validity of secret trusts for land, and a fourth, though not specifically aimed at the Jesuits, could be used against them. It reserved the right to deny granting land to any person whom Lord Baltimore chose to exclude.

These points eliminated the possibility of Jesuits owning land as a Society but stopped short of prohibiting them from owning it as individual planters. Lord Baltimore was willing to recognize them as gentlemen, not as part of a larger church. This would become the pattern of Jesuit land ownership until the American Revolution. Father Peter Attwood, writing in 1727, described the system:

> Each tract was purchased . . . and descends by conveyance or will; for all other rights of succession or inheritance in common we are deprived of by the Statute of Mortmain. Hence it is advisable that each possessor have always a will by him, whereby he bequeaths all his estate, both real and personal, to N. N. and his heirs for ever . . . lest possibly our land become escheat.[7]

Although Lord Baltimore, the Society of Jesus, and the inhabitants of Maryland all thought of these lands as Jesuit property, legally they were owned by one individual. Other difficulties would arise between Lord Baltimore and the Jesuits in the ensuing years, but the land controversy faded from view with the Jesuit acceptance of these conditions. Maryland, at least on the surface, conformed to English law regarding church property.

The rebellion pointed out potential difficulties other than land ownership. The fact that the governor and the entire Council of Maryland were Catholics raised great suspicions in England. Any concentration of power in the hands of "Papists" led Protestant Englishmen to readily accept even the wildest tales regarding their actions or intentions. If the Ordinance for Maryland had passed, it would have replaced the government with one that was exclusively Protestant. Under the political conditions of the time, Lord Baltimore could no longer rely only on Catholics. He had to find able but loyal Protestants to appoint to the council. Nor could he allow Thomas Greene to remain as governor.

On 17 August 1648, Lord Baltimore issued a new commission for the council and named five men to compose that body: Thomas Greene, John Price, Thomas Hatton, John Pile, and Robert Vaughan. Of the five, only Greene and Pile were Catholics. In this commission, Lord Baltimore created a council with a Protestant majority and thereby undercut one of the potential charges his enemies could make against him. Equally important was the fact that all but one of these men had already proven themselves loyal to Cecil Calvert. Thomas Greene had handled the Assembly of 1648 and protected the custom duty on tobacco. Although he could no longer be governor, Baltimore named him first in the commission and he served as deputy governor. John Price was captain of the soldiers that Leonard Calvert had led to Maryland and had been instrumental in bringing peace after the rebellion. John Pile and Robert Vaughan had been steadfastly loyal throughout the rebellion and were now rewarded for it.[8]

The one person who had not been settled previously in Maryland was Thomas Hatton. On 12 August 1648, Baltimore had appointed him to be provincial secretary. What association Hatton had with Lord Baltimore before his appointment is unknown. He seems to have had connections in the court system in London. Given all of the recent legal work in defense of the Maryland charter, he may have met Lord Baltimore in this area or he may have been recommended in the same way that William Stone seems to have been. In any case, Hatton would justify Lord Baltimore's confidence in him by loyally upholding the rights of the proprietor under difficult circumstances. Eventually, Hatton died defending those rights at the Battle of the Severn. By appointing a Protestant to the second most important office in the province, Lord Baltimore again undercut his opponents' ability to use the religious issue against him.[9]

The commission for the council marks a major change in the type of men appointed to high office in Maryland. This change goes beyond the simple inclusion of Protestants and reflects a shift in the social conditions of Maryland society. Prior to this time, each of the councils had been made up of manor lords. While some served on the council without owning a manor, most of the men filling the office had held large tracts of land in fealty to Lord Baltimore. What makes the council appointed in 1648 unique is that no one on it owned a manor. The recent "time of troubles" had destroyed the manorial system and the gentry associated with it. Although manors would continue to be erected sporadically, their owners would not play the same central role in the government. That was an enduring legacy of Ingle's rebellion.

The new council was an important step in defusing criticism of the Maryland government but, for the strategy to work, the office of governor had to be filled by a Protestant. Lord Baltimore had to find a Protestant whose loyalty to Parliament could not be questioned yet one who could also be loyal to him. Furthermore, the governor had to be someone familiar with the conditions of the Chesapeake and able to command the respect of both Protestants and Catholics. None of the Protestants resident in Maryland could meet these requirements. Most had recently been in rebellion, and Lord Baltimore did not trust them. Those who had remained loyal, like Robert Vaughan, were tainted by their association with the previously all-Catholic, Royalist government. The governor would have to be someone from outside Maryland.

Lord Baltimore chose Captain William Stone of Accomac, Virginia. Stone had many of the qualities Baltimore thought essential. He was familiar with the Chesapeake. Stone had been in Virginia since the 1620s and over that twenty years had risen to become a prominent planter and politician. He had patented more than five thousand of land and was recognized as a leading tobacco merchant. Stone had been sheriff of his county three times, served continuously on the county court, and had been a burgess in the Virginia Assembly of 1642. He was already a man of wealth and power.[10]

What made him even better suited for Lord Baltimore's plan was that he not only was a Protestant but he was well connected with the Parliamentary faction. His uncle, Thomas Stone, was one of the leading tobacco merchants of London and closely allied with the cause of Parliament. The Stone family, as well as his in-laws, the Cottons, were intimately related to the Independents in New England. By appointing Captain Stone,

Lord Baltimore would make his government much more acceptable to Parliament and to the Independent faction in the army.

Yet this appointment was not without risks. Captain Stone represented a potential threat or at least an uncertainty to Baltimore's control of the province. First, Cecil Calvert probably had no direct knowledge of William Stone. Throughout the late 1630s and 1640s, Stone seems to have been continuously in Virginia, and the two men probably never met. Stone's appointment may have been based on his uncle's recommendation. Baltimore was trusting the province to someone he did not know. Neither was Stone well-known in Maryland at the time. He is only mentioned once in the pre-1645 records, and then he was represented by Nathaniel Pope. He does not appear as a creditor in the early estate accounts. The lack of such records strongly indicates that Stone's involvement in Maryland before his appointment was minimal.

The most serious objection to William Stone must have been his business connections in Virginia and England. At various times between 1630 and 1645, Stone had been closely allied with Lord Baltimore's enemies. He had worked with William Claiborne on the Accomac County Court in the 1630s, and his brother-in-law, William Cotton, was Claiborne's minister on Kent Island. His uncle, Thomas Stone, had been closely allied with Maurice Thompson, a strong supporter of Claiborne and Lord Baltimore's most virulent enemy in the London merchant community. More recently, Stone had served as Richard Ingle's factor on the Eastern Shore. In April 1645, as Ingle was leaving the Chesapeake with the plundered spoils of Maryland, Stone delivered to him seventy hogsheads of tobacco he had collected in exchange for goods Ingle had left with him.[11]

These business and personal connections were not the sort to inspire confidence in Stone's loyalty to Lord Baltimore. How then did Stone come to be governor? His appointment was the result of his being the middle-man in a web of unique connections in Virginia and England during a very important time. A number of groups could only achieve their ends by working through him. This reshuffling of alliances was only temporary, but it was enough to get him the office of governor and to set Maryland on course for another decade of troubles.

The most likely factor influencing Lord Baltimore's choice for governor was William Stone's promise to bring five hundred new settlers to Maryland. This was an extremely attractive offer given the depopulation of Maryland. If Stone could deliver on his promise, he would in a very short time double the population, add substantially to the rent receipts, and provide greater stability to the colony. But the immigrants that Stone would procure had other advantages in Baltimore's eyes. The community Stone hoped to entice to Maryland were the Puritans or Independents from the area south of the James River and were important to Baltimore's plan for two reasons. First, they were already well established and familiar with the Chesapeake. They would need no period of adjustment and could become productive members of the colony right away. Many were already prosperous, and their accumulated wealth would make the whole province richer. Just as important was the political advantage they would give Lord Baltimore. By accepting these persecuted refugees from a colony that still would not accept Parliamentary control, Baltimore hoped to establish his loyalty to the government and confound his critics.

It seems in hindsight that by inviting radical Protestants into Maryland Lord Baltimore was asking for trouble. They barely tolerated other Protestants, let alone Catholics. This was Baltimore's biggest gamble and one he would soon lose, but at the time the chances of success appeared to be good. In England, Catholics and Independents were still negotiating toleration and had arrived at a tentative consensus. Lord Baltimore hoped that these sentiments would translate to the Chesapeake. The potential gains seemed to outweigh the risks.

For the Virginia Independents, the offer of a safe haven in Maryland and freedom to worship as they pleased could not have come at a better time. Throughout the early history of Virginia there had been no real established church. Although the colony was nominally Anglican, many forms of dissenting worship had been tolerated. This de facto toleration had ended with the arrival in 1642 of Sir William Berkeley, who was not only a Royalist but believed that conformity in worship was vital to a peaceful colony.[12]

Late in 1642 the Virginia Independents sent to New England for ministers to care for their growing church. After a long and difficult voyage, three arrived in Virginia. Berkeley was not pleased, and the following March he had the Assembly pass an act requiring all ministers to conform to the practices of the Church of England. If they did not, the governor and council were authorized to expel them from the colony. Within a short time after the passage of this act, all three ministers were forced to leave Virginia.[13]

The Indian troubles that came shortly thereafter distracted Berkeley during the mid-1640s, but he still pressed the Independents to conform. It was at this time that they first began to think about leaving Virginia, and they received several offers from New England and the Bahamas to join like-minded settlements. Even Lord Baltimore, always looking for a way to increase the population of his colony, made an offer through Edward Gibbons, a prominent Boston merchant. After considerable discussion, the Independents chose to stay in Virginia.[14]

Despite political changes in England, Governor Berkeley would not relinquish his support of the king nor his desire to make the Independents conform. In November 1647 the Assembly, under Berkeley's leadership, passed an act requiring all ministers to read from the English Book of Common Prayer during Sunday services. This had been the approved form of worship before the Civil War, but Parliament had outlawed the book's use in England. Forcing the Independents to use the Book of Common Prayer struck directly at their form of worship. When the governor later exiled their minister and two of their elders, the Independents began to realize that they could not stay in Virginia.[15]

Although specific information is not available, it is probable that the second offer of a safe haven in Maryland was made through Thomas Stone, the uncle of William Stone and a prominent London tobacco merchant. Thomas Stone had been in the trade for twenty years and was one of a handful of merchants who controlled the market. He was himself an Independent and was well-connected to the churches in New England. Stone had worked closely with Maurice Thompson and William Claiborne in the 1630s. Significantly, his name was not on the 1646 petition of the London tobacco merchants that castigated Lord Baltimore and his government in Maryland. Thomas and William Stone were both familiar to the Virginia Independents and were respected by them. It was their involvement in the process that probably made the offer acceptable.[16]

Lord Baltimore signed the commission appointing William Stone as governor on 6 August 1648. The commission was generally like those previously issued to Leonard Calvert but included some changes related to recent events. Lord Baltimore left no doubt why Stone had been appointed. Right after Stone's name was first mentioned, Lord Baltimore repeated the captain's promise to bring five hundred people of British or Irish descent into the province within a short time. Yet, much as Baltimore wanted this influx of new settlers, he was wary of Stone's personal connections. In describing Stone's powers as governor, Baltimore placed a number of restrictions on his actions. Stone could not, under any circumstances, pardon William Claiborne, Richard Ingle, or John Durford. Cecil Calvert was taking no chances that Stone's former business partners would be given the opportunity to cause more trouble in Maryland.[17]

The most serious restrictions placed on Stone had to do with religion. From the founding of Maryland, Lord Baltimore had tried to keep religion a private matter not subject to state interference. So long as his brother was governor, this had remained a minor issue. Leonard Calvert was also a Catholic, and it was in his interest to see that a policy of religious toleration was actively pursued. Lord Baltimore could not be so sure that William Stone would continue to uphold this policy. To prevent the establishment of the Church of England as the state supported religion in Maryland, Stone's commission forbade his approving any laws dealing with religion, the collection of tithes, or the establishment of parishes without specific permission from Lord Baltimore.[18]

In the new oath prescribed for the governor, Lord Baltimore went even further. Governor Stone had to swear that he would not allow anyone professing in Christ to be bothered, molested, or otherwise questioned on account of their religion, and specifically for being a Roman Catholic. He was to appoint individuals to government positions without concern for their religion but only on their merit. Stone was ordered to prosecute anyone who disturbed another person because of their religion.

Lord Baltimore clearly thought of religion as a private matter and strove to keep his government from interfering in it.[19]

The commissions for the governor, the council, and other specific positions were completed late in August and given to Thomas Hatton, the new secretary, to transport to the province. Hatton probably sailed with the London tobacco fleet in November 1648, but the date of his arrival in the province is uncertain. He was still in London as late as 5 September 1648. A later land claim reported that Hatton and his family arrived in Maryland in 1648. If we assume that upon his arrival the commissions he carried became effective, then he could not have arrived until late in February of 1648/9. Court records indicate that Thomas Greene continued to act as governor as late as 10 February. At that same court, Margaret Brent was still referred to as Lord Baltimore's attorney, which would not have been the case if Hatton had arrived. Also, William Stone was in court during this period but was not acting as governor.[20]

Even before Hatton arrived, rumors of the impending changes in the government must have filtered across the Atlantic. William Stone, who was barely mentioned in court records before 1645, was suddenly very active. Many of his appearances related to the estate of Thomas Weston, who owed a great debt to Stone. It may be that Stone came early to Maryland to settle this case, but surely he was not unaware of and perhaps was even anticipating Hatton's imminent arrival.

As Stone prepared to settle in Maryland, Giles Brent was leaving. Brent had regularly sat as a judge in the provincial court through 1648 and made his last appearance there on 7 December 1648. From that point on, he was represented by an attorney, usually his sister, and was never in court personally. He soon moved across the Potomac to Virginia, where Margaret Brent joined him in the early 1650s. Giles Brent's departure from Maryland broke the last tie with the pre-rebellion, manorial government.[21]

The first official act of the new government seems to have been the holding of an Assembly, which met from 2 to 21 April 1649. No record of its sessions has survived, but a list of expenses and the laws passed by the freemen were recorded. The beginning of the session was marked by an entry Thomas Hatton made in the council minutes, reporting that on 2

April, which he named as the first day of the Assembly, he received the book of council minutes. This marks the transfer of power from the old government to the new and brings the Plundering Time to a close.[22]

The Plundering Time vastly changed Maryland's political and social environment. The council that sat in the Assembly of 1649 was fundamentally different from those that had ruled before the rebellion. Neither the governor nor any of the councilors were manor lords. Two councilors had arrived as indentured servants, and several were of very modest means. By destroying the manorial system and the hierarchical society on which it was based, the rebellion opened society in a way that was not possible in the first decade of settlement. Maryland in the 1650s and 1660s has been described as a "good poor man's country," in which, with hard work and luck, an immigrating servant could attain prosperity and respect.[23]

Another important development was the first codification of the concept of religious toleration. Lord Baltimore had already expressed his concern that the policy be continued under Governor Stone. This concern led to his drafting, and the Assembly's passing, the famous Act Concerning Religion. For the first time, government recognized that religion was a private matter so long as it did not disturb the peace of the community. Modern eyes can find many flaws in this legislation: it extended toleration only to Christians and enforced harsh penalties against non-believers. Nevertheless, it was an important step on the road to a civil government.[24]

This act has led to much discussion concerning its authorship and purpose. It has been argued that, rather than establishing or expanding toleration, the act limited an already existing spirit of toleration. Some have seen it as a way of protecting Catholic rights in a changing political climate. The lack of any records detailing the membership of the 1649 Assembly has led to arguments over whether the act was passed by Catholics or by Protestants. Much of the confusion results from the view that this legislation was unique to Maryland, but to understand the meaning of these events it is necessary to place them in contemporary political context.

The period 1647–49 saw numerous contacts between English Catholics and Independents concerning religious toleration, an issue important to both groups. Legislation similar to the Maryland act had already been prepared for the Parliament. Cecil Calvert was ahead of his time in proclaiming religious toleration from the founding of the colony, but surely the Act Concerning Religion owed at least some of its inspiration to the ongoing discussion of the issue in England.

An equally serious question is why it was important to enact this legislation at all. Historians have assumed that Cecil Calvert was forced to codify toleration because of the political changes in England or because he was changing the government of Maryland. Neither really answers the question. Throughout this period, Calvert was trying to make Maryland conform to English law and to appear personally loyal to Parliament. This act runs counter to the whole thrust of his program and made Maryland unique and different from England. The act passed not because of the political climate in England but in spite of it.

The second cause, the appointment of a Protestant government, could have spelled disaster for Maryland Catholics. Yet up to this point Lord Baltimore had relied on his governor and officers to enforce toleration. He made certain that William Stone, the new governor, would continue the same policy by changing his commission and oath of office. So long as Lord Baltimore controlled the government, his officers would have to follow his wishes. This should have been enough to guarantee toleration without the politically inexpedient passage of an act whose substance had already been rejected in England.

Could it be that the Act Concerning Religion was created not to protect Catholics, for whom Lord Baltimore had already provided, but to satisfy the apprehensions of the Virginia Independents? That group was certainly as suspicious of a Catholic proprietor as the Catholics were of a Protestant governor. While the Catholics had recourse to Lord Baltimore, a co-religionist, if his officers should disturb their religious freedom, the Independents could not count on the same kind of sympathy. It has been suggested that someone rewrote the beginning of the Act Concerning Religion to give it a distinctly Puritan flavor. This revision has been assumed to be the work of the 1649 Assembly, but that cannot be demonstrated. Regardless of when such a change took place, it is interesting to note that of the seventeen reproachful and banned terms, nine directly relate to the Independents and two others relate to Protestants in general. Only four of these terms could specifically be applied to Catholics. The preponderance of terms associated with Puritans in this revision suggests that it was for their benefit that it was passed. It is perhaps not coincidental that the Virginia Independents did not migrate until after this act was approved by the Assembly. Perhaps they were not willing to leave a Protestant colony, even if they were persecuted, for a Catholic one without some such assurance.[25]

Connections between the English political situation and the changes in the Maryland government emphasize an important point about the whole episode of the Plundering Time. This investigation began with the statement that the cause of these sometimes violent events was neither the revenge of a single man nor simply the extension of the English Civil War into Maryland. We must realize that although the colonists were three thousand miles from their homeland, they shared the cultural expectations of their relatives back in England. It should come as no surprise that they reacted in the same way to the events and currents of their day. There is a tendency to see in Maryland's isolation a history divorced from events in England. The one thing that this study has made clear is that Maryland history cannot be viewed in isolation. It may have taken eight or ten weeks for news to travel to the New World, but the colonists were aware of what was going on at home and shared the same prejudices and political grudges that most Englishmen did. For example, we can see in the Maryland Assembly, during this period, many of the same political issues that strained the relationship between king and Parliament.

What made Maryland's experience unique was that the conflict between Royalist and Roundhead was recast into the mold of religious intolerance. Thomas Cornwaleys, whom even Richard Ingle praised as a supporter of Parliament, was the first person to have his estate plundered by the rebels acting for Parliament. The impetus for the rebellion was clearly the English Civil War, but in Maryland these events were quickly translated into existing conflicts between Catholics and Protestants. Although the actors aligned themselves under national banners for king or Parliament, they acted their roles in response to local conditions. Scholars of the English Civil War have noted just such a dichotomy on a county level in England. Traditional county leaders fought each other in the name of God and Country to settle age-old disputes over place and precedence that had nothing to do with king or Parliament.[26]

Had Maryland been united, as was Virginia, the Plundering Time would never have happened. Richard Ingle may have brought the script of the Civil War, but Marylanders acted out the drama. Ingle's actions struck like a wedge on the fault line that separated Catholic Royalists and Protestant Parliamentarians. If that fissure had not already existed in Maryland society, Ingle would be remembered only as a disgruntled ship's captain.

The Plundering Time was not, as it is so often portrayed, a period of general anarchy. The Protestants who overthrew the government were not mercenaries from Virginia or anywhere else. They were Marylanders intent on establishing their own government. Many estates were looted, but this was a common act of war in England and should be viewed as such. What Thomas Arundel, brother-in-law of Lord Baltimore, lost in the siege of Wardour Castle makes all of the Maryland losses seem paltry by comparison. The Plundering Time destroyed most of the Catholic estates but barely affected those of the Protestants. Among the Protestants no indentured servants were freed, business relationships continued, and there was the expectation of a settled government. If this was anarchy, it was very selective anarchy.

There has also been a tendency to view this episode as something imposed on Maryland from the outside, either as the revenge of Richard Ingle or as a result of the English Civil War. Because of this, the rebellion of 1645 has been looked upon as an aberration in the general course of Maryland's development. Yet the root cause of the rebellion was the division between Catholics and Protestants. When viewed in this light, the Plundering Time fits well in the main flow of Maryland history. It was only the first of several rebellions that rocked the colony in the seventeenth century.

APPENDIX

Inventory of Cross House

Fenwick's description of this room tends to support this conclusion. It apparently had two doors that opened to the exterior, each of which had a "great lock" worth five shillings. In the center of the room was a table with a carpet on it worth together £2. In the seventeenth century, carpets were put on the table rather than on the floor. Against one wall was a large cupboard with press and drawers and its own locks and keys. This was valued at £3 and contained goods valued at £5. The cupboard contained spices, wax candles, drugs, shoes, and two new rugs. Against another wall was an iron-bound, painted chest that contained clothing and more carpets. Specifically reported in this chest was a new satin damask petticoat decorated with gold and silver lace. The trunk and its contents were listed at £30. The room also contained a great chest on a frame that contained more clothing. Of interest here was a bearing mantle of crimson taffata, trimmed with gold lace. The chest also contained a Chinese porcelain voider. The great chest and its contents were valued at £10. Finally, there was a trunk containing ordinary household linen including sheets, pillowbears, table cloths, and napkins, the whole valued at £5. The declared value of goods in the Hall was £55, 10s.

The next listed room is the parlor, a private room usually reserved for the master and his family. This room had a fireplace that was equipped with a pair of "great" andirons, a fire pan, and tongs, among other things. The door between the hall and the parlor had a spring lock on it. The lock and the fireplace equipment were valued at £15. The parlor also had a round table with a carpet on it. This must have been a better quality table than the one in the hall since it was valued at £3. The major piece of furniture in this room was described as a great cabinet cupboard filled with fine linen for tables and beds, thread, tape, and other things. The whole was worth £50. The parlor also held a cypress chest containing linens valued at the high price of £150 and a round, iron-bound trunk with fine and coarse linens valued at £50. Unlike the more formal hall, the parlor contained a number of smaller items including a cedar table, linen-covered stools and chairs, and an inlaid form with a back. Together these totaled only £3. Finally, the windows in the parlor were covered by new Darnix hangings and window curtains with iron rods. There were four new cushions and three green cloth carpets. The window cloths and carpets were valued at £15. The total value of goods in the parlor was £286.

The parlor chamber was described next, and this appears to have been Cornwalyes's bedroom. The central item of this room was a large bedstead with its curtains of green cloth decorated with lace and valued at £10. In addition, the bed comprised a large down mattress, a quilt made of holland linen, three fine blankets, and other things to the value of £15. Other furniture in the room included a couch with bed pillows and coverlet, £5, a cedar table and carpet, two stools, a leather chair and cushion, £3. On the walls were six pair of tapestry hangings with forest scenes valued at £25. The room had two windows, each with curtains and rods worth £1. There was a fireplace equipped with a pair of greater and a pair of lesser andirons, fire pans, and other items. The door to the parlor chamber was held by a double spring lock. The lock and fireplace equipment was valued at £2 and the total claimed for the parlor chamber was £61.

Going back to the other end of the hall was a room described as the "Great Chamber." This room was also used as a bedroom as it had a bedstead and a set of blue serge bed curtains with a silk fringe worth £6. The bed was composed of a down bed tick, boulsters and pillows, a holland quilt, three blankets, a bed rug, and a canvas mattress, the whole valued at £12. The room also held a table and carpet, £1, a cedar cabinet containing writings, £2, and a stool, chair and cushions, £1. The major piece of furniture in this room was a great cabinet cupboard with drawers. In this cupboard were a diverse group of goods including linen, thread, needles, silk, pins, laces, chains and bracelets valued at £35. The walls were decorated with a suit of striped stuff hangings and the window had curtains and a rod valued at £5. The three doors in this room each had a double spring lock to the value of 10s. The value of the goods in the "Great Chamber" was set at £62 10s. This may have been Cuthbert Fenwick's room.

Adjacent to the Great Chamber were two little rooms or "closets." The first held four shelves of books, £20, a cabinet holding spices, sugar, fruit and soap, £5, and a chest with cupboard containing clothes and fine linen, £10. The other "closet" had a writing desk, and casks of sugar and fruit, £7, a little inlaid cabinet, £2. This room also had a tapestry hanging on the wall and a taffeta curtain on the window, £2. The contents of the first closet were valued at £35 and the second closet at £11.

Above the hall, in a loft were the makings of two beds including blankets, boulsters and pillows and some tapestry valued at £10. This room was used to store some of the more expensive household items including: a chest of new pewter, £12, a box of porcelain and china dishes and two boxes of drinking glasses, £5, a dozen brass and copper pots, two copper watering pots, a new jack with line and pulleys for the fireplace, £10, a bag of cotton, divers quilted coats and other things worth £15. The loft above the hall held goods valued at £52.

There was a loft above the loft above the hall that was also used for storing valuable items. This loft contained two great, round trunks that held two new bed ticks, two hammocks, three "Turkey work" carpets, a long Arras carpet, five red and green sage curtains, a pair of Fustian blankets, a suit of stained calico hangings and other things worth £40. Captain Cornwalyes's silver plate was kept here before Fenwick hid it in the woods. It included a basin, two bowls, one can (a drinking vessel), one French cup & cover, one salt cellar, twelve spoons, one sugar box & spoon. All of the silver was worth £60. The loft also contained brass, pewter, spits, racks, pots, kettles, and other furniture for a kitchen worth £15. The contents of the upper loft were valued at £115.

Next to the hall were two small chambers that were used as bedrooms. Each contained a bedstead complete with feather bed tick, boulster, blanket, pillow, and bed rug. Together, these beds were valued at £25. Each of these rooms had a Darnix hanging and a table. One of the rooms had a fireplace with fire pan and tongs. These materials were valued at £5 and the two chambers had a total value of £30. The loft above these chambers held the makings of two more beds valued at £3.

Near the main house was a bake house containing pots, kettles, pestles, and other appropriate items valued at £3. There was a separate servants house that had one feather bed and six flock beds worth £12. In a storehouse Cornwalyes kept beer, wine and "stronge waters" worth £20, a smith's forge and tools, £6, iron ware, £10, carpenter's tools, trading axes, hoes, locks, hinges, the brass and iron for a mill, £20, a new cable, £10, a wagon, plow, jacks, and chains, £10. The plantation had a barn and granary which contained wheat, barley, oats, and Indian corn worth £60. In the loft of the granary was bacon worth £20. For livestock, Cornwalyes had 120 head of cattle, £500, goats, £70, sheep, £50, swine £150, horses and mares, £150. He had hogsheads of tobacco worth £200. The new pinnace, with all her rigging, cables, tools, kettles, anchor, small guns, and bedding was worth £200. There were three smaller boats in the creeks worth a total of £30. Finally, he had three blacks and twelve English servants to the value of £200. To this list was added the £160 of goods that Cornwalyes shipped over on the *Reformation* that were never delivered.

References

Introduction: "They came in arms . . . and ransacked every place"

Chapter title from Henry Foley, S.J., *Records of the English Province of the Society of Jesus,* 8 vols. (London, 1877), 3:391. The quote is from a Jesuit letter of 1670 and reportedly describes events at St. Inigoes in 1646.

1. Russell R. Menard, "Maryland's 'Time of Troubles': Sources of Political Disorder in Early St. Mary's," *Maryland Historical Magazine,* 76 (1981): 140, note 54, attributes this phrase to John Lewgar. It is one of many descriptive terms used in the Maryland records to describe this violent period. Others include: "the troubles," "the Plundering Year," "the Plunder," and "the rebellion." William Hand Browne, et al., eds., *Archives of Maryland* (hereafter *Archives*), 72 vols. (Baltimore, 1883–), 4:357, 362, 422, 427.

2. Russell R. Menard, "Economy and Society in Early Colonial Maryland" (Ph.D. diss., University of Iowa, 1975), 146, suggests that the population of St. Mary's County was approximately 470 in 1642. In 1648, after the restoration of proprietary rule, the population was approximately 280. During the period of the troubles, he estimated that the population may have been as low as 100. Garry Wheeler Stone, "Manorial Maryland," *Maryland Historical Magazine,* 82 (1987): 30, estimated a total population of 700 for Maryland, including Kent Island before Ingle came. Beauchamp Plantagenet, *A Description of the Province of New Albion* (London, 1648), 29, reprinted in Peter Force, *Tracts and Other Papers Relating Principally to the Origin, Settlement, and Progress of the Colonies of North America from the Discovery of the Country to the Year 1776,* 4 vols. (Gloucester, Mass.: Peter Smith, 1963), reported that after the rebellion there were only 20 men left on Kent Island. Russell R. Menard, "Economy and Society," (1975), 146, states that only 11 out of 87 freemen resident on the island in 1642 were still there in 1652.

3. Garry Wheeler Stone comments that before 1645, Maryland's commerce was firmly in the hands of the manorial lords. After Ingle's rebellion, their power was greatly reduced and the economy was dominated by English merchant - mariners. See Stone, "Manorial Maryland," 25–26. Lois Green Carr, Russell R. Menard, and Lorena S. Walsh, *Robert Cole's World: Agriculture and Society in Early Maryland* (Chapel Hill: University of North Carolina Press, 1991), 8–9, 11–12, note that after the rebellion, the manor was "something of a dinosaur." Maryland would develop a more egalitarian look based on ordinary planters rather than manorial lords.

4. Given the dramatic events that took place and their impact on Maryland's later development, it is surprising that this period has been given so little popular attention. One of the earliest attempts at understanding the episode was Edward Ingle, "Captain Richard Ingle, the Maryland 'Pirate and Rebel,' 1642–1653," Maryland Historical Society Fund Publication Number 19 (Baltimore, 1889). In this defense of Richard Ingle, the author attempts to explain away his actions and refute the charge that he was a pirate.

This study was based on limited information and was biased in its approach. The most complete presentation of the published material is Matthew Page Andrews, *Tercentenary History of Maryland* (Baltimore, 1925), 1:171–87.

5. Menard, "Maryland's 'Time of Troubles,'" 136; Stone, "Manorial Maryland," 31.

6. Lois Green Carr, "Sources of Political Stability and Upheaval in Seventeenth Century Maryland," *Maryland Historical Magazine,* 79 (1984): 55.

7. Steven D. Crow, "'Your Majesty's Good Subjects': A Reconsideration of Royalism in Virginia, 1642–1652," *Virginia Magazine of Biography and History,* 87 (1979): 164, reports that in 1644, the year before Ingle's raid, Parliament's admiral, the Earl of Warwick, proposed that sympathetic Virginians use the London tobacco fleet to overthrow their royalist governor.

8. Menard, "Maryland's 'Time of Troubles,'" 135–36.

9. Menard, "Economy and Society," 43–44; John D. Krugler, "Lord Baltimore, Roman Catholics and Toleration: Religious Policy in Maryland During the Early Catholic Years, 1634–1649," *Catholic Historical Review,* 65 (1979): 49–75. Lord Baltimore's instructions to the colonists are reprinted in Clayton Coleman Hall, ed., *Narratives of Early Maryland, 1634–1684* (New York: Barnes & Noble, Inc., 1967), 11–24.

10. The case against William Lewis is described in *Archives,* 4:35–39.

11. *Archives,* 4:36.

12. *Archives,* 4:38–39. Lewis is specifically charged with offensive speeches committed against a public proclamation prohibiting unreasonable religious disputes.

13. Nathaniel C. Hale, *Virginia Venturer: A Historical Biography of William Claiborne, 1600–1677* (Richmond: Dietz Press, Inc., 1951), 130–47.

14. J. Frederick Fauz, "Merging and Emerging Worlds: Anglo-Indian Interest Groups and the Development of the Seventeenth-Century Chesapeake," in *Colonial Chesapeake Society*, Lois Green Carr, Philip D. Morgan, and Jean B. Russo, eds. (Chapel Hill: University of North Carolina Press, 1988), 47–98.

15. Hale, *Virginia Venturer,* 195–209, 219–27; deposition of Cuthbert Fenwick, answers 25 and 26, 20 October 1646, in Cornwaley *vs.* Ingle, Chancery, C24 690/14, Public Records Office (hereinafter PRO); Leonard Calvert to Cecil Calvert, 25 April 1638 in *Calvert Papers,* 3 vols., Maryland Historical Society Fund Publication Number 28 (Baltimore, 1889), 1:182–89.

16. Claiborne's petition, and a wealth of information on Kent Island, are published in *Archives,* 5:157–239. Fausz, "Merging and Emerging Worlds," 47–98, explores the extent of Claiborne's plots against the Calverts. The question of Claiborne's connection to Ingle will be explored more fully in a later chapter. Some have seen the two taking advantage of one another's actions but have not suggested a direct link, Hale, *Virginia Venturer,* 260; Raphael Semmes, *Captains and Mariners of Early Maryland* (Baltimore: Johns Hopkins University Press, 1937), 157.

17. Menard, "Economy and Society," 22–24, describes Lord Baltimore's "vision" for Maryland. John Bossy, *The English Catholic Community, 1570–1850* (London: Darton, Longman & Todd, 1975), 102–3, points out that English Catholicism was essentially rural and conservative.

18. Lawrence Stone, *The Family, Sex, and Marriage in England, 1500–1800* (New York: Harper Colophon Books, 1979), 100.

19. Lois Green Carr, "Sources of Political Stability and Upheaval," 45–46, discusses

the development of kinship and community networks as lending stability to the government. However, these developments took place in the 1660s. At the time of Ingle's rebellion these institutions were only in their incipient stage.

20. Menard, "Maryland's 'Time of Troubles,'" 134–35; Stone, *The Family, Sex, and Marriage in England*, 97–108.

21. The literature on the English Civil War is extensive and detailed. In discussing aspects of this conflict, I have relied heavily on a selected number of works. An excellent popular account of the period is J. P. Kenyon, *The Civil Wars of England* (New York: Alfred A. Knopf, 1988). A more detailed but still readable account is Ivan Roots, *The Great Rebellion, 1642–1660* (London: Botsford, 1966). The classic and still most complete study is Samuel R. Gardiner, *History of the Great Civil War, 1642–1649* (London, 1893). A contemporary account with important details is Edward Hyde, Earl of Clarendon, *The History of the Rebellion and Civil Wars in England Begun in the Year 1641*, ed. W. Dean Macray (Oxford, 1888). An important discussion of the Civil War on a local level is J. S. Morrill, *The Revolt of the Provinces: Conservatives and Radicals in the English Civil War, 1630–1650* (London: Allen & Unwin, 1976). For technical aspects of the military campaigns and armies, an excellent, readable source is Phillip Haythornthwaite, *The English Civil War, 1642–1651: An Illustrated Military History* (Dorset: Blandford Press, 1983).

22. The period leading up to the civil war is detailed in a number of biographies of Charles I, including John Bowle, *Charles I: A Biography* (Boston: Weidenfeld & Nicolson, 1975) and C. V. Wedgewood, *The King's Peace* (London: Macmillan, 1955). The dramatic events surrounding the end of the king's life are presented in C. V. Wedgewood, *A Coffin for King Charles: The Trial and Execution of Charles I* (New York: Macmillan & Co., 1964; repr. with an introduction by A. L. Rowse, Alexandria, Va.: Time-Life Books, 1981).

23. The text of the Grand Remonstrance, as well as most other government documents of major importance for this period, is published in Samuel R. Gardiner, *The Constitutional Documents of the Puritan Revolution, 1625–1660* (Oxford: The Clarendon Press, 1906).

Chapter 1: "Our present estate every day bettering itt selfe . . ."

Chapter title from Andrew White, S.J., to Cecil Calvert, 20 February 1638, in *Calvert Papers*, 1:202.

1. Menard, "Economy and Society," 57–60, 81.

2. Carr, "Sources of Political Stability and Upheaval," 55; Stone, "Manorial Maryland," 3–36.

3. Stone, "Manorial Maryland," 7–11.

4. Menard, "Maryland's 'Time of Troubles,'" 125–26; Stone, "Manorial Maryland," 29.

5. Menard, "Maryland's 'Time of Troubles'" 135.

6. Menard, "Economy and Society," 73–77; Lois Green Carr, Russell R. Menard, and Louis Peddicord, *Maryland at the Beginning* (Annapolis: Hall of Records Commission, 1975), 28.

7. Leonard Calvert's age has been a source of some controversy. It had long been thought he was born in 1606, as published in Edward C. Papenfuse, Alan F. Day, David

W. Jordan, and Gregory A. Stiverson, *A Biographical Dictionary of the Maryland Legislature, 1635–1789,* 2 vols. (Baltimore: Johns Hopkins University Press, 1979–85), 1:190. However, Harry Wright Newman, *The Flowering of the Maryland Palatinate* (Baltimore: Genealogical Publishing Co., 1984) published a birth record dated 1610 that probably refers to Leonard Calvert. A birth date in 1610 would explain the confusion in the will of George Calvert over what Leonard was to inherit. Mrs. Russell Hastings, "Calvert and Darnell Gleanings from English Wills," *Maryland Historical Magazine,* 20 (1925): 320, suggested a birth date of c. 1610 because Leonard is first treated as a minor and later as an adult. She concluded that he had just reached the age of 21. Leonard Calvert's sea voyages and much information on the Avalon Colony, are summarized in J. Thomas Scharf, *History of Maryland,* 3 vols. (repr. Hatboro, Pa.: Tradition Press, 1967), 1:42–49. Scharf reported that Calvert accompanied his father to Newfoundland in 1628, returned to England later that year, and sailed again for Newfoundland in 1629. He probably sailed with his father back to England in 1630. His trip to Maryland in 1633, when he was only 23 years old, was his fifth transatlantic voyage.

8. This information on Leonard Calvert is presented in testimony taken in relation to the question of Catholic priests in Newfoundland as published in R. C. Anderson, ed., *The Book of Examinations and Depositions, 1622–1644,* Publications of the Southampton Record Society, 2 vols. (Southampton, 1929), 2:38–42.

9. Leonard Calvert to Cecil Calvert, 25 April 1638 in *Calvert Papers,* 1:182–93.

10. Stone, "Manorial Maryland," 29, 31, argues that Calvert could not inspire loyalty among the settlers and contrasts him with William Claiborne's efforts. Lois Green Carr, "Sources of Political Stability and Upheaval," 55, points out the religious gulf that separated Calvert from the people he was trying to govern. In 1644 and again in 1646, William Claiborne tried to induce the Kent Islanders to attack St. Mary's. Most of what is known about Claiborne's attempts on Kent Island in the 1640s comes from two depositions given by Thomas Bradnox on 7 December 1648, *Archives,* 4:458–59.

11. Leonard Calvert to Cecil Calvert, 25 April 1638, in *Calvert Papers,* 1:182–193.

12. The powers and responsibilities of the governor are detailed in various commissions sent to Maryland by Lord Baltimore. For the period under consideration, these are published in *Archives,* 3:49–55 (1637), 108–14 (1642), and 151–57 (1644).

13. The duties and responsibilities of the council were given in the same commission given to Leonard Calvert in 1637. The members of the council early in 1642 were those sworn in on 20 March 1639 and there is no record of any additions until late in 1642, *Archives,* 3:53, 85, 114.

14. Lewgar's appointment as secretary was part of Leonard Calvert's commission in 1637, *Archives,* 3:53. Garry Wheeler Stone, "Society, Housing and Architecture in Early Maryland: John Lewgar's St. John's" (Ph.D. diss., University of Pennsylvania, 1982), extensively researched the career of John Lewgar and described the house and plantation he built in Maryland. Lois Green Carr, "John Lewgar, biography file" (unpublished mss., Research Department, Historic St. Mary's City, n.d.) has abstracted most of the references to Lewgar's Maryland career.

15. Anthony Wood, *Athenae Oxonienses,* 4 vols., Philip Bliss, ed. (London, 1813), 4:696–97; Sidney Lee, ed., *Dictionary of National Biography,* 22 vols. (London, 1909) 11:1046–47.

16. Gregory Panzini, Papal Nuncio to England, described Lewgar's almost penniless state in London during 1635, as published in Thomas Hughes, S.J., *The History of the*

Society of Jesus in North America, 4 vols. (London, 1907), Text 1: 359–60.

17. Lewgar arrived in Maryland on 28 November 1637, accompanied by his wife, Ann, his son, John and 7 servants. "Land Notes, 1634–1655," *Maryland Historical Magazine,* 5 (1910): 166.

18. Stone, "Society, Housing and Architecture in Early Maryland," 135.

19. Lois Green Carr, "Thomas Cornwaleys, biography file" (unpublished mss., Research Department, Historic St. Mary's City, n.d.); Papenfuse, et al., *Biographical Dictionary of the Maryland Legislature,* 1:234–35; Jane Cornwaleys, *Private Correspondence of Jane Lady Cornwaleys, 1613–1644* (London, 1842); Edward D. Neil, *The Founders of Maryland as Portrayed in Manuscripts, Provincial Records and Early Documents* (Albany, 1876), 4; f. 522v, 18 May 1640 in Hawley *vs.* Cornwallis, Chancery, Decrees and Orders, C33/177, PRO.

20. The Battle of the Pocomoke is described in *Archives,* 1:17–18 and in deposition of Cuthbert Fenwick, answer 25, 20 October 1646 in Cornwaleys *vs.* Ingle, Chancery C24 690/14, PRO, as transcribed in Edward W. Beitzell, ed., *Chronicles of St. Mary's,* 26 (1978): 8. The invasion of Kent Island is reported in Leonard Calvert to Cecil Calvert, 25 April 1638, in *Calvert Papers,* 1:182–89.

21. Thomas Cornwaleys to Cecil Calvert, 14 April 1638, in *Calvert Papers,* 1:174, describes problems with the mill and the construction of his house. This structure was probably the house on Cross Manor. John Lewgar to Cecil Calvert, 5 January 1639, in *Calvert Papers,* 1:197–98, discusses Cornwaleys's involvement with the fur trade. Also see Stone, "Manorial Maryland," 16–17, for the history of the fur trade in Maryland during this period. Menard, "Economy and Society," 81, 87, discusses Cornwaleys's tobacco trading and his extension of credit to the planters.

22. Thomas Cornwaleys to Cecil Calvert, 14 April 1638, in *Calvert Papers,* 1:172, 179. The record of the first Assembly that rejected Lord Baltimore's code of laws is in *Archives,* 1:2–24.

23. One exception is Edward W. Beitzell:

He [Cecil Calvert] was most fortunate in obtaining the services of Cornwaleys—here was a man of confidence, cool in the hour of danger, firm, frank and determined, a molder of public opinion and a center to which all eyes turned in cases of emergency and doubt. In all activities, whether legislative, judicial or military with which his name is linked, he stands out as fearless and undaunted in expressing his views and as a brave defender of the rights of the Proprietor as well as those of the colonist. In debates of the Assembly he was ever a leader and in every military expedition, he was the ablest commander.

See Beitzell, "Captain Thomas Cornwaleys, Forgotten Leader in the Founding of Maryland," *Chronicles of St. Mary's,* 20, no. 7 (1972): 1.

24. William B. Chilton, "The Brent Family," *Virginia Magazine of History and Biography,* 14 (1906–7): 95–101; 15 (1908):194–97. Giles Brent's headrights and arrival in Maryland are published in "Land Notes, 1634–1655," *Maryland Historical Magazine,* 5 (1910): 167, 265.

25. Stone, *The Family, Sex, and Marriage in England,* 69–89, discusses the traditional lineage-based family. "Ingle in Maryland," *Maryland Historical Magazine,* 1 (1906): 136.

26. Brent's defense of the freemen's right to depart out of the province was in September 1642 (*Archives,* 1:173–74).

27. Carr, "Sources of Political Stability," 49; Menard, "Economy and Society," 111.

28. For the case of Thomas Gerrard, see *Archives,* 1:119. Menard, "Maryland's 'Time

of Troubles,'" 134–35, discusses the heightened expectations and increasing ambition of the ordinary planters in opposition to the gentry.

29. On 4 August 1645, Ingle gave a deposition in the High Court of Admiralty concerning 40,000 pipestaves Leonard Calvert took from Kent Island in 1640. He described himself as 36 years of age and living in Stepney, Middlesex County. Deposition of Richard Ingle, High Court of Admiralty, Examinations, HCA 13/60, PRO. The 1644 indictment against Ingle is in *Archives,* 4:238. For Radcliff and Stepney, see Ben Weinrib and Christopher Hibbert, eds., *The London Encyclopedia* (Bethesda: Adler & Adler, 1986), 637–38, 824; Michael Power, "Shadwell: The Development of a London Suburban Community in the Seventeenth Century," *The London Journal,* 4 (1978): 29–45; and William Lowe, "The Master of the Ark: A Seventeenth-Century Chronicle," *Maryland Historical Magazine,* 95 (2000): 261–89.

30. Ralph Davis, *English Merchant Shipping and Anglo-Dutch Rivalry in the Seventeenth Century* (London: H.M.S.O., 1975), 22. John Winthrop, *History of New England, 1630–1649,* James K. Hosmer, ed., 2 vols. (New York: Barnes & Noble, Inc., 1966), 2:75, reports Ingle's claim to have been in the Virginia trade for ten years in 1642.

31. Ingle's command of a ship is recorded on 10 September 1639 in Port Book, London, Exports by Denizens, Christmas 1638–Christmas 1639, E 190/43/6, f. 98, PRO. Cornwaleys's description of Ingle is in Bill of Thomas Cornwaleys, 22 August 1645 in Cornwaleys *vs.* Ingle, Chancery, Bills and Answers, C24 15/23, PRO. Thomas Gerard returned to England in the *Blessing* early in 1640 (*Archives,* 41:542). Cornwaleys, who had been in Maryland in January 1640, was in England by October 1640 (*Archives,* 4:58, 41:543). That he sailed with Ingle is likely. Gerrard exported 22 hogsheads of tobacco on the *Blessing* (*Archives,* 41:542).

32. Port Book, London, Exports by Denizens, Christmas 1639–Christmas 1640, E 190/43/1, f. 150,152, PRO. Deposition of Richard Ingle, High Court of Admiralty, Examinations, HCA 13/60, PRO.

33. Port Book, London, Exports by Denizens, Christmas 1639–Christmas 1640, E 190/43/1, f. 153, PRO. Ames, ed., *County Court Records of Accomack-Northampton, Virginia, 1640–1645* (Charlottesville: University Press of Virginia, 1973).

34. Ames, ed., *County Court Records of Accomack,* 164. Winthrop, *History of New England,* 2:75.

35. Ingle's association with Parliament was charged in the 1644 indictment against him and by his own testimony in 1645. See *Archives,* 4:238; Answer of Richard Ingle, 29 September 1645, in Copley et al. *vs.* Ingle, High Court of Admiralty, Answers, HCA13/119, PRO.

36. One of Lord Baltimore's secular priests came to Maryland in 1643 on the *Reformation.* See Cecil Calvert to Leonard Calvert, 21 November 1642, in *Calvert Papers,* 1:212; Ames, ed., *County Court Records of Accomack,* 270; *Archives,* 4:251–52.

37. Ames, ed., *County Court Records of Accomack,* 164, 405–6.

38. Bernard Capp, *Cromwell's Navy: The Fleet and the English Revolution, 1648–1660* (Oxford, 1989), 159.

Chapter 2: "They slew the men . . . we had there and carried away our goods"

1. Fausz, "Merging and Emerging Worlds," 47, 68–69; Francis Jennings, *The Ambiguous Iroquois Empire* (New York: W. W. Norton & Co., 1984), 116–21.

2. Stone, "Manorial Maryland," 14–16; Fausz, "Merging and Emerging Worlds," 59–61; Jennings, *Ambiguous Iroquois Empire,* 118.

3. Andrew White, S.J., "A Briefe Relation of the Voyage unto Maryland," in Hall, ed., *Narratives of Early Maryland,* 42; Semmes, *Captains and Mariners of Early Maryland,* 140–41. Whether or not it was Claiborne who incited the Maryland Indians against Calvert's settlement is a question that can never be settled. According to Claiborne's supporters, the conference held at Patuxent on 20 June 1634 entirely cleared Claiborne of the charges. See, for example, *Virginia Venturer,* 179–81. Calvert's supporters see this as a contrived vindication, directly against the orders of Virginia's governor, Sir John Harvey. Claiborne did publicly threaten that, if provoked, he would "be revenged though he be joined with the Indians in a canoa." Toby Young to Sir Toby Matthew, July 1634, in Hall, ed., *Narratives of Early Maryland,* 55–58.

4. The Marylanders sent another vessel up to Palmer's Island the next year but it was seized by the Virginians. Hale, *Virginia Venturer,* 196–97. This trade continued as late as March 1641, *Archives,* 4:138.

5. Fausz, "Merging and Emerging Worlds," 73.

6. Jennings, *Ambiguous Iroquois Empire,* 116–19; Plantagenet, "A Description of the Province of New Albion," 24.

7. Fausz, "Merging and Emerging Worlds," 76–77

8. Stone, "Manorial Maryland," 16–17; Fausz, "Merging and Emerging Worlds"; "From the Annual Letter 1639," in Hall, ed., *Narratives of Early Maryland,* 124; "From the Annual Letter 1640" in Hall, ed., *Narratives of Early Maryland,* 131.

9. *Archives,* 3:99; 4:138.

10. *Archives,* 3:103–4.

11. *Archives,* 1:127–64.

12. *Archives,* 3:85–86, 106.

13. *Archives,* 3:258; 4:71, 94–95, 146.

14. "A Narrative Derived from the Letters of Ours, Out of Maryland, [1642]" in Hall, ed., *Narratives of Early Maryland,* 136.

15. *Archives,* 3:149; 4:94.

16. *Archives,* 1:167–98; 4:128.

17. *Archives,* 1:173; William W. Henning, ed., *The Statutes at Large, Being a Collection of All the Laws of Virginia from the First Session of the Legislature in the Year 1619* (New York, 1823), 228.

18. Krugler, "Lord Baltimore, Roman Catholics and Toleration," 20; Samuel R. Gardiner, *History of the Great Civil War, 1642–1649* (London, 1893), 1:114–15.

19. Billings, *Old Dominion in the 17th Century* (Chapel Hill: University of North Carolina Press, 1975), 51–52.

20. *Archives,* 1:180–81.

21. *Archives,* 3:116–17; 4:125.

22. Lewgar's account for the expedition is in *Archives,* 3:119–21. The case against Giles Brent is played out in *Archives,* 4:128–40.

23. *Archives,* 4:140.

24. *Archives,* 4:151–61.

25. *Archives,* 4:155. Prior to this case, the composition of the court is only mentioned twice and each time there were three judges. Following this case, the number of judges varies but is often just two, the governor and the secretary. Of the men on the jury, Cuthbret Fenwick and John Price had appointed Thomas Cornwaleys as their proxy. Thomas Greene, Nicholas Harvey, and Francis Posie voted with Cornwaleys. On the other side, David Wickliff, George Pye, and Walter Beane gave their votes to Thomas Weston who voted with the governor. Also, George Binx and Thomas Hebden voted with the government party. The final two jurors, James Neale and Peter Macrill, were not at the Assembly. *Archives,* 1:167–82.

Chapter 3: "Security of contiens was . . . expected from this government . . ."

1. Cecil Calvert to Leonard Calvert, 21 November 1642, in *Calvert Papers,* 1:217.

2. Krugler, "Lord Baltimore, Roman Catholics and Toleration," 65–66; John Bossy, "Reluctant Colonists: The English Catholics Confront the Atlantic," in David Quinn, ed., *Early Maryland in a Wider World* (Detroit: Wayne State University Press, 1982), 162–63; Russell R. Menard, "Economy and Society," 32; John Bossy, *The English Catholic Community,* 259.

3. Bossy, "Reluctant Colonists," 152, 156.

4. Francis Edwards, S.J., *The Jesuits in England from 1580 to the Present Day* (London: Burns & Oates, 1985), 58–61; Hughes, *History of the Society of Jesus in North America,* 1:201–2.

5. Bossy, *The English Catholic Community,* 51–52, 174–75; Krugler, "Lord Baltimore, Roman Catholics and Toleration," 54.

6. Hughes, *History of the Society of Jesus in North America,* Text, 1:256–57; Krugler, "Lord Baltimore, Roman Catholics and Toleration," 66.

7. White, "A Briefe Relation," 40.

8. *Archives,* 1:5; Thomas Copley to Cecil Calvert, 3 April 1638, in *Calvert Papers,* 1:163.

9. Krugler, "Lord Baltimore, Roman Catholics and Toleration," 57; Russell R. Menard, "Economy and Society," 36–37; Cecil Calvert, "Instructions to the Colonists by Lord Baltimore, 1633," in Clayton Coleman Hall, ed., *Narratives of Early Maryland, 1633–1684,* 16–17; Thomas Copley, S.J., to Cecil Calvert, 3 April,1638 in *Calvert Papers,* 1:157–69; Hughes, *History of the Society of Jesus in North America,* Text, 1:386–87.

10. Thomas Copley, S.J., to Cecil Calvert, 3 April 1638, in *Calvert Papers,* 1:162.

11. Copley to Calvert, 3 April 1638, ibid., 1:157.

12. Thomas Cornwaleys to Cecil Calvert, 14 April 1638, ibid., 1:172.

13. Thomas Copley, S.J., to Cecil Calvert, 3 April 1638, ibid., 1:158.

14. John Lewgar, "The Cases of John Lewgar, twenty in number," in Hughes, *History of the Society of Jesus in North America,* Documents, 1:158–61.

15. General Vitelleschi, S.J., to Philip Fisher, S.J. (Thomas Copley), 3 September 1639; General Vitelleschi, S.J., to Edward Knott, S.J., 3 September 1639 in Hughes, *History of the Society of Jesus in North America,* Documents, 1:22–23, Text 1:458–459.

16. John Lewgar to Cecil Calvert, 5 Jan 1639 in *Calvert Papers,* 1:194–201; *Archives,* 1:27–84.

17. "Land Notes, 1634–1655," 267–68.

18. Hale, *Virginia Venturer,* 176. Final determination of the issue came on 4 April 1638 when the Lords Commission on Plantations decided in favor of Lord Baltimore, *Archives,* 3:71–73. The act for maintaining Lord Baltimore's title is in *Archives,* 1:41–42.

19. Thomas Copley, S.J., to Cecil Calvert, 3 April,1638 in *Calvert Papers,* 1:164–65.

20. Extracts of the Jesuit Annual letters for the 1630s, on which this discussion is based, are in Hall, ed., *Narratives of Early Maryland,* 119–31 and Foley, *Records of the English Province of the Society of Jesus,* 3:367–81.

21. Father Andrew White, S.J., to Cecil Calvert, 20 February 1638, in *Calvert Papers,* 1:201–11.

22. *Archives,* 3:88.

23. John Lewgar to Cecil Calvert, 5 January 1639, in *Calvert Papers,* 1:194.

24. *Archives,* 1:2–3; "Land Notes,1634–1655," 166.

25. Edward C. Papenfuse and Joseph M. Coale III, *The Hammond-Harwood House Atlas of Historical Maps of Maryland, 1608–1908* (Baltimore: Johns Hopkins University Press, 1982), 2.

26. Stone, "Manorial Maryland," 7–8, argues that there was little dispersion of settlement before 1637. However, Henry Fleet had a grant dated 9 May 1634 from the Commissioners of Maryland. See "Land Notes, 1634–1655," 68. St. Inigoes, the Jesuit manor south of St. Mary's, had been purchased from Richard Gerard. He left Maryland well before the 1636 Conditions of Plantation were proclaimed. His grant must have been early. See Henry W. Newman, *Flowering of the Maryland Palatinate,* 211. Jerome Hawley's grant on the Patuxent dated to August 1636. *Archives,* 51:497.

27. Patents 1, ff. 40–41 on microfilm produced by the Genealogical Society, "Maryland Patents, 1637–1650" (Salt Lake City, 1947).

28. Walter Morely arrived in Maryland on 22 November 1638. "Land Notes, 1634–1655," 167.

29. The Jesuits had transported a total of 62 individuals. Of those, 8 were Jesuits. In submitting his demand for land, Father Poulton did not claim headrights for the Jesuits but only for the servants. The 11,700 acres claimed were much lower than what was actually due to them. "Land Notes, 1634–1655," 267–68.

30. Bossy, "Reluctant Colonists," 151.

31. John Lewgar to Cecil Calvert, 5 January 1639, in *Calvert Papers,* 1:200.

32. Hughes, *History of the Society of Jesus in North America,* Text, 1:459.

33. Cecil Calvert to Leonard Calvert, 21 November 1642, in *Calvert Papers,* 1:219; Patents 1, ff. 40–41 on microfilm produced by the Genealogical Society, "Maryland Patents, 1637–1650."

34. "From the Annual Letter 1640," in Hall, ed., *Narratives of Early Maryland,* 131–34; John Lewgar to Cecil Calvert, 5 January 1639, in *Calvert Papers,* 1:194; Hughes, *History of the Society of Jesus in North America,* Text, 1:459–60.

35. *Archives,* 1:88; "Land Notes, 1634–1655," *Maryland Historical Magazine,* 5 (1910): 366–67.

36. Hughes, *History of the Society of Jesus in North America,* Text, 1:477–92, provides a discussion of the "seizure" of Jesuit lands. "From the Annual Letter 1640," 132.

37. "From the Annual Letter 1642," in Hall, ed., *Narratives of Early Maryland,* 136; *Archives,* 3:149.

38. Hughes, *History of the Society of Jesus in North America,* Documents, 1:166–68; The Provincial's objections are listed in the same source, Text, 1:513–14.

39. Ibid., Text, 1:495–99.

40. Ibid., Documents, 1:190–91.

41. Ibid., Documents, 1:172–78; Text, 1:570–73.

42. Ibid., Text 1:499–501. The conditions as published in Maryland are in *Archives,* 3:99–100.

43. Bossy, "Reluctant Colonists," 151.

44. Hughes, *History of the Society of Jesus in North America,* Documents, 1:164–65.

45. Ibid., Text, 1:489–90.

46. Ibid., Text, 1:505–15; Documents, 1:169–72.

47. Ibid., Text, 1:515–18.

48. Ibid., Text, 1:520.

49. Ibid., Documents, 1:172–78.

50. Ibid., Documents, 1:187–90.

51. Cecil Calvert to Leonard Calvert, 21 November 1642, in *Calvert Papers,* 1:221.

52. "Baltimore's draft of a Jesuit assignment," in Hughes, *History of the Society of Jesus in North America,* Documents, 1:190–91; Text 1:529–31.

53. General Vitelleschi, S.J., to Edward Knott, S.J., 22 November 1642 and 6 December 1642, in Hughes, *History of the Society of Jesus in North America,* Documents, 1:27, Text, 1:532.

54. Cecil Calvert to Leonard Calvert, 21 November 1642, in *Calvert Papers,* 1:211–21.

55. "Land Notes, 1634–1655," *Maryland Historical Magazine,* 6 (1911): 202–3.

56. Cecil Calvert to Leonard Calvert, 21 November 1642, in *Calvert Papers,* 1:219; *Archives,* 3:99–101.

57. Cecil Calvert to Leonard Calvert, 21 November 1642, in *Calvert Papers,* 1:220–21.

58. "Land Notes, 1634–1655," 262.

59. Hughes, *History of the Society of Jesus in North America,* Text 1:477–92.

Chapter 4: "The tymes now doe seeme perillous . . ."

1. The beginning of the war is well covered in Kenyon, *The Civil Wars of England,* 23–62, and Ivan Roots, *The Great Rebellion, 1642–1660,* 73–82.

2. It is possible that Lord Baltimore had informed his brother of current events in an earlier dispatch sent on the *Reformation.* See, Cecil Calvert to Leonard Calvert, 21 November 1642, in *Calvert Papers,* 1:211.

3. Hughes, *History of the Society of Jesus in North America,* Text, 1:562.

4. J. C. H. Aveling, *The Handle and the Axe: The Catholic Recusants in England from Reformation to Emancipation* (London: Blond & Briggs, 1976), 169; Margaret Blundell, *Cavalier: Letters of William Blundell to his Friends, 1620–1698* (London: Longmans, Green & Co., 1933), 11; Vicary Gibb, ed., *The Complete Peerage of England, Scotland, Ireland, Great britian and the United Kingdom,* 13 vols. (London, 1910), 1:264.

5. Quoted in Hughes, *History of the Society of Jesus in North America,* Text, 1:562.

6. Parliament passed an ordinance on 18 August 1643 that allowed sequestration of two-thirds of an estate if a person harbored a priest, had been to Mass, had been con-

victed of popish recusancy, brought their children up as papists or refused to take an anti-papal oath, C. M. Firth and R. S. Rait, eds., *Acts and Ordinances of the Interregnum, 1642–1660*, 3 vols. (London, 1911), 1:254–60.

7. *Dictionary of National Biography*, 1:615–21; S. John Edwards, *Some Old Wiltshire Homes* (London, 1894), 55. It was from Woodhouse that Lady Blanche Arundel supposedly escaped in a coffin.

8. *Dictionary of National Biography*, 18:640–42; Aveling, *The Handle and the Axe*, 166–67.

9. Davis, *English Merchant Shipping and Anglo-Dutch Rivalry*, 8.

10. Ralph Davis, *The Rise of the English Shipping Industry in the 17th and 18th Centuries* (Norton Abbot: David & Charles, 1962), 286; Davis, *English Merchant Shipping and Anglo-Dutch Rivalry*, 8–9.

11. Davis, *Rise of the English Shipping Industry*, 45.

12. Examination of Hatrick Cornelison Cocke, answer 8, 13 June 1645, in Ingle *vs.* The Looking Glass, Examinations, section E, High Court of Admiralty, HCA 13/60, PRO; Davis, *The Rise of the English Shipping Industry*, 59.

13. The *Reformation* crew included Richard Ingle, master, John Durford, master's mate, Thomas Greene, boatswain, Thomas Eves, cooper, Pascho Panton, cooper, Richard Garnett, gunner, Gilbert Chubb, gunner, Robert Rawlins, surgeon and William Edrupp, servant to Ingle.

14. Davis, *Rise of the English Shipping Industry*, 110–13.

15. Ibid., 59–60.

16. John Durford, Thomas Greene and William Edrupp all testified about Ingle's voyage in 1644 as well as events in 1645.

17. Davis, *Rise of the English Shipping Industry*, 143.

18. *Archives*, 4:238.

19. Arthur Pierce Middleton, *Tobacco Coast: A Maritime History of Chesapeake Bay in the Colonial Era* (Baltimore: Johns Hopkins University Press, 1984), 8–10.

20. Ames, *County Court Records of Accomack*, 251–53.

21. Ibid., 263. The connection between Mrs. Troughton and Father Poulton is in Foley, *Records of the English Province of the Society of Jesus*, 1:155. (Pedigree chart of the Poulton family.)

22. Ames, *County Court Records of Accomack*, 269–70, 301, 304–5.

23. *Archives*, 4:233, 238–39.

24. *Archives*, 4:189, 197, 203.

25. Ames, ed., *County Court Records of Accomack*, 270.

Chapter 5: "Whereas I am determined to goe for England . . ."

1. *Archives*, 3:126–129; 4:180–181.

2. *Archives*, 3:130.

3. "A Narrative Derived from the Letters of Ours, Out of Maryland, [1642]" in Hall, ed., *Narratives of Early Maryland, 1633–1684*, 140.

4. Cecil Calvert to Leonard Calvert, 21 November 1642 in *Calvert Papers*, 1:212.

5. Ibid., 1:216; "A Narrative Derived from the Letters of Ours, Out of Maryland, [1642]," 140.

6. Hughes, *History of the Society of Jesus in North America,* Documents, 1:28; *Archives,* 4:292.

7. Lois Green Carr, "Chapel Field Land Use History File," mss. on file, Department of Research, Historic St. Mary's City, 1992.

9. Hughes, *History of the Society of Jesus in North America,* Documents, 1:28.

9. Ibid., Documents, 1:28–29.

10. Ibid., Text, 1:557.

11. *Archives,* 3:130.

12. Ibid., 1:201, 4:196; "Land Notes,1634–1655," *Maryland Historical Magazine,* 5 (1910): 368.

13. *Archives,* 1:143; Pope claimed Thomas Baker and Thomas Oliver as his servants while they were actually transported by Leonard Calvert in 1641, *Archives,* 4:174,221; "Land Notes,1634–1655," *Maryland Historical Magazine,* 5 (1910): 262–63. Calvert's clearing of the fort area is based on *Archives,* 4:159.

14. *Archives,* 4:189.

15. Ibid., 3:131; 4:196, 201.

16. Ibid., 3:139.

17. Leonard Calvert left Maryland soon after 12 April 1643. With favorable conditions, he could have been back in England by mid-June. He returned to Maryland by mid-September 1644. Again, under the best conditions, he would have left England by mid-July 1644. He could only have been in England for a year. A discussion of the use of wet nurses is in Antonia Fraser, *The Weaker Vessel* (New York: Vintage Books, 1984), 77–79.

18. The idea of a connection between the Calvert family and the Brent family was mentioned in John L. Bozman, *The History of Maryland,* 2 vols. (Baltimore, 1837), 2:307. I have been unable to trace the origin of this idea but it has clearly been around since the early nineteenth century. In a series of articles on the Calvert-Darnall genealogy, this connection, especially Ann Brent's marriage, has been questioned. See Mrs. Russell Hastings, "Calvert and Darnall Gleamings from English Wills," *Maryland Historical Magazine,* 20 (1925): 321; 22 (1927): 307. Newman, *The Flowering of the Maryland Palatinate,* 181, reported searching in England for a marriage certificate for Leonard Calvert but without success.

19. William B. Chilton, "The Brent Family," *Virginia Magazine of History and Biography,* 14 (1906–7): 99–100.

20. Ibid., 427.

21. Hugh Aveling, "the Marriage of Catholic Recusants, 1559–1642," *Journal of Ecclesiastical History,* 14 (1963): 68–83.

22. *Archives,* 3:130. In 1982 and 1983, Historic St. Mary's City conducted extensive excavations on the site to define its history. These excavations confirmed that it was the site of Governor Calvert's residence and uncovered the foundation of a truly impressive structure, measuring 67.5 feet long and forty feet wide. The house was divided into two long rows of rooms separated by a corridor that ran its length. The southern section was eighteen feet wide, the northern section 16.5 feet wide. It was also clear that the structure had undergone many modifications during its long history.

The archaeological evidence suggests that Calvert built the southern section of the house in the 1630s and that the northern section was added to it about 1639 as the "townhouse" authorized by the Assembly in that year. This probably was connected directly to the north wall of Calvert's house with no corridor between the sections. Later, when the house was used as an ordinary in the 1660s, the central corridor was created to provide privacy between the two halves of the house.

In the summer of 1995 archaeologists returned to the site to explore the origin and history of the central corridor. The current foundation of the Calvert house consists of brick that was added in the late seventeenth century. The original foundation, preserved in places under the brick, was made of a ferrous sandstone. Evidence of this stone has been found under the south, east, and north exterior walls. If, as had been suggested, the northern section of the house was added to a standing structure, there should be a sandstone foundation under one of the brick walls of the central corridor. Much to the archeologists' surprise, there was no sandstone foundation, or any continuous foundation trench other than the one for the brick.

The new archaeological evidence created an interpretive problem for the Calvert house. If there was no evidence of a continuous sandstone foundation in the center of the house, then neither corridor wall could have ever been an exterior wall. This suggested that the house was built to its present size all at one time and that the central corridor was an integral part of the design. The archaeology pointed to a very different history for this house than one built in stages would imply. It gave rise to questions concerning the dating of this house and Calvert's purpose in building it.

Of these two issues, the dating of the construction is the easiest to handle. In the northern section was a large room without a fireplace and open to the rafters. This was later referred to as the St. Mary's Room and the Assembly used to meet here. Scholars have always suspected that Calvert built this room specifically for that purpose. The earliest date that the Assembly could have met in this room was March 1642. As late as January 1642, Calvert was calling for the Assembly to meet at the fort of St. Mary's. It is unlikely that Calvert would have let the Assembly meet elsewhere if he had a suitable space in his own house. Thus the construction of the house can reasonably be dated to 1642.

An earlier date in the 1640s would fit the historical record better. While the property was called was called the Governor's Field as early as 1639, Calvert did not patent the land until 13 August 1641. Significantly, the surveyor did not refer to a house on the property, as he did in every other early patent in St. Mary's. It is inconceivable that the surveyor would not mention the house if it were standing. This strongly suggests that the house was built after the date of the patent. However, the price Nathaniel Pope agreed to pay for the property in August 1642 was high enough to include the house. The most likely date for the construction of the house then would be between August 1641 and August 1642.

For information on these findings, see H. Chandlee Forman, *Jamestown and St. Mary's: Buried Cities of Romance* (Baltimore: Johns Hoplins University Press, 1938), 268–73; Henry M. Miller, "Discovering Maryland's First City: A Summary of the 1981–1984 Archaeological Excavations in St. Mary's City, Maryland," *St. Mary's City Archaeology Series,* No. 2 (St. Mary's City, 1986), 13–46; Timothy B. Riordan, "Preliminary Report on the 1995 Excavations at the Calvert House (18ST13), St. Mary's City, Maryland," ms. on file, Department of Research, Historic St. Mary's City,1995; Stone, "Society, Housing and Architecture in Early Maryland," 378–81; and "Land Notes, 1634–1655," *Maryland Historical Magazine,* 6 (1911): 264.

23. *Archives,* 1:75; Miller, "Discovering Maryland's First City," 20–23.

24. Examination of Giles Brent, answer 7, 7 August 1645, in Cornwaleys *vs.* Ingle, Examinations, section K, High Court of Admiralty, HCA 13/60, PRO.

25. *Archives,* 4:203.

26. The council records abruptly stop on 24 April and begin again on 13 December 1643, *Archives,* 3:134–35. The court records show Brent gone during this period as well, *Archives,* 4:203–14. The lack of land patented in this period is evident in "Land Notes, 1634–1655," *Maryland Historical Magazine,* 5 (1910): 166–74, 261–71, 374; 6 (1911): 60–70, 195–203, 262–70.

27. *Archives,* 3:135–37.

28. Ibid., 3:131–32.

29. Ibid., 3:133–34.

30. Ibid., 3:133.

31. Fausz, "Merging and Emerging Worlds," 77. Jennings, *The Ambiguous Iroquois Empire,* 120.

32. Barry C. Kent, *Susquehanna's Indians* (Harrisburg, Pa.: Pennsylvania Historical & Museum Commission, 1989), 342. The place is known today as the Roberts site.

33. Peter Lindestrom, *Geogrophia Americae* (1691), translated and edited by Amandus Johnson (Philadelphia: Swedish Colonial Society, 1924), 241; Johan Printz, "Report of the Governor, 1644," in Albert C. Myers, ed., *Narratives of Early Pennsylvania, West New Jersey, and Delaware, 1630–1707* (New York: C. Scribner's Sons, 1912), 102; Plantagenet, "A Description of the Province of New Albion," 24.

34. *Archives,* 4:209–10.

35. Plantagenet, "A Description of the Province of New Albion," 24.

36. Peter Lindestrom, *Geogrophia Americae,* 244.

37. *Archives,* 3:137, 146–47.

38. Ibid., 3:137.

Chapter 6: "Which bills . . . I have thought fit not to accept . . ."

Chapter title from *Archives,* 3:136.

1. This period of the Civil War is covered in Kenyon, *The Civil Wars of England,* 62–73; Roots, *The Great Rebellion,* 72–82; and Haythornthwaite, *The English Civil War,* 59–74.

2. The death of Thomas Arundel has been confused by Clarendon's statement that he was killed at the battle of Landsdowne, on 5 July 1643. His monument erected at Tisbury Church records that he died at Oxford on 19 May 1643 of wounds suffered at the battle of Stratton, which occurred on 16 May. Hyde, *History of the Rebellion and Civil Wars in England,* 3:92; *Dictionary of National Biography,* 1:621; Gibb, *Complete Peerage,* 1:264. For the political situation in Wiltshire during 1643, see Morrill, *Revolt of the Provinces,* 43–44.

3. A good account of the first seige of Wardour Castle is in James Everard, Baron Arundel, and Sir Richard C. Hoare, Bart., *A History of Modern Wiltshire,* 6 vols. (London, 1829), 4:156–59.

4. Fraser, *The Weaker Vessel,* 165–66.

5. *Dictionary of National Biography,* 12:255–61.

6. A. R. Bayley, *The Great Civil War in Dorset, 1642–1660* (Taunton, U.K.: The Wessex Press, 1910), 75.

7. Everard, et al., *A History of Modern Wiltshire* (London, 1829), 4:159–68.

8. A description of Hook House is in: Bryden B. Hyde, "New Light on the Ark and the Dove," *Maryland Historical Magazine,* 48 (1953): 185–90.

9. *Archives,* 3:49, 137.

10. Ibid., 3:139.

11. A description of this seal is given in *Archives,* 3:214–15. The information on the extant seal fragment is from a personal communication with Gregory Stiverson of Historic Annapolis Foundation, who has extensively researched the various early seals, on 3 May 1994. The earliest seal fragment is at Georgetown University.

12. Hughes, *History of the Society of Jesus in North America,* Text, 1:529–31; Documents, 1:190–91.

13. *Archives,* 3:143.

14. Ibid., 3:136.

15. Ibid., 3:135–37.

16. Ibid., 3:140–43.

17. Ibid., 4:275–79.

18. Ibid., 3:143.

19. Hughes, *History of the Society of Jesus in North America,* Text, 1:544.

20. The full text of this commission is presented in "Two Commissions," *Maryland Historical Magazine,* 1 (1906): 211–16.

21. Davis, *English Merchant Shipping and Anglo-Dutch Rivalry in the Seventeenth Century,* 8; Davis, *Rise of the English Shipping Industry,* 86–87, 286–88, 372–75.

22. Middleton, *Tobacco Coast,* 107, 265; John R. Pagan, "Dutch Maritime and Commercial Activity in Mid-Seventeenth-Century Virginia," *Virginia Magazine of History and Biography,* 90 (1982): 491.

23. Firth and Rait, *Acts and Ordinances of the Interregnum,* 1:347–51.

24. *Archives,* 1:91; 4:377; H. E. Nott, ed., *The Deposition Books of Bristol,* 2 vols. (Bristol: Bristol Record Society, 1935), Volume 1 (1643–47), 64–65.

25. Nott, ed., *Deposition Books of Bristol,* 1 (1643–47): 64–65; *Archives,* 4:377.

Chapter 7: "The highest fine that . . . can or ought to be assessed . . ."

1. Ames, ed., *County Court Records of Accomack,* 304–5.

2. *Archives,* 4:221, 223.

3. Ames, ed., *County Court Records of Accomack,* 304.

4. *Archives,* 4:185–86, 203.

5. Answer of Richard Ingle, answer 17, 29 September 1645 in Copley et al. *vs.* Ingle, High Court of Admiralty, Answers, HCA13/119, PRO; *Archives,* 4:133, 237–41.

6. Examination of Thomas Greene, answer 4, 10 July 1645, in Ingle *vs.* The Looking Glass, Examinations, section I, High Court of Admiralty, HCA 13/60, PRO. The warrant for Ingle's arrest is in *Archives,* 4:231.

7. *Archives,* 4:231–32.

8. Examination of Richard Garrett, answer 4, 11 July 1645, in Ingle *vs.* The Looking Glass, Examinations, section I, High Court of Admiralty, HCA 13/60, PRO.

9. Examination of Thomas Eves, answer 4, 4 July 1645, in Ingle *vs.* The Looking

Glass, Examinations, section G; examination of Thomas Greene, answer 4, 10 July 1645, in Ingle vs Looking Glass, Examinations, section G; examination of Thomas Greene, answer 4,10 July 1645, in Ingle *vs.* The Looking Glass, Examinations, section I, High Court of Admiralty, HCA 13/60, PRO.

10. While the marginal note in *Archives,* 4:231 states that this proclamation was never issued, some similar proclamation was nailed to the mast of the *Reformation* as evidenced by the testimony of William Edrupp who specifically mentioned a paper nailed to the mast. Examination of William Edrupp, answer 4, 5 July 1645, in Ingle *vs.* The Looking Glass, Examinations, section G, High Court of Admiralty, HCA 13/60, PRO.

11. Examination of John Durford, answer 8, 26 June 1645, in Ingle *vs.* The Looking Glass, Examinations, section E; examination of William Edrupp, answer 4, 5 July 1645, in Ingle *vs.* The Looking Glass, Examinations, section G, High Court of Admiralty, HCA 13/60, PRO.

12. *Archives,* 4:245–46.

13. When Ingle was arrested, he was brought to Brent's house and held there until his release. The only house Brent was connected with in St. Mary's was that of his sister Margaret. The details of Ingle's arrest are in Examination of Richard Garrett, answer 4, 11 July 1645, in Ingle *vs.* The Looking Glass, Examinations, section I, High Court of Admiralty, HCA 13/60, PRO.

14. *Archives,* 4:248, 251, 258; examination of John Lewgar, answer 10, 6 August 1645, in Cornwaleys *vs.* Ingle, Examinations, section K, High Court of Admiralty, HCA 13/60, PRO.

15. *Archives,* 4:258.

16. Ibid., 4:234, 247; examination of Richard Garrett, answer 4, 11 July 1645, in Ingle *vs.* The Looking Glass, Examinations, section I; examination of Thomas Greene, answer 4, 10 July 1645, in Ingle *vs.* The Looking Glass, Examinations, section I; examination of Thomas Eves, answer 5, 4 July 1645, in Ingle *vs.* The Looking Glass, Examinations, section G, High Court of Admiralty, HCA 13/60, PRO.

17. *Archives,* 4:247–48.

18. Bill of Thomas Cornwaleys, 22 August 1645 in Cornwaleys *vs.* Ingle, Chancery, Bills and Answers, C24 15/23, PRO.

19. Examination of Henry Stockton, answer 4, 22 October 1645, in Glover *vs.* Ingle, Examinations, section Q, High Court of Admiralty, HCA 13/60, PRO.

20. Examination of John Durford, answer 7, 26 June 1645, in Ingle *vs.* The Looking Glass, Examinations, section E, High Court of Admiralty, HCA 13/60, PRO.

21. *Archives,* 4:231–32, 248.

22. Ibid., 4:234.

23. The indictments against Ingle were made between 1–8 February and are presented in Ibid., 4:235–52.

24. Examination of Thomas Cornwaleys, answer 8, 8 August 1645, in Copley et al. *vs.* Ingle, examinations, section K, High Court of Admiralty, HCA 13/60, PRO.

25. *Archives,* 4:251; examination of Thomas Eves, answer 7, 4 July 1645, in Ingle *vs.* The Looking Glass, examinations, section G; High Court of Admiralty, HCA 13/60, PRO.

26. Examination of Thomas Cornwaleys, answer 20, 8 August 1645; examination of John Lewgar, answer 19, 6 August 1645, in Copley et al. *vs.* Ingle, examinations, section

K, High Court of Admiralty, HCA 13/60; answer of Richard Ingle to a libel of Thomas Copley et al., answer 20, 29 September 1645, answers, HCA 13/119, PRO.

27. *Archives,* 4:256–57, 261.

28. Ibid., 4:261, 265, 271; Ames, ed., *County Court Records of Accomack,* 330–31.

29. For a discussion of the development of mercantile law see Theodore P. T. Plucknett, *A Concise History of the Common Law,* 5th ed. (London: Butterworth, 1956), 657–69; David M. Walker, *The Oxford Companion to Law* (Oxford: Oxford University Press, 1989), 130–31.

30. *Archives,* 3:136.

31. Ibid., 4:216.

32. Ibid., 3:143, 4:217–18.

33. Ibid., 4:221.

34. Ibid., 4:236, 243–44.

35. Ibid., 4:259–60.

36. Ibid., 4:262–67.

37. Ibid., 4:270, 276.

38. Bill of Thomas Cornwaleys, 22 August 1645 in Cornwaleys *vs.* Ingle, Chancery, Bills and Answers, C24 15/23, PRO.

Chapter 8: "Our Rebellious subjects . . . drive a great trade . . . in Virginia"

Chapter title from: "Two Commissions," 211.

1. Helen J. Crump, *Colonial Admiralty Jurisdiction in the Seventeenth Century* (New York: Longmans, Green, & Co., 1931), 41–51.

2. Charles M. Parr, *The Voyages of David De Vries, Navigator and Adventurer* (New York: Crowell, 1969), 252–53.

3. Hale, *Virginia Venturer,* 246–47; Helen C. Roundtree, *Powhatan Foreign Relations, 1500–1722* (Charlottesville: University Press of Virginia, 1993), 194.

4. *Archives,* 3: 137–38, 4:235–36, 282.

5. Ibid., 4:180–81.

6. Ibid., 3:146, 4:255, 260.

7. John Winthrop, *History of New England,* 2:167–68.

8. *Archives,* 3: 144, 4:235.

9. Ibid., 1:136, 3:147–48, 4:269.

10. Ibid., 3:148–50.

11. Ibid., 3:163.

12. Ibid., 3:150–51.

13. Calvert carried commissions for the government of Maryland that were signed by Lord Baltimore on 2 July and published in St. Mary's on 6 September (*Archives,* 3:151–60). Weston's saga continues in *Archives,* 4:377; Nott, ed., *Deposition Books of Bristol,* 1 (1643–47):134–35.

14. Brainthwaite's commission was issued on 30 September but he was not sworn until 3 October. He became a member of the council on 2 November, *Archives,* 3:160; 4:286.

15. "Virginia and Maryland, Or the Lord Baltimore's Printed Case Uncased and Answered, 1655," in Hall, ed., *Narratives of Early Maryland,* 228–30.

16. The membership of this Assembly is listed in Henning, ed., *The Statutes at Large,* 1:282–83.

17. Steven D. Crow, "Your Majesty's Good Subjects," 167; examination of Thomas Eves, answer 10, 4 July 1645, section G; examination of Robert Rawlins, answers 9–10, 2 July 1645, section G; examination of John Durford, answer 10, 26 June 1645, section E, in Ingle *vs.* The Looking Glass, Examinations, High Court of Admiralty, HCA 13/60, PRO.

18. Ames, ed., *County Court Records of Accomack,* 405–6.

19. Henning, ed., *The Statutes at Large,* 1:296.

20. Examination of Josias Casswell, 15 August 1645, section L, in Cornwaleys *vs.* Ingle, Examinations, High Court of Admiralty, HCA 13/60, PRO.

21. The events of the Civil War for the year 1643 are well covered in Kenyon, *The Civil Wars of England,* 89–122; Roots, *The Great Rebellion,* 83–94; Haythornthwaite, *The English Civil War,* 76–99.

22. Examination of George Horsfall, 16 August 1645, section L, in Cornwaleys *vs.* Ingle, Examinations, High Court of Admiralty, HCA 13/60, PRO.

23. *Archives,* 10:102–3.

24. Examination of Thomas Greene, answer 1, 10 July 1645, section I; examination of Richard Garrett, answer 1, 11 July 1645, section I, in Ingle *vs.* The Looking Glass, Examinations, High Court of Admiralty, HCA 13/60, PRO.

25. Firth and Rait, eds., *Acts and Ordinances of the Interregnum,* 1:347–51; examination of Robert Rawlins, answer 2, 2 July 1645, section G; examination of John Durford, answer 3, 26 June 1645, section E, in Ingle *vs.* The Looking Glass, Examinations, High Court of Admiralty, HCA 13/60, PRO.

26. Leo F. Stock, *Proceedings and Debates of the British Parliaments Respecting North America,* 2 vols. (Washington: Carnegie Institution of Washington, 1924), 1:155–56; Pagan, "Dutch Maritime and Commercial Activity in Mid-Seventeenth-Century Virginia," 493.

Chapter 9: "If Ingle or any other. . . should come . . . hee would hang them"

1. The size of the ship is mentioned in a contract recorded in the Rotterdam archives and reprinted in Noel Currer-Briggs, *Colonial Settlers and English Adventurers* (Baltimore: Genealogical Publishing Co., 1971), 332. That she was a relatively new ship is based on her captains's testimony that he "knew the building" of the ship. See examination of Hatrick Cornelison Cocke, 13 June 1645, in Ingle *vs.* The Looking Glass, Examinations, section E, High Court of Admiralty, HCA 13/60, PRO.

2. This list of crew members is derived from various depositions. However, most of these names come from the testimony of Gabrant Ouckerson, the steersman, who kept the record of goods loaded for these people in the hold of the ship. Many of the ordinary seamen did not have this advantage and so remain anonymous.

3. Examination of Gabrant Ouckerson, answer 1, 13 June 1645, in Ingle *vs.* The Looking Glass, Examinations, section E, High Court of Admiralty, HCA 13/60, PRO.

4. Davis, *Rise of the English Shipping Industry,* 48–50; George Masselman, *The Cradle of Colonialism* (New Haven: Yale University Press, 1963), 48, 111.

5. John R. Pagan, "Dutch Maritime and Commercial Activity in Mid-Seventeenth-

Century Virginia," *Virginia Magazine of History and Biography,* 90 (1982): 485–501.

6. Ibid. 494.

7. Ibid., 489–91.

8. Examination of Hatrick Cornelison Cocke, answer 1, 13 June 1645, in Ingle *vs.* The Looking Glass, Examinations, section E, High Court of Admiralty, HCA 13/60; Pagan, "Dutch Maritime and Commercial Activity," 489.

9. Currer-Briggs, *Colonial Settlers and English Adventurers,* 332.

10. Pagan, "Dutch Maritime and Commercial Activity," 491; *Archives,* 4:294–99; Currer-Briggs, *Colonial Settlers and English Adventurers,* 332; "Notes from the Records of York County," *William and Mary Quarterly,* 22 (1913): 240, 23 (1914): 10–15, 24 (1915): 38.

11. Currer-Briggs, *Colonial Settlers and English Adventurers,* 331–33, 341–42. That Brookes was a Catholic is supported by John Lewgar's testimony in examination of John Lewgar, answer 4, 6 August 1645, in Cornwaleys *vs.* Ingle, Examinations, section K, High Court of Admiralty, HCA 13/60, PRO.

12. Currer-Briggs, *Colonial Settlers and English Adventurers,* 341; *Archives,* 4:201–2, 282, 303.

13. Examination of Robert Reeves, answer 1, 13 August 1645, in Cornwaleys *vs.* Ingle, Examinations, section L, High Court of Admiralty, HCA 13/60; Currer-Briggs, *Colonial Settlers and English Adventurers,* 331–32; examination of Henry Stockton, answer 1, 22 October 1645, in Glover *vs.* Ingle, Examinations, section Q, High Court of Admiralty, HCA 13/60, PRO.

14. Currer-Briggs, *Colonial Settlers and English Adventurers,* 332.

15. Examination of Robert Rawlins, answer 1, 2 July 1645, in Ingle *vs.* the Looking Glass, Examinations, section G, High Court of Admiralty, HCA 13/60, PRO.

16. Examination of Thomas Eves, answer 10, 4 July 1645, in Ingle *vs.* the Looking Glass, Examinations, section G, High Court of Admiralty, HCA 13/60, PRO.

17. Examination of John Durford, answer 3, 26 June 1645, in Ingle *vs.* the Looking Glass, Examinations, section G, High Court of Admiralty, HCA 13/60, PRO.

18. Examination of Pascho Panton, answer 1, 16 July 1645, in Ingle *vs.* the Looking Glass, Examinations, section I, High Court of Admiralty, HCA 13/60, PRO.

19. *Archives,* 4:458.

20. Ibid., 3:161.

21. Ibid., 4:288.

22. Ibid., 3:161–62; 1:205.

23. Ibid., 4:292.

24. Ibid., 3:162–63.

25. Ibid., 4:292–94.

26. Ibid., 4:301–302, 307.

27. Ibid., 1:205; examination of Giles Brent, answer 1, 7 August 1645, in Cornwaleys *vs.* Ingle, Examinations, section K, High Court of Admiralty, HCA 13/60, PRO.

28. Examination of Giles Brent, answer 8, 7 August 1645, in Cornwaleys *vs.* Ingle, Examinations, section K, High Court of Admiralty, HCA 13/60, PRO.

29. *Archives,* 1:205.

Chapter 10: "A most pitifull ruines, spoiled and defaced"

1. Examination of Henry Stockton, answer 4, 22 October 1645, in Glover *vs.* Ingle, Examinations, section Q, High Court of Admiralty, HCA 13/60; *Archives,* 4:303.

2. *Archives,* 4:307.

3. Examination of Hatrick Cornelison Cocke, answer 2; examination of Gabrant Ouckerson, answer 2, 13 June 1645, section E; examination of Michael Albertson, answer 4, 23 June 1645, section F, in Ingle *vs.* The Looking Glass, Examinations, High Court of Admiralty, HCA 13/60; examination of John Lewgar, answer 10, 26 September 1645, in Cornwaleys *vs.* Ingle, Chancery, Examinations, C24 690/14.

4. *Archives,* 4:294–99.

5. Examination of Gabrant Ouckerson, answer 11, 13 June 1645, section E, in Ingle *vs.* The Looking Glass, Examinations, High Court of Admiralty, HCA 13/60; "Ingle in Maryland," *Maryland Historical Magazine,* 1 (1906): 134.

6. Examination of Gabrant Ouckerson, answer 11, 13 June 1645, section E, in Ingle *vs.* The Looking Glass, Examinations, High Court of Admiralty, HCA 13/60, PRO.

7. Examination of Cuthbert Fenwick, answer 12, 20 October 1646; examination of John Lewgar, answer 10, 26 September 1645, in Cornwaleys *vs.* Ingle, Chancery, Examinations, C24 690/14.

8. Examination of John Lewgar, answer 10, 26 September 1645, in Cornwaleys *vs.* Ingle, Chancery, Examinations, C24 690/14.

9. Public Records Office (PRO), Bill of Thomas Cornwaleys, 22 August 1645 in Cornwaleys *vs.* Ingle, Chancery, Bills and Answers, C24 15/23.; examination of John Lewgar, answer 14, 26 September 1645, in Cornwaleys *vs.* Ingle, Chancery, Examinations, C24 690/14.

10. *Archives,* 3:161; Public Records Office (PRO), Bill of Thomas Cornwaleys, 22 August 1645 in Cornwaleys *vs.* Ingle, Chancery, Bills and Answers, C24 15/23.; examination of Henry Williams, answer 12, 11 August 1645, section L, in Cornwaleys *vs.* Ingle, Examinations, High Court of Admiralty, HCA 13/60, PRO.

11. Examination of John Lewgar, answer 12, 26 September 1645, in Cornwaleys *vs.* Ingle, Chancery, Examinations, C24 690/14; "Ingle in Maryland," 130.

12. Examination of John Lewgar, answer 12, 26 September 1645, in Cornwaleys *vs.* Ingle, Chancery, Examinations, C24 690/14.

13. Examination of Hatrick Cornelison Cocke, answer 9; 13 June 1645, section E; examination of Michael Albertson, answer 4, 23 June 1645, section F, in Ingle *vs.* The Looking Glass, Examinations, High Court of Admiralty, HCA 13/60, PRO.

14. Examination of Henry Stockton, answer 12, 5 August 1645, section K; examination of Henry Williams, answer 12, 11 August 1645, section L in Cornwaleys *vs.* Ingle, Examinations, High Court of Admiralty, HCA 13/60, PRO.

15. Examination of Thomas Green, answers 7–14, 10 July 1645, section I; examination of Robert Popeley, answer 12, 26 June 1645, section G; examination of Pascho Panton, answers 12–14, 16 July 1645, section I; examination of Richard Garnett, answers 14, 11 July 1645, section I; in Cornwaleys *vs.* Ingle, Examinations, High Court of Admiralty, HCA 13/60, PRO.

16. Examination of Giles Brent, answers 8, 7 August 1645, section K; examination of Henry Stockton, answer 12, 5 August 1645, section K; examination of Henry Williams,

answer 12, 11 August 1645, section L; in Cornwaleys *vs.* Ingle, Examinations, High Court of Admiralty, HCA 13/60; examination of John Lewgar, answer 12, 26 September 1645, in Cornwaleys *vs.* Ingle, Chancery, Examinations, C24 690/14.

17. Examination of Hatrick Cornelison Cocke, answers 3 and 5, 13 June 1645, in Ingle *vs.* The Looking Glass, Examinations, section E, High Court of Admiralty, HCA 13/60, PRO.

18. Examination of Robert Rawlins, answers 15, 2 July 1645, section G, in Ingle *vs.* The Looking Glass; examination of Henry Williams, answer 4, 7 July 1645, section H, in Cornwaleys *vs.* Ingle, Examinations, High Court of Admiralty, HCA 13/60; Geoffrey J. Marcus, *Naval History of England* (Boston, 1961), 137–38.

19. Examination of Gilbert Chubb, answers 15–16, 28 June 1645, section G; examination of Michael Albertson, answer 3, 23 June 1645, section F, in Ingle *vs.* The Looking Glass, Examinations, High Court of Admiralty, HCA 13/60, PRO.

20. Examination of Hatrick Cornelison Cocke, answers 3 and 5, 13 June 1645, section E, in Ingle *vs.* The Looking Glass, Examinations, High Court of Admiralty, HCA 13/60, PRO.

21. Examination of Hatrick Cornelison Cocke, answer 13, 13 June 1645, section E; examination of Gabrant Ouckerson, answer 13, 13 June 1645, section E; in Ingle *vs.* The Looking Glass, Examinations, High Court of Admiralty, HCA 13/60; Firth and Rait, eds., *Acts and Ordinances of the Interregnum,* 1:350.

22. Examination of Thomas Greene, answer 14, 10 July 1645, section I; examination of William Little, answer 16, 1 July 1645, section G; examination of Pascho Panton, answer 14, 16 July 1645, section I, in Ingle *vs.* The Looking Glass, Examinations, High Court of Admiralty, HCA 13/60, PRO.

23. Examination of Thomas Greene, answer 14, 10 July 1645, section I; examination of Richard Garnett, answers 14–17, 11 July 1645, section I; examination of Gilbert Chubb, answer 16, 28 June 1645, section G; examination of Pascho Panton, answer 14, 16 July 1645, section I, in Ingle *vs.* The Looking Glass, Examinations, High Court of Admiralty, HCA 13/60, PRO.

24. *Archives,* 4:300; examination of Thomas Greene, answer 13, 10 July 1645, section I; examination of Gilbert Chubb, answer 13, 28 June 1645, section G; in Ingle *vs.* The Looking Glass, Examinations, High Court of Admiralty, HCA 13/60; "Land Notes, 1634–1655," *Maryland Historical Magazine,* 5(1910):171–172; Nott, ed., *Deposition Books of Bristol,* Volume 1 (1643–1647), 134–35.

25. Thomas Cornwaleys to Cecil Calvert, 14 April 1638, in *Calvert Papers,* 1:174.

26. Examination of Hatrick Cornelison Cocke, answer 17, 9 August 1645, section L, in Cornwaleys *vs.* Ingle, Examinations, High Court of Admiralty, HCA 13/60; examination of John Lewgar, answer 16, 26 September 1645, in Cornwaleys *vs.* Ingle, Chancery, Examinations, C24 690/14.

27. *Archives,* 10:12, 362–63, 371–72.

28. Examination of John Lewgar, answers 12 and 16, 26 September 1645; examination of Cuthbert Fenwick, answer 15, 20 October 1646 in Cornwaleys *vs.* Ingle, Chancery, Examinations, C24 690/14.

29. *Archives,* 10:371–72; examination of William Little, answer 3, 1 July 1645, section G, in Ingle *vs.* The Looking Glass, Examinations, High Court of Admiralty, HCA 13/60, PRO.

30. Examination of William Edrupp, answer 4, 5 July 1645, section G, in Ingle *vs.* The Looking Glass, Examinations, High Court of Admiralty, HCA 13/60; examination of John Lewgar, answer 18, 26 September 1645, in Cornwaleys *vs.* Ingle, Chancery, Examinations, C24 690/14, PRO.

31. Examination of William Little, answer 3, 1 July 1645, section G, in Ingle *vs.* The Looking Glass, Examinations, High Court of Admiralty, HCA 13/60, PRO.

32. Examination of Henry Williams, answer 13, 11 August 1645, section L, in Cornwaleys *vs.* Ingle, Examinations, High Court of Admiralty, HCA 13/60, PRO; examination of John Lewgar, answer 18, 26 September 1645, in Cornwaleys *vs.* Ingle, Chancery, Examinations, C24 690/14, PRO.

33. The description which follows is based on examination of Cuthbert Fenwick, answer 19, 20 October 1646 in Cornwaleys *vs.* Ingle, Chancery, Examinations, C24 690/14, PRO.

34. Stone, "Society, Housing and Architecture in Early Maryland," 40.

35. Gloria L. Main, *Tobacco Colony: Life in Early Maryland, 1650–1720* (Princeton: Princeton University Press, 1982), Table II.6. on page 61.

36. Ibid., 48–62, 287.

37. Thomas Cornwaleys to Cecil Calvert, 14 April 1638, in *Calvert Papers,* 1:176.

38. Main, *Tobacco Colony,* 152.

39. Examination of Henry Williams, answer 20, 11 August 1645, section L; in Cornwaleys *vs.* Ingle, Examinations, High Court of Admiralty, HCA 13/60; examination of John Lewgar, answer 18, 26 September 1645, in Cornwaleys *vs.* Ingle, Chancery, Examinations, C24 690/14, PRO.

40. Examination of Michael Albertson, answer 20, 9 August 1645, in Cornwaleys *vs.* Ingle, Examinations, section L, High Court of Admiralty, HCA 13/60, PRO.

41. Examination of William Edrupp, answer 12, 5 July 1645, section G; in Ingle *vs.* The Looking Glass, Examinations, High Court of Admiralty, HCA 13/60; examination of John Lewgar, answer 18, 26 September 1645, in Cornwaleys *vs.* Ingle, Chancery, Examinations, C24 690/14, PRO.

Chapter 11: "Burn them Papists Divells . . ."

1. Donald B. Shomette, *Pirates on the Chesapeake* (Centerville, Md.: Tidewater Publishers, 1985), 30; Hale, *Virginia Venturer,* 261.

2. Menard, "Maryland's 'Time of Troubles,'" 136.

3. *Archives,* 10:372.

4. Examination of Robert Popeley, answer 15, 26 June 1645, section G; examination of Richard Garnett, answer 14, 11 July 1645, section I; in Cornwaleys *vs.* Ingle, Examinations, High Court of Admiralty, HCA 13/60, PRO.

5. C. G. Cruickshank, *Elizabeth's Army* (Oxford: The Clarendon Press, 1966), 24–25.

6. References to the Maryland militia are in *Archives,* 1:77, 159; 3:107, 118.

7. The roster of the expedition is listed in Ibid., 3:119–20.

8. Examination of Ralph Beane, answer 7, 16 August 1645, section L; in Cornwaleys *vs.* Ingle, Examinations, High Court of Admiralty, HCA 13/60, PRO; Archives 4:453.

9. "Land Notes, 1634–1655," *Maryland Historical Magazine,* 5 (1910): 264; Lois Green Carr, "The Founding of St. Mary's City," *Smithsonian Journal of History,* 3 (1968–69): 90.

10. Although it is generally assumed that St. Inigoes Fort was one of the first places captured by Ingle, I can find no references to this in the original records. See Edward F. Beitzell, *The Jesuit Missions of St. Mary's County* (Leonardtown, Md.: Privately published, 1960), 16, and Shomette, *Pirates on the Chesapeake,* 30. In contrast to this view, several of the Looking Glass crew testified that Maryland was not fortified before Ingle arrived. See examination of Hatrick Cornelison Cocke, answer 9, 13 June 1645, section E; examination of Gabrant Ouckerson, answer 9, 13 June 1645, section E; in Ingle *vs.* The Looking Glass, Examinations, High Court of Admiralty, HCA 13/60, PRO.

11. *Archives,* 1:20; 3:107–8; Thomas Copley to Cecil Calvert, 3 April 1638, in *The Calvert Papers,* 1:163.

12. A good summary of the evidence regarding the guns at Fort Point is Frank L. Howard, "The Guns of St. Mary's," in *Chronicles of St. Mary's,* 6 (1958): 217–29.

13. For example, *Archives,* 1:292–93.

14. Howard, "The Guns of St. Mary's," 217–29; *Archives,* 3:107.

15. *Archives,* 1:222.

16. Ibid., 4:336, 380–83.

17. Examination of Gilbert Chubb, answer 3, 28 June 1645, section G; examination of William Edrupp, answer 3, 5 July 1645, section G; in Ingle *vs.* The Looking Glass, Examinations, High Court of Admiralty, HCA 13/60, PRO.

18. *Archives,* 4:336, 381, 423, 453.

19. Examination of Thomas Greene, answer 4, 10 July 1645, section I; examination of William Edrupp, answer 12, 5 July 1645, section G; in Ingle *vs.* The Looking Glass; examination of Ralph Beane, answers 14, 18, 16 August 1645, section L; in Cornwaleys *vs.* Ingle, Examinations, High Court of Admiralty, HCA 13/60, PRO; *Archives,* 4:348–49, 370, 372, 375–76, 513.

20. Answer of Richard Ingle to a libel of Thomas Copley et al., answer 11, 29 September 1645, Answers, HCA 13/119, PRO; *Archives,* 4:415; 10:12.

21. Foley, *Records of the English Province of the Society of Jesus,* 3:387; 7(1):163, 343; 7(2):650.

22. Examination of Henry Stockton, answer 17, 5 August 1645, section K, in Cornwaleys *vs.* Ingle, Examinations, High Court of Admiralty, HCA 13/60, PRO.

23. *Archives,* 4:415.

24. The discussion of the Jesuit losses is based on the schedule published in "Ingle in Maryland," 139–40.

25. *Archives,* 4:435–36, 440–41.

26. "Ingle in Maryland," 136.

27. Ibid., 139.

28. Firth and Rait, eds., *Acts and Ordinances of the Interregnum,* 1:35.

29. On 5 October 1647, Cuthbert Fenwick was appointed administrator of Brooks's estate. See *Archives,* 4:336.

30. Examination of Henry Williams, answer 10, 7 July 1645, section H; examination of Robert Reeves, answer 10, 8 July 1645, section H; examination of Henry Stockton, answer 10, 5 August 1645, section K; in Cornwaleys *vs.* Ingle; examination of Gabrant Ouckerson, answer 10, 13 June 1645, section E; examination of Hatrick Cornelison Cocke, answer 10, 13 June 1645, section E; in Ingle *vs.* The Looking Glass, Examinations, High Court of Admiralty, HCA 13/60, PRO.

31. Examination of Robert Popeley, 26 June 1645, section G; examination of Robert Popeley, 28 June 1645, section G; in Ingle *vs.* The Looking Glass, Examinations, High Court of Admiralty, HCA 13/60, PRO; "Ingle in Maryland," 135; *Archives,* 4:372.

32. Examination of Ralph Beane, answer 13, 16 August 1645, section L; in Cornwaleys *vs.* Ingle, Examinations, High Court of Admiralty, HCA 13/60, PRO.

33. Ames, ed., *County Court Records of Accomack,* 437.

34. Answer of Richard Ingle to a libel of Thomas Copley et al., answer 16, 29 September 1645, Answers, HCA 13/119, PRO; "Ingle in Maryland," 135–36.

Chapter 12: "These had protection in a certain fortified citadel . . ."

Chapter title from Force, *Tracts and Others Papers,* 4:45.

1. Examination of Cuthbert Fenwick, answer 12, 20 October 1646; examination of John Lewgar, answer 12, 26 September 1645, in Cornwaleys *vs.* Ingle, Chancery, Examinations, C24 690/14, PRO.

2. *Archives,* 4:513.

3. Ibid., 10:362.

4. "Petition of Richard Ingle to the House of Lords," 24 February 1646, printed in *Archives,* 3:165–66; examination of Giles Brent, answer 7, 7 August 1645, in Cornwaleys *vs.* Ingle, Examinations, section K, High Court of Admiralty, HCA 13/60, PRO; *Archives,* 4:381; 10:253–54.

5. *Archives,* 1:89; 3:85, 108, 178; 4:453; John Bailey Calvert Nicklin, "Immigration Between Virginia and Maryland in the Seventeenth Century," *William and Mary Quarterly,* 18 (1938): 440.

6. Papenfuse, et al., *Biographical Dictionary of the Maryland Legislature,* 2:656.

7. "Land Notes, 1634–1655," *Maryland Historical Magazine,* 5 (1910): 365.

8. *Archives,* 4:22, 72.

9. Ibid., 1:143; 4:270.

10. "Land Notes, 1634–1655," *Maryland Historical Magazine,* 5 (1910): 264; Thomas Oliver, whom Calvert said was transported in 1641, was one of Pope's servants.

11. *Archives,* 4:188, 191, 207, 233; "Land Notes, 1634–1655," *Maryland Historical Magazine,* 5 (1910): 170.

12. *Archives,* 1:129; 3:148–49; 4:241, 245; Giles Brent refers to the Assembly meeting at Mr. Pope's House in St. Mary's in examination of Giles Brent, answer 7, 7 August 1645, section K, in Cornwaleys *vs.* Ingle, Examinations, High Court of Admiralty, HCA 13/60, PRO.

13. *Archives,* 4:418; 10:96–97.

14. Ibid., 4:423.

15. Examination of Thomas Greene, answer 4, 10 July 1645, section I, in Ingle *vs.* The Looking Glass, Examinations, High Court of Admiralty, HCA 13/60, PRO.

16. Henry M. Miller, "Discovering Maryland's First City: A Summary of the 1981–1984 Archaeological Excavations in St. Mary's City, Maryland," *St. Mary's City Archaeology Series,* Number 2 (St. Mary's City 1986), 47–66; Timothy B. Riordan, "Summary Report of the 1986 Excavations at Pope's Fort in the Village Center, St. Mary's City, Maryland," Ms. on file, Department of Research, Historic St. Mary's City,1986.

17. G. A. Hayes-McCoy, ed., *Ulster and Other Irish Maps, c. 1600* (Dublin: Irish Manuscripts Commission, 1964), 5–7.

18. Force, *Tracts and Others Papers,* 4:45; Charles Fithian, "'Master Pope's Fort': An English Civil War Fortification on the Chesapeake Frontier," paper presented at the 20th Annual Meeting of the Society for Historical Archaeology, Savannah, Georgia, January 1987. The description of cannon sizes varies considerably. See Harold L. Peterson, *Roundshot and Rammers* (Harrisburg, Pa.: Stackpole Books, 1969), 14 and W. G. Ross, *Military Engineering During the Great Civil War, 1642–1649* (1887, repr.; London: Ken Trotman, 1984), 35.

19. Howard, "The Guns of St. Mary's," 217; examination of Cuthbert Fenwick, answer 20, 20 October 1646, in Cornwaleys *vs.* Ingle, Chancery, Examinations, C24 690/14, PRO.

20. Bernard C. Steiner, "New Light on Maryland History from the British Archives," *Maryland Historical Magazine,* 4 (1909): 251–62.

21. Fithian, "'Master Pope's Fort.'" Throwing away parts of the armor and retaining only the back and breast plate is a well-documented tradition for English armies sent to France. See Cruickshank, *Elizabeth's Army,* 117–18.

22. Harold L. Peterson, *Arms and Armor in Colonial America, 1526–1783* (Harrisburg, Pa.: Stackpole Co., 1956), 140–41; Ivor Noël Hume, *Martin's Hundred* (New York: Alfred a. Knopf, 1982), 205; "A Relation of Maryland, 1635," in Hall, ed., *Narratives of Early Maryland, 1633–1684,* 94.

23. Haythornthwaite, *The English Civil War,* 25; *Archives,* 4:320.

24. Ibid., 3:85–86.

25. Clifford Lewis III, "Some Recently Discovered Extracts from the Lost Minutes of the Virginia Council and General Court, 1642–1645," *William and Mary Quarterly,* 20 (1940): 69.

26. *Archives,* 10:211–13.

27. Ibid., 1:238–43.

Chapter 13: "To hold yourself upright and hang from the gibbet at Tyburn . . ."

1. Foley, *Records of the English Province of the Society of Jesus,* 7(1):527–28; Joseph N. Tylenda, S.J., *Jesuit Saints and Martyrs* (Chicago: Jesuit Way, 1984), 29–32.

2. Lawrence Harper, *The English Navigation Laws* (New York: Columbia University Press, 1964), 89–90.

3. Firth and Rait, eds., *Acts and Ordinances of the Interregnum, 1642–1660,* 1:351.

4. Ibid., 1:442–43.

5. Harper, *English Navigation Laws,* 89.

6. Examination of John Lewgar, September 1645, in Cornwaleys *vs.* Ingle, Chancery, Examinations, C24 690/14, PRO.

7. Hughes, *History of the Society of Jesus in North America,* Text, 2:12.

8. *Archives,* 4:479; Hughes, *History of the Society of Jesus in North America,* Text, 2:13; Documents 1:36.

9. Plucknett, *A Concise History of the Common Law,* 176–77, 663–64; Crump, *Colonial Admiralty Jurisdiction in the Seventeenth Century,* 1–23.

10. Harper, *The English Navigation Laws,* 109–10; Walker, *Oxford Companion to Law,* 31–32.

11. This first group included Hatrick Cocke, the master of the *Looking Glass,* Michael Albertson, the gunner, and Gabrant Ouckerson, the steersman. See 14–23 June 1645, sections D, E, and F, in Ingle *vs.* The Looking Glass, Examinations, High Court of Admiralty, HCA 13/60, PRO.

12. Examination of Hatrick Cornelison Cocke, answers 11 and 13, section E, 13 June 1645, in Ingle *vs.* The Looking Glass, Examinations, High Court of Admiralty, HCA 13/60, PRO.

13. Examination of Robert Popeley, answers 3, 8, 14 and 15. 26 June 1645, section G; examination of Robert Popeley, answers 1 and 2, 28 June 1645, section G; in Ingle *vs.* The Looking Glass, Examinations, High Court of Admiralty, HCA 13/60, PRO.

14. Hale, *Virginia Venturer,* 163–64, 250; *Archives,* 5:225–27; "Abstracts of Virginia Land Patents," *Virginia Magazine of History and Biography,* 7 (1899): 193.

15. Examination of Robert Popeley, answer 12, 26 June 1645, section G, in Ingle *vs.* The Looking Glass, Examinations, High Court of Admiralty, HCA 13/60, PRO.

16. Robert Popeley testified in the case of Ingle *vs.* the Looking Glass on 26 June 1645 and was called back to testify in Cornwaleys *vs.* Ingle on 28 June 1645. John Durford testified in both cases on 26 June 1645. The *Looking Glass* crew, who had testified a week earlier, did not give testimony in Cornwaleys *vs.* Ingle until early August.

17. Examinations of John Durford, Gilbert Chubb, William Little, Robert Rawlins, Thomas Eves, and William Edrupp, section G, in Ingle *vs.* The Looking Glass, Examinations, High Court of Admiralty, HCA 13/60, PRO.

18. Examinations of Henry Williams, Robert Reeves, Dionisius Corbin, section H, in Cornwaleys *vs.* Ingle, Examinations, High Court of Admiralty, HCA 13/60, PRO.

19. Examinations of Thomas Green, Richard Garnett, and Pasho Panton, section I, in Ingle *vs.* The Looking Glass, Examinations, High Court of Admiralty, HCA 13/60, PRO.

20. Crump, *Colonial Admiralty Jurisdiction in the Seventeenth Century,* 21.

21. *Dictionary of National Biography,* 2:1170–1172; William B. Chilton, "The Brent Family," *Virginia Magazine of History and Biography,* 14 (1906–1907): 95.

22. Answer of Richard Ingle to a libel of Thomas Cornwaleys and Alan Lane, 31 July 1645, in Cornwaleys *vs.* Ingle, Answers, High Court of Admiralty, HCA 13/119, PRO

23. Examinations of Henry Stockton, John Lewgar, Giles Brent, and Thomas Cornwaleys, section K, in Cornwaleys *vs.* Ingle; Copley et al. *vs.* Ingle, Examinations, High Court of Admiralty, HCA 13/60, PRO.

24. Examination of John Lewgar, answers 1, 6, 9, 11, and 18, 6 August 1645, section K, in Copley et al. *vs.* Ingle, Examinations, High Court of Admiralty, HCA 13/60, PRO.

25. Examination of John Lewgar, answer 22, 6 August 1645, section K, in Cornwaleys *vs.* Ingle; examination of John Lewgar, answer 13, 6 August 1645, section K, in Copley et al. *vs.* Ingle Examinations, High Court of Admiralty, HCA 13/60, PRO.

26. Examination of Giles Brent, answers 1, 8, 9, 7 August 1645, section K, in Copley et al. *vs.* Ingle Examinations, High Court of Admiralty, HCA 13/60, PRO.

27. Examination of Thomas Cornwaleys, answers 17, 20, 8 August 1645, section K, in Copley et al. *vs.* Ingle Examinations, High Court of Admiralty, HCA 13/60, PRO.

28. Examination of Thomas Cornwaleys, answer 10, 8 August 1645, section K, in Copley et al. *vs.* Ingle Examinations, High Court of Admiralty, HCA 13/60, PRO.

29. Examinations of Hatrick Cocke, Michael Albertson, Dionisius Corbin, Henry Williams, Robert Reeves, section L, in Cornwaleys *vs.* Ingle; Copley et al. *vs.* Ingle, Examinations, High Court of Admiralty, HCA 13/60, PRO.

30. Examination of Josias Casswell, answers 9–11, 15 August 1645, section L, in Cornwaleys *vs.* Ingle Examinations, High Court of Admiralty, HCA 13/60, PRO.

31. "Suit of Thomas Cornwaleys against Richard Ingle," in *Archives,* 3:167–68; Bill of Thomas Cornwaleys, 22 August 1645; in Cornwaleys *vs.* Ingle, Chancery, Bills and Answers, C24 15/23; examination of John Lewgar, 26 September 1645, in Cornwaleys *vs.* Ingle, Chancery, Examinations, C24 690/14, PRO.

32. 'Petition of Richard Ingle to the House of Lords," 24 February 1646, in *Archives,* 3:165–66; Plucknett, *A Concise History of the Common Law,* 663.

33. Plucknett, *A Concise History of the Common Law,* 176–77, 662–64.

34. Answer of Richard Ingle to a libel of Thomas Copley et al., answer 10, 29 September 1645, Answers, HCA 13/119, PRO.

35. Hughes, *History of the Society of Jesus in North America,* Text, 1:346; Documents 1:25.

36. Answer of Richard Ingle to a libel of Thomas Copley et al., answers 11, 16, 29 September 1645, Answers, HCA 13/119; *Archives,* 10:12; examination of John Durford, answer 3, 26 June 1645, in Ingle *vs.* The Looking Glass, Examinations, section G, High Court of Admiralty, HCA 13/60, PRO.

37. Answer of Richard Ingle to a libel of Thomas Copley et al., answers 8, 21, 29 September 1645, Answers, HCA 13/119, PRO.

38. Examinations of Henry Stockton, Robert Reeves, Henry Williams, Dionisus Corbin, Willaim Rameshall, Thomas Cross, section Q, in Glover *vs.* Ingle, Examinations, High Court of Admiralty, HCA 13/60, PRO; "Suit of Thomas Cornwaleys against Richard Ingle," in *Archives,* 3:167–68; "Petition of Mary Ford to the House of Lords, 25 April 1646," *Archives,* 3:171.

39. Answer of Thomas Cornwaleys to a libel of Richard Ingle, answer 4, 30 September 1645, Answers, HCA 13/119, PRO.

Chapter 14: "The Soldiers were to expect no pillage . . ."

1. Henning, ed., *The Statutes at Large,* 1:236, 283, 289, 321.

2. *Archives,* 3:171–72; 4:389.

3. Ibid., 3:188–89; 4:315–16.

4. Ibid., 3:189–90.

5. Ibid., 3:188–90.

6. Leo F. Stock, *Proceedings and Debates of the British Parliaments Respecting North America,* 2 vols (Washington, D.C.: Carnegie Insitution of Washington, 1924), 1:183.

7. *Archives,* 1:239; 4:332.

8. Ibid., 1:209, 301.

9. Ibid., 4:368–69.

10. Fausz, "Merging and Emerging Worlds," 79–80, described this company as being composed of "Puritan mercenaries from south of the James River," and attributes their leadership to "Colonel" Richard Bennett. However, based on the surviving records, this

would seem to be a stretch of the truth. The following list is as complete as possible and describes whether the soldier was a Catholic or had been settled in Maryland before the rebellion:

Name	Ref (Arch.)	Religion	Pre 1645 Res.
Captain John Price	4:412	Protestant	Maryland
Lt. William Evans	4:358	Catholic	Virginia
Lt. William Lewis	1:209	Catholic	Maryland
Sgt. Mark Pheypo	4:313		Maryland
Sgt. Thomas Jackson	4:323		Maryland
William Johnson	4:311		Maryland
Walter Guest	4:311		Maryland
James Lindsey	4:311		Maryland
Stanop Roberts	4:323		Virginia ?
John Jarboe	4:362	Catholic	Virginia?
William Bretton	4:367	Catholic	Maryland
John Ward	4:373		Virginia?
Edward Hull	4:377		Virginia?
John Salter	4:375		Virginia
Adam Stavely	4:411		Virginia?
William Whittle	4:449		Virginia?
George Manners	4:463	Catholic	Virginia?
Nicholas Gwyther	4:480		Maryland
William Hungerford	1:226		Virginia?
Robert Sharp	1:209		Virginia?
Willaim Clare	1:209		Virginia?
Thomas Kingwell	1:209		Virginia?
Henry Adams	4:365	Catholic	Maryland
Henry Clay	4:394		Virginia?
Thomas Payne	4:407		Virginia?
Nicholas Keytin	4:469		Maryland
Henry Pourtney	4:489		Maryland
Walter Peake	4:366	Protestant	Virginia?

11. *Archives,* 4:338, 362, 469.

12. The three who disappear from the records are William Clare, Thomas Kingwell and Adam Stavely. Thomas Payne died before 8 April 1649. In October 1646, only shortly before the invasion took place, Bennett was still titled Mr. in the Virginia Assembly not Colonel. See Henning, ed., *The Statutes at Large,* 1:322.

13. For Richard Bennett's trading partners see *Archives,* 4:269, 304; 10:36; Fausz, "Merging and Emerging Worlds," 80.

14. *Archives,* 4:344, 432.

15. John Lewgar's account for this expedition is in *Archives,* 3:119.

16 In March 1643, the Virginia Assembly passed an act restricting settlement north of the York River, Henning, ed., *Statutes at Large,* 1:274. Those who settled in the area, despite the restriction had a rough reputation. See Wilcomb E. Washburn, *Virginia Under Charles I and Cromwell, 1625–1660* (Williamsburg: Virginia 350th Anniversary Celebration Corporation, 1957), 35.

17. *Archives,* 1:209.
18. Ibid., 1:209, 239.
19. Ibid., 1:239–40.
20. Ibid., 4:315, 371.
21. Ibid., 1:209.
22. Ibid., 1:184, 210.
23. Ibid., 10:96–97. The same language was later part of the Act of Oblivion in 1650, *Archives,* 1:301.
24. Ibid., 1:268, 416; 3:302, 310.
25. Ibid., 1:268.
26. Ibid., 1:226.
27. Ibid., 3:176–77.
28. Ibid., 41:454.
29. Ibid., 4:351, 368.
30. Ibid., 1:320; 4:389.
31. Ibid., 10:94.
32. Ibid., 3:175–76.
33. Ibid., 3:176; 10:458–59.
34. Ibid., 3:176.
35. Ibid., 3:177.
36. Ibid., 3:178.
37. Ibid., 3:179–80.
38. Ibid., 3:179–80.

Chapter 15: "Catholicks of this nation . . . have deemed it necessary . . ."

1. The final days of the First Civil War are summarized in Kenyon, *The Civil Wars of England,* 123–57; Ivan Roots, *The Great Rebellion,* 90–100; Haythornthwaite, *The English Civil War,* 100–12. The title of this chapter is quoted from "Declaration of the Lay Catholic Gentlemen, 1647," published in Thomas H. Clancy, S.J., "he Jesuits and the Independents:1647," *Archive Historicum Scriptorum Societatis Iesu,* 40 (1971): 77.
2. C. H. Firth, *Cromwell's Army* (London: Methuen, 1962), 16–18, 31–33, discusses the difficulties of dealing with locally raised troops.
3. *Archives,* 3:164.
4. Stock, *Proceedings and Debates of the British Parliaments,* 1:171–73; *Archives,* 3:179.
5. *Archives,* 3:173–74.
6. *Archives,* 3:165–166; Stock, *Proceedings and Debates of the British Parliaments,* 1:180, n280.
7. Stock, *Proceedings and Debates of the British Parliaments,* 1:178, 183–84.
8. *Archives,* 3:172–173; Stock, *Proceedings and Debates of the British Parliaments,* 1:184, 186, 194–95.
9. *Archives,* 3:181; Stock, *Proceedings and Debates of the British Parliaments,* 1:195.
10. *Archives,* 10:211–13.
11. Kenyon, *The Civil Wars of England,* 158–62.
12. Clancy, "The Jesuits and the Independents:1647," 67–69; Kenyon, *The Civil Wars of England,* 164–75.

13. Kenyon, *The Civil Wars of England,* 166.

14. W. K. Jordan, *The Development of Religious Toleration in England,* 4 vols. (1940, repr.; Gloucester, Mass., 1965), 3:443.

15. Ibid., 3:443–46.

16. Bossy, *The English Catholic Community, 1570–1850,* 64–67; Clancy, "The Jesuits and the Independents:1647," 67–90; Hughes, *History of the Society of Jesus in North America,* Documents, 1:34.

17. An excellent history of English Catholic education in the seventeenth century is A. C. F. Beales, *Education Under Penalty* (London: Athlone Press, 1963). Philip Calvert's association with the Lisbon College was communicated to me by Lois Green Carr in 1994.

18. Beales, *Education Under Penalty,* 151–52.

19. Ibid., 153.

20. Hughes, *History of the Society of Jesus in North America,* Documents, 1:184; Text, 1:498. The connection of Jerome White and Thomas White is mentioned in John Evelyn 's Diary.

21. Aveling, *The Handle and the Axe,* 116; Cecil Calvert to Leonard Calvert, 21 November 1642 in *Calvert Papers,* 1:218–19.

22. Clancy, S.J., "The Jesuits and the Independents:1647," 68.

23. Ibid., 76.

24. For lay Catholics in England, professions of loyalty to the government were an important part of their quest for toleration, Jordan, *The Development of Religious Toleration in England,* 3:458–60.

25. Clancy, "The Jesuits and the Independents:1647," 77–78.

26. Ibid., 82–84.

Chapter 16: "The said Mrs. Brent protesteth against all proceedings . . ."

1. *Archives,* 4:458–59.

2. Ibid., 3:178.

3. Ibid., 1:145; 3:179; Menard, "Maryland's 'Time of Troubles,'" 137.

4. Skordas, *Early Settlers of Maryland.*

5. *Archives,* 10:100.

6. Ibid., 3:192–93; 4:460.

7. Ibid., 4:417.

8. Ibid., 3:181–82.

9. Plantagenet, "A Description of the Province of New Albion," 29, reprinted in Force, *Tracts and Others Papers*; *Archives,* 1:143–44.

10. *Archives,* 3:182–83.

11. Ibid., 3:187; 4:308–9, 313–14.

12. Ibid., 4:314.

13. Ibid., 4:388; 10:96.

14. Gilbert Watson, *Theriac and Mithridatum: A Study in Therapeutics* (London: Wellcome Historical Medical Library, 1966).

15. *Archives,* 4:315, 388, 401.

16. *Archives,* 4:388; Clare Gittings, *Death, Burial and the Individual in Early Modern England* (London: Croom Helm, 1984), 116–18.

17. Gittings, *Death, Burial and the Individual in Early Modern England,* 29; "Inventory of Patrick Innis, 9 February 1686," Inventories and Accounts, f. 306–310, typed transcription on file, Department of Research, HSMC; "Inventory of Justinian Snow, 24 May 1639," *Archives,* 4:79–88.

18. *Archives,* 4:388.

19. The suggestion that Leonard Greene was born during the Plundering Time is important because it emphasizes the closeness of Thomas Greene and Leonard Calvert during this period. However, the Greene genealogy is very confused in the literature. Papenfuse, et al., *A Biographical Dictionary of the Maryland Legislature,* 1:373–74, suggests that Greene first married Ann Cox, then in 1643, he married Millicent Brown, and finally, by 1647 he married Winifred Seyborn, who was further identified as the widow of Nicholas Harvey. Greene had four sons, Thomas, Leonard, Robert and Francis. In contrast, Harry Wright Newman, *The Flowering of the Maryland Palatinate,* 213–18, states that Greene married Ann Cox and then Winifred Seyborn. He attributes the first two children to Ann Cox and the last two as the children of Winifred Seyborn.

The documents suggest that both of these reconstructions are inaccurate in some aspects. Ann Cox came to Maryland in 1634 under her own name but is referred to as Thomas Greene's first wife in a land claim dated 1 December 1648, "Land Notes, 1634–1655," *Maryland Historical Magazine,* 7 (1912): 195. This marriage had to take place before 1638 as a letter from Thomas Copley, S.J., refers to Greene and his wife, Thomas Copley to Cecil Calvert, 3 April 1638 in *Calvert Papers,* 1:163. Newman suggests that Cox died in 1638 and was the "noble matron" mentioned in the Jesuit Annual Letter (*Flowering of the Maryland Palatinate,* 190). In 1643, Thomas Greene swore that there was no impediment to his marrying Millicent Brown, *Archives,* 4:192. This is the only reference in any early Maryland record to Millicent Brown. Winifred Seyborn came to Maryland in 1638 and by 1648 she was married to Thomas Greene. She cannot have been the widow of Nicholas Harvey. As late as January 1645, Harvey's wife was named Jane, *Archives,* 4:318. Harvey died c. 1646–47 and in numerous court cases after his death, his daughter Francis is mentioned but not a widow, *Archives,* 4:318. Is it possible that the transcription of the name Millicent Brown might be wrong? If Thomas Greene married Winifred Seyborn in 1643, it would be more understandable.

This issue relates to the age of Greene's children. Newman uses Greene's will, dated 18 November 1650, to demonstrate that neither Thomas Greene, Jr., nor Leonard Greene were 18 years old in that year. Greene's will is recorded in *Archives,* 10:88–90. For Newman, this proved they were born in Maryland and were the children of Ann Cox. He referred to a land claim made on 1 September 1648 which states that Thomas and Leonard were transported to Maryland in 1644. See "Land Notes, 1634–1655," *Maryland Historical Magazine,* 7 (1912): 186. He suggests that after the death of their mother, they were sent back to England and did not return until 1644. There is no documentation for these movements.

The will of Thomas Greene strong suggests the age of his sons but this evidence was ignored because it did not fit Newman's reconstruction. Thomas Greene, writing in 1650, stated that each of his sons was to receive his portion when he reached the age of 18 years. He then went on to elaborate lengths to explain how and when the estate was to be divided. His eldest son, Thomas, was to receive his portion in ten years from the date of the will or 1660. He would be 18 years old in that year, meaning that he was born c.

1642–43. Leonard Greene, his second son, had to wait 13 years for his portion which means he was born c. 1645–46. Using the same information, Robert was born c. 1647–48 and Francis was born c. 1649–50. Interestingly, there is another indication of these birth dates in the pattern of Thomas Greene's gifts of cattle to his sons, *Archives,* 4:310, 373–74; 10:14. On 7 April 1650 Greene deeded a cow to his son Francis. If the sequence derived from the will is correct, Francis would have been about one year old. Slightly earlier, on 24 February 1648, Greene gave a cow to his son Robert. Again, Robert would have been a year old at the time. Finally, on 1 June 1647, Greene gave a cow to his son Leonard, who would have been about a year old at that time. These gifts indicate a pattern of Greene's deeding a cow on or close to the first birthday of his sons and supports the contention that Leonard Green was born during the Plundering Time.

20. *Archives,* 4:132–33, 192, 259.

21. Ibid., 1:239.

22. Fraser, *The Weaker Vessel,* 167.

23. *Archives,* 4:314, 320–21.

24. Ibid., 4:318–19, 327; Main, *Tobacco Colony,* 55.

25. *Archives,* 4:388–89; Main, *Tobacco Colony,* 55.

26. *Archives,* 1:108–10, 154–56, 188–90.

27. Ibid., 3:187.

28. Ibid., 4:321–22, 324.

29. Ibid., 4:314–15.

30. Ibid., 4: 315–16.

31. Ibid., 3:188–90.

32. Ibid., 4:313, 338.

33. Ibid., 4:348, 355–56.

34. Stone, "Manorial Maryland," 19, suggests that a laborer could produce 800–1000 lbs of tobacco a year. Using this figure, it would have taken 350–400 full time laborers to grow enough tobacco for the custom duty to pay the soldiers wages.

35. *Archives,* 1:226–27; 4:309.

36. Ibid., 4:331, 350, 365.

37. Ibid., 4:355–56; 365.

38. Ibid., 4:357–58.

39. Soldiers claims for wages are recorded in *Archives,* 4:362, 366, 373, 374, 383, 384, 394, 411, and 469.

40. *Archives,* 4:388.

41. Ibid., 1:217.

42. Ibid., 1:215.

43. Ibid., 1:218.

44. Ibid., 1:220–21.

45. Ibid., 1:221–27.

46. Ibid., 1:218, 320.

Chapter 17: "I will not . . . trouble . . . any person . . . in respect of his religion"

1. "A Relation of Maryland, 1635," in Hall, ed., *Narratives of Early Maryland, 1633–1684,* 101; *Archives,* 3:157. Chapter title taken from *Archives,* 3:210.

2. *Archives,* 4:275–78; Brent's sale of cattle is recorded in *Archives,* 4:367–68, 373–74, 378, 449, 480, 489–90.

3. The Assembly charges for early 1648 were 7752 lbs. of tobacco. The total was to be paid by the freemen at a rate of 55 lbs. per head. This would indicate 140 taxable persons in the county. See *Archives,* 1:231–32. Kent Island was not mentioned, but as previously described, it was reported that there were less than 20 freemen on the island.

4. Hughes, *History of the Society of Jesus in North America,* Text, 2:13; Documents 1:191–96.

5. Ibid., Documents 1:35–36.

6. *Archives,* 3:221–28.

7. Hughes, *History of the Society of Jesus in North America,* Text, 2:13; Documents 1:211.

8. *Archives,* 3:211–12.

9. *Archives,* 3:217–18; 10:86; Papenfuse, et al., *Biographical Dictionary of the Maryland Legislature,* 1:422–23.

10. Ibid., 2:788–89; Newman, *Flowering of the Maryland Palatinate,* 7–10.

11. Hale, *Virginia Venturer,* 193, 209; Ames, ed., *County Court Records of Accomack,* 437.

12. John H. Latané, *The Early Relations Between Maryland and Virginia,* Johns Hopkins University Studies in Historical and Political Science, 13th series (repr.; New York: Johnson Reprint Co., 1973), 3:31–40; Henry R. McIlwaine, *The Struggle of the Protestant Dissenters for Religious Toleration in Virginia,* Johns Hopkins University Studies in Historical and Political Science, 12th series (repr.; New York: Johnson Reprint Co., 1973), 4:15–17.

13. Henning, ed., *The Statutes at Large,* 1:277.

14. Latané, *Early Relations Between Maryland and Virginia,* 3:42–43.

15. Henning, ed., *The Statutes at Large,* 1:341–342; Latané, *Early Relations Between Maryland and Virginia,* 3:45.

16. Robert P. Brenner, "Commercial Change and Political Conflict in the Merchant Community in Civil War London" (PhD. diss., Princeton University, 1970), 110–12, 369–70.

17. *Archives,* 3:201, 205.

18. Ibid., 3:204.

19. Ibid., 3:210–24.

20. Ibid., 4:468–69, 471, 476; 10:9; "Land Notes, 1634–1655," *Maryland Historical Magazine,* 8 (1913): 186.

21. *Archives,* 4:456, 469, 475.

22. Ibid., 1:237–38; 3:229.

23. Menard, "Economy and Society," 213; Lois Green Carr, "Sources of Political Stability and Upheaval in Seventeenth Century Maryland," 47; Carr, Russell R. Menard, and Lorena S. Walsh, *Robert Cole's World,* 8–9, 15.

24. *Archives,* 1:244–47; Gerald W. Johnson, *The Maryland Act of Religious Toleration: An Interpretation* (Annapolis: Hall of Records Commission, Department of General Services, 1973); Lois Green Carr, "Roman Catholics and Toleration in Seventeenth Century Maryland," Ms. on file, Department of Research, HSMC, n.d.

25. *Archives,* 1:245; Johnson, *Maryland Act of Religious Toleration,* 8. The banned terms were: heretic, schismatic, idolator, Puritan, independent, Presbyterian, popish priest, Jesuit, jesuited papist, Lutheran, Calvinist, Anabaptist, Brownist, Antinomian, barrowist, Roundhead, and separatist.

26. Morrill, *Revolt of the Provinces,* 42–45.

Bibliography

Primary Sources

Maryland, Province of. [1639] Patents 1, ff. 40–41 on microfilm produced by the Genealogical Society. "Maryland Patents, 1637–1650" (Salt Lake City, 1947).

"Inventory of Patrick Innis, 9 February 1686." Inventories and Accounts, f. 306–310. Typed transcription on file. Department of Research, HSMC.

Public Records Office, Chancery Court, London. Hawley *vs.* Cornwallis, Decrees and Orders, C33/177 [1640].

Cornwaleys *vs.* Ingle, Bills and Answers, C24 15/23 [1645].

Cornwaley *vs.* Ingle, Examinations, C24 690/14 [1645].

Public Records Office, High Court of Admiralty, London.

Port Book, London, Exports by Denizens, Christmas 1638–Christmas 1639, E 190/43/6, f. 98.

Port Book, London, Exports by Denizens, Christmas 1639–Christmas 1640, E 190/43/1, f. 150,152.

Deposition of Richard Ingle [1640], Examinations, High Court of Admiralty (HCA) 13/60.

Copley et al. *vs.* Ingle [1645], Answers, High Court of Admiralty (HCA) 13/119.

Copley et al. *vs.* Ingle [1645], Examinations, High Court of Admiralty (HCA) 13/60.

Cornwalyes *vs.* Ingle [1645], Bills and Answers, Court of Chancery, C24 15/23

Cornwalyes *vs.* Ingle [1645], Answers, High Court of Admiralty (HCA) 13/119.

Cornwaleys *vs.* Ingle [1645], Examinations, High Court of Admiralty (HCA) 13/60.

Glover *vs.* Ingle, Examinations [1645], High Court of Admiralty (HCA) 13/60.

Ingle *vs. The Looking Glass* [1645], Examinations, High Court of Admiralty (HCA) 13/60.

Secondary Sources

"Abstracts of Virginia Land Patents." *Virginia Magazine of History and Biography,* 7 (1899): 190–94.

Ames, Susie M., ed. *County Court Records of Accomack-Northampton, Virginia, 1640–1645.* Charlottesville: University Press of Virginia, 1973.

Anderson, R. C., ed. *The Book of Examinations and Depositions, 1622–1644.* 2 vols. Southampton, U.K.: Publications of the Southampton Record Society, 1929.

Andrews, Matthew Page. *Tercentenary History of Maryland,* 4 vols. Baltimore: S. J. Clarke Publishing Co., 1925.

Aveling, J. C. H. "The Marriage of Catholic Recusants, 1559–1642." *Journal of Ecclesiastical History,* 14 (1963): 68–83.

———. *The Handle and the Axe: The Catholic Recusants in England from Reformation to Emancipation.* London: Blond & Briggs, 1976.

Bayley, A. R. *The Great Civil War in Dorset, 1642–1660.* Taunton, U.K.: The Wessex Press, 1910.

Beales, A. C. F. *Education Under Penalty*. London: Athlone Press, 1963.

Beitzell, Edward W. *The Jesuit Missions of St. Mary 's County*. Leonardtown, Md.: Privately published, 1960.

"Captain Thomas Cornwaleys, Forgotten Leader in the Founding of Maryland." *Chronicles of St. Mary's*, 20, no. 7 (1972): 1-12.

Billings, Warren M. *The Old Dominion in the 17th Century*. Chapel Hill: University of North Carolina Press, 1975.

Blundell, Margaret. *Cavalier: Letters of William Blundell to his Friends, 1620–1698*. London: Longmans, Green & Co., 1933.

Bossy, John. *The English Catholic Community, 1570–1850*. London: Darton, Longman & Todd, 1975.

———. "Reluctant Colonists: The English Catholics Confront the Atlantic," in David Quinn, ed., *Early Maryland in a Wider World*. Pp. 149–64. Detroit: Wayne State University Press, 1982.

Bowle, John. *Charles I: A Biography*. Boston: Weidenfeld & Nicolson, 1975.

Bozman, John L. *The History of Maryland*, 2 vols. Baltimore: J. Lucas & E. K. Deaver, 1837.

Brenner, Robert P. "Commercial Change and Political Conflict in the Merchant Community in Civil War London." PhD. dissertation, Department of History, Princeton University, 1970.

Browne, William Hand, et al., eds. *Archives of Maryland*, 72 vols. Baltimore: Maryland Historical Society, 1883–.

Capp, Bernard. *Cromwell's Navy: The Fleet and the English Revolution, 1648–1660*. New York: Oxford University Press, 1989.

Carr, Lois Green. "Biography files." Unpublished mss., n.d. Research Department, Historic St. Mary's City.

———. "Roman Catholics and Toleration in Seventeenth Century Maryland." Mss. on file, Department of Research, Historic St. Mary's City.

———. "The Founding of St. Mary's City." *Smithsonian Journal of History*, 3 (1968–69): 77–100

———. "Sources of Political Stability and Upheaval in Seventeenth Century Maryland." *Maryland Historical Magazine*, 79 (1984): 44–70.

———. "Chapel Field Land Use History File." Mss. on file, Department of Research, Historic St. Mary's City, 1992.

Carr, Lois Green, Russell R. Menard, and Louis Peddicord. *Maryland at the Beginning*. Annapolis: Hall of Records Commission, 1975.

Carr, Lois Green, Russell R. Menard, and Lorena S. Walsh. *Robert Cole's World: Agriculture and Society in Early Maryland*. Chapel Hill: University of North Carolina Press, 1991.

Chilton, William B. "The Brent Family." *Virginia Historical Magazine* 14 (1906–7): 95–101.

———. "The Brent Family." *Virginia Historical Magazine* 15 (1908): 194–97.

Clancy, Thomas H., S.J. "The Jesuits and the Independents:1647." *Archive Historicum Scriptorum Societatis Iesu*, 40 (1971): 67–90.

Cornwallis, Jane. *Private Correspondence of Jane Lady Cornwallis, 1613–1644*. London, S. & J. Bentley, 1842.

Crow, Steven D. "'Your Majesty's Good Subjects': A Reconsideration of Royalism in

Virginia, 1642–1652." *Virginia Magazine of Biography and History,* 87 (1979): 158–73.
Cruickshank, C. G. *Elizabeth's Army.* Oxford: The Clarendon Press, 1966.
Crump, Helen J. *Colonial Admiralty Jurisdiction in the Seventeenth Century.* New York: Longmans, Green, & Co., 1931
Currer-Briggs, Noel. *Colonial Settlers and English Adventurers.* Baltimore: Genealogical Publishing Co., 1971
Davis, Ralph. *The Rise of the English Shipping Industry in the 17th and 18th Centuries.* Norton Abbot, U.K.: David & Charles, 1962.
English Merchant Shipping and Anglo-Dutch Rivalry in the Seventeenth Century. London: H.M.S.O., 1975.
Edwards, Francis, S.J. *The Jesuits in England from 1580 to the Present Day.* London: Burns & Oates, 1985.
Edwards, S. John. *Some Old Wiltshire Homes.* London: Charles J. Clark, 1894.
Everard, James, Baron Arundel, and Sir Richard C. Hoare, Bart. *A History of Modern Wiltshire.* 6 vols. London: J. Nichols, 1829.
Fauz, J. Frederick. "Merging and Emerging Worlds: Anglo-Indian Interest Groups and the Development of the Seventeenth-Century Chesapeake," in *Colonial Chesapeake Society,* Lois Green Carr, Philip D. Morgan, and Jean B. Russo, eds. Pp. 47–98. Chapel Hill: University of North Carolina Press, 1988.
Firth, C. H. *Cromwell's Army.* London: Methuen, 1962.
Firth, C. M. and R. S. Rait, eds. *Acts and Ordinances of the Interregnum, 1642–1660.* 3 vols. London: H.M.S.O., 1911.
Fithian, Charles. "'Master Pope's Fort': An English Civil War Fortification on the Chesapeake Frontier." Paper presented at the 20th Annual Meeting of the Society for Historical Archaeology, Savannah, Georgia, January 1987.
Foley, Henry, S.J., *Records of the English Province of the Society of Jesus.* 8 vols. London: Burns & Oates, 1877.
Forman, H. Chandlee. *Jamestown and St. Mary's: Buried Cities of Romance.* Baltimore: Johns Hopkins University Press, 1938.
Fraser, Antonia. *The Weaker Vessel.* New York: Vintage Books, 1984.
Gardiner, Samuel R. *History of the Great Civil War, 1642–1649.* London: Longmans, Green & Co., 1898.
The Constitutional Documents of the Puritan Revolution, 1625–1660. Oxford: The Clarendon Press, 1906.
Gibb, Vicary, ed. *The Complete Peerage of England, Scotland, Ireland, Great Britain and the United Kingdom.* 13 vols. London: St. Catherine Press, Ltd., 1918.
Gittings, Clare. *Death, Burial and the Individual in Early Modern England.* London: Croom Helm, 1964.
Hale, Nathaniel C. *Virginia Venturer: A Historical Biography of William Claiborne, 1600–1677.* Richmond: Dietz Press, Inc., 1951.
Hall, Clayton Coleman, ed. *Narratives of Early Maryland, 1634–1684.* New York: Barnes & Noble, Inc., 1967.
Harper, Lawrence. *The English Navigation Laws.* New York: Columbia University Press, 1964.
Hastings, Mrs. Russell. "Calvert and Darnell Gleanings from English Wills." *Maryland Historical Magazine,* 20 (1925): 303–24.

Hayes-McCoy, G. A., ed. *Ulster and Other Irish Maps, c. 1600*. Dublin: Irish Manuscripts Commission, 1964.

Haythornthwaite, Phillip. *The English Civil War, 1642–1651: An Illustrated Military History*. Dorset: Blandford Press, 1983.

Hening, William W., ed. *The Statutes at Large, Being a Collection of All the Laws of Virginia from the First Session of the Legislature in the Year 1619*. New York: printed for the editor, 1823.

Howard, Frank L. "The Guns of St. Mary's," in *Chronicles of St. Mary's,* 6 (1958): 217–29.

Hyde, Bryden B. "New Light on the Ark and the Dove." *Maryland Historical Magazine,* 48 (1953): 185–90.

Hyde, Edward, Earl of Clarendon. *The History of the Rebellion and Civil Wars in England Begun in the Year 1641*, ed. W. Dean Macray, Oxford: Clarendon Press,1888.

Ingle, Edward. "Captain Richard Ingle, the Maryland 'Pirate and Rebel,' 1642–1653." Maryland Historical Society Fund Publication Number 19, Baltimore, 1889.

Jennings, Francis. *The Ambiguous Iroquois Empire.* New York: W. W. Norton & Co., 1984.

Johnson, Gerald W. *The Maryland Act of Religious Toleration: An Interpretation.* Annapolis: Hall of Records Commission, Department of General Services, 1973.

Jordan, W. K. *The Development of Religious Toleration in England.* 4 vols. Gloucester, Mass.: P. Smith, 1965.

Kent, Barry C. *Susquehanna's Indians.* Harrisburg, Pa.: Pennsylvania Historical & Museum Commission, 1989.

Kenyon, J. P. *The Civil Wars of England.* New York: Alfred A. Knopf, 1988.

Krugler, John D. "Lord Baltimore, Roman Catholics and Toleration: Religious Policy in Maryland During the Early Catholic Years, 1634–1649." *Catholic Historical Review,* 65 (1979): 49–75.

Latané, John H. *The Early Relations Between Maryland and Virginia,* Johns Hopkins University Studies in Historical and Political Science, 13th series. New York: Johnson Reprint Co., 1973.

Lee, John W. M., ed. *The Calvert Papers.* 3 vols., Fund Publication No. 28. Baltimore: Maryland Historical Society, 1889.

Lee, Sidney, ed. *Dictionary of National Biography,* 22 vols., London: Smith, Elder & Co., 1909.

Lewis, Clifford, III. "Some Recently Discovered Extracts from the Lost Minutes of the Virginia Council and General Court, 1642–1645." *William and Mary Quarterly,* 20 (1940): 62–78.

Lindestrom, Peter. *Geogrophia Americae,* (1691), translated and edited by Amandus Johnson. Philadelphia: Swedish Colonial Society, 1924.

Lowe, William W. "The Master of the Ark: A Seventeenth-Century Chronicle." *Maryland Historical Magazine,* 95 (2000): 261–89.

Main, Gloria L. *Tobacco Colony: Life in Early Maryland, 1650–1720*. Princeton: Princeton University Press, 1982.

Marcus, Geoffrey J. *Naval History of England.* Boston: Little Brown, 1961.

"Ingle in Maryland." *Maryland Historical Magazine,* 1 (1906): 125–40.

"Two Commissions." *Maryland Historical Magazine,* 1 (1906): 211–16.

"Land Notes,1634–1655." *Maryland Historical Magazine,* 5 (1910): 166–74, 261–71, 365–74; 6 (1911): 60–70, 195–203, 262–70, 365–73.

Masselman, George. *The Cradle of Colonialism.* New Haven: Yale University Press, 1963.

McIlwaine, Henry R. *The Struggle of the Protestant Dissenters for Religious Toleration in Virginia.* Johns Hopkins University Studies in Historical and Political Science, 12th series. New York: Johnson Reprint Co., 1973

Menard, Russell R. "Economy and Society in Early Colonial Maryland." PhD. dissertation., Department of History, University of Iowa, 1975.

———."Maryland's 'Time of Troubles': Sources of Political Disorder in Early St. Mary's." *Maryland Historical Magazine,* 76 (1981): 124–40.

Middleton, Arthur Pierce. *Tobacco Coast: A Maritime History of Chesapeake Bay in the Colonial Era.* Baltimore: Johns Hopkins University Press, 1984.

Miller, Henry M. "Discovering Maryland's First City: A Summary of the 1981–1984 Archaeological Excavations in St. Mary's City, Maryland." *St. Mary's City Archaeology Series,* No. 2. St. Mary's City, Md., 1986.

Morrill, J. S. *The Revolt of the Provinces: Conservatives and Radicals in the English Civil War, 1630–1650.* London: Allen & Unwin, 1976.

Neil, Edward D. *The Founders of Maryland as Portrayed in Manuscripts, Provincial Records and Early Documents.* Albany: J. Munsell, 1876.

Newman, Harry Wright. *The Flowering of the Maryland Palatinate.* Baltimore: Genealogical Publishing Co., 1984.

Nicklin, John Bailey Calvert. "Immigration Between Virginia and Maryland in the Seventeenth Century." *William and Mary Quarterly,* 18 (1938): 440–46.

Noël Hume, Ivor. *Martin's Hundred.* New York: Alfred A. Knopf., 1982.

"Notes from the Records of York County." *William and Mary Quarterly,* 22 (1913): 240–48.

"Notes from the Records of York County." *William and Mary Quarterly,* 23 (1914): 10–15, 24 (1915): 38.

"Notes from the Records of York County." *William and Mary Quarterly,* 24 (1915): 37–43.

Nott, H. E., ed. *The Deposition Books of Bristol,* 2 vols. Bristol: Bristol Record Society, 1935.

Pagan, John R. "Dutch Maritime and Commercial Activity in Mid-Seventeenth-Century Virginia." *Virginia Magazine of History and Biography,* 90 (1982): 485–501.

Papenfuse, Edward C., Alan F. Day, David W. Jordan, and Gregory A. Stiverson. *A Biographical Dictionary of the Maryland Legislature, 1635–1789.* 2 vols. Baltimore: Johns Hopkins University Press, 1979.

Papenfuse, Edward C. and Joseph M. Coale III. *The Hammond-Harwood House Atlas of Historical Maps of Maryland, 1608–1908.* Baltimore: Johns Hopkins University Press, 1982.

Parr, Charles M. *The Voyages of David De Vries, Navigator and Adventurer.* New York: Crowell, 1969.

Peterson, Harold L. *Roundshot and Rammers.* Harrisburg, Pa.: Stackpole Books, 1969.

Plantagenet, Beauchamp. *A Description of the Province of New Albion* (London, 1648). Reprinted in Peter Force, *Tracts and Other Papers Relating Principally to the Origin, Settlement, and Progress of the Colonies of North America from the Discovery of the Country to the Year 1776,* 4 vols. Gloucester, Mass.: Peter Smith.

Plucknett, Theodore P. T. *A Concise History of the Common Law,* 5th ed. London: Butterworth, 1956.

Power, Michael. "Shadwell: The Development of a London Suburban Community in the Seventeenth Century." *The London Journal,* 4 (1978): 29–45.

Printz, Johan. "Report of the Governor, 1644," in Albert C. Myers, ed., *Narratives of Early Pennsylvania, West New Jersey, and Delaware, 1630–1707.* New York: C. Scribner's Sons, 1912.

Riordan, Timothy B. "Summary Report of the 1986 Excavations at Pope's Fort in the Village Center, St. Mary's City, Maryland." Mss. on file, Department of Research, Historic St. Mary's City.

———. "Preliminary Report on the 1995 Excavations at the Calvert House (18ST13), St. Mary's City, Maryland." Mss. on file, Department of Research, Historic St. Mary's City.

Roots, Ivan. *The Great Rebellion, 1642–1660.* London: Botsford, 1966.

Ross, W. G. *Military Engineering During the Great Civil War, 1642–1649.* London: Ken Trotman, 1984.

Rountree, Helen C. *Powhatan Foreign Relations, 1500–1722.* Charlottesville: University Press of Virginia, 1993.

Scharf, J. Thomas. *History of Maryland,* 3 vols. Repr. Hatboro, Pa.: Tradition Press, 1967.

Semmes, Raphael. *Captains and Mariners of Early Maryland.* Baltimore: Johns Hopkins University Press, 1937.

Shomette, Donald B. *Pirates on the Chesapeake.* Centerville, Md.: Tidewater Publishers, 1985.

Skordas, Gust. *Early Settlers of Maryland.* Baltimore: Genealogical Publishing Co., 1968.

Steiner, Bernard C. "New Light on Maryland History from the British Archives." *Maryland Historical Magazine,* 4 (1909): 251–62.

Stock, Leo F. *Proceedings and Debates of the British Parliaments Respecting North America,* 2 vols. Washington: Carnegie Institution of Washington, 1924.

Stone, Garry Wheeler. "Society, Housing and Architecture in Early Maryland: John Lewgar's St. John's." PhD. dissertation. University of Pennsylvania, 1982.

———. "Manorial Maryland." *Maryland Historical Magazine,* 82 (1987): 3–36.

Stone, Lawrence. *The Family, Sex, and Marriage in England, 1500–1800.* New York: Harper Colophon Books, 1979.

Tylenda, Joseph N., S.J. *Jesuit Saints and Martyrs.* Chicago: Jesuit Way, 1984.

Walker, David M. *The Oxford Companion to Law.* Oxford: Oxford University Press, 1989.

Washburn, Wilcomb E. *Virginia Under Charles I and Cromwell, 1625–1660.* Williamsburg: Virginia 350th Anniversary Celebration Corporation, 1957.

Watson, Gilbert. *Theriac and Mithridatum: A Study in Therapeutics.* London: Wellcome Historical Medical Library, 1966.

Winthrop, John. *History of New England, 1630–1649,* James K. Hosmer, ed., 2 vols. New York: Barnes & Noble, Inc., 1966.

Wood, Anthony à. *Athenae Oxoniensis,* 4 vols., Philip Bliss, ed. London: F. C. & J. Rivington,1813.

Wedgewood, C. V. *The King's Peace.* London: Macmillan, 1955.

———. *A Coffin for King Charles: The Trial and Execution of Charles I.* Alexandria, Va.: Time-Life Books, 1981.

Weinrib, Ben and Christopher Hibbert, eds. *The London Encyclopedia.* Bethesda: Adler & Adler, 1986.

Index